GRIGORI SAVVICH SKOVORODA

Prior to his death, Skovoroda bequeathed his burial to occur on high ground, near a forest and flourmill, and requested the following epithet to be inscribed on his grave marker:

The world tried to catch me but could not.

GRIGORI SAVVICH SKOVORODA

OTHER BOOKS BY DANIEL H. SHUBIN:

History of Russian Christianity in 4 volumes:
From the Earliest Years through Tsar Ivan IV
The Patriarchal Era through Tsar Peter the Great: 1586 to 1725
The Synodal Era and the Sectarians: 1725 to 1894
The Orthodox Church of the 20th Century: 1894 to 1990

Daniel and Alla Andreev

Leo Tolstoy and the Kingdom of God within You

Helena Roerich: Living Ethics and the Teaching for a New Epoch

Russia's Wisdom

Tsiolkovski: The Cosmic Scientist and His Cosmic Philosophy

Concordia Antarova

Andrei Bely

Tsars and Pseudo-Tsars: Russia's Era of Upheavals

Monastery Prisons

The Gospel of the Prince of Peace

Kingdoms and Covenants

Attributes of Heaven and Earth

Rose of the World (Tr.)

The Grey Man, Menace Eastern-Light (Tr.)

The Third Testament (Tr.)

SKOVORODA

THE WORLD TRIED TO CATCH ME, BUT COULD NOT

A Biography and Analysis of the Itinerant Philosopher, Scholar and Christian Humanist, Grigori Savvich Skovoroda, and a Translation of Selected Writings.

Daniel H. Shubin

(BIOGRAPHER AND TRANSLATOR)

Cover: Artist's conception of Skovoroda in his early years, based on the recollections of those who knew him. He holds a book in his hand with the title *Alphabet*, which was his favorite composition.

ISBN 978-0-9662757-3-5
Copyright 2012.
All rights reserved.
Daniel H. Shubin

danhshubin at yahoo dot com

February 24, 2021

TABLE OF CONTENTS

1. Introduction — 7
2. Brief Chronology of Skovoroda's Life — 19
3. Biography — 23
4. Legends and Unverifiable Accounts — 61
5. Skovoroda's Compositions — 65
6. Notes on the Translation — 71

GRIGORI SAVVICH SKOVORODA

(translated from the Russian)

7. Introduction to Christian Morality — 73
8. Battle between Archangel Michael and Satan — 85
9. Narcissus or Comprehending Yourself — 115
10. Lot's Wife — 169
11. Dialogue named The Serpent's Flood — 201
12. Symphony or the Book Achsah — 237
13. Conversation regarding True Happiness (selection) — 333
14. Garden of Divine Songs (selections) — 337
15. Poems (selections) — 345
16. Kharkov Fables (selections) — 351
17. Letters (selections) — 361

18. Bibliography — 399

INTRODUCTION

The introduction and subsequent biography will provide the reader with background information in order for the reader to be able to read and understand Skovoroda's compositions and be able to draw their own conclusions. Too many articles have been written on Skovoroda where the author provides the reader his personal interpretation of Skovoroda, but this does not allow the reader to draw their own conclusions, as the conclusion is provided by the commentator. A personal and intensive study of Skovoroda is necessary in order to understand the depth and value of such a philosophic genius and Christian humanist.

I have provided some basic concepts of Skovoroda's philosophy in the introduction, but only enough to stimulate the reader's appetite. Some interpretation is also provided, but again only as much as necessary to understand Skovoroda's life.

Grigori Savvich Skovoroda is the person that all philosophers wish to become, but for whatever personal reasons they never do. Skovoroda was a mental giant and scholarly genius, and the exceptional talents he possessed provided him the means for philosophic success: his profound mind, phenomenal memory, poetic and prosaic creativity, excellent singing voice, and his ability to play several musical instruments. Skovoroda composed music and was also an artist. Along with knowing the Russian and Ukrainian languages, Skovoroda was fluent in Hebrew, German, Latin and Greek, and translated works of Cicero and Plutarch from Greek into Ukrainian. He also had a photographic memory of the Bible.

Skovoroda was raised in the Cossack environment where all able bodied men were expected to continue the militarist tradition of their forefathers, but he showed an intelligence and ethos that deviated from what was expected of him. So his father – a parish priest – enlisted him in a formal school in Kiev where he excelled, and beyond anybody's expectations. But he was far ahead of what the school could provide and so he then traveled in Europe, and there learned foreign languages and their culture. Returning to Ukraine he continued his education and then began to teach himself, but he was again far beyond his contemporaries. Again traveling and again teaching he was offered positions of security in higher educational institutions, but he could not conform to the regimentation of institutionalized learning.

The era of Skovoroda's adolescence was affected by the upheavals of the Russo-Turkish war of 1735-39. The region of Skovoroda's home was the area that Russian military forces used to conscript tens of thousands of Cossacks and peasants into makeshift armies and mobilized them to fight the infidels. Fatalities from the war reached about 35,000, a very high figure relative to the estimated total population of Ukraine of about 1.2 million. The war also bled Ukraine's economy and finances dry. Skovoroda's age was 13 through 17 during the war, with the war ending just prior to his own possible conscription into the military.

The horrifying impact of the war on the landscape as well as human suffering possibly led Skovoroda to being a pacifist. In letter 49 to Mikhail Kovalinski he urges him to be strong in the face of those who criticize him for refusing military service. Skovoroda's philosophy of harmony, reconciliation, cooperation and peaceful coexistence no doubt had its origins in the devastation of war that enveloped the region of his family and Cossack society. (This would be parallel to the effect that the Crimean War of 1855-1858 had upon Leo Tolstoy, to also motivate him toward a philosophy of Christian pacifism.)

A second Russo-Turkish War occurred 1768-1775, and Skovoroda would have been age 46 to 53 these years, but he began his nomadic life in 1769 and would not have permitted himself to be conscripted. Ukraine during the intervening years between the 2 Russo-Turkish Wars was under Russian political occupation with a puppet-government under the domination of Empress Catherine II the Great's favorites, such as Grigori Potemkin and Lord Byron. This likewise led to the suppression of independent Cossack military forces by the Russians to force them to subjection. The Cossacks fought the Russians regularly during this period and up to 1783 the area was rampant with strife.

Even though the war for independence under Emilian Pugachev, 1772-1774, was further east and involved the Ural Cossacks, reports would have funneled into Ukraine regularly and independence-minded Cossacks did travel and join his resistance to Russian incursion. Skovoroda was 50 to 52 years of age during Pugachev's rebellion.

All of these events and the historical environment would have molded Skovoroda's thinking.

Eventually at about age 46, Skovoroda abandoned everything he had and took to the road as a mendicant philosopher for the next 26 years. He felt he could accomplish more with his talents by visiting the homes of thousands much like an itinerant preacher having in his bag a Bible and teaching them his form of Christian humanism. Skovoroda's Christianity was stripped of theology, ceremony and supernaturalism, and he concentrated on a moral code, and a very conservative one, for all his listeners. Proper conduct was ethic and ethos based on the Bible.

No doubt Skovoroda saw many in Cossack society adapting to what was expected of them and of which they felt a duty, but not what their inner person felt they should become. In the religious and ecclesiastical institutions he saw people adapting to the form of life that was expected of them in their clerical position, and so they could lead a comfortable life, even though deep in their hearts it was not what they wanted. But for reasons of a life-long security they embraced it and defended it and so sold their souls to the devil for bread. In the educational institutions he saw the same with the prestige that accompanied the positions, but the educators demanded a regimented form of instruction because they were themselves unable to grasp any depth beyond the written word. The rich were for the rich at the expense of others, and exploited the underprivileged and desperate, while the lower-income families lived hand to mouth with no escape from their dilemma.

Skovoroda's hallmark was "Comprehend Yourself." What did this mean? Every person had to develop his own purpose in life based on his inner inclinations. To know what you want in life was necessary in order to obtain the basic or most fundamental of all life's needs – happiness – and without happiness nothing could be further gained. For Skovoroda philosophy had to be practical to be effective and this meant the ability to attain happiness. The origin of his statement was Socrates' "The Unexamined Life is not Worth Living."

With a person first comprehending himself, defining a goal and purpose for his life, a new start could be made, much like the Christian cliché To be Born Again. Skovoroda's equivalent of being Born Again was the moment in a person's life that he or she gains this metaphysical comprehension of their personal self. This was attaining God's Kingdom within you; this was the return of Jesus Christ; this was finding peace with God; this was mortifying the body and attaining the resurrection. This inner spark of Christian humanism would then extend to others to join together and create a righteous society. Although Skovoroda was fluent in the early philosophers and ecclesiastical fathers, the Bible was always the final authority and the foundation of all his concepts, since it provided the moral code by which people's life could succeed, and temptation could be defeated.

The philosophy of Skovoroda can be capsulated as the attainment of morality and ethic by constant self-examination and self-improvement. The loss of his teaching vocation caused him to lose what little respect still remained in him for the Orthodoxy. The greed and hypocrisy of the clergy and their lack of concern for the welfare of the people was repulsive to Skovoroda, and seemed to him to lead the people into further corruption rather than improving their morality and ethic. Skovoroda also noticed the cruel treatment of serfs by landowners and aristocrats, and their drive to increase their property and wealth and political domination, and he condemned them for it.

The goal that Skovoroda hoped that his listeners would attain was contentment with themselves and personal happiness. He emphasized an acetic mode of existence, impressing upon his readers and listeners the necessity to overcome sin and temptation in order to inherit blessings of God. The fundamental conclusion that Skovoroda drew was that the universe was created by a God of providence having a love and sincere concern for the welfare of all this creatures. As a result, this same God has provided all the necessities for a person and in an easy manner to acquire in order to attain happiness. What is not necessary for happiness or personal success in life is difficult to acquire. So has God arranged it.

Skovoroda allegorized the Bible for a deeper meaning than the superficial and shallow understanding of the clergy and Orthodoxy of his era. The rites and theology of Orthodoxy he felt interfered with a person's capability of depth. The institution of religion, any religion, constrained a person's ability of free thought and confined him to a specific order of tenets and routines that did nothing for his spiritual advancement.

The basic understanding by which Skovoroda's teaching of the human is analyzed is the understanding of the heart. "Every person is what his heart is," wrote Skovoroda. "The heart is all that a person possesses in his head, and this is the true person. The entirety of the ostensive person is nothing else but a mask that covers every member and is hidden in his heart as though in a seed." Skovoroda taught that every person possesses a body made of earth and a second inner and invisible body that is spiritual, secret, hidden and eternal. Skovoroda writes that in every person the divine Spirit in secluded and it is a divine power.

"The entire universe consists of 2 natures. One is visible: creation. The other is invisible, the divine. God penetrates all creation and retains it," he writes. As a result nothing can actually perish, but all in its own right is eternal. God is the eternal head and secret law in created entities. He is the tree of life while all else is nothing but its shadow.

Every person needs to enter into a struggle against himself, because in him lives "the guide of a blessed nature." And, "We must not interfere with the wisdom that resides in us." The spiritual path of a person must secure the triumph of the mystical spirit residing in him. The strength of the superficial person interferes with spiritual growth and it constantly entangles a person in snares. Skovoroda wrote, "Do not blame the world: this corpse is innocent. The root of sin lies in the person and in Satan. The will is an insatiable hell. It is to you poison and you are poison to all. Every person that deifies his will is a enemy of the divine will and cannot enter into God's kingdom."

The secret law of a person's own development resides in the depths of himself. As a result and first of all a person must find himself, "Comprehend yourself." All sufferings and anguish that a person endures as he journeys through life occur as a result of a person conducting himself opposite to the reason he was created. "Such misery is imposed in heterogeneous acts. Nature and affinity signify a congenital divine blessing, God's secret law that governs all created entities." As a result, we must "first of all seek within ourselves that spark of divine truth, while it, overwhelming our darkness, cleanses us."

Skovoroda's life's experience convinced him that a person's true value did not consist of a social expression of success. The concept of ostensive progress, just as with the concept of ostensive equality, was alien to Skovoroda. Quite often Skovoroda satirizes this concept as in the following passage,

> "We have measured the oceans, earth, atmosphere and heavens. We have secured the underground in our search for metals, we have discovered countless worlds in outer space, we built machinery beyond our dreams. There seems to be not a day where we do not experience or develop something new. What is it we cannot do? But the sorrow in all of this lies in that the greatest we cannot attain."

He refers to our attainment of personal happiness and liberation from the superficial world in his conclusion. In regard to death, Skovoroda said the following,

> "Fear of death falls upon every person in their old age. It is necessary to prepare for this at a opportune time early in life as a weapon against the enemy, to develop a peaceful attitude of the will toward this event. Such a psychological peace is prepared at a distance from the event, quietly in a secret conclave of heart where it grows and increases with a feeling of goodness. This feeling is a crown of life."

For Skovoroda friendship was an established metaphysical and religious fact. He understood Christianity as a covenant of the most consummate friendship possible. As he wrote:

> "What can be more destructive than restrained or feigned love? And what is more divine than Christian love, that is, true love? And what is this that is called Christian religion except the most true and consummate friendship? Did not Christ indicate that the distinction of his disciples would be mutual love? Does not friendship unite all things, while it is animosity that dissipates and ruins? Does not the

beloved disciple John call Jesus God?¹ Are not all the gifts, even Angelic languages, nothing without love? What causes abundance? Love. What creates? Love. What preserves? Love, and more love. What sweetens? Love, love! Love is the beginning, middle and end."

In another area Skovoroda speaks to his friend Kovalinski regarding his most coveted desire and his worry over the destiny of others.

"I worry over the riches of the spirit, over that bread and that clothing without which a person cannot enter into the most beautiful chambers of the heavenly groom. All of my strengths, all of my drives I direct there. And you would like me to further and more openly disclose to you my soul? Listen. I abandon all things and am abandoning all thinks, and there is only one thing I want to attain in all my life: this is to understand of what the death of Christ consists and what his resurrection signifies. We do know that a person cannot rise with Christ if he has not first died with him. Woe to our stupidity. We think that we hold in our hands the ark of Sacred Scripture, when we really do not know what baptism is or what the sacred meal is. If we understood these matters right from the first, would we then call them mysteries?² And is it not foolish for us to call secret and hidden what is unveiled to only the uneducated? The ancient Pharisees and scribes flattered themselves, thinking of themselves that they were the law of Moses, but nonetheless Christ called them blind. Who has known the mind of the Lord?³ Paul speaks of this referring to Sacred Scripture where the mind of the Lord is located, but it is inaccessible and hidden because of figures. This is what, my friend, my spirit strives for and thirsts for. This is what it strains to attain. Now you can ask no more as to what my effort is dedicated."

As far as literature was concerned it was antiquity to which Skovoroda was attracted. The primary piece of literature of which Skovoroda had a mastery and which was his main philosophical and moral guide was the Bible: the Old Testament in its original Hebrew, and the New Testament in

---

[1] 1 John 5:20
[2] In the Russian the word *mystery* is the root of the word *sacrament* in Orthodoxy.
[3] 1 Cor 2:16

its original Greek. Skovoroda's compositions reflect his photographic memory of almost its entirety. Skovoroda's many quotations also evidence his knowledge of the Greek Septuagint Old Testament and the Church Slavonic Bible, just recently published.

There was probably no other soul in Russia in the 18th century who was so comparably fluent as Skovoroda in the ancient classics, and including Plato, Isocrates, Demosthenes, Epicurus, Aristotle, Philo Judaeus, and Plutarch, all in Greek. In addition Skovoroda was also fluent in much Latin literature, namely Horace, Virgil, Cicero, Seneca, Lucretius, Persius, and Terentius. In addition to the above, Skovoroda studied the patristic fathers and later theologians Clement of Alexandria, Origen, Dionysius the Areopagite, Maksim the Confessor, Gregory the Theologian, John Chrysostom, Basil the Great, and Augustine. Skovoroda's fluency in languages included German, Latin, Greek, Hebrew and some Italian and Hungarian, in addition to his native Russian and Ukrainian. He also translated works of Cicero and Plutarch from Greek into Ukrainian.

Of the newer or more contemporary literary figures whom Skovoroda studied and who are noted in his compositions are Newton and Copernicus, and he mentions the circulation of blood, electricity, astronomical observatories, and the Copernican planetary system.

European enlightenment was a facet of polity and philosophy that Skovoroda rejected or to which he paid no attention, although it was very popular during that era.

Skovoroda wrote 77 letters to Kovalinski in Latin and about 15 letters in Greek as a testimony to his fluency in those languages. Several of his compositions in his *Garden of Divine Songs* were also composed in Greek. In other compositions Skovoroda has large selections in Hebrew.

Even though Skovoroda was a graduate of the Kievo-Brethren School he was self-educated for the most part, because the vast amount of texts he consumed and his mastery in several languages were not courses taught to that extent in the school, but were developed from personal study and his travels. The language of about half of Skovoroda's compositions was his native Ukrainian, which was equally balanced with Russian being the other half. Of foreign languages, Skovoroda indicated his favorite as Greek.[4]

---

[4] For the general reader the Russian translation is the most popular, and is herein utilized as the basis into English in this volume.

The genius of Skovoroda also intends into music, being able to write music and also playing a number of instruments, namely the violin, flute, lute, and piano (harpsichord).

Some debate surfaces as to why Skovoroda never married. Skovoroda was very much an ascetic: he avoided gaiety, alcohol, tobacco, immorality and situations that would lead to temptation. (His one attempt at marriage will be discussed later.) The evidence and reliable testimony is inclined toward Skovoroda taking personal vows similar to those of the priesthood: celibacy, poverty and obedience, and as a result of his seminary training and close association with many monks. But his vow was to an authority transcending institutional Christianity. With his rigorous asceticism and diet and travels and studiousness, marriage would have become alien to his nature.

Only one portrait of Skovoroda was composed during his life, and he was already 72 years old and ill from his decades of travel and mendicancy. Others – such as the cover photograph – were done later based on the amount of descriptive information from the few that knew him.

After Skovoroda's death his closest friend and confidant Mikhail Kovalinski wrote a biography, and which is distinct from other biographies because it is saturated with an understanding of his psyche. Kovalinski wrote in 1796, 2 years following Skovoroda's death.

If it were not for this biography written by the closest associate of Skovoroda, the historian would hardly find enough information from scattered fragments in the notes of other people of the era, and many of which are more fiction and legend than fact, as well as contradictory, as with the later biographies composed by Vernet, Gess de Kalvi, Sreznevski and others. But hardly enough attention is actually paid to Kovalinski's account of Skovoroda by later biographers, who seem to prefer legend rather than fact.

A second valuable source of biographical information are the letters that Skovoroda sent to Kovalinski and to many associates over the years, and right up to just a few days before his death. Skovoroda was a profusely brilliant communicator in his letters, expressing his opinions and convictions and experiences and hopes in a sincere manner.

What type of impression did Skovoroda leave on his contemporaries as a result of the fascinating and remarkable life of a philosophic nomad? Apparently immense. Kovalinski writes regarding the beginning of Skovoroda's wilderness residence. "The report about him spread through the entirety of Ukraine and Maloruss and the surrounding region." Gess de Kalve notes, "His composed verses became national songs." Snegireb says, "In the areas he visited, many of his statements became regular proverbs." Sreznevski indicates that the greater portion of the hymns sung with a harp were Skovoroda's compositions.

There is no doubt that over the decades of Skovoroda's travels and visits he was able to gain a spiritual connection with several thousand people. Excerpts of scattered notes and letters compiled during Skovoroda's era and after reflect the opinion of people toward him:

> "I would call him a Russian Socrates."
> "He was a Stoic philosopher and the Diogenes of Kharkov."
> "His allegorical association with Spinoza astonished me."
> "Skovoroda was a clandestine father of early Slavanophilism."
> "One of the first peasant democrats in Russia."
> "The first philosopher on Russian soil in the true sense of the word."
> "An apostle of rationalism."
> "He delved into the dark abyss of mysticism."
> "A rationalistic mystic if he can be explained in such a manner."
> "A true son of the rationalist age of enlightenment."
> "A version of Christian Platonism in the patristic tradition."
> "As an eclectic, loose collection of ideas."

These will serve sufficiently to provide the reader the contradictory characteristics of our subject that each of them viewed in their personal investigation.

Pavel Miluikov in Volume 2 of his *History of Russian Culture* wrote the following about Skovoroda:

> It is impossible not to notice that the era prior to the reformation pertains to the lively preaching of the famous Ukrainian philosopher

and mystic Grigori Savvich Skovoroda. Not affiliating himself with any sect, and not severing himself openly from the Orthodox Church, Skovoroda in soul was a sectarian. His views, with the exception of the teaching of the preexistence of souls, were completely aligned with the views of Dukhabors. In intimate letters to 2 or 3 friends, he straightaway identified himself as an Abrahamian, a student of Bohemian sectarians. "Let them get involved in whatever they want," he wrote to his closest friend, "but I have dedicated myself to the search for divine wisdom. For this reason we are born, by this I live, of this I meditate day and night, and with this I die." Many of the compositions of Skovoroda, valued highly by the sectarians, are nothing more than the inspired propaganda of Spiritual Christianity.

Skovoroda considered himself among their number, equating his inner voice with the genius of Socrates, and was unconditionally obedient to all that the spirit commands him. His closest of friends were prepared to accept the command of this inner spirit as prophesy, as Skovoroda did himself. Skovoroda was not alien to that mystic perception of the inner fire that convinced Spiritual Christians of all eras that the spirit of God resided in their soul. After one such ecstasy, Skovoroda conclusively believed in his calling. His attitude in relation to superficial forms of Christianity can be deduced from his opinions. He decided to fulfill Orthodox rites prior to his demise only to condescend to the conscience of the weak. Scripture he interpreted according to spiritual intellect, viewing He who exists as though a literal thought. The Bible, according to his opinion, consisted of pictures and figures that had to be understood spiritually and interpreted allegorically.

Nikolai Kostomarov summarizes his impression in the following passage:

"His portrait hangs in many homes of the entire region from Ostrogozhk[5] to Kiev. Every educated Ukrainian knows of him; and even among many of the uneducated his name is popular. His nomadic life is the subject of tales and anecdotes. In some places fathers and grandfathers have related the places where he visited, where he liked to reside, and shown them with honor. The good attitude that

---

[5] In Voronezh province.

Skovoroda showed those contemporaries he visited now comprises the family pride of their grandchildren."

Danilevski said in 1862 that at that time there was hardly a corner of his homeland that did not remember him with compassion. He states,

> "The best proof of Skovoroda's social significance consists in the fact that without him and to a widespread extent, a new university would not have been established as soon as it was. The effort of Karamzin to open the Kharkov University, which was easily finished in 1803, had as its first financial supporters landlords who donated the inconceivable among of 618 thousand rubles in silver to found this university, and they were for the most part either students of Skovoroda or his friends, or else were brief associates that knew him during his travels."

So did Skovoroda in the meek form of a destitute nomad attain being one of the most influential Russians of the 18th century.

In another respect, the tradition of Skovoroda grew because the people provided him more fable than fact, more legend than substance, and the need for this type of national folk hero was in demand, since he was a native Ukrainian. It was more of the second generation following Skovoroda that made him to be the person they wanted in their history.

DANIEL H. SHUBIN
FEBRUARY 24, 2021

BRIEF CHRONOLOGY OF SKOVORODA'S LIFE

1722 December 3	Skovoroda born in the village Chernukha, Lubyanski region, Kiev province.
1738 September	Enters Kievo-Brethren Academy.
1742	Sent to St Petersburg as a singer in an *a capella* choir.
1744 July and August	Empress Elizabeth Petrovna travels to Ukraine and Skovoroda returns and enters again the Kievo-Brethren Academy.
1745	His father dies.
1750	Departs abroad to Hungary and travels though Europe.
1753	Returns from abroad to Ukraine and attends Pereyaslav Seminary.
1754	Leaves the Pereyaslav Seminary. Stepan Tomara hires Skovoroda as a tutor.
1755	Travels to Moscow and Troitza-Sergeev Monastery.
1755-1758	Second employment of Skovoroda at Tomara in Kovrai.
1759	Invited to teach at the Kharkov Seminary.
1760 summer	Departs from Kharkov seminary.
1760-1761	Resides in the village Staritza.
1761 summer	Returns to Kharkov Seminary and meets Mihail Kovalinski.
1761-1764	A teacher of linguistics and Greek language at Kharkov Seminary
1764 August	Travels with Kovalinski to Kiev.
1764 autumn	Leaves Kharkov seminary a second time.

1766	Composition of *Introduction to Christian Morality*. He isolates himself in the Gusinski Forest near Kharkov, and there composes his first philosophic treatise *Narcissus*.
1767	Date of composition of *Achsah*.
1767 June	Residence at the Kuryazhski Preobrazhenski Monastery.
1768-1769	Teaches catechism at Kharkov Seminary.
1769	Conclusion of Skovoroda's teaching career at Kharkov Seminary and the beginning of his mendicant period.
1770	Final visit of Skovoroda to Kiev. He resides 3 months at the Kitaevoi Monastery and he then moves to Akhtirshi Troitzi Monastery.
1772	Writes *Discussion of the Ancient World*, and subsequent to it, *Conversation of Five Travelers regarding True Happiness in Life*.
1773	At the beginning of the year Skovoroda lives in the village Babaev outside of Kharkov. He writes *Kharkov Fables* during the summer, and also *Ring*.
1775 January 1	Finishes his *Alphabet*.
1776	Writes *Ikon of Alkiviad* (*Ikona Alkiviadski*)
1780	Writes *Lot's Wife* and resides shortly at the Sennyanski Monastery near Belgorod.
1781	Travels to Taganrog.
1783	Completes his *Struggle between Archangel Mikhail and Satan*.
1783-1785	Composes 3 treatises: *Observartorium, Observatorium Specula*, and *Dialog of the Deadom and Varsava*.
1785-1790	Lives in 3 villages: Gusinka, Manachinovka, and Veliki Burluk.
1787 November	Completion of dialogs *The Crippled Lark* (*Ubogi Zhaivoronok*), and *The Grateful Stork* (*Bladodarni Erodi*).
1790 April 13	Composes his *Plutarch's Book on the Soul's Contentment*.

1790 September 26	His new residence in the village Ivanivka.
1790 End of	Composes his final philosophic dialog *Serpent's Flood* (*Potop Zmiin*).
1792	Returns to live in Gusinka.
1794 Autumn	The artist G. Lukyanov paints Skovoroda's portrait.
1794 Early August	Meets Kovalinski for the final time in Orel Province in the village Khotetovo.
1794 August 26	Departs for Kiev but instead returns to Ivanivka in September.
1794 October 29	Dies in the village Ivanivka, bequeathing the statement *The World Tried to Catch Me but Could Not* on his tombstone.

GRIGORI SAVVICH SKOVORODA

BIOGRAPHY

In eastern Ukraine and south-east Russia the farmer from ancient times built homes in areas that were protected from wind and the elements and observing eyes. The unfamiliar person could long travel in the steppes with full assurance that it was unpopulated. Yet, on occasion a village located in some valley forgotten to the balance of civilization will sprout.

The village of Chernukh of the 18th century was typical of the era and region. Located along a river with a few mills for grinding wheat, it would have matched any of hundreds that populated the Ukraine landscape, and the next village far beyond the horizon. Other local villages had similar Tatar or Cossack names such as Sukhonosovka, Kovalinskii, Bondari, Kharsiki and Nekhristivka. The residents of the present Chernukh even to the present are not total definitive of the exact location of the house where on December 3, 1722, a son was born to Savvi and Pelagia Skovoroda, whom they named Grigori.

He could have even been born in Kharsiki since there to the present time the family name of Skovoroda still persists. If we were also to believe 2 of the earlier biographers who stated that the father was a priest, this would provide more evidence of his birth in Kharsiki instead of Chernukh, because the former village was large enough to justify an elder's or village counsel which would also provide sufficient income for a resident priest.

The earliest of biographers, Mikhail Kovalinski, states that Grigori was born into a Cossack family who possessed only a small parcel of farmland. Our subject in no area of any of his writings that are extant ever provides details of his family's social status. There is no reason to doubt any of Kovalinski's record since he knew Skovoroda much better than any of Skovoroda's other contemporary biographers.

According to Kovalinski, Skovoroda's parents "were people of the land with a decent income, and had a proper, honest, devout and friendly attitude toward the others in their circle." So Skovoroda inherited in this manner from his parents not only Cossack genes but also proper attributes of conduct and attitude toward society.

One biographer worth mentioning in this matter is Gess de Kalve, an Austrian-Hungarian who migrated to Ukraine at the beginning of the 19th century, who also composed a short biography of our subject. He states that the father of our subject was a village priest. Based on the characteristics of Ukrainian Cossack village life of the 18th century the father could well have been a priest from among the Cossacks. In village parishes the rank of priest was one that was nominated by the villages, and could be held in some dire situations by just about any male who was educated, knew the rites and traditions and had the trust of the village populace.

Such a capacity as meager as it may have been for the subject's family, it would have provided a means for his decent education and beyond that of the balance of village Cossack children. According to the accounts, at the age of 3 our subject was already humming ecclesiastical hymns, and later in adolescence he was spending time thumbing through ancient texts and studying the icons. This provided the parents some evidence that the future of their son would be the priesthood or education. The brief information of his childhood indicates Skovoroda had no physical defects and was a healthy and active child.

Based on the words of Kovalinski, the young Skovoroda is recorded as having done well in the local village school. "Skovoroda by the time he was 7 was noticeable inclined toward religious ceremony, was gifted in music, had an inclination toward science and was serious." Of course, such meager testimony is not substantial enough for a good observation of our subject and would appear to be bias to justify Skovoroda's later life. Apart from the above few meager statements there is nothing more reliable about Skovoroda's childhood. For all practical purposes it would have been identical with that of the balance of Cossack children of the era.

The balance of Skovoroda's education was learned from the father in his vocation or travels or village involvement, or from the mother based on household responsibilities. With the evidence of Skovoroda's father being a parish priest – to whatever extent this may be true – it would have been a benefit in his home schooling. He would have learned ecclesiastical texts enough to be a reader and some history of Russia and Ukraine and Russian Orthodoxy. The lives of Orthodox saints were a favorite for story-telling in the long and silent winter evenings. All of this would have increased Skovoroda's knowledge and served as a basis for his future education.

Life in a village exposed him to the elements of nature and various weather patterns, to the crops grown in the region along with the heavy labor needed for sowing, harvest, storage and distribution. By the time Skovoroda was in his late teens and like the other Cossack boys of the era and region, he would have been strong and developed endurance to survival typical of Cossacks. Superstitions, old wives' tales and the stories of travelers would have also been part of Skovoroda's diet of information.

Skovoroda's entrance into the Kievo-Brethren Academy in September 1738 at the ago of 16 and his advancement is recorded by Kovalinski.

> "At the request of his father, Skovoroda was willingly enrolled at the Kiev Academy, which at the time boasted of its sciences. Grigori quickly advanced beyond his contemporaries with his successes and merits."

Not including a 2-year interruption our subject spent a total of 10 years at the Kiev Academy, but apart from the short mention of Kovalinski above, nothing more is definitively known. Skovoroda's academic studies can only be indirectly stated.

When Skovoroda entered Kievo-Brethren it listed 444 names. In some archival documents the name of Skovoroda is found. Aristotelian philosophy was taught and in Latin more than any other philosophy, and he would have developed an understanding of Latin as well as Greek and Hebrew while attending.

The school likewise boasted of its choir of which Skovoroda was a member. When Gavril Matveev arrived from St Petersburg he selected Skovoroda as a singer for his royal *a capella* choir along with 6 others, the best singers of the school choir. In 1842, the 20-year old Skovoroda was selected for the environment of the elegant royal court of the Empress Elizabeth Petrovna.

He did not remain in St Petersburg long and the Empress Elizabeth traveled to Kiev during the summer of 1744, and brought her entire royal court with her including her choir. Skovoroda was able to acquire a release from the royal capella choir and so remained in Kiev, and returned to the academy. He continued to have an excellent singing voice his entire life.

Now back at the Kievo-Brethren School at age 22 Skovoroda zealously tackled Hebrew, Greek and Latin, mastering them over the next 6 years. He also intensely studied rhetoric, philosophy, metaphysics, mathematics, natural science and theology. Gess de Kalve records an interesting incident that occurred during the conclusion of this academic portion of his life.

> "He had absolutely no inclination toward a religious vocation, which his father had especially intended for him. And his repulsion toward a religious vocation grew to such an extent that when he noticed the Archbishop of Kiev wanting to ordain him as a priest, [Skovoroda] turned to subtlety. He pretended mental retardation, lowered the pitch of his voice and began to stutter in his speech. The deceived archbishop excluded him from the list of subsequent applicants to the seminary, as though he was not teachable and unqualified for a religious vocation, and left him to his own intents. And this is exactly what Skovoroda wanted. Once freed he considered himself well rewarded for the intolerable previous 6 years of his study at the academy, especially in the sciences, and which he put to a completely different use, and an intent that was other than what his contemporaries at the academy felt he would do."

This statement is valuable in 2 areas. First it definitively states that Skovoroda, having returned from St Petersburg, re-entered the Kievo-Brethren School and spent another 6 years there, intensely studying languages and various sciences Secondly, it focuses our attention on a crystallization of his internal attitude. It is apparent that Skovoroda, intently having studied the sciences, was at this time seized with a drive toward quest, and was not at all content with settling for a life-time secure position of a priest. Skovoroda was 28 years of age and felt he was still young enough to plan his life ahead of him and discover his purpose in life and society. It was during this period of intense study that Skovoroda's father died in 1745.

So Skovoroda graduated from the school and immediately decided to travel. This was about 1750. He first went to Hungary, to the Tokai gardens.[6] While visiting there, he was introduced to the general-mayor of the region, Vishnevski. He took an interest in Skovoroda, feeling he could be valuable to him in the local Greek Orthodox Church that needed clergy capable of directing the liturgy and choir, so Skovoroda became music director. Vishnevski also could utilize Skovoroda's fluency in the ancient languages to his advantage. Skovoroda willingly accepted his offer and while there he also learned German very fluently and some Italian and Hungarian.

While there, Skovoroda traveled with Vishnevski to Vienna, Ofen, Pressburg and other major cities where he in his inquisitive nature learned as much as possible about the populace, culture and scholastics. Skovoroda attended lectures at the local universities, visited German museums, and attempted to acquire as much as possible of central European enlightenment.

After his few formal visits and travels with Vishnevski, Skovoroda started on his own travels through central Europe as a philosophic nomad. All he took with him was a staff and a small purse hanging from his neck with the least of personal necessities. He traveled on foot though Poland, Prussia, Germany, Italy and the intervening countries and where he could with at the least expense. In Rome he spent personal time studying Cicero, Seneca and Cato, and visited the Vatican. He visited likewise St Peter's Square, Tatian's Triumphal Arch, the ruins of the Roman Baths of Caracalla, and as much as he could that was in contradistinction to the contemporary edifices constructed by the modern age.

The able body of a Cossack heritage provided Skovoroda with the fortitude he needed to transverse the long distances under various weather patterns and exposure to the elements (and which also benefited him in later life doing the same in Ukraine and southern Russia).

In his writings, Skovoroda never lauded the foreign countries he visited or even indicate reminiscence for them. On the contrary, he wrote that happiness was within a person and could not be attained by travels in foreign countries. This statement would be somewhat a paradox, although travel would be beneficial for exposure and experience, true contentment was something to be acquired in his Russian and Ukrainian homeland.

---

[6] Tokaj-Hegyalja: an area in north-eastern Hungary and south-western Slovakia famous for its vineyards.

At the conclusion of his European travels Skovoroda returned to his home base at the estate of Vishnevski and requested his severance in order to return home. This point was the conclusion of the initial period of Skovoroda's life – his educational – at the age of about 30, with his return home from Europe.

With Skovoroda's return to Ukraine in 1753 from Europe he first went to his home village. He stopped at the cemetery and studied all the tombstones erected since his departure for Kiev some 14 years earlier. He noticed that his entire family was buried except for one brother. After entering the village he was informed that his brother had left at some early time and there was no information to his whereabouts. After a short stay in his home village, Skovoroda again took his nomad's staff and purse and slowly by a serpentine path journeyed on foot to Kharkov.[7] For the first time in his life Skovoroda felt orphaned and a foreigner in his native land, or as one biographer described it, "A link in a chain removed and discarded by humanity."

This event began a second period of Skovoroda's life: his teaching career. Even though Skovoroda had his pockets filled with scholarship, experience and zeal, his pockets were devoid of money and he was dependant on the kindness of earlier friends and acquaintances and even strangers, and lodging at their homes. Several extended this effort to put him to work, attempting to find something in his vocational field, but of course this excluded what most of the populace did at the time, which was farming or a trade or manual labor. The bishop of Pereyaslav heard of the plight of Skovoroda and offered him a teaching position at the Pereyaslav Seminary, the reputation of Skovoroda still intact as far as his academics was concerned.

Arriving in Pereyaslav-Khmelnitzki and settling in his new position, Skovoroda wrote a dissertation (now lost) to the bishop explaining his method of teaching, and which he felt he had to do because his education far surpassed any of the provincial teachers and his experience led him to teaching in a manner that was not the regimented manner of provincial schools.

Of course, Skovoroda's proposition was alien and incompatible with the manner that the bishop operated his school system and he replied

---

[7] Or, Charkiv or Kharkiv.

telling Skovoroda that he would have to change his approach to teaching and conform to the traditional manner if he wanted the teaching position. But if Skovoroda did want to implement his new approach he would have to document it and present it to the local Episcopal consistory with a personal inquest for their approval. Skovoroda, assured that his approach to teaching was superior to that of the bishop's, responded, informing him of his refusal to agree to the bishop's demands and that he was not about to allow them to put him to trial for his beliefs, as he viewed the inquest.

The bishop in a report to the consistory called Skovoroda arrogant and made a decision to expel the newly-arrived Skovoroda from teaching, and he was asked to leave. Skovoroda's expulsion, as he states in one of his letters, was a sorrowful day in his life, and because he was hoping to remain at the school and teach. Skovoroda felt they were mistaken in their evaluation of him, considering his firmness and self-confidence as arrogance. Skovoroda had spent about a year teaching there.

Even though his pockets remained empty and he was total destitute Skovoroda remained firm in his convictions and moved to live with a local acquaintance. His entire material possessions at this time consisted solely of 2 worn shirts, one colored pair of pants, one pair of shoes and one pair of black wool stockings. The year was 1754 and Skovoroda was 32 years old.

As with previous situations, an opportunity again arose, and now with a popular Ukrainian nobleman who lived not to distant from Pereyaslav. Stephan Tamara needed a private tutor for his son Vasili. Skovoroda's acquaintances recommended him to Tamara and he was invited to the village Kovrai, located across the Dnepr River from Cherkassy, where the nobleman entrusted his son to Skovoroda's care and education.

The nobleman Tamara was gifted with an immense intellect and was self-taught for the most part. During his national service he had direct contact with many foreigners and acquired over the years familiarity with other cultures and civilizations. Skovoroda understood the disposition of his employer and so followed the same vein with regard to the son's education: first with rudimentary topics of history and grammar, and then later with introduction into the sciences. Eventually the son developed a fond affection for Skovoroda. The agreement was made for one year.

Even though the elder Stephan and Skovoroda and the son Vasili sat at table for dinner every day, not once did the elder begin a conversation with

Skovoroda and did not say even one word to him. Skovoroda felt humiliated at this condescension, but decided to tolerate the arrogance of Tamara and serve his one year of tutoring. Tamara's wife was a coarse and audacious woman and was very insecure with Skovoroda in their household. Often times, she would have her servants spy on Skovoroda during his off-hours.

On one occasion while discussing some topic, Skovoroda asked the son to be open and frank in regards to this particular topic and disclose his thoughts. His pupil responded in a manner that Skovoroda felt was improper and unsuitable. Skovoroda's response was to tell him that his thinking was like something coming from a pig's head. The servants immediately relayed this to the mistress and she to her husband. The elder Tamara, as much as he valued the tutoring of Skovoroda, capitulated to the demands of his wife and informed Skovoroda of his termination and expulsion from their home. The only words the elder Tamara said to Skovoroda were, "Forgive me for having to do this. This is sorrowful for me." Now it was 1755.

As Kovalinski recorded:

"Skovoroda remained without a home, food, clothing, but not without hope. Maimed, destitute and in need he arrived at the home of his friend, a military captain in Pereyaslav, a person magnanimous and hospitable. All of a sudden he was presented with the opportunity to travel to Moskva with a calligrapher, who was going to the Moskva Academy as an artist, and so he left. After arriving in Moskva, he traveled to the Troitza-Sergeev Monastery, where at the time the rather educated Kirill [Florinski], who was earlier Bishop of Chernigov, was Father Superior. Seeing Skovoroda, whom he knew by reputation, he noticed he was a person excellently gifted and educated. Kirill attempted to convince him to remain at the monastery and to take a teaching position at their seminary. But love of his homeland drove him back to Ukraine. He returned to Pereyaslav."

So typical of Skovoroda was this incident to suddenly travel, visit places and people of philosophic and theological interest and return to his homeland. Of course he could have found security with a long-term teaching position and entering the Orthodox priesthood, but again this would have curbed his freedom. The period between his expulsion from tutoring the son of Tamara to his return from Moskva was about 2 to 3 years in Skovoroda's life.

Immediately after describing Skovoroda's journey to Sergeev Monastery Kovalinski wrote the following:

"His spirit distanced him from any ties and caused him to be a nomad, a migrant, wanderer, creating within him the heart of a world-wide citizen. Not having relatives or ties or a corner where he can rest his head he consumed the satisfaction of nature, the eternal treasures that were simple, chaste, worriless, true and the source of a pure and untroubled mind."

Kovalinski knew Skovoroda best of any person of the era and such words reflect the soul of Skovoroda. But they are not idyllic as Skovoroda was experiencing much upheaval internally with his search for purpose after his return from Moskva.

About this time Skovoroda composed his series of 30 poems titled *Garden of Divine Songs*, most of them in Greek. Having sung himself in the *a cappella* choir, his arrangements were to be sung in the same manner. This collection of Skovoroda's songs unveils a soul full of depth, sorrow, passion, chaos and difficulty. (Selections of his songs are in this volume.)

The elder Tamara, having read some of Skovoroda's songs and poems and fables, and understanding that this was Skovoroda's pastime, told him, "My friend, God has blessed you with the gift of spirit and word."

No sooner did Skovoroda return to Pereyaslav from Moskva that Tamara had some acquaintance contact him and convince to return to the employment of being his son's tutor. Initially Skovoroda rejected the offer remembering the bad experience of Tamara's capitulation to his wife to terminate his employment and the treachery of the other employees. However a friend told Skovoroda to go with him for a ride at night and while he was sleeping in the carriage they arrive at Tamara's home.

Tamara's attitude changed over the course of Skovoroda's absence and he developed a more friendly and courteous approach to requesting his return as a tutor. The new attitude and frankness won Skovoroda's confidence in the nobleman and he agreed to return to employment, but now without any reservations or conditions. The new term of teaching was from 1755 to 1758.

On a regular basis and after finishing his daily tutoring routine at the city home of Tamara Skovoroda would flee to the countryside. There among his beloved nature and living among people who cherished him, and free from the stress and demands of the Tamara household, he was able to concentrate and focus on his personal deliberations of philosophy and theology. As Kovalinski described it:

> "Quite often during his free hours from his obligations did he depart into the fields, forests and gardens for meditation. Early in the morning dawn he would wander among oak trees, and talking to them as though they were his interlocutors. The vanity and stress of the secular world was a turbulent sea incessantly violent and was never able to bring him to a calm haven for his soul."

Scherbinin, the Governor of Kharkov, heard of Skovoroda and summoned him asking him why he had not accepted some permanent vocation or employment. Kovalinski records the conversation.

> Skovoroda replied, "Merciful sir. The world is like a theater: to put on a play with success and acclaim people who accept roles according to their abilities. Long have I meditated on this matter and after testing myself in many areas I came to the conclusion that I am unable to take any role in the theater of this world successfully, except as a lowly, simple, carefree and self-sufficient individual. This is the role I have chosen, taken and with which I am satisfied."
>
> "My friend," responded Scherbinin leading him aside, "Perhaps you have capabilities in other areas, in community work, but I think it is because of your habits, opinions, prejudices that are hindering you."
>
> "If I was to feel today," interrupted Skovoroda, "that I could kill Turks without my timid character, then I would today tie a hussar sword to my side and don a military dress hat and depart to serve in the army. The difficulty I have with a congenital inclination has served to my benefit. A dog will guard the flock day and night due to its congenital love and will attack a wolf due to its congenital inclination disregarding the fact that it has subjected itself to danger and could die

at the jaws of the aggressor. Inclination, willingness, satisfaction, nature, divine strength is all of God. Evil inclinations and natures are a manifestation of divine wrath. A person is an instrument that willingly and voluntarily subjects itself to the activity and love of God, that is, either to the love or to the wrath of God, that is, a judgment that is either good or bad, light or darkness. This is sealed tangibly on the rotation of day and night, summer and winter, life and death, eternity and temporary. God is the god of life or love and God is judgment or wrath. All creatures are coarse servile instruments of the personality of the Supreme Essence. Only people are His noble instruments having primarily freedom and free will of choice, and as a result they must answer for the use of this privilege."

Kovalinski records a note that Skovoroda left with him that pertains to this period of his life. It was a revelation that molded and accompanied Skovoroda the balance of his life.

"While at the home of Tamara in the village Kovrai during the late night of November 24, 1758, I had a dream where I saw the various things that people wanted for their life. In one place I visited there were royal palaces, decorations, music, dancing, and people that loved to sing, and looking at themselves in a mirror and running from room to room taking off their masks, sitting on expensive blankets, and so on.

"Then some power led me to simple people where I noticed the following activities. People walked along the street with glassware in their hands, shouting, happy, shaking, just as you would usually find among rifffaff. And then I noticed something unusual in matters of love-making. Men were lined in one row and opposite them women were lined in a row and they would inspect each other and decide who was good for whom as a pair.

"From this place I went to some out-buildings, where horses, their harnesses and hay were stored and where I heard arguments and disputes.

"Finally this force let me to some type of church, large and beautiful, and I was there as if on the day of the descent of the Holy Spirit and I performed the liturgy with the deacon and I remember that

I shouted out loud, 'For holy is our God.' And then the lengthy response of a choir on both sides, 'Holy God.' Both I and the deacon bowed low to the ground in front of the altar, and I felt an inner sweet satisfaction which I cannot describe. However this place was defiled with the sins of humans. They drug into it their love of money and their purses, and the priest himself unconsciously was deep into the charity box.

"Then I saw the following terrifying scene as several people dressed in black clothes, but above their knees, did not have enough foul and animal meat to eat, and they would hold raw meat over a fire and eat the fat as it poured out of the meat. To me this seemed repulsive and I could not tolerate the bestial and shameful conduct of the ecclesiastical servants and so I turned my eyes away from them and left.

"This dream scared me more than any comfort it provided."

It was this year of 1758 in the village Kovrai that played a life-changing decisive role in Skovoroda's life. His dream is unusually characteristic: it was not simply a dream but disclosed the meaning of Skovoroda's struggle. He turned his eyes away from the complexities of life, he exited from the normal conditions of existence. Kovalinski further describes the matter:

"Not deciding to have any steady income, he fixed it firmly in his heart to furnish his life with restraint, satisfaction with little, prudence, humility, industriousness, patience, magnanimity, integrity, honestly, and abandon all desire for vanity, all cares for acquisition, all the complications of superfluity."

Skovoroda was faithful to this decision his entire life.

In the same year 1758, the young Vasili Tamara also decided on a different course in life apart from Skovoroda's philosophic and theological meanderings, and Skovoroda decided to depart from employment as his tutor and this time permanently and on good terms. He leaves the now-hospitable Stephan Tamara and village Kovrai.

On March 6, 1788, some 30 years later, the son Vasili Tamara wrote to Skovoroda:

"My beloved teacher Grigori Skovoroda. I received your letter sent via our mutual friend Kisilov with great admiration and heartfelt fondness for you. My friend, I hope you remember your Vasili at least superficially and not a person who is unfortunate, but who inwardly needs counsel more today than he did when he was with you. O, if the Lord would only allow you to live with me more. If you were only to listen to me just for a while you would not be very happy with your former pupil. Do I yearn for you in vain? If not, then dedicate some time and reply to me, telling me how we can again see each other. Farewell my best friend Skovoroda. And do not deny some spare time of yours to your former pupil Vasili Tamara."

Now it was 1759 and Skovoroda was invited to teach at the Kharkov Seminary and had 3 periods there as a teacher: 1759 to the summer of 1760; summer of 1761 to autumn of 1764; and 1768 to 1769. Kovalinski writes:

"Joasaph Mitkevich ascended the Episcopal cathedra in Belgorod.[8] He was a person having a kind heart, philanthropic, and very educated. He was likewise close friends with the monk Gervasi Yakubovich who was residing at the time in Pereyaslav.

"Joasaph invited Gervasi to share some of the Episcopal responsibilities with him and the more friendly atmosphere of the bishop's residence. Gervasi arrived in Belgorod and seeing Joasaph's zeal toward the sciences he highly recommended Skovoroda to him. The bishop summoned Skovoroda, and who soon arrived. Skovoroda was offered a position teaching at the Kharkov Seminary in 1759, which he accepted.

"His excellent ability to synthesize ideas, his education and attitude toward life quickly drew toward him the attention of the local religious community. He dressed plainly and modestly. His diet consisted of fruits and vegetables and milk products, and usually only one meal a day after sunset. He did not eat meat or fish; not due to superstition but because of his personal disposition. He only slept 4 hours a day. He rose before dawn and if the weather permitted he

---

[8] Presently in the Russian Federation, north of Kharkov.

would walk on foot about the city enjoying the fresh air and gardens. He was always happy, vigilant, relaxed, temperate, prudent, content with what he had, magnanimous, was kind to everybody he met, a good conversationalist where he was not forced to converse, having a high ethic, treating people of all social levels well, visiting the sick, comforting those in sorrow, sharing what little he had with the underprivileged, he selected his friends based on their character, having a devotion but without superstitions, he would not flaunt his education and would not tolerate flattery.

"A year passed and having met his obligations he requested Joasaph a review of his effort. The bishop, wanting to keep him at the seminary indefinitely entrusted Gervasi – as an intermediary and common friend – to convince him to become a monk and which would allow him to further advance in rank. Gervasi spoke with Skovoroda telling him the bishop's proposition and all its advantages, and the honor, merit, income and veneration he would acquire as well as a secure future."

But the attempt was unsuccessful, as Kovàlinski records.

"These were not the type of advantages that should have been proposed to incline Skovoroda. Having heard all Gervasi had to say, he zealously replied, 'Do you want me to increase the number of Pharisees? Eat the fatty, drink the sweet, clothe yourselves comfortably and live as monks?' But Skovoroda considered monasticism as a life that should be without compensation, content with little, restrained, and deprived of all that was unnecessary, in order to acquire what is absolutely necessary by the denial of desire, in order to preserve yourself whole, defeating ambition, in order to fulfill the commandment of love toward associate, seeking the merit of God, and not merit of people."

Gervasi attempted to convince him on behalf of the bishop, what a benefit it would to the church, but Skovoroda was firm in his attitude and principles, and declined the invitation.

Gervasi, knowing Skovoroda's material destitution and his need for income, figured that eventually he will agree to the proposition, and asked

Skovoroda to think about it for a while. After 3 days of meditation on the offer Skovoroda made his decision. He confronted Gervasi and told him very kindly, "I ask that his Highest Reverend bless me on my way." Gervasi, hardly looking at him, blessed him reluctantly. Gervasi reported Skovoroda's rejection of their proposition and his exit to Bishop Joasaph, who was displeased with the conclusion of the matter and as a result grieved for Skovoroda.

Skovoroda departed peacefully that very moment to the village Staritza[9] south of Belgorod to his new friend.[10] Staritza was a region abundant in forests, streams, meadows, and pleasant profound solitude. Skovoroda settled here in order to continue writing.

Kovalinski described Skovoroda's period there:

"There is no place that a person can reflect upon himself except in solitude, and not in vain did the ancient sages states that when in solitude a person must be either a king or a beast. To defeat boredom, any cursed progeny of dissatisfaction, mental anxieties or lonesomeness, is a matter that only a wise person in total possession of his faculties can accomplish, a person who is a king over his seclusion, a priest of God, filled with the Spirit of our Lord and who can worship Him in spirit."

So Skovoroda selects solitude but not of a monastic type in order to walk the path of thousands of other saints and ascetics. What was it about Orthodoxy that repulsed Skovoroda? Several items will come to our mind at this point: his individualism, independence, refusal of regimentation, rejection of institutionalized religion, as well as recognizing the power struggle and moral corruption inherent in the ecclesiastical hierarchy.

It was the summer of 1760 and he lived there until his return to Kharkov Seminary in the summer of 1761.

His forest hermitage was interrupted when rumors of his reputation began circulation: his asceticism, scholarship and hermitage motivated people to seek him and enter into edifying conversation.

---

[9] Or, Starycja, located in the Volchanski Region of Kharkov Province, along the Severni Donets River, and near the present border with the Russian Federation.
[10] Kovalevski

It was about this time that Skovoroda met the person who would become in his life his closest friend, confidant, biographer and promoter of his compositions, Mikhail Kovalinski. They did not meet incidentally. It was Kovalinski's uncle Grigori Ivanovich who heard of his reputation and met with him and then asked that when Skovoroda would have his next opportunity to be in Kharkov, to visit him and say a few words of encouragement to his nephew. Some short time later Skovoroda did visit Kharkov to visit some friends and took the time to visit the young man recommended to him. At first glace Skovoroda took a serious liking to Mikhail Kovalinski, while later Kovalinski wrote that their meeting was arranged "by the finger of God from a distance." Skovoroda attached himself to Kovalinski as a mentor and friend and to the end of his life.

Bishop Joasaph, who had never let Skovoroda out of his direct sight and had continually sought a manner to lure him back to his Kharkov Seminary and make use of his talents, propositioned him at this time, during this visit to return as a teacher. Skovoroda combined his meeting with Kovalinski and the new request of Bishop Joasaph as being divine agreed to do so and very willingly and voluntarily.

Immediately Skovoroda abandoned Staritza and returned to Kharkov Seminary as a teacher. Such a move is very characteristic of Skovoroda, but now his reasoning to return to teaching was not to want his education and experience to be wasted in exclusion from others. He realized that his knowledge of philosophy and theology and foreign languages could be transmitted to others for a beneficial use by returning to Kharkov seminary and teaching. In this case he was assigned to teaching linguistics and Greek.

The young Kovalinski was likewise captivated and enchanted by Skovoroda's philosophic life. Between the 2 of them an original mystical novel immediately began. Skovoroda would visit Kovalinski regularly and impressed on him the study of music and reading of various books, which then became the basis of their intense and lengthy conversations. Often during the summer they took long walks late in the evening outside the city, and sometimes in the city cemetery wandering about. In a nearby forest they would sit together as Skovoroda would play his flute. A close spiritual and fraternal relationship developed between the 2 of them.

But it was difficult for Skovoroda to visit Kovalinski as regularly as he wanted due to his obligations at the seminary, but wanting to educate him and impress upon him the search for truth and drive for study Skovoroda would write to him almost every day. Many of these letters survive to the present and allow us insight into their relationship and Skovoroda's desire for the person who became the son he never had (some of the letters are translated in this volume). We have no knowledge of Kovalinski's family or why it was easy for him to attach himself to Skovoroda and for Skovoroda to take him as a pupil and perhaps foster-child. The relationship between Apostle Paul and Timothy would be a good analogy.

The relationship between the 2 created a profound and undefiled joy and radiance in Skovoroda's life. The letters of Skovoroda to Kovalinski allowed Skovoroda to project his philosophic convictions to a second party whom he felt would be able to utilize them and in this manner provide Skovoroda with a manner of unearthing and disclosing his ideas in a more personal manner than in the composition of bland and colorless philosophical treatises. This also indirectly relieved Skovoroda's internal struggle by as if shifting this load to a second party whom he knew would understand his predicament and dilemma, yet Kovalinski was himself unaffected. How many of Skovoroda's letters did Kovalinski actually read and how many did he take seriously cannot be ascertained and it would not matter anyway, except that we have in these letters Skovoroda's honest and sincere reflections on various facets of his life and an understanding of his philosophy that is personal and non-pretentious.

Skovoroda's letters to Kovalinski are infused with his desires for the young man: to lead him into knowledge, to summon in him a correct and honorable attitude toward life. Skovoroda senses in him the capacity of becoming "a graduate of the most gracious Christian philosophy," and so strives to plant in his soul seed. This is a consistent vein of thinking in Skovoroda's letters to Kovalinski.

Skovoroda taught Kovalinski Greek and Latin, and impressed upon him the possibility of acquiring the treasures of ancient and patristic literature in their original languages. Skovoroda familiarized Kovalinski with Plutarch, Philo, Cicero, Clement of Alexandria. Origin, Dionysius the Ariopagite, and Maxim the Confessor, and most of all of them the Bible.

Skovoroda's letters had an enormous impact on Kovalinski. Some 30 years later, Kovalinski wrote to Skovoroda. "Just looking at the letters you sent me ignites a fire in me. It is difficult for me to erase these first impressions."

Skovoroda continued to live in Kharkov to 1766, teaching and privately tutoring his pupil and friend Kovalinski, until the Kharkov seminary added more classes to its agenda, and which were assigned to Skovoroda to teach. He willingly accepted the additional teaching load but only with the condition that he would not accept payment for his efforts. Skovoroda was now age 44 and settled in his ways and his thinking.

A student recorded a few excepts of one of his lectures.

> "All the world sleeps! It has stretched itself out, and as if is sewn closed in its blanket. Not only do pedagogues not awaken it, but stroke them, saying, 'Sleep, do not fear, this is a good place, there is nothing to be afraid of.'

As a result a scandal arose and his lectures were critiqued from another angle and interpreted in a most perverted manner.

As with the previous situation and conflict with Bishop Joasaph, the same arose with his additional teaching responsibilities and the Bishop required an investigation and inquest into all of his lectures, and a review of his lectures prior to their delivery. Unable to again tolerate the suppression of his independent thought, Skovoroda was terminated from his position.

He moved to the Gusinski forest near Kharkov, where he wrote *Introduction to Christian Morality*: his first philosophic composition, *Narcissus*: and subsequently *Achsah* in early 1767. In June of 1767 Skovoroda moved to live at the Kuryazhski Preobrazenski Monastery.

However once again he returned for a final year of teaching at Kharkov Seminary, from 1768 to 1769, now teaching catechism. Subsequently the second period of his life – his teaching career – abruptly ended and never would he again follow such a path. The final period of his life – from 1769 to his death in 1794 – was his period of mendicancy, an ascetic severance from all the normal comforts of human continuance and also his teaching career.

Skovoroda wrote of this moment

> "Opinions are like the wind, they are not visible among the elements, but are firmer and stronger than waters that can uproot trees, overturn buildings, create massive waves and force ships; it can rust metal and

erode rock, and extinguish and quench fire. So are the thoughts of the heart, they are not seen, and exist as if they do not, but from such a spark a large fire will start, or revolt or destruction. The entire life of our tree depends on such a seed."

And so did Skovoroda in 1769 at age 46 consummate an alteration in his life, now transformed into a nomad, a bird without a nest, a nomad without a place to rest his head, without possessions and entirely dependant on the will of God, meaning, the kindness and hospitality of Ukrainian and Russian villagers. Initially in 1770 Skovoroda visited Kiev and resided 3 months at the Kitaevoi Monastery, and then relocated to the Akhtirski Troitzki Monastery.

When the 83-year-old Leo Tolstoy abandoned his home and departed to parts unknown, the entire world sighed in amazement. All the world raised questions about the incident; he was followed until found at Astopova, where a new telegraph office and wires had to be installed to forward the latest news of the famous author turned nomad. But when Skovoroda abandoned all and took his staff, no one noticed and no one of those that knew him even expressed any emotion, and no one even cared. But this does not make the exodus of Skovoroda any less significant than that of Tolstoy. The difference was the popularity of each figure, but the intents were the same: to depart from the secular and complex world and live a life of simplicity and unworried travel. But Skovoroda's exodus was far more significant and intensive than Tolstoy's, because Tolstoy left after having lived all that the world could offer him: family, wealth, real estate, security, financial success and popularity, and he had little life remaining at his age of 83. Skovoroda's departure was far more significant since it occurred at the prime of his life, denying himself the future possibilities of an equal satisfaction of all that Tolstoy had already received and experience. With his equal genius, Skovoroda could also have attained all that Tolstoy had, but he foresaw the detriment it would have on himself as a philosopher, and would force him to compromise or capitulate to the secular demands of Ukrainian society or the Orthodox religious establishment. (Tolstoy did not have the genius that Skovoroda had in regard to foreign languages or music, but Tolstoy did excel Skovoroda in history and composition. Their knowledge of the Bible and the Christian religion was about equal.)

Perhaps Skovoroda felt he could accomplish more with his life as a nomadic philosopher and itinerant preacher, traveling where he wanted and communicating with whomever would want to discuss any matter or subject with him, and without censure and without worry about being pretentious. Perhaps Skovoroda felt he could accomplish more with his life by not being a professor in some seminary, delivering structured lectures that had to comply with the established policy of the academy. Tolstoy left with a dissatisfaction of his life as it was, realizing it had come to a stalemate, while for Skovoroda it was a new beginning with a wide future ahead of him. Tolstoy left to meet death in peace; Skovoroda resurrected unto life abundant and left spiritual death behind him. Tolstoy's demise was 2 weeks after his departure from Yasnaya Polyana, while Skovoroda inherited 26 years.

Having taken his nomad's staff, Skovoroda would now never release it. He becomes a true nomad wandering with passion, with the most part with a calm sense of a calling. Mendicancy for Skovoroda was a voluntary feat of severance from the regular conditions of life that interfered with his inner life of spirit.

The region of his roaming was not a large one. It was the eastern half of Ukraine and the southern portion of Russia for the most part. He traveled as far south to Taganrog on the Black Sea coast and as far north as Voronezh and Orlov Provinces. His letters and compositions of this era were composed in the most diverse of places. Due to the lack of chronological data there is little manner of defining when Skovoroda was at some specific place, how long he stayed there or where he stayed when there, and when he departed. Only an assortment of places within the general time frame is known for sure, and this information is meager, and mostly based on the letters he sent, often containing the date and the city where he composed them. Being attracted to some forest or grove, Skovoroda would improvise and build for himself a hamlet or hovel and remain there until some inner motivation would force him to take his nomad's staff and depart.

He was completely dependant on nature during summer and good weather periods. Much of the time with ill weather or winter he would reside at the home of anyone who would receive him, or someone having heard of him, or those whose confidence or trust he would gain. The records of those who saw him confirm that all his traveling was on foot, never once seeing him in a wagon or carriage or on horseback.

His possessions during this nomadic period were his gray bag containing some books and some provisions. His books were a Hebrew Bible and a Greek Old and New Testament, along with papers and writing materials that became his manuscripts and compositions. A flute that he hand carved was a permanent fixture. (Reports of later generations displayed Skovoroda as a Piped-Piper with a stream of young devotees behind him walking some country path, stopping on occasion to discuss philosophic topics. But there is more legend to this than fact.)

Skovoroda related to his Hebrew Bible as his bride,

"I have loved you from my youth. My sweetest musical instrument. My Bible is my beloved dove. For this reason I was born. For it I eat and drink. With it I live and I will die with it."

His words were prophetic because when dying Skovoroda placed his bag containing his Hebrew Bible and other books under his head. The nomad read it at every occasion he had over the years of his nomadic travels.

Regarding subsidence, Skovoroda repeats with pride Socrates' words, "Many live to eat, while I eat to live."

Skovoroda strove to not be in debt to his benefactors. He taught their children grammar, entertained them with his fables, and played music. More than all he philosophized with them and discussed the Bible and its application, and especially in regard to the Christian denominations of the era: Orthodoxy and the iconoclast sectarians. People had so much respect for Skovoroda that they considered it a blessing should he visit their home and take asylum there for a while. As Sreznevski reported, "The respect for Skovoroda was so great that the home he resided in for even just a few days was considered a special blessing of God. In this manner did Skovoroda resolve his economic difficulty. He repaid his benefactors for their material support with his metaphysical and spiritual contribution."

In one letter Skovoroda clearly explains in what his involvement was and how his time was occupied, and what the goal was of his isolationism.

"My guardian Angel rejoices with me here in the wilderness. I was born for this. Old age, destitution, humility, worry-free, and consideration are all my cohabitants. I love them and they me. Not long ago someone asked of me, 'Tell me, what does he do there?' If I was in the wilderness to heal myself of some bodily illness, or to watch beehives, or to trap animals, then Skovoroda would seem to them to be occupied. But since I do not any of this, they figure I am idle and are amazed at this. It is true that idleness is heavier than the Caucasus Mountains. Is all there is to a person an occupation to sell, buy, marry, enjoy, war, sew clothes, build, and trap animals? Is our heart inescapable from all this? Now we can recognize clearly the reason for our destitution: we have delved with all our heart into acquisition of secular possessions, and into the sea of bodily necessities, and as a result we have not the time to delve within ourselves, to cleanse and heal the master of our body – our soul. We have an over-abundance of such items. It seems that all goodness needs to be corporeal. But we are like a carriage without wheels: it is our soul that we do not possess.

True, we do possess a soul, but for some it is the same as swelling or gout of the foot. It has become weakened, cruel, capricious, cowardly, envious, selfish, dissatisfied in us, angry at itself, gaunt, pale, like a patient at a mental asylum who is buried there, sentenced by the state although is alive. So if such a soul is clothed in velvet, then is not its coffin also lined in velvet? If it feasts in bright chambers, is this not its hell? If its entire world exalts paintings and songs, which the offspring of Adam magnifies, then the following prophetic sonnet is pitifully applied to it, 'In secret does my soul weep.' If the very secret, meaning the very center of the soul anguishes and hurts, who or what will console it? Ah my master! Swim to the shore and raise your eyes to the harbor. Do not forget yourself in the midst of your abundance. A person does not just live by bread."

Kovalinski supplements the following regarding this angelic bread about which Skovoroda day and night was concerned.

"Philosophy, having settled in Skovoroda's heart, provided him sustenance, the ability to live off the land. Liberated from the shackles of every compulsion, futility, acquisition, anxiety, he found a fulfillment of all his wants in the mortification of the above. Rather than worrying about the reduction of natural necessities, and not about expansion, he ate satisfaction that was incomparable with any secular prosperity. When the sun, having shined its infinite rays on the emerald shroud, stretched its generous hand with the sensation of its dinner table, then he, accepting the cup of enjoyments, undiluted with any kind of life's sorrows, any kind of passion's moans, any kind of dissolute vanities, and tasting the ecstasy of a supreme intellect, in the full calm of his soul's contentment, he spoke, 'Gratitude to the all-gracious God, because he made easy what is necessary, and difficult what is unnecessary.' The night for him was a place of tranquility from his mental concentrations, which unconsciously exhausted his bodily strength. An easy and quiet sleep was a time for reflection, a harmony of nature as he imagined it."

So was the discovery of this angelic bread and that inherent calm that provided Skovoroda with the harmony of nature, and so became the primary idea pervading his roaming. Indirectly and unconsciously Skovoroda passed all of this on to others.

The ascetic vein so characteristic of Skovoroda increased during this period. Skovoroda's destitute condition was in itself an extreme view of asceticism. Willingly accepting such a vocation he very seldom departed from it, however occasionally he did, since he was always ready to dine in the company of friends. One occasion at the home of a businessman Yurypin, Skovoroda drank enough of some alcoholic beverage that he was involved in a brawl. But in general Skovoroda abstained from alcohol altogether and such an occurrence was rare and unusual, but as the account provided by an associate Kvitko Osnovyanko indicated, Skovoroda was not opposed to or withdrawn from the gatherings of friends and associates who would feast and drink to enliven their conversations. Such associations also testify to Skovoroda's freedom in discussion and debates, and his opposition to pedantry and dry rhetoric, yet doing his best not to condescend to or condone irresponsible behavior. Skovoroda's letters to Kovalinski testifies to his high morality and ethic as he warns Kovalinski about the temptation of youth and the vices that are so easy for a young person to acquire.

Kovalinski records the discredit and criticism that Skovoroda endured because of his refusal to indulge in alcohol and irresponsible behavior and vices.

"The pseudo-philosophic haughtiness was not strong enough to harm him using discredit and would often turn to another weapon – slander. They taught that Skovoroda condemned the use of meat and wine and so abstained from this himself. But we know that such a teaching was that of the Manicheans, condemned by the holy councils. But these accusers label him as a Manichean disciple. In addition to this, they prove that he categorically calls harmful gold, silver, valuable items, and nice clothing."

Skovoroda, having heard of this, strove to dissipate such rumors, and in front of a large group of people, publicly stated,

"There was a time and on occasion even at the present, that for my internal preservation I restrained myself from all meat and wine. This can be compared to a doctor recommending against certain foods if you are ill, such as garlic. All was created good by the all-generous Creator, but not all of it is always beneficial. It is true that I counseled some that they be careful with the amount of wine and meat they consume, and occasionally that they completely abstain from it, understanding the zeal of their youth. But when a father snatches a knife from a child and does not allow him to play with gunpowder, is it not clearly obvious that his son is still not mature enough to correctly handle these items and to properly use them for the beneficial intent for which they were designed? It is false that every type of food and drink is beneficial and good. But it is necessary to take into consideration time, place, amount and personal fitness. Would it not be repulsive to offer a breast-feeding child a glass of strong vodka? When God assigned me as a lowly character in the theater of this world, then he also assigned to me the ability to remember my condition in my clothing, actions; and attitude with the middle class, officials, famous and honored people; and to preserve order and obligation and respect."

Gess de Kalve states that Skovoroda only ate the most coarse of food, and did not want to depart from his extreme ascetic habits even to his old age. But Skovoroda's asceticism had another more important facet: the soul's restraint and inner spirit's working. To Skovoroda his asceticism was not a self-imposed deprivation of life's benefits, but the removal of restraints and chains that hindered his expression of life in its fullness. His attainment of what life had to offer him was discovered in existence as a roamer and mendicant philosopher, having liberated himself from the bonds of unnecessary obligations and responsibilities.

Kovalinski writes,

> "He had a custom of always dedicating to prayer the deepest midnight. During such tranquil periods of profound silence his sense of nature was accompanied by divine meditation. Then he, gathering his senses and thoughts in one circle within himself and having reflected with his discerning eye the gloomy residence of his earthly person, he would cry to God as his principal, 'Arise lazy and consistently melancholy thoughts of my mind! Ascend and rise to the mountains of eternity.' Immediately a struggle evolved within him and his heart became the battlefield. Ambition was armed together with the sovereigns of this age, secular reason, individual mortality of human – and that of all creatures – frailty, all of which powerfully attacked his will in order to enslave him and ascend the throne of his freedom and be like the Supreme. His divine meditations summoned his will to His eternal, sole, true goodness. What a struggle! What a heroic feat! Heaven and hell fought in the sage's heart. And so he passed the midnight hours in battle armor against the powers of the dark world. The radiant morning encompassed him in the light of virtue, and in triumph of spirit he exited the battlefield and shared his accolades with all nature."

Almost always in all his motions Skovoroda indicated that he was subjecting his will to his spirit. Phrases such as 'the spirit orders,' 'the spirit summons,' 'the spirit speaks,' are regular expressions of Skovoroda. That these are not just metaphors and simple expressions of motivation is testified to by the following interesting incident that occurred with Skovoroda.

In 1770 he arrived in Kiev to the home of a relative name Justin. He suddenly noticed within himself a strong motion of spirit, one not comprehendible, compelling him to leave Kiev. Justin begged him not to leave. Friends also gathered there attempted to restrain him, but he responded that the spirit was positively commanding him to depart Kiev. So Skovoroda ascended some local hill on his way out of the city and as he descended the other side he suddenly stopped, and sensed the strong smell of dead corpses, so strong he could not endure it, and immediately turned to his home. The spirit in a convincing and forceful manner was herding him out of the city. By the next day he had departed and was gone.

After arriving in Akhtirka, 2 weeks having passed, he heard news that plague overcame Kiev, and so intense that such had never occurred in the history of the city, and that the city had closed its gates as a result.[11]

It is obvious that nature or deity was benevolently inclined to Skovoroda in sharing with him this special and extreme sense of impending distress.

What role did women play in the life of Skovoroda? Kovalinski completely diminishes the issue. Gess de Kalve states that Skovoroda had no inclination toward the female gender. Sreznevski condenses previous records and says, "Grigori Savvich was terrifyingly afraid of young women, especially girls." Nonetheless, Sreznevski in one of his narratives relates Skovoroda's one romance, the only one he knows about, that he seemed to have gleaned from a multitude of sources, and most of then unreliable second-hand accounts. Yet there is no good reason not to accept its validity, since in general it coincides with Skovoroda's character. Sreznevski's narrative is as follows:

> Toward the end of the 1760s, Skovoroda entered a Cossack village and where he saw a young girl singing; her name was Elena Pavlovna. Skovoroda settled in an apiary not far from the village. The girl's father – whose name was Paul, but his nickname was Mayor – fell ill. The girl had heard rumors that Skovoroda had the ability to heal and personally went to fetch him and begged him to come visit her father. Skovoroda went and a friendship developed between him and the girl. The father had also heard of Skovoroda and was quite satisfied to enter

---

[11] This spread of plague in Kiev in 1770 is historically documented.

into discussions with him on various subjects. After his illness passed and he regained his health Mayor did not want Skovoroda to leave. He proposed that Skovoroda educate his daughter. Skovoroda felt that women had equal rights to education as did men and so should acquire and equal education. Then Skovoroda began personally tutoring the girl, and often just the 2 of them being together and so the 2 became close. The father likewise continued his discussions with Skovoroda, the 2 of them reading the Bible together and time flew happily and harmlessly by. Elena eventually fell in love with Skovoroda. The father, noticing this, saw nothing wrong with Skovoroda marrying his daughter and so began deliberations with him on this matter.

Skovoroda became afraid, sensing a dislike for a settled life and began to incur doubt and an internal struggle. Skovoroda several times gathered his belongings in order to leave, but at the same time he felt a strong tie to the home where he had found such love and hospitality and so could not arbitrarily leave. After some conversations and intense thinking he finally decided to become a groom, and they began arrangement for a wedding. The father joyfully awaited this fulfillment of his deepest desire. But then the wedding day arrives and Skovoroda stands beneath the crown.[12] Suddenly he runs out of the church and flees without looking back.

Eventually, as Sreznevski records, Elena did marry and became quite happy. Of course, once Skovoroda heard about it, this also made him happy.

Exactly when this occurred is up to debate, but probably in about 1766 or 1767 at the beginning of Skovoroda's decision to become a roamer and his departure from secular involvement. His mind would still not have been fully crystallized regarding a nomadic and ascetic life. But the experience gained in this incident stayed with Skovoroda as there was never another. Even though he avoided the private company of women, he enjoyed their public company, as a letter sent my Myagki to Danilevski mentions Skovoroda's association with the wife of landlord Andrei Ivanovich Kovalinski, and later Skovoroda mentions himself his enjoyable friendship with Mikhail Kovalinski's wife.

---

[12] In the Russian Orthodox Church, a crown is placed on the head of groom, a reference to Proverbs 12:4.

Bagali in his record of Skovoroda records the statement made by a person – whose name is long lost – who met Skovoroda during his period of roaming.

"He was an intelligent and good person, teaching and admonishing what was good; he had the fear of God in him and relied on the kind-heart of Him of who was crucified for our sins, the Lord Jesus Christ. When he would start to discuss the passion of our Lord, or the parable of the wayward son, or the good shepherd, he would become emotional to such a point and begin to weep. May the memory of Skovoroda be eternal."

In February 1772, Kovalinski left Ukraine to visit Europe. After visiting France, he traveled to Switzerland in 1773. While in Lauzanne, Kovalinski met a certain man named Daniel Meingard who had in Kovalinski's opinion a natural intellect, eloquence, special education and wide knowledge, and had a philosophy that pertained to morality and ethic. In addition to these intellectual traits, his character was much like Skovoroda's and he even had a physical resemblance to him. The 2 of them immediately created a friendship and Meingard invited Kovalinski to his home for a stay during his visit and give him access to his library, which was very large for the era and of which Kovalinski took advantage.

Returning from Europe and visiting with Skovoroda in 1772, Kovalinski told him about this unusual meeting and the number of similarities that existed between Skovoroda and Meingard, intellectual, character and physical, and the subsequent friendship that evolved as a result. Skovoroda was so enthused over the fact that there existed someone else in another country with parallel traits that he decided to utilized his name somewhat modified as a pseudonym. The character of Grigori Barsabbas Meingard appears in letters number 77 and 78 and also in the tractate *Struggle of Archangel Michael against Satan*. The patronymic Barsabbas is a union of the Hebrew Bar – meaning son – and Sabbas – Skovoroda's artificially-created Hebraic form of the son of Savva, which in Russian is Savvich.

The years passed as well as decades, Skovoroda still with his staff and bag containing his Bible along with his manuscripts always walked visiting friends. The severity of exposure of course took its toll on Skovoroda, but being of Cossack substance his body endured the travel.

From letters and poems it seems that initially boredom would set in and he would feel himself to be the foam on the top of a wave, moving about and rising and lowering without a goal roaming about. But he felt the fruit of his decision to be his compositions and the discussions he shared with others.

In 1784, at the age of 60 and 15 years a nomad, he wrote,

"From a distance I look at his land with eyes of belief as though through a telescope at an astronomical observatory, at all of my upheavals and storms and sorrows and I am delighted at the spectacle I view, singing the song of Habakkuk, Upon my guard I rise and ascend the rock."[13]

And in 1788, toward the end of his life, now 64 with 20 years as a nomad, Skovoroda wrote to Kovalinski:

"Many say that what Skovoroda is doing with his life is just a joke. But I rejoice in the Lord; I am happy in God my salvation.[14] The eternal mother of holiness is the nursemaid of my old age, I nurse on her breasts without fatigue and I hunger for more and more.[15] I will be with her for ages and she with me. All will pass, but never will the love of my beloved."

This vein of thinking regarding inextinguishable love is expressed in a letter to an unknown person who sent Skovoroda a pair of leather boots.

"I thank the good heart for the fiery-inspiring letter to me, and even the entire world did not bring me the satisfaction that did its contents and your leather boots. Have you taken consideration of Paul's words? I seek you and not your possessions.[16] The good spirit within me praises you because you have been constant in love and have condescended to help me in my destitute mendicancy, and that you

---

[13] Hab 2:1
[14] Is 61:10
[15] Is 66:11
[16] 2 Cor 12:14

were not seeking of my flesh and blood. You, man of God, flee these things, hold fast to love. All passes but love will never, all will leave you except what is beloved residing within you. This stands at our walls, in a prison it is light. If the sea is turbulent, of the flesh and blood is agitated, if the waves of the fear of death rise, do not run to find help in the streets and in stranger's homes, enter within yourself"

Bishop Gavriil, having become acquainted with Skovoroda during this period, wrote of him,

"The spirit of Skovoroda in his enthusiasm seems to be carried about an ocean of limitless ideas, as if touching the world and its infinity. He was prophetic, experiencing all migrations of inspiration."

Skovoroda described one of these inspirational ecstasies to Kovalinski in a letter.

"Having tempered thoughts and a feeling of reverence and gratitude in my soul, I arose early and went to take a walk in the garden. The first feeling that touched me in my heart was a certain relaxation, freedom, cheerfulness, hope with abundance. Entering into this mood of my spirit, my entire will and all my desires, I felt within myself an extreme movement which overwhelmed me with some indefinable power. It suddenly filled my soul by pouring into it something so sweet, from which my entire inner person began to fervently burn and it seems that in my blood vessels a flaming flow was circulating. I began not to walk, but to run, as if carried by some ecstasy, not feeling either my hands or feet, but as if I entirely consisted of a fiery composition transported in the expanse of my surroundings. The entire world vanished before me. Solely the feeling of love, tranquility, eternity, livened my existence. Tears poured from my eyes in streams and spread causing a special meek harmony enveloping my entire composition. I examined myself and sensed the assurance of a love that a son would have."

During these minutes when eternity approached Skovoroda's soul he clearly felt the progress of time and with joy concluded his description,

"The scene of this world departs, and perishes like a dream when a person awakens."

Skovoroda described himself in a letter to Kovalinski he wrote while in the forest.

"I do not plow, I do not sow, I do not buy, I do not war, I reject every sorrow caused by livelihood. So what do I do? This is what. Always blessing the Lord, I sing to his resurrection. I learn gratitude, my friend. This is my work. I learn to be content with all that proceeds from the providence of God and given to me for my life. The ungrateful will is the key to infernal torment; the grateful heart is the paradise of sweetness. O, my friend. Learn of gratitude while sitting at home, walking the road, when falling asleep and when waking. Accept and convert all you have into goodness and contentment. And never attribute error to God for any of your experiences. Rejoice always, be thankful for all, pray."

Foreseeing the advent of these words Kovalinski bitterly stated after reading them, "There was a time when we could call Skovoroda's life a life." But it was no longer this way with Kovalinski his friend. In earlier years the friendship was fervent, but now began its dissipation. Life divided the 2 friends: Skovoroda to roaming, while Kovalinski entered the customary course of life of a young man, drawn by the voice of "the sirens." The final opportunity they had to visit with one another was in 1775 when Kovalinski returned from abroad, and then not again until August of 1794, 19 years later and 2 months before Skovoroda's death. During this interval they regularly communicated through letters.

Because of Kovalinski's departure there exists little information regarding the final 20 years of Skovoroda's life, except for what can be gleaned from his letters and compositions. He moved to Babaev outside of Kharkov in 1773 until 1778, when he moved to Veliki Burluk. For the winter of 1780 he stayed at the Sennyanski Monastery outside of Belgorod. He traveled to Taganrog in 1781. From 1785 to 1790 he lived in Gusinski Forest and in the neighboring villages of Gusinski, Manachinovka and Veliki Burluk. He then moved to Ivanivka to the estate of Kovalevski. In

1792, he returned to the Gusinski Forest. During the intervals he managed to travel as far north into Russia as Orlov and Voronezh.

Skovoroda worried over Kovalinski, and in a letter to an unnamed recipient while residing in Gusinski Forest in 1787 he wrote at the end of the letter, "Write Mikhail and give him and her a kiss from me. I have received all that he sent me. But his human voice I still wait for, not yet having received it. Do this for our mutual friend." The *her* no doubt referred to Kovalinski's wife. Such a statement of wanting to hear Kovalinski's voice echoes Skovoroda's sincere grief and desire to again see him.

Nineteen years passed after Kovalinski's departure. It was in about April 1794 that Kovalinski left St Petersburg and went to Orel Province to look at purchasing property. While there he sent word to Skovoroda of his temporary residence in the village Khotetovo, about 15 miles from Orel. The 73-year old Skovoroda, suffering from old-age and disregarding the distant journey and extreme sultry weather, traveled from Ivanivka to Khotetovo, a journey of about 110 miles, arriving early August, and traveling as always on foot. Skovoroda brought to him compositions, and many of which were dedicated to Kovalinski. They read them together, discussed them, interpreted them as people both searching for truth, not only in theory but likewise in conduct.

For the next 3 weeks the 2 friends discussed philosophy and religion. After their stay together Skovoroda decided to return to Ukraine, leaving on August 26, 1794. As Kovalinski wrote again in the 3rd person:

> "Old age, autumn season, the continuous wet weather increased the lack of immunity in Skovoroda's health: his coughing increased and his body became noticeably frail. His friend asked him to remain there and pass the winter with him living at his home, and there conclude life. He replied that his spirit was ordering him to go home, and his friend assisted him with departure."

Kovalinski offered him monetary assistance but Skovoroda refused. Skovoroda's final words at their departure are recorded in a letter written shortly after.

"Perhaps my illness will become worse along the road and I will have to stop someplace and so will have to pay. O, my friend, have I not yet acquired such trust of God, assured that His Providence will truly take care of me and provide me all that I need for the time. Perhaps I will not see you again. Forgive me. Remember me always in all your experiences of life and in all of what we often conversed: the light and darkness, good and bad, eternal and temporal."

Skovoroda for quite a while thought about his demise and so inwardly prepared himself for the occasion. Various illnesses and maladies plagued him for several years, but his spirit was vigilant and he was able to overcome his weaknesses and calmly awaited the end of his journey. In 1792 Skovoroda wrote to priest Pravitzki:

"O, God! Yes! It has been lonesome for me for a long while, not having conversed with you. But during the winter or spring I will not be able to leave my body's comfortable nest to encourage you and see you and have pleasure with our conversation in Christ, and we are in him and he in us. At the present I only visit you with the love of a dove's wings. Forgive me my beloved for not answering your or your child's letter. My heart fervently desired to do so, but old age and laziness is the result of cold weather on my blood. But I still write to you although I am ill. Blessed is my God! Although I am feeble, I am strong with Paul. My illness is my old age, poor blood circulation and fervor. This is occurring due to a poor diet, and not because of a lack of food."

About this time during weakness and illness Skovoroda again wrote to Kovalinski.

"Have you ever had pleasant or terrifying dreams? A feeling of these dream-filled pleasures or fears that only lasted until you awakened? All ends with a dream. Awakening destroys all joys and fears acquired in dreams. So it is with a person and death. The temporal life is a dream of our thought power. The time will come when the dream ends, the thought power will be excited and all temporal joys, pleasures, sorrows and fears of the era will vanish. Our spirit will enter another sphere of existence, and all that is temporal disappears like awakening from a dream. A woman barely gives birth and the child enters into a new order of existence, a new connection to his essence, in place of what he had which in his mother's womb. The mother's womb is this great world. When he exits it and into a new one, all the previous, the darkness, constriction of movement, and unsanitary state is severed from his existence and destroyed."

Such inherent clarity and a clear view of death provided Skovoroda with a calm and fearless exit. If he lived as he taught, and taught as he lived, then he died in the manner he lived and taught: resolutely, without complaint, contently.

After departing Kovalinski in Orel, he journeyed south, as Kovalinski records.

"Having arrived in Kurst,[17] he resided for a short while with the local archimandrite Ambrosia, a pious individual. He stayed there due to the incessant rain and waited for better weather, and then he continued his journey but not to where he intended. At the end of his road he felt an inspiration to travel back to the point he left to visit his friend. It was the city Ivanivka[18] at the estate of Kovalevski where he decided to reside, where he previously had lived for a while and where he arrived to finally conclude his journeying."

Sreznevski describes the final minutes of Skovoroda's life in the following.

"The final residence of Skovoroda was outside a village on the estate of landlord Kovalevski, a small but comfortable one-room hut with windows directed toward the orchard. It was a beautiful day. Several neighbors had gathered at the landlord's estate to walk and enjoy themselves. Some also had the purpose of visiting Skovoroda and talking with him. After lunch Skovoroda was unusually cheerful and conversational, and even joked telling them about his earlier years, about his roaming, his experiences. The visitors were impressed with

---

[17] About 100 miles north of Kharkov, and 50 miles south of Orel.
[18] Today known as Skovorodynivka, near Kharkov.

his eloquence and they left after lunch, while Skovoroda hid from them. He went into the orchard. For a long while he walked along the paths with the sun's rays penetrating through the trees, picked some fruit from the trees and gave them to workers' children. Toward evening Kovalevski went to look for Skovoroda and found him under a large-branched linden tree. The sun by now was already setting and its last rays were hardly showing through the leaves. Skovoroda had a spade in his hands and was digging a hole, a long and narrow grave. The landlord approach the elder and asked him, 'What are you doing, my friend Grigori?' Skovoroda replied, 'The time has arrived my friend to end my roaming. It is time for my rest.' The hair on Skovoroda's gaunt head fell over his face. The landlord then told him, 'You talk vanity, brother. Enough joking, let's go.' 'I go but I ask you first as my benefactor, let this place be my final grave.' So they went into the house. Skovoroda remained there only a little while and then he went to his room, changed the sheets of his bed and prayed to God. He placed a stack of his compositions under his pillow along with his gray knapsack, laid down, and folded his hands in the form of a cross. Others long waited for him to come to dinner, but Skovoroda did not show. He likewise did not show for breakfast or tea or lunch. This struck the landlord as unusual. He decided to enter Skovoroda's room to awaken him, but he lay there cold and mortified."

Kovalinski records a somewhat different account about Skovoroda's demise.

"Living there over a month Skovoroda was always on his feet and he often conversed with a good nature saying, 'The spirit is vigilant but the body is weak.' The landlord, noticing his extreme exhaustion, proposed to him having rites performed to prepare himself for death. He, like Apostle Paul, considering the rite of circumcision unnecessary for the true believer, replied that this only pertained to Jewish ceremonialism. But because of his weak conscience and bodily weakness, as well as due to his Christian love, he fulfilled the religious rites and passed away at dawn on the morning of October 29, 1794."

Although Kovalinski was not present at Skovoroda's death, he claims that Skovoroda complied with the ceremony of last rites according to Russian Orthodoxy, but beside his words there is no indication anywhere that Skovoroda did this or that he would do this, considering his repulsion toward sacraments and ritual. Kovalinski may have written this to protect Skovoroda's reputation by having him reconciled with the established church. Perhaps Kovalinski felt that in the future this would lead to less censorship of Skovoroda's compositions. Skovoroda was 2 months short of 72 when he died.

Prior to his death, as Kovalinski also notes, Skovoroda bequeathed his burial to occur on high ground, near a forest and flourmill, and requested the following epithet to be inscribed on his grave marker:

The world tried to catch me but could not.

So in one phrase Skovoroda concluded the attitude of the world toward his life, quest and philosophy. So profound the statement that it continues to be echoed to the present as consummate of all that Skovoroda represents.

However the following verse was inscribed instead (which rhymes in Ukrainian):

> A zealot for truth, spiritual worshipper of God,
> And a philosopher in word and mind and life,
> A lover of simplicity with freedom from vanity.
> An upright person without guile, satisfied always with everything.
> Attaining supreme knowledge, recognizing the spirit of nature.
> An example worthy of the heart, Skovoroda.

LEGENDS AND UNVERIFIABLE ACCOUNTS

In 1764 Skovoroda visited the Kievo-Pecherski (Caves) Monastery, and while there several monks surrounded him and attempted to convince him to remain and take monastic vows, saying, "Enough of you wandering about the world! Time to shelter yourself in a harbor. We are aware of your talents, you will be a pillar and decoration for our residence." Skovoroda responded with, "You have enough crudely hewn pillars here without me."

We must not think that Skovoroda associated with every person that wandered by wanting to become his disciple. It was quite the opposite. He was very particular in his selection of disciples, and his candid and often cruel responses would repel possible devotees. But some would change their attitude and return to him in a different frame of mind that would cause Skovoroda to reconsider and this would begin a friendship of several years.

One biographer Vernet relates what occurred initially with the landlord Stepan Tamara. "I was not insulted when he called me a man with a grandmother's mind and a high society woman's subjective thinking. I took the route of becoming liked by him and liking him, which worked to my advantage and prosperity. Later I bequeathed the plot of ground that became the grave of Skovoroda, where the perishable remains of that unforgettable person lie."[19]

---

[19] The property was actually owned by Kovalenski, which is noted in the Biography.

One legend that circulated in later years regarding Skovoroda was the following. Empress Catherine II the Great heard of Skovoroda and was impressed with his life and the respect he earned from people. So she sent her emissary Grigori Potemkin, who was vice-governor of Novo-Rossiya (as she referred to Ukraine), to invite him to migrate and live in her capital. The emissary met Skovoroda with his flute at the shoulder of some road near where a flock of sheep were grazing, a place the philosopher felt pleasant to rest. After hearing of the invitation, Skovoroda replied, "Tell the mother-queen that I will not abandon my homeland. My flute and sheep are more valuable to me than any royal crown."

Nonetheless, it was destined for them to meet. Traveling though Kharkov in 1787, Empress Catherine saw Skovoroda in his dingy and stained clothes and asked, "Why are you so black?" Skovoroda answered, "O, sovereign-mother, have you even seen a skillet that was white, since it is always in the fire cooking or baking?" (His response was a play on words: the word skovoroda in Russian is a skillet.)

One of Skovoroda's adherents lived in Taganrog, a resort city on the Black Sea at its west end. To visit him it was over a year's travel. When he arrived in Taganrog, his disciples invited a large group of guests, among which was one person who was famous. But after seeing such a large group, all of whom he considered nothing more than patronizing, he immediately left the room and no one was able to find him. He hid in the cellar and lied in a wheelbarrow until all become quiet in the house.

In a similar manner did he deal with people who were insincere or whose purpose was not serious or dedicated to his principles and concepts. Skovoroda avoided such people when he divined their attitude being, "A philosopher is just a monkey on a rope begging money from people." He would not waste his time with them.

A certain Mr. G. who was an intelligent person but an atheist had an urge to ridicule Skovoroda and told him, "It is a pity that you, being such an educated person, live like a retarded person, without having a purpose, and without providing any benefit for our society."

Skovoroda replied, "You may be right. Up to now I have not done anything beneficial, but at the same time, I have done nothing harmful. But you, sir, have done much harm with your atheism. A person without beliefs is a poisonous insect." Mr. G. eventually died in his atheism.

On one occasion the Kharkov governor was riding through the street in an elegant carriage and accompanied by many attendants and he saw Skovoroda sitting in the street in front of a hotel. The governor sent his assistant to him, "Your excellency desires your presence!"
"What excellency?" was Skovoroda's reply.
"His excellency the governor," the official replied back.
"Tell him that we are not acquainted," Skovoroda stated.
The official, excusing himself, told the governor Skovoroda's response. The governor then sent him back a second time and he said, "Evdokim Alexandrovich Scherbinin requests your presence!"
"Yes, I have heard of him and he is also musically talented." And Skovoroda removed his hat and approached the carriage. At this minute they became acquaintances.

In about 1794, not long before Skovoroda's death, Kovalinski discussed with him the various Russian sectarian groups and asked him about the new and fashionable Martinists. Skovoroda replied, "I do not know the Martinists, and every sect smells of individualism! And where individualism resides, there is no primary goal or principle tenets of philosophy." The irony of Skovoroda's philosophy is apparent as he was also very much an individualist. (The Martinists were a Masonic lodge in Moscow founded in 1780, and they named themselves after Saint Martin Louis-Claude, a French mystic philosopher.)

After Skovoroda's death rumors were circulated that his grave possessed certain strange unusual characteristics. When new owners of the garden or orchard that was adjacent to Skovoroda's grave forgot about his grave, misfortunes occurred to them, or their wife died, or they drank themselves to death. So the rumors circulated. The following is one example that was documented. In a letter of N. Myagki to Danilevski he wrote:

> "On the other side of the ditch where Skovoroda's hut was located, a gardener built for himself a home and told me about a strange incident

that occurred to him. On one occasion after his relocation to this new residence a strong wind appeared from nowhere and with a howl and thunder entered the window, through the open door and almost tore the door off its hinges and scared his wife to death. The poor gardener did not know that earlier this was the residence of the extraordinary elder Skovoroda."

SKOVORODA'S COMPOSITIONS

During his life, Skovoroda published nothing. All of his labors were copied by hand by his disciples. As his biographer Kovalinski recorded,

> "Skovoroda had so many genuine devotees. These were serious people who were not easily inclined or manipulated. Skovoroda wrote in a difficult, ambiguous and alien language regarding subjects that were abstract and nebulous and only capable of drawing a small circle of esoteric and almost unnoticeable persons. This means that his compositions were only copied by people who had the same direction and purpose in life as he did. A few of his halfway-religious and halfway-satirical poetic compositions were modified to fit music and were sung by mendicant troubadours in the market places and crossroads. Some of these became popular folk songs. But the greater influence on the people – more than any of his prosaic or rhyming compositions – was the person of Skovoroda himself."

For this reason Skovoroda preferred to work with people directly, and not though some educational establishment. One promised goal in all his conversations is the repeated intent of motivating people to a spirit-filled life, to a heart-filled nobility, to enlightenment of thought.

Skovoroda understood culture not in the usual intellectual sense in the light if European culture, but in terms of the great ancient thinkers and early Christianity. So once departing from secular obligations and associations with his ascetic and nomadic life he began composing, putting his personally developed Christian humanistic and philosophic conclusions and deliberations on paper. Many of his compositions are pseudo-dialogues or fictitious conversations, each of the persona interjecting views as the mouthpiece of Skovoroda, and some of them appearing as his alter-ego. In addition to his pseudo-dialogues, as a talented musician Skovoroda also composed several songs; as a story-teller he composed fables; and as a poet he composed many poems.

As Gess de Kalvi wrote, "He taught children using stories of an immaculate life while the adults with admonitions." As Kovalinski recorded, "He often lived at someone's home not at all pleased with the vices of his hosts. So he would converse with them for them to gain of better knowledge of themselves, in the love for truth, to impress on them a repulsion toward evil, and used his own life as an example of love and virtue."

His songs were composed early for the most part, from 1750 to 1758, before he departed as a nomad. He gathered them all together into one notebook and gave them the general title of *Garden of Divine Songs, Sprouting from the Seed of Sacred Scripture*. These were written in Russian or Ukrainian.

Skovoroda's poems were written primarily for his friend Kovalinski and were part of his letters to him. Most of them are prosaic while a few a admonishing in content. Skovoroda used dactylic hexameter as the format for the rhyme and composition. His poems were written in Latin, Greek, Russian and Ukrainian.

Skovoroda also created a number of fables that he collected into one notebook and titled *Kharkov Fables*. They follow the pattern and logic as Aesop and are simple to understand with each one having some moral conclusion.

Skovoroda highly valued the moral code of the Bible, and the most famous single tractate of his is the *Introduction to Christian Morality*. It was originally written in 1766 for the young gentry of Kharkov province as an introduction to understanding morality through self-examination, and by the use of the Ten Commandments. After its publication, the tractate was reviewed by the bishop of Belgrade, who censored it, claiming it departed from the standard Orthodox concept of morality. Skovoroda's reply to the inquisitor was that the aristocracy and gentry should have an identical standard of morality as that which was required of clergy and serfs by Orthodox prelates, and nothing less.

Skovoroda was likewise a prolific letter writer, with 124 letters extant and presently published. Most of them, 75, were written to his friend

Kovalinski, while the balance was to a number of other associates. The identity of the recipient of some letters is not known.

Of exceptional interest are Skovoroda's compositions of a philosophic and theological character. As mentioned about, they are composed as dialogues or conversations, each of the persona interjecting Skovoroda's thoughts and conclusions. Just as Skovoroda was accustomed to share his thoughts in conversations, so did he do the same in his compositions by conversing with fictitious friends.

Kovalinski wrote:

"Skovoroda, moved by the spirit, departed to deep solitude. Near Kharkov there is a place called Gusinski forest which belonged to the landlord Zemborski, whom he loved due to their benevolence. It is covered with thick forests, and an apiary in the center of it and a small hut. Here Skovoroda settled sheltering himself from the noise of everyday mundane existence and discredit from the Orthodox clergy. Devoting himself to freedom of thought and barricading his tranquility of spirit with silence, security and effectiveness he wrote his first composition here in the form of a book titling it *Narcissus or The Need to Comprehend Yourself*. Previous to this, his earlier compositions were only either fragments, or his poems and fables."

Prof. Bagali correctly notes:

"It was in such an environment that Skovoroda began his philosophic activity. His hut served as his study, located near the apiary. The quiet of such a corner was violated only by the echo of bees and sound of his personal flute. His entire library consisted of a Greek or Hebrew Bible and perhaps some favorite classic authors in Latin and Greek. His food was a plain village or country style. The paper on which he composed his compositions was whatever quality he could acquire under the circumstances. We have in our personal possession his original manuscripts composed while at the Zemborski apiary: these are a few notebooks consisting of coarse paper. Skovoroda wrote solely during the summer."

Skovoroda wrote in a letter to Priest Pravitzki,

"I hurry to compose while there is time, because surely at my doors stands the muses of a dangerous winter. I will be spending my time not in writing but in keeping my hands warm."

Skovoroda composed his manuscripts in unusually large letters and its legibility was almost the same as typeset letters. It was a strange style of handwriting where every letter was entered unhurriedly, carefully, with true patience. It is apparent that Skovoroda was in no hurry to go anywhere – his time passing slowly for him – and concentrated on recording his thoughts in a manner to be absorbed by readers.

Why and for whom did Skovoroda write? He wrote the following in regard to Narcissus, "This is my first-born son, born in the 7th decade of this century." And just as it is impossible to avoid birth once he is conceived, so Skovoroda had to write his first-born. Skovoroda as if entered into a spiritual marriage with the most beautiful of all humanity's daughters – the Bible – and from this marital union all of his compositions of the spirit were born. Skovoroda wrote, "The more intense and deserted my solitude, the more fortunate my cohabitation with this beloved wife. She provided me a child of the male gender, a true and complete person, and so I do not die childless."

The philosophic compositions of Skovoroda was the true and complete person that was born of him in his sublime mystical union with the Bible; his offspring was, 'flesh of my flesh and bone of my bone,' as he states in a letter.

In another respect, his compositions were spiritual gifts to friends, as Skovoroda wrote in the dedication to his *Dialogue regarding the Ancient World*, "My beloved friend Mikhail. Accept from me this small gift. You were born to have love towards God. Accept this charity. Read it, become wise from it, grow in it and let it blossom in you."

In the prologue to *Grateful Stork*, dedicated to S.N. Dyatkov, Skovoroda writes, "Behold a gift for you my friend. May this basket be a mirror of my heart and for a memory of our friendship in these final years."

One item noticeable with an intense investigation into Skovoroda's compositions was that it was never his intent for them to be published and distributed. During his life not one composition of his ever reached a printer. There is no doubt that he could have done this, should he have wanted to: because of his popularity a publisher could have been found. Prof. Bagali felt that Skovoroda protected his manuscripts from "literary thieves."

It seems there was some inherent psychological fear within Skovoroda with his compositions being read by those who would not understand their content or perhaps would misinterpret them or even discredit him for some reason. But this does not apply to his fables, songs or poems. Only one composition was specifically written for general use and this pertained to improving the morality of the Ukrainian gentry, *Introduction to Christian Morality*, and this was early in his nomadic career, in 1766.

In 1766 and 1767 respectively he wrote *Narcissus* and *Achsah*, both of them dealing with the topic of knowing one's personal self. In 1772, Skovoroda wrote his *Discussion of the Ancient World* and *Conversation of the Two Travelers*. In the early part of 1774 Skovoroda wrote A *Friendly Conversation regarding the Spiritual World*. Toward the end of 1774 was his *Discussion called Alphabet*, which was his favorite composition. In 1776 he wrote *The Snake of Israel*, subtitled as *The Ikon of Alkiviad*. In the winter of 1780 was *Lot's Wife* composed during his stay at the Sennyanski Monastery near Belgorod. In 1783 was the *Battle between Archstratigist Michael and Satan*, which is the most autobiographical of all of Skovoroda's composition. In 1787 was *The Grateful Stork* and *The Crippled Lark*. At the end of the 1780s Skovoroda wrote his *Serpent's Flood*, and which he edited and completed in 1791.

Skovoroda's compositions were personally disseminated; he would expend time to carefully copy them over and over and give them as gifts to close friends or to those to whom he was financially obligated. As mentioned above, he had an inherent fear of the publishing process for his compositions. In reality there were few copies made of his compositions by himself or by others due to the narrow audience at this time, the few who were attracted to Skovoroda's unorthodox and spiritualized thinking.

Of course, once Skovoroda became popular in the mid-19th century, it was not unusual for other authors to ascribe some of their own writing to Skovoroda. For example, Olga Pravoslavnaya has passages in her book on self-realization that she ascribes to Skovoroda, except that they are her own composition. Sreznevski claims that he had in his library several books claiming Skovoroda's authorship, but all of them were counterfeit.

One forgery even made its way into the Kharkov Jubilee Edition of Skovoroda's collection, and later Prof. Balagi exposed it as a fake. One popular composition was titled *The Righteousness of Faith*, and was circulated until exposed as a fraud. The identity of these authors are either unidentifiable or are long lost in history, but no doubt hoping to earn a few rubles by publishing under Skovoroda's name, or gaining some personal recognition by being recognized as an successfully equivalent philosopher.

In regard to his letters, Skovoroda was only able to teach what he had passionately crystallized within himself. As a result they are an echo of his life's dedication and without any dissidence at all.

Skovoroda's letters though fall into a different category of composition entirely from the longer pseudo-conversations. They also reflect his high regard for those whom he called and considered his friends, including some who did not approve of his nomadic life. In these letters he encourages, comforts and inspires. Skovoroda does not moralize or theorize. Instead he passionately responds to questions from his friends offering his aspect of the moral and Christian humanist life. His friends valued his letters, copying them and considering them a common treasure. His final letter was to a certain Ivan Vasilyevich and was in the collection of other letters addressed to Kovalinski.

NOTES ON THE TRANSLATION

If Skovoroda is difficult to read or comprehend in English, this is because it is difficult to read or comprehend in Russian. If the topic is unintelligible or irrational in English, this is because it is unintelligible or irrational in Russian. If it is nebulous or ambiguous in English, this is because it is nebulous or ambiguous in Russian. And so does Skovoroda also quite often write in contradictory language.

The depth lies in his ability to synthesize a subject by using various stories, passages and events in the Bible, and derive a meaning that is beyond the grasp of the regular Sunday School level reader. Quite often Skovoroda invents new words by combining Russian words, and because he wrote during the 2nd half of the 18th century, his language is just as archaic, utilizing the language of the peasants and uneducated, and which is even more difficult for us today in the 21st century. Skovoroda had a photographic memory of the Bible, and quoted his own version of verses translated from the Hebrew or Greek texts. The reader will notice that Skovoroda's quotation will be from the most literal to what would be considered a complete mistranslation of the text or even rendering a verse opposite to its obvious intent. So in the majority of Bible verses quoted, Skovoroda takes the liberty of arbitrary translation to suit his own purpose. But this is Skovoroda and the method he used to convey some concept that is beyond the superficial statement.

That Skovoroda used the Greek Septuagint is evidenced by his quotations from Sirach and Wisdom of Solomon and the apocryphal sections of Daniel, which are not in the Hebrew text.

I, as translator, have done my best to render Skovoroda in a manner that is understandable in modern English but without sacrificing the uniqueness that is Skovoroda.

The only additions to the text by the translator are indicated in [brackets], otherwise no other words have been added.

The passages selected for translation are first, those that were the most circulated and published after his lifetime, and second, those that will provide the reader with a good cross-section of his various philosophic and Christian humanist concepts. Included is an assorted selection of his songs, poems, fables and letters. Of the entire text that comprises the 2-volume *Collected Works* of 1972, Moscow, in Russian, which is the most comprehensive collection of Skovoroda's compositions, this translation contains about 40% of the material. What was especially not selected was redundancy: Skovoroda very often repeated concepts and subject matters in his different compositions, so I have done my best not to include repetitious material.

Skovoroda's letters are an excellent source of basic comprehension of his concepts, since they were written in a more informal setting or mental state than the intensity of his philosophic and humanist compositions.

I have attempted to locate as many quotations from the Bible as reasonably possible. Many are popular passages already known to the student of the Bible and so are not referenced.

GRIGORI SAVVICH SKOVORODA

SKOVORODA

(SELECTED WRITINGS
TRANSLATED FROM THE RUSSIAN)

INTRODUCTION TO CHRISTIAN MORALITY

Foreword

Gratitude to the blessed God because He has made easy what is necessary, and difficult what is unnecessary.

There is nothing sweeter for a person and nothing more needful than happiness, and there is nothing easier to acquire than this. Gratitude to the blessed God. God's Kingdom is within us. Happiness in the heart, the heart in love, love is the eternal law.

This is continuous fine weather and a sun that never sets which enlightens the abyss of the darkness of the heart. Gratitude to the blessed God.

What would occur if happiness, so needed and so loved by all, was dependent on place, on time, on flesh and blood? I will say it more clearly: What would occur if God was to confine happiness in America or on the Canary Islands or in Asian Jerusalem or in the chambers of a king or during the age of Solomon or in wealth or in the desert or in rank or in science or in health? Then our happiness would be meager. Who can travel to these places? How can all be born during the same era? How can we all fit in one rank and file? What type of happiness is this if founded on the sand of someone' s flesh, or in limited space and time, or on a mortal person? Is this not difficult? Yes. Difficult and impossible. Gratitude to the blessed God because He has made the difficult unnecessary.

Do you want to be fortunate at present? Do not seek happiness across the sea, do not ask it of a person, do not journey throughout the planet, do not ramble yard to yard, do not drag yourself across the earth, do not worry over Jerusalem. With gold you can buy a village, an item difficult to find, something you could not find and live without, but happiness as an indispensable necessity is everywhere free and gifted always.

The air and sun are always with you, everywhere and free. All that flees away from you, know that it is someone else's and do not consider it yours. All of this is alien and superfluous. What are your needs? For this reason it is difficult. If it was undependable it would never have parted from you. Gratitude to the blessed God.

Happiness is not from heaven, nor does it depend on the earth. Say together with David, "What do I have in heaven? And what do I want from you on earth?"[20]

What is required of you? That which is very easy. But what is it that is easy? O, my friend, all that is difficult is hard and bitter and evil and false. There is something easy. That my friend is what is needful. What is needful? Only one item is needful. One thing only is necessary for you, one thing only that is good and easy; all the rest is labor and illness.

What is this one thing? God. All creation is utensils, furniture, miscellaneous, trash, mixture, debris, assortment, riffraff, fragments, nonsense, solidarity, and flesh and cages. But that which is amiable and needful is the same everywhere and always. And all of this you can hold in your hand and the dust of your flesh will retain it.

Gratitude to the blessed God for He allows us access to all, and makes difficult for us, except for that which is needful, amiable and required. Much that is indispensable for the body awaits you, but happiness is not there. But for your heart only one thing is required, where God and happiness reside. It is not distant. It is near, in your heart and in your soul.

Into this ark is led our sermon of 10 chapters, as if through 10 doors. But I wish for your soul what the dove of Noah represents, to rest anywhere and return to the heart, to him who rests in your heart. So the Scripture would be fulfilled, "Your foundations will be eternal, generations after generation, and you will be called a builder of walls, and you will rest in your paths."[21]

This desires Grigori, son of Savvi Skovoroda.

---

[20] Ps 73:25
[21] Is 61:4

Foundation of the Sermon

The truth of the Lord abides forever.
Forever Lord, does Your word abide.
Your law resides in my inner person.
The Word became flesh and resided with us.
In the midst of You stands one whom you know not.

Chapter 1

About God

The entire world consists of 2 natures: one is the visible, the other is the invisible.

The visible nature is named creation, while the invisible is named God. This invisible nature or God penetrates and retains the entire creation; it has existed and will exist everywhere. For example, the human body is visibly apparent, but what penetrates and retains the mind is not visible or apparent.

For this reason the people of antiquity called God the world-wide mind. They had various names for Him, for example, nature, Genesis of things, eternity, time, fate, indispensability, luck, and others. But among Christians the most popular names are the following: Spirit, Lord, King, Father, Mind, Truth. The latter 2 names appear to be more personal than the rest, because the mind is entirely immaterial, while truth with its eternal residence is completely opposed to temporal material. Even at the present, in another land God is called Truth.

There is likewise not just one name pertaining to the visible nature, for example: material or objects, earth, flesh, shadow, and others.

Chapter 2

About the Ecumenical Belief

Just as there are few who presently comprehend God, so it is not surprising that in antiquity they often venerated objects as God, which was a common error, and for this reason their entire worship service was ludicrous.

However, during all these ages the peoples still believed and were in agreement that there is a secret someone, a power effusing everywhere and possessing all. For this reason to honor and remember Him throughout the entire earthly sphere, buildings were publicly dedicated, so at present He everywhere continues. And although for example, the subject may in error display veneration to the personal attendant instead of the master, but he is not argumentative, because he realizes he has a sovereign over him, whom perhaps has never seen in public. His subject is every nation, and everyone likewise recognizes their enslavement in His presence. This type of faith is common and simple.

Chapter 3

About the Common Providence

This most blessed nature or spirit keeps the entire world in movement, just like the ingenuity of the mechanism of a mechanical clock on a tower. The existence of all creation follows the consideration of the Father. He Himself enlivens, feeds, arranges, repairs, protects and according to His own will, which is called the general law or statute, and then He returns it to its original coarse material or soil, which we call death.

For this reason the intelligent antiquity equated it with mathematics or geometry, because it could always be arranged proportionately or measured, or molded into various figures, for example: grass, trees, animals and all else. While the Jewish sages compared him to a potter?[22] This is common providence because it pertains to the welfare of all creatures.

Chapter 4

About Providence Especially for a Person

He has poured out on us – this most pure, worldwide community mind of all the ages and nations – like from a fountain, all wisdom and culture to accompany the existence of what is necessary. But in no manner is any nation in debt to Him, in as much as He has given to us His supreme wisdom that is His natural portrait and seal. It surpasses other intellect spirits or understandings as much as the heir surpasses the servant.

---

[22] Rom 9:21

It is identical to the most elegant architectural symmetry or model, expanding throughout all material, though not sensed, making every structure firm and pleasant and maintaining all other implements. So is it migrating from word to word, throughout all members of a political confederacy, from people, and not composed of stones, secretly spreading out, making it firm, peaceful and prosperous. If for example, some family name, or city or government is founded and established on this model, at that time it becomes a paradise, heaven or house of God, and other objects. And if some person or other should build his existence according to it, at this time it becomes in him the fear of God, holiness, piety and other items. And just as there is in the human body one mind, although it may act in various manners based on its different facets, so in cohabitation bound by this wisdom God through various members accomplishes activity for the general advantage.

Soul, benefit and beauty resides in all of our deeds and conversations, and without it all is dead and vile. All of us are born without it, although for it. Who is more naturally inclined and willing towards it, he is more noble and sharper; and who has greater participation with it, he is the more genuine, but it is not the assistant who inwardly senses the bliss or satisfaction. Those set apart depend on it alone in developing thought for the human race. It is the most beautiful face of God, which He, at some time sealing it upon our souls, turns us from wild and ugly monsters or deformed humans that are wild beasts, towards companionship and into testifiable, coexisting people, valuable, passive, temperate, magnanimous and equitable.

And if it should reside in the inclination of the human heart, at this very time the following will occur just like the movement of the mechanisms of a clock: correctness and reliability. And then it abides in the soul as chastity and a pure heart, just like the spirit of paradise and a taste that captivates leading to friendship. It makes us distinct from wild animals by way of kindness and equity, and from animals through temperance and reason. And this could be nothing else except the most blessed face of God written secretly upon the heart, the strength and rule of all our movements and deeds. At this time our heart becomes a pure fountain of philanthropy, the indescribable soul of those who rejoice.

And then we become true in our soul and in the human body similar to those having worth for building with the cornerstone, with which the living house of God is constructed, in which He in a special way reigns mercifully. It is difficult to penetrate and observe this priceless treasure, although this one is still not easy to love and find. To the extent it is superficial and distained, to the same extent it is inwardly magnanimous and looks like a small seed of a fig in which an entire tree with fruit and leaves is contained, or a small plain pebble in which an entire fire is concealed. To display it, it was always signified with signs, and it was as if some type of prince having his portraits, seals, and various parcels in various ages and nations. It was the parcel, for example, the snake hanging on the stake in the presence of Jews.

Its emblem is a dove holding an olive branch in its mouth. It has appeared in the image of a lion and lamb, while the royal scepter was its sign, and other items. It was hidden within the sacred ceremonies they had, for example, eating the Passover, circumcision, and others. It secluded itself as though under various masquerades and civil histories, for example, under the narratives about Esau and Jacob, Saul and David, and others. And only with its secret presence did it make these books sagacious. While in the progressing eras it appeared in the image of a male who became the god-person.

By what ability was this wisdom of God born from a father without a mother and from a virgin without a father, and then it resurrected and again ascended to its father, and other items, please, do not be curious. There are in this case, as in other studies, dormant subtleties, only in this un-real faith can it find a place for itself, which is called speculative. Conduct yourself here just as you would at an opera and be satisfied with what is presented before your eyes, but do look behind the screens and scenery of the theater.

Why should you ask, for example, about the resurrection of the dead, if the very gift of the ability to resurrect is of no benefit to the inactive soul-which will not be resurrected, nor can be resurrected. Out of these curious people has evolved sectarianism, superstition and other plagues, as a result of which all Europe is uneasy. The most important word of God is to enliven the disordered soul with the spirit of His commandments, rather than develop a new earthly world out of nothing, populated with criminals. It is not the person who strives to look into His secrets that is faithful to the Sovereign, but the person who fervently fulfills His will. This eternal wisdom of God continues its speech without ceasing throughout all the ages and nations. And it is none other than the ubiquitous nature of the invisible face of God and living word, secretly thundering secretly inside all of us. But we do not want its counsel: some because of deafness, but the majority because of unfortunate obstinacy, because of dependence on a poor upbringing.

Among the Jews, wise individuals called prophets fulfilled with most profound apprehension what was commanded them, listening intently to this immaterial voice. It is the beginning and end of all prophetic books: all written in them is from it, through it and for it. For this reason it received several names. It is called the image of God, glory, light, word, counsel, resurrection, life, path, rectitude, peace, fate, justification, grace, truth, power of God, name of God, will of God, rock of faith, Kingdom of God, and others. The very first Christians called it Christ, that is, King, because he alone directs the entire state, all inhabitants and every person individually to eternal and temporal prosperity. And besides, during antiquity all that was supreme and primary was venerated as royal.

Abraham foresaw its most blessed light and trusted it. He became righteous with his entire family and successful with all his subjects, although it lived before Abraham in all those who loved it. While Moses as though accepted a plan from this invisible divine image and drew it plainly and coarse in the manner he was able and founded the Jewish community based on it. He made it prosperous and victorious. He wrote all of it in the language of that era on stone plaques and made it such so the invisible wisdom of God, although a visible and perishable human, possessed an ability to speak to them all with genuine voice.

This speech was named the Ten Words since it was divided by Him into 10 ideas or points.

Chapter 5

About the Ten Words

I

"I am the Lord your God; There will be no other gods among you."

More clearly stated in this manner: I am the head of your good-fortune and the light of mind. Watch out, that you not base your life on other counsels, thinking or reasoning, even if they should evolve from the minds of angels. Follow Me blindly. If you should circumvent Me you will load your eternity onto some other wisdom, which then will be your god, but not a true one. Then your happiness can be compared to stolen money.

II

"Do not make for yourself an idol."

I no longer command you to build upon perceptible items, just as upon rocks. All that is perceptible is flesh; all that is visible is an idol.

III

"Do not use the Name in vain."

Watch first that you not fall into a trap of stupidity, as though there is nothing in the world other than the visible, and as though His name, God, is vain. In this abyss reside false oaths, hypocrisy, deceit, guile, treachery, and all the secret and obvious abominations to scare others with. And in place of all this write upon the heart that everywhere and always resides the secret judgment of God, ready in every place to invisibly scorch and whip your invisible parts, affecting even the smallest, for all the deeds, words and thoughts where I was not present.

IV

"Remember the Sabbath Day to keep it holy."

You must everywhere and inwardly crumble before the majesty of God and not to forget to glorify Him with faith and reverence on Sunday. Do not worship Him in meaningless ceremonies, but in conduct, imitating Him in our heart. His activity and every minute of His entire past time is spent meditating on the benefit of all creatures. From you He does not require anything more except having a sincere kind heart toward close associates. And this is very easy.

V

"Honor your father and mother."

Before anything else honor father and mother and attend to their needs. They are visible portraits of the invisible entity who has obligated Himself so much to you.

And this is who your father and mother are: First be loyal and zealous to the Sovereign, obedient to the city mayor, polite to the priest, submissive to parents, grateful to your teachers and benefactors. Here is the true path to your eternal and temporal prosperity and to establish your family name.

That which concerns other facets of society, beware of the following:

VI

Do not murder.

VII

Do not be immoral.

VIII

Do not steal.

IX

Do not witness falsely, or Do not slander.

We sentence the guilty and slander the innocent. This is the most terrible malice, and slanderer in Greek is Devil.

X

Do not envy.

But since evil intentions are the root of all evil actions, an innumerable amount, while the heart of the slave is an inexhaustible source of bad intentions. It would be impossible during the course of your life for you to be honorable unless you allow God to give a rebirth to your heart. Dedicate this to unfeigned love. Immediately at this time crime will be confined in the abyss within you. God, the word of God, love toward His word – is all the same.

The heart set aflame by the Trinitarian fire will never sin, because they cannot possess the evil seed or intention.

Chapter 6

About True Belief

If a person was able to quickly understand the invaluable price of this great counsel of God, he would suddenly accept and love Him. But because bodily and crude reasoning is an obstacle, for this he needs faith. It is a bliss closed to all counsel, viewing it from a distance as though through a telescope, and with which he identifies himself.

In its presence it is necessary that hope exist. It blindly and violently retrains the human heart in the presence of His only-born truth, not allowing it to be troubled by the vile winds of foreign opinions. For this reason she is presented in the image of a woman holding an anchor. These virtues as though reliable winds, finally bring the heart of a person, the ship, to a haven of love and is entrusted to it.

At this time with the opening of the eyes the Holy Spirit secretly cries in the soul the following, "Your virtue is forever virtue, and your law is truth."

Chapter 7

Piety and Ceremony - The Difference

The entirety of the strength of the 10 addresses can be concluded in one appellation – love. It is the eternal union between God and a person. It is an invisible fire by which the heart bums fervently to the word or will of God, and for which reason is itself God.

This divine love possesses external appearances or tokens. These are called ceremony, ritual or the image of piety. So ceremony is near piety just as a leaf is near fruit, or the husk on grain, or as a complement for a favor. If this mask is deprived of its strength, then at that time it remains only as hypocritical deceit, while the person is a decorated coffin. This is all there is to ceremony, which can hardly rectify the most unfortunate miscreant.

Chapter 8

The Law of God and Tradition - The Difference

The law of God resides forever, while the traditions of people are local and temporal. The law of God is the tree of Paradise, while tradition is its shadow.

The law of God is the fruit of life, while tradition is like the leaves. The law of God is God in the heart of a person, while tradition is the leaf of a fig tree, often covering a viper. The door of the temple of God is the law of God, while tradition is the front porch connected to the temple. As far as the entrance to the altar and as far as the tail from the head, so is the distance of tradition from the law of God.

Among us and almost everywhere this incomparable difference is equated with people forgetting the law of God and mixing it with the dirt of humanity into one, even to the point that a persons' babble is held higher. And now depending on it, they do not think about love, in order to fulfill this, "Hypocrites. For the sake of your traditions you have destroyed the law."[23] If it is not the law of God, then it is all tradition.

Chapter 9

About Passions or Sins

Passion is the atmosphere of plague in the soul. It is immoral desire for what is visible, while named an unclean or tortuous spirit. The chief of them all is envy, the mother of other passions and crimes. It is the chief center of the crevasse where the soul is tormented. In no manner can it be colored or utilized. Light is not attractive to it, neither is honor. But harm is so sweet, that it will eat a dozen of itself.

The sting of this dragon's hell is the entire generation of sins, and these are its family names: hate, vengeance, pride, deceit, dissatisfaction, melancholy, regret, boredom, grief and the other insatiable maggots that reside in the soul.

---

[23] Matt 15:6-7

Chapter 10

About Love or the Clean Heart

The condition of a clean heart opposes the abyss. It is a calm breath in the soul and the wind of winnowing, the Holy Spirit. It is like a beautiful garden, soft winds, fragrant flowers and fulfilled pleasures, where the imperishable tree of life flowers.

And these are its fruits: wishing the best for another, gentleness, a good disposition, meekness, sincerity, assurance, providing safety, satisfaction, encouragement, and other inalienable traits.

Whoever has such a soul, peace be upon him and mercy, and eternal joy upon the head of this true Christian.

STRUGGLE BETWEEN ARCH-STRATIGIST MICHAEL AND SATAN REGARDING: GOODNESS IS EASY

Written in the year 1783.

My beloved Mikhail!

Accept from me this booklet as a gift to you, although the title includes a champion having your name.[24] If you have accepted the name Michael then also accept his heart, singing from the Books of the Kings this song, "My heart is yours, and yours is mine." At that time, you Mikhail, will exist as a friend to your protector Michael, and in one heart will exclaim, "Who is like our God?"[25]

I began this book in Burluka but finished it in Babaev. I do not furrow, I do not sow, I do not purchase, I do not war, and I reject every form of livelihood sorrow. So what do I do? This is what: I always bless the Lord and sing of his resurrection.

This is my dish full of wheat dough and my reliance! What is the resurrection? The land of Israel is the resurrection. To say this directly, it is the entire Bible in a small world, the new and ancient Eve. In this land Jacob slept peacefully. And how not peacefully? He had a rock in place of a pillow. The most uncomfortable item was the softest for him there, where later Samson found honeycomb. Yes, I say! I found it also, and I also rest there, am consoled, rejoice. I sing, "God has gifted us this holiday."

Even more do I sing with David, "I fell asleep and slept and arose." And with my Isaiah, "God has given us rest upon this mountain."[26] This I know for a truth fact as the elders of Solomon's time said, "Old age is the crown of praise."[27] They eat and suck the breasts of 2 mothers and brides who were never brides: the progenitor Eve and Mary the mother of our

---

[24] This booklet was written for Mikhail Kovalinski.
[25] Ps 113:5
[26] Is 25:10
[27] Pr 16:31

Lord, as it writes, "They sucked honey out of the rock."[28] Then you will ask me: Why is it that all residing in this land seek consolation, yet hunger, complain and curse it?

The answer: Because this small portion of land has 2 parts: valleys and mountains, the local and the distant, the cursed and the blessed, the demonic and the Lord's, like 2 nipples or 2 fountains. "Jacob evolved from the source of the promise." Do you heed this? "And I have acquired the place." Do you heed this? "And he slept there." Do you heed this? If the places were the same he would not have searched for a second and would not have departed from here. Not in vain does Isaiah say, "Not only, he says, in this land, but on its mountain." There! Tell me, who chooses the better portion?

The answer: For this reason this booklet extracts 2 hearts to show on the scene what is under the heavens: the Angelic and the Satanic, which struggle between themselves. These 2 kingdoms conduct an eternal war within every person. When the pure heart defeats the malicious abyss, then the gates of hell are destroyed. The captives are liberated. The road to the resurrected mountain and out of the abyss is unveiled, "Who will ascend the mountain of the Lord?"[29] What is the sweetness and consolation on this mountain? Tell us, Isaiah! "God will provide us rest on this mountain."[30] This is enough! Is there more? "They will drink wine. They will drink joy on this mountain." O, this is more than enough. "They will be anointed with peace upon this mountain." O, this is more than enough, enough! Behold the place where our Jacob rested! "And there he slept." He slept in Haran, in the city of love he slept. "There I will provide you my nipples."[31]

Do you see, my beloved Mikhail, the place where your friend rests? The elder Barsabbas Daniel Meingard.[32]

July 19, 1788.

---

[28] Deut 32:13
[29] Ps 24:3
[30] Is 25:6
[31] Is 66:11
[32] This name was a pseudonym that Skovoroda used to refer to himself, as noted in the Biography, in order to occasionally project himself as a person into his own narratives.

Preface to the Composition

He will kill the dragon that resides in the sea.[33]
O, how you have fallen, morning star![34]
The criminal who curses Satan, curses his own soul.[35]
Until the morning star arises and the dawn shines in your hearts.[36]

The Struggle and Dispute over the Statement:
Is it Difficult to be Bad. It is Easy to be Good.

Satan, having flown with bat's wings from the nether-regions to the celestial, he stopped at the regions of the atmosphere. Having seen with this night-time eyes the radiant house, ("Wisdom has built for itself a house and strengthened the pyramid 7 times."[37]) he howled with his infernal roar like thunder, "Why was this house built?"

At this display of cowardly turbulence, Michael with his silvery wings having gold trim descended like an eagle for the spoils and cried.

Michael: O, enemy of God! Why are you here? And what business do you have here? In ancient times you vomited blasphemy upon the body of Moses in my presence.[38] Now you vomit the same poison upon God's house. Who is like God? And what is as good and as beautiful as His house? Let my Lord rebuke you, in whose presence I now stand.

Satan: It is not proper for the Archangel of the heavenly hosts to act quarrelsome; he is supposed to be quiet and meek.

Michael: O, snake! You soften your words more than butter even though they are arrows. But you cannot grasp that opportune anger is God's love, and that importune mercy is your heart.

Satan: This is such a strange song you sing!

---

[33] Is 27:1
[34] Is 14:12
[35] Sirach 21:27
[36] 2 Pet 1:19
[37] Proverbs 9:1
[38] Jude 9

Michael:	The heavenly hosts sing the strange, new and glorious in God's city. This is truth.
Satan:	So what do the hosts of the nether-regions sing?
Michael:	Your hosts sing of what is vile, secular and sacrilegious. I can only repeat what Peter said in the Acts.[39] In short, this is the market place dirt and the excrement of Ezekiel.[40]
Satan:	Ha, ha, ha! What the heavenly hosts sing is strange.
Michael:	O, blasphemer! Why do you ridicule this song? Your guile is not hidden from me. Calling this strange, secretly slandering the heavenly glory and its dogmas, attributing to it some imaginary ugliness and impropriety, or plainly said, nonsense.
Satan:	Not circumventing the issue, you now have announced the reason why the residents of the nether-regions number a thousand times more than your heavenly.
Michael:	You lie and obscure statements. Open more if you can the abyss of your heart.
Satan:	O, discrediting dogmatic difficulties, crooked in your path, difficult in your actions. This is the tri-natured source of your heavenly desert.
Michael:	Can you not even be a little bit more frank?
Satan:	It is more than difficult to be a resident of heaven. Do you heed this? Behold the reason for the desolation of your heavens.
Michael:	From where did this stone come and who placed it as a foundation?
Satan:	Behold I speak! It is more than difficult to be and has been this way.
Michael:	Are you the creator of this dogma?
Satan:	This dogma is indestructible diamond.
Michael:	Take heed, heaven and listen, earth.[41] Even the nether-region must hear! Of them all who is the greatest blasphemer and greatest slanderer of the supreme Lord? Behold the city that snares all! Behold the key that opens the gates of hell to all. Behold the deceit that interferes with all who are on the

---

[39] Acts 13:10
[40] Eze 4:12
[41] Is 1:2

heavenly path! O, you decorated royal coffin, full of dead bones and dust and the adulterous world! You deceive the aged, young and children. You snare them in guile like birds in a net.

The entire world breathes his spirit. He is the world's heart and an unclean heart, a carnal heart. Behold the sacrilegious trinity: Satan, flesh, world. Who will give me God's sword so I can pierce this Midianite who is fornicating with the immoral and adulterous of this world, and I will rebuke her shamelessness.[42]

And Michael raised his spear – bright as lightning and hard as a diamond – and struck Satan right in his heart and discarded him into an evening cloud. He, falling head first, cried, "Hooray, hooray! I have won! I have won!" From the center of that cloud he howled, "O, O slanderer. Call heaven and earth as witnesses. I will not subject myself to you and I will continue strong in my dogma."

Michael:	O, bat! Woe unto you who turns light into darkness, and darkness into light, calling what is sweet – bitter, and what is easy – difficult.[43]
Satan:	Is it not written? "What is first necessary is God's Kingdom."
Michael:	Be silent, lying dog! Satan. And you add violence to attain your intents. Bark, bark now, dog. You are far from the sun. Lord my God, your righteousness is like the sun at noon. Who is like you? You have barricaded the jaws of this dragon who consumes all he can, not just for one day, but for a thousand years. Amen.

At the sound of the noise and roar there descended Gabriel, Raphael, Uriel and Barachiel to Michael flying just as a stork's fledglings fly to their mother at her nest who has just trampled upon a snake and is carrying it in her claws. Michael like a stork beloved of God tramples and tortures the household enemy, giving gratitude to the master's house who is pleased to reside in the 7 towers that view his wisdom-filled house from the heights, a

---

[42] Num 25:7-8
[43] Is 5:20

place where birds can nest, as it is written, "How beloved are your settlements."[44] The bird has acquired for herself a home. There the birds nest. The stork's residence proceeds ahead of them. Blessed are they who reside in your house."

Angelic Discourse regarding the Devil's Slander and regarding the Intrigues that cause Departure from True Consolation

The heavenly arch-warriors made seats for themselves on the rainbow. Michael produced the statement, "Our battle is not against blood and flesh."[45] A person's heart is an unfathomable abyss. It is like the atmosphere carrying the floating planets. This abyss is dark and the fulfillment of the following words has not yet occurred, "It shined upon my darkness. God, who commanded the light to shine from darkness, who shined in our hearts."[46]

Then it becomes poison, meaning a prison, and materializes as night birds, gloomy dreams and illusions. The night owl, king and father of all the others, is Satan. These empty dreams are evil spirits, while evil spirits are evil thoughts. And so this is written, "Our battle is against the sovereigns of the darkness of this age, meaning that our battle is against evil spirits that have the dominion over the unenlightened world and over all criminal disarray." What does it say further? The beginning of all garden fruit trees is a seed. The seed of all evil activities is evil thoughts. And so it is written, "Against authorities and principalities, the spirits of malice under heaven." These spirits of malice under heaven are dreams of human and animal and beast hearts whose eyes are pierced by the sharp sword of God's righteousness. "Satan, you do not think about the matters of God, but about the matters of people."[47]

My beloved brethren! Do you see the extent that Satan has sown his seed throughout the entire world? From his type of seed the adulterous Sirens have evolved and their immoral songs.

---

[44] Ps 84:1
[45] Eph 6:12
[46] John 1:5. 2 Cor 4:6
[47] Matt 16:23

It is a difficult and tough work
To become a resident of heaven.
It is a happy and smooth path
To live as the world lives.
The holy person suffers without comfort.
While malice everywhere sees success.
What benefit is it to be holy?
It is a more successful life for all the wicked.[48]

As he is vomiting such sweetened waters of his from heavenly windows, your Angelic eyes sharply see how subtlety he extinguishes the divine fire in all hearts, "Who will give me wings? I will fly and I will rest. Love is as strong as death. Its wings are wings of fire. Who will separate us from God's love? My heart is warmed and a fire is ignited in my instruction."

The world is compressed with his basilisk's poison: deaf like an asp and cold as ice. But the created was made for our mother, God's wisdom which warms us in its bosom and comforts us. "Son, if you sleep long, sweetly sleep. If you travel somewhere, be fearless and joy will accompany you on all your paths."[49] For this reason it is not surprising how all lean together. To say, God is not sweet, and, There is not God, is the same. They have become morally corrupt and detestable in their sources and seeds and even to the very root of their heart.

Who can raise upon the path gold or a pearl that thinks of itself as nothing useful? What grouse would deliberately jump into a trap, thinking that captivity is abundance? What lamb would not be afraid of its mother should she turn into a wolf? Or would not attach itself to a wolf should it turn into its mother? Do not blame the world; you cannot blame this corpse. The passion of this captive is removed, the eye is pierced, the path is barricaded; the anguish of his heart is tied with eternal chains.

What anguish? When thoughts love and want something, then the carnal heart within us expands, inflates, rejoices; while at times of pressure it contracts, withdraws, cowers, and repulses food as if deflated and tightens its lips. Satan, having extinguished the divine fire in the secular heart, has bound anguish using anguish so that it eternally will loathe the divine kingdom and forever not extend to acquire it. So that the song of

---

[48] Malachi 3:14-15
[49] Pr 3:24

victory would never be sung, "The snare is destroyed. The path of your commandment flowed when you expanded my heart. The wants and fulfillment of my soul! My heart and my flesh rejoiced."

And when it writes, "Let my heart rejoice," this means, "Let it be courageous." "My rejected heart will be comforted," means that it will not accept courage and demands. To remove the courage and then bring upon it terror means to oppress, to close and bind the soul so it will not rejoice, but will anguish when confronted with some charitable need. To morally corrupt a person's thoughts and heart is the most terrible offense, captivity and murder, intruding into his seed and root, just as it is written, "They have become morally corrupt and detestable in their sources," meaning their principles. They are as if guided by a demon-possessed chariot driver or ship captain. The corpse is not guilty; it is the murderer who is guilty. The world is a nut having a worm in it, a blind person without eyes and guide, a bear led by a muzzle over its snout, a slave of Satan, a captive of the devil, a lion-like fence. What type of fence? Listen to a parable.

The Lion-like Fence

A lion guards a sleeping oak tree and its shoots, and which has access only by one gate and he lies there nearby in secret. He guards it not with a wall or roar, but with his pacing. When it is hungry it roars. Animals become terrified and seek deliverance and arriving at a road of deliverance they drive in a direction opposite form the lion's pacing, who is already breathing intolerable fear at them and attempting to barricade the road.

There was no fear earlier, but now there is and they seek a safe path to that gate as they approach it. They do not see his pacing and do not sense his justifiable threat. Here they are caught! Here are the gates of hell! Here is the exit of all the world and its end. Like a lion in his yard residing in secret Satan captures all of those of whom it is written, "They were afraid of fear where there was no fear."[50]

In this terrifying place Michael was silent. His celestial military officials, sitting on the beautiful circular clouds, gave themselves to meditation, looking at the earth's sphere and downcast as though staring at the destroyed Sodom and Gomorrah. At this very absent-minded time,

---

[50] Lev 26:36

needing courage instead of bleakness, joy instead of fear, Gabriel unexpectedly broadcast the following statement.

Path of Salvation

He first began to sing the song and all the Archangels followed him:

> The Archangel has descended into Nazareth to the virgin.
> He brings joy to the supreme mother Eve.
> Greetings, Eve! Greetings, young girl!
> She is happy. The Lord is with you!
> You will provide joy for many.

He then opened his flourishing lips having an imperishable fragrance, proclaiming day to day the salvation of our God, "I am a messenger but not only to the girl Mary, but to all in the world who are like her. Lord, you have conceived in our womb." He has conceived all in their womb, and having made a place in their hearts for the 2 commandments of the Lord. I visit, bless and kiss with the following kiss, "Greetings, gracious person! The Lord is with you! Blessed are you among women."[51]

These are the virtuous divine mothers who birth children not of blood, not of carnal lust, not of male lust, but of God. What is born of the flesh is flesh, while what is born of the spirit is spirit that has sanctified our hearts and our wombs.[52] Lord! This spirit is your law residing within our womb: the path, truth and life. Peace upon the many who love him, and there is no guile in him. Peace upon Israel and upon all who live according to this rule. Peace upon them and mercy! Heed this, heaven and tell the earth. Life is safe, that is, the sweet path is the Lord's path. My beloved brethren! Turn your Angelic eyes away from the Sodomites and gaze upon the wanderer traveling in the land and who is in your presence. He travels many places with the iron staff of joyful feet and calmly sings, "I am a migrant in the land; do not hide from me your commandments."[53]

---

[51] Luke 1:42
[52] John 1:13, 3:6
[53] Ps 119:19

While singing he turns his eyes to the left, then to the right, then at the entire horizon. Resting on the hill, at a spring, at green grass, eating genuine food, but like a talented singer of a simple song, he provides it taste. He sleeps sweetly and is comforted with divine visions in his sleep and when he is awake. He arises in the morning fresh and filled with hope, singing Isaiah's song, "Adolescents will hunger and young men will tire and the elect may lose their strength. The patient of the Lord will renew their strength and develop wings like the eagle. They will run and not exhaust, proceed and not become weary."[54]

His day is as long as an age and like a millennium and even after a millennium the criminal will not sell him. Of all in the world he is the most destitute, but according to God he is wealthier than all. And is there anything better than a person's life being joy in his heart? His staff is the Lord's passion and his desire, and no one will deprive him of his happiness. He has acquired the entire world but not in the manner that a person will typically gain it. He has long the divine path and glory. This is true peace and eternal life while His gospel is proclaimed, "Let all the earth hear the words of my lips."

This wanderer roams on foot through the land while his heart with us is turned toward the heavens and he finds consolation, "The souls of the righteous are in the hands of God. Among foolish people they are considered ruined and lost, but they rest in peace."[55] Although as bodily individuals they were irritated and discomforted, but this loss is made up to them with a greater reward of their hope, filled with immortality. And the Lord will reign among them forever. "Do you not hear what this walking traveler is singing?"

"How can we not hear?" answered the Archangels. He waves his hands and sings this song, "I take comfort upon the path of your revelations just as in all wealth." He alone is the most contrite spectacle and more than all the Sodomites. We have comprehended him. He is our friend, Daniel Barsabbas.

And all of them began to laugh. Then Gabriel stretched his emerald-long wings and, having flown, sat at the side of Raphael while smelling a fragrant lily of the field he was holding in his hands. Raphael, looking at Barsabbas and laughing like Sarah remembered his spiritual son, the

---

[54] Is 40:30-31
[55] Wisdom of Solomon 3:1, 3

beloved traveling companion Tobias the son of Tobit. He created a long tale about it, the manner that the father entrusted to him his son, the various calamities and adventures that befell them along the journey, and how happy the son was when he married and spent the night with his divine bride. "When he was afraid of the water or the fish," narrated Raphael, "Then I taught him: My son Tobias. My son, do not fear. This water will not drown you, but water vomited by the snake will. Such flooding speeches are secular counsel and turbulent waves of carnal intentions. This is the worldwide ancient flood that devoured everything. Yes, I tell you. This is what you must fear. But a slave or son will not devour you. But the stomach, the throat and your intestines are the hell and whale that swallows all. For them their stomach is their god and their glory is their shame.[56] Yes, I say to you, this is what you should fear. But the inner parts of a fish and some smoke from it will not save you. But the smoke of smoke and the spirit of spirit, yes, it will save you I tell you."

"Listen, Israel! The Lord God is in the midst of you, inside of you, in your heart and in your soul." This is the smoke of smoke and spirit of spirit. The smoke from your inner self from the burning of Sodom that ascended to heaven, and the spirit that does not separate itself from you but transcends the fat of the flesh and slenderness of your soul, this will save you. This is myrrh and tree sap from the cassia of your entrails. This will descend, appear to you and conceive in your heart and instill itself in your heart, and it will flow as a fragrance of peace, so that the demonic stench and the secular stink does not suffocate your soul.

To burn the intestines as Moses commanded and to kill the body's members created from dust is the same. This all occurs with faith, meaning to consider yourself dead according to the flesh while being alive according to God. Comprehend what it means to burn and kill your soul: remove from it authority and power. Then only divine incense will remain in you, the fragrance of salvation, the myrrh of peace and the Lord's spirit will anoint you and the following will fulfill, "He will direct your feet upon the path of peace."

---

[56] Phil 3:19

The Path of Peace is Called Empty

"Now ignited with my good words," Raphael continued, "My Tobias went to the right to the path of peace, by which presently our Barsabbas is traveling. This is the royal path, the supreme path, the celestial path. By this path Enoch, Elijah, Habakkuk and Philip were raptured, no longer were they found in the world. By this path Abraham ascended the mountain bringing Isaac as a sacrifice and accepted from God the sign of faith. By this path Moses ascended the mountain Pisgah and passed away. By this path all of Israel traveled to the promised land. By this path David entered Zion, was filled with eating the sacred bread and distributed it to others just like crepes from a skillet.[57] By this path Mary ascended the hill country, kissed Elizabeth and was blessed by her. By this path Christ went into the wilderness and defeated Satan. By this path the apostles ascended the mountain of Galilee and viewed the light of resurrection. This is the Sabbath path – understand this – the peaceful. By this path journeyed Luke and Cleopas while a third and blessed interlocutor joined them, and who broke heavenly bread with him and opened their eyes to see his invisible fragrance.

Finally, by this path the eunuch in the chariot was traveling to Queen Candace and became acquainted with Phillip. He unveiled to the eunuch the person inside a person, the essence within the essence, the fragrance of Christ and the new gospel. He ignited his heart like lighting special incense, and washed him top to bottom from the elemental water by using imperishable water and released him to his home. He departed to his path rejoicing. This is the joyful path, but it is empty, empty, but joyful, and outside of it there is no salvation. It is empty because it is disclosed only to elect people. The world imagines it to be empty, meaning vain, but this is slander. It imagines it again to be celestial, meaning bitter, but this is slander.[58] The mountain signifies ascendancy, not difficulty and sorrow. Woe to those who call the sweet – bitter, and the opposite. The Lord's path is judgment, to ascertain what is bad and to choose what is good. The beloved path! "The sun will not descend upon you and the moon will not

---

[57] This passage is a play on words. The name Skovoroda in Russian means frying pan or skillet and Russian blini are crepes that are cooked in a skovoroda.
[58] This passage is poetic. In Russian empty and vain rhyme, and celestial and bitter rhyme.

deprive you. The Lord will be your light until the days of your wailing have vanished."

Having announced all this Raphael fell silent. Then Uriel shouted, "Extend your gaze into the distance and see the number of traveling companions that are following Barsabbas." But Raphael began to press on them, "My beloved brethren! Look at how many there are on the left path and the amount of goats traveling upon their unfortunate path."

The Archangels cried, "O, he wants us to look the other way, away from the beautiful scene to the horrible one." Gathering together they sang this song.

O, world, world, decorated world.
Completely a pretense,
Like an ornamented coffin.
You deceive the aged, young and children.
Binding them in deceit
Just as birds in a snare.
The world seems decorated,
But it is an ornamented coffin.
Only if you open it, will you see its rot.[59]

The Path on the Left, called The Trawl

"This path," said Raphael, "is called a trawl. Fishermen use one style of trawl that is shaped in the form of a funnel: it is wide at the entrance and narrow at the exit. This path, declining from the east, hides its end not in a radiant southern region, but in midnight darkness.

"Here is the path," said Tobias' leader, "And here his unfortunate traveler walks ahead of you! Judge him! The heavenly hosts, looking upon the traveler with empathy and a kind heart, announced, "O, destitute martyr! He is a lover of money. My God! Completely burdened with bags, purses, suitcases, wallets, and he can hardly move, just like an over-loaded camel. Every step for him is torture. Woe unto you, rich people, for you have departed from your comfort."

---

[59] The lines of this song rhyme in Russian.

"But he does not sense any of this," justifies Raphael, "But on the contrary he consoles himself and considers this path to be blessed forever. He is magnanimous as he travels and sings."

"It this possible?" cried the spirits.

"Please heed his song," pleaded Raphael.

The Rich Person Traveling Sings a Song

It is fine for me to be corrupt in society,
As long as I am rich.
Today conscience is not in style,
But gold is considered fine.
How I earned it, do not ask,
As long as the crumb is buttery.
As long as I am wealthy, I am everybody's brother
And respected and welcome.
Is there anything really dishonorable in the world?
Only if your purse is empty.

Should the destitute live?
I would rather descend into the fatal mire.
And death is sweet, as long as I swim
For one dollar after another dollar.[60]
O, holy gold! There is nothing is the world that surpasses you.
A dear father is not worth you,
A dear mother is not worth you.
Beloved and happy children are not worth you.
And if this is the beauty of Venus,
It is not surprising that all of creation
Has fallen in love with you.

The Angelic hosts were terrified, seeing that Satan was so subtle to be about to corrupt his demonic soul, to deify what was dead and be reliant on an idol. "O, Satan!" they cried sympathetically. "A genuine divine monkey." In place of the words, Woe unto you the rich, and, Blessed are

---

[60] The Russian Ruble is used in this line.

the poor, and he has inserted others in his heart as the basis of his stench, Blessed are the rich for theirs is the kingdom of every type of consolation. Such a soul is an asp, no longer hearing merciful words directed to it, "Come unto me you who are laboring and burdened and I will provide you rest."

"My God," cried Uriel. "This unsettling path is completely filled with trash – crowds of people who are merchants. Listen, Raphael! Who are these, the closest crowd?"

"The rattle of chariots," he replied, "The noise of whips, the hoof beats of horses and the trumpet blare expose this armada as a regiment of ambitious men. The crowd behind them is celebrating promiscuity. They are betrayed by the blowing and whistling of musical instruments, the exciting cries of celebration and bleating of goats, and prepared perfumes, vapors and incense. The others further in the distance are the rabble and indiscriminant. There is war, battle, theft, pillage, deceit, buying and selling, and dishonestly.

"Brethren! Now turn your gaze to the right side. There they are! Not many travelers have severed themselves from the left path and run over jagged places to the peaceful path. "I, as God, have tested them and acquired them, those worthy of Me."

"What a strange spectacle I see," cried Barachiel unexpectedly and like lightning. "Aside from them are 5 men in extensive frocks so long they are dragging behind them several feet. On their heads are hoods. In their hands are not staffs but spears. Around the neck of each of them is a rope with a bell, and they are holding bags with icons and worn books. They can hardly move, they are like oxen dragging the patriarchal bell. These are definitely the labored and burdened. Woe unto them, woe!"

"These are the hypocrites," said Raphael, "monkeys of true holiness. They pray long in churches, chant incessantly in a low monotone voice from the Psalms, they build edifices and furnish them, wander as pilgrims about Jerusalem as though they are saints in the midst of criminals. They are money-lovers, ambitious, promiscuous, flatterers, panderers, ruthless, irreconcilable, rejoicing at their neighbor's misfortunes, posing as pious people with their immense property. All day they kiss the Lord's commandments while selling themselves behind the altar. Appearing as domestic animals they are inside snakes fierce as tigers, crocodiles and basilisks. Such bats between the right and the left path are neither male or female gender. They are enemies of both, crippled in both feet, not hot, not cold, not animal, not bird. The left side estranges them because they have a superficial appearance of piety; the right side rejects them because they deny its power. In their handbags they carry sand from the Jordan River with their money. Their worn books are ecclesiastical rites and liturgies. Their recitation of prayer consists of complaining to God and requesting bodily comforts. Now they are stopping, praying and beginning to sing. Let's listen to their godless song unto God."

The Hypocrites, Praying, Sing.

God, arise, why are You sleeping?
Why are You negligent toward us?
Behold how the path of criminals flourishes!
There are no destitute on their paths.
We have lit candles on Your behalf.
Every day we direct requiems and matins.
And You have forgotten all of us.
Twice do we fast in the week.[61]
During the fast days we abstain from alcohol.
We journey through holy cities,
Praying there in those homes.
We do not need the words of the Psalms,
Even though we know them by memory.[62]
And you have forgotten all of us.

Hear, God, the wail and groans!
Give to us the wealth of all the nations!
Then will we glorify You.
Golden candlesticks will we set for You,
And all of our gilded churches will
Proclaim loudly in song unto You,
Only give us gold during our life.

---

[61] The Russian Orthodox Church has 2 meatless days per week: Wednesday and Friday.
[62] Orthodox priests learned Psalms by memory, from a few to all of them.

"O, they are nothing but stench-filled coffins with their prayers," cried Barachiel. "Under the guise of holy religion Satan is deified in such immorality-filled monasteries. Malice wearing the garments of superficial reverence is this Satan transformed into an angel of light.[63] There is nothing more evil in the entirely of hell: the desolation of kingdoms, undermining of churches, deceit of God's elect. Let us turn our eyes away from such sacrilegious complainers, beggars, deceivers and hypocrites. Do you not hear the noise, echo, roar, wail, war cry, scream, smoke, brimstone and Sodom's stench that emanates from this path?

The Archangels turned their radiant faces from the north to the clear south and sang this song.

The Song of the Archangels:
The Abyss Summons the Abyss

It is impossible to discard the ocean's abyss like a handful of dust.
It is impossible to quench the fiery camp with a mere drop of water.
It is impossible for an eagle to soar in a dark cave,
Just as it does in the high sky.
    So the carnal spirit will never be satisfied.

The spirit of the abyss resides in a person,
Waters most expansive than the skies,
You will never satisfy it ever.
Better the chance of taking all the world captive.
So evolves boredom, internal gnashing, melancholy, sorrow.
So evolves dissatisfaction, and anything will cause immense fire.
    Know this: the carnal spirit will never be satisfied.

O, generation of bodily attitude! Ignorance!
How long will your heart be hard?
Lift the eyelids of your heart.
Look above and beyond the firmament of the heavens.
If you do not want to seek this, then why are you asking God?
What do you not coerce, in order to acquire it yourself?
    The abyss will satisfy the abyss and suddenly.

---

[63] 2 Cor 11:14

Slander

In Greek, slander is Devil.

Having sung this, they asked, "So what is slander? Tell us, Barachiel, the divine lightning."

He answered in the following, "Slander is to call bitter what is sweet, and the opposite.[64] It is the same as stealing, because stealing steals items but slander steals thoughts. Thinking is a person's guide and path. The Devil, stealing a person's good thought, casts it as if into a net and installs a barricade across the good path, while installing a route to direct him to the bad path. This is why the Greek word *diabolos*, also known as fugitive and a panderer or a reviser, is given the name slanderer. In Slavonic to slander means to mix, meaning to interchange the meanings of bitterness with sweetness, and the opposite. This occurs when they place something bitter and call it sweet, and the opposite. This is one source of all infernal torments."

Intrigue

"You, Uriel, are divine light! Explain to us what intrigue means."

Uriel answered, "Intrigue is a form of slander, a means by which it is sown and grows. It is the same as a machine that moves objects, while the devil's intrigues move thoughts. Nets catch birds and fish, while he catches using intrigues. An intrigue is a capable machine, for example an ambush, trap, pit, trawl, creel, referring to subterfuge and loop-holes. Among the ancient architects as well as the present, one machine was called a trestle. Today it is clearly apparent that subtlety in theft and intrigue in slander is the same."

O, what a seditious street! Having become insane on it, the human will is terrified of virtue and strives for stupidity, like a deer wounded in the torso, and not seeing its slow death. Such souls deceive themselves by singing such songs:

---

[64] Is 5:20

The ancient age was for saints,
The present age is not the same.
Spit, brother, on Zion.
Sing a secular tune.
Will you live long enough to be holy?
The present live is what you have earned.

And again:
Earn society while you are young.
What the greed of society will do for a young person.

And again:
When you are old there is no rest.
Only illness with calamity.
Even if you were to acquire some prosperity,
But in old age it will provide you no mercy.

What good is happiness to me if all of this will betray me when I become aged, since it will fail as a trusting and eternal friend? A friend is trustworthy, but blood is stronger.[65] Do not abandon me in my time of old age. All things will pass but love will continue.[66] God is love. Listen, Israel! The Lord your God is in the midst of you. What is necessary is God's kingdom and those that exert the effort will attain it.[67]

The evil tempting hook is visible and catches insane souls. And as a wolf attacks sheep at pasture and while being watered, so does the secret flatterer in his chamber and at his dinner table, but it is like a worm inside a nut eating from the inside out, and so does the devil at such green pastures. He subtly snares by replacing mother's milk for children with his poison. The Holy Bible states that in Eden's divine paradise he did the same by installing his taste and his spirit inside the fragrant fruit.

Satan corrupted this oracle, and in it defiled the fragrance of Christ. He stole the spirit of Christ and replaced it with his soul-killing taste. He redefined what is necessary as what is difficult. The German's sing this proverb, "God builds a chapel, but the devil stands there as sentry." While

---

[65] This is a Russian proverb that relatives are more dependable in the long run than any non-relative even if you consider him a friend.
[66] 1 Cor 13:8
[67] Matt 11:12

Christ sings, "What is necessary is God's kingdom." The devil adds as the chorus, "God's kingdom is difficult."

O, obscene monkey! Using this bridge to cross, but to a different city. Using this bell to ring, but for a different meaning; the Angelic tune becomes an infernal reflection; the voice of Jacob becomes the heart of Esau; he kisses like a friend but betrays like Judas. And the laughter and weeping for us is like a divine marmoset. "Heed this, heaven, and I will speak!" What slander against the Lord Almighty! The necessary and the difficult cannot be intermixed, just as light with darkness. The sun is necessary, is it difficult? Fire is necessary, is it difficult? Air is necessary, is it difficult? Land and water is necessary, and who does not have any? Do you see what is necessary? The difficultly to obtain what is close to you has disappeared!

There is no place for difficulty in chaste chambers and blessed necessity! Its house is the house of peace, house of love and sweetness. Show me where the difficulty lies. Is it in hell? I believe, Lord, that labor and sickness reside there and sorrow and sigh. But are the necessities to be found there? Ah, they have never been found there. With their presence hell is immediately transformed into paradise. In hell all is turned into what is unnecessary and superfluous, indecent, improper, repulsive, harmful, damaging, vile, stupid, indecent, disgusting, painful, dishonest, sacrilegious, cursed, secular, bodily, perishable, temporal, expensive, rare, fashionable, destructive, worrisome, ruinous and infernal, and including other persistent parasites.

From the heavenly circles and from the celestial regions this beloved queen erased all misery and labor and sorrow and sigh. Satan with all of his 10 thousands was cast into hell. What power cast him out? The one that determined that life there does not depend on vain futility and futile vanities. There lives only the one item that is necessary: it is natural and easy and beautiful and reputable and happy and useful, without money and with acquired charity, as it says, "Freely you were given, freely give."[68] Take heed, earth! Listen, humanity! Write it using a diamond pen upon the eternal tablets of your heart unto the Lord's glory, Blessed is he who made what is necessary easy and what is difficult unnecessary.

---

[68] Matt 10:8

As soon as Uriel finished delivering his accolade of the supreme Lord, a blasphemous noise, roar, battle cry, whistle and groan arose from the nether regions, like the type that comes from wild animals in the forest, or nighttime birds, or frogs in the swamps during an earthquake. Compressing, twisting and developing into innumerable convolutions this infernal snake was pierced with a strong and sharp arrow and with the flames of fiery coals dumped upon him.

First of them all Michael killed Satan's promiscuous heart with a spear.

Then upon Uriel's wings a precious supreme sapphire light of a blue color matching the beautiful and clear sky was seen. This divine mind, having released from his lips a double-edged sharp sword, struck Satan directly in his stomach and killed immorality. Barachiel shot lightning like an aimed arrow and pierced the dragon right in his eye and killed the lust of the eyes,[69] as it is written, "Let the raven of the forest pluck out the eye that insults the father and vexes the mother."[70] From this hour his kingdom and intrigues were shredded.

The Infernal Kingdom

Upon what is it founded?

Raphael extended his jasper-appearing wings with Gabriel and, having flown, sat at the side of Barachiel. Then, having laughed a while, joyfully said, "My spirit rejoices, as does Uriel's, as did Phinehas when he pierced their sides,[71] and as did Jael when she punctured Sisera's head."[72] The appearance of Barachiel's wings were like the appearance of burning hot coals, "The arrows of the strong are sharpened with consuming coals. Your word provides heat and your slave loves it. The word became flesh and resided in us."

Then this flaming eagle, the divine Barachiel, a servant in the highest of lightning, extended his wings and waving them he proclaimed, "This is the victory that has defeated the world, flesh and devil: our love. Love is as strong as death; it is as fierce as hell, jealous as God. Its wings are wings of

---

[69] 1 John 2:16
[70] Proverbs 30:17
[71] Num 25:8
[72] Judges 4:21

fire. Fiery coals set it aflame. O, burning coals! O, our beloved onyx! The gold of that land is good and onyx is there."[73]

This is his voice, "O, humble and afflicted! You have not been comforted. Behold I prepare for you onyx – a precious stone – and will provide sapphire as your foundation. I will use jasper as your pinnacles and your gates will be made of crystal, and your walls will be built of select jewels, and you will be rewarded with virtue. And every weapon turned against you and every voice that summons you to war will fail. Over them all you will gain the victory. All of your sons will be taught of God and he will provide the prosperity of many children. This is the legacy of those who serve the Lord and you will be a righteous people unto me, says the Lord."

Today our expectations have materialized. Today our three-part prayer of Sirach has been heard.[74]

> Lord, father and God of my life!
> Let not the secular abyss devour me!
> Raise your eyes on their deceits,
> Let not the precipice of my stomach swallow me
> Which they venerate as though a god.
> And let not shameful conduct bind me,
> Seeking sweetness in dead delights.

The infernal kingdom stands upon the following three-part prayer. Today wisdom has defeated malice, and all have started to sing:

> O, son born of a virgin,
> In the impassionate depths!
> Drown the three-part malice of the soul
> As I pray playing on my cymbals.
> I sing this song of victory
> Residing in this dead body.

"O, three-lipped tongue," shouted Barachiel, "that has destroyed the cities and overturned the homes of rulers. Blessed is he who possesses you. This

---

[73] Gen 2:12
[74] Sirach 23:1-6

is God's kingdom. There is nothing easier to acquire, and nothing more necessary and nothing more innate. And what is God if not the fiery essence within us, burning like spark-emanating hot coals. Blessed is this beauty. Without me you cannot accomplish anything. What is this? It carries mountains and waters and all our burdens. It grabs and holds the intangible heaven with the fire of its right hand.

"Lord, we devote unto You our effort. You are our joy and happiness, peace and rest. Your virtue is like the sun, while Satan blackens. The world testifies to falsity. Lord! If it be possible, let this bitter cup bypass me.

The Childless Weeper

At that time a pitiful voice was heard in heaven. A widow, wandering about the land, clothed in dark clothes, must give birth to a son and she is seeking a place but cannot find it, since she is pursued by a snake that wants to devour the fruit of her womb as soon as it can and then to vomit a flood.[75] For this reason she wanders, wailing and weeping this song:

> Who will give unto me wings?
> Who will cover them with silver?
> Who will provide me strong shoulders?
> Who will attach feathers to them?
>> Let me fly directly to God,
>> From the edge of the earth and even to paradise,
>> And there to rest.
>
> Behold the viper runs in my direction!
> He is attacking me!
> He opens his infernal jaws at me.
>> To swallow me, to infect me with his poison.
>> The formidable basilisk, the subtle viper.
>> Woe is me!
>
> The bitter waters shamefully vomit what is black.
> Behold the darkness!
> Behold how the nighttime cloud has covered me!

---

[75] Rev 12:4-6, 15

Woe unto me! Alas I am alone!
He pursues me with all his poison.
I have no peace.

Sorrow, sorrow. What is occurring?
Whom can I boldly call for help?
I am desperate. I must pray.
Woe unto me! Alas I am alone.
He pursues me with all his poison.
I have no peace.

God! Look upon me from your holy heights.
And descend to the distant person,
Consider my tears.
Provide me with fortitude and strength lest I fail,
Lest the fangs of the snake devour Your slave.
Alas! O, God.

Who will now provide me wings?
Let me rise like a cloud from the depths of hell.

The Archangels loved this beautiful bride of God wandering about the earth and not having a place to lay her head, and they had sympathy for her. Michael, fired with zeal, expanded his silver wings and soared like an eagle to guard its nest, and grabbed the woman and sat her on the rainbow. Now this prudent lily was hovering over the fatalists of the earth, so that malice would not interfere with her thinking, or allow deceit to manipulate her soul. The busy woman sang with her son sitting on the beautiful circular arch of clouds while she was protected from this flood by the rainbow.

Look upon the arch and bless he who created it.
Beautiful in its radiance.

Her critics are the following, "The wisdom and punishment that desolates is cursed and their hope is futile and their efforts are fruitless and their actions are unnecessary. Their wives are stupid and their children criminal. Cursed is their birth, and blessed is the unmarried woman never violated."

Then from the cloud Michael thundered to those on the earth with the following voice, "Offspring of humanity! Why do you love falsity, consuming dirt all the days of your life? Are you the retarded sons of Israel? Not having ascertained, not comprehending truth, you have condemned the daughter of Israel. O, you are dilapidated due to your evil days. Why do you unjustly judge and not hear God speaking to you, Do not kill the innocent and righteous. Who has ears, let him hear!" After his thunderous voice the celestial hosts were heard singing this song in the distance.

Song

The snake released from his lips water
like a river after the woman in order to
drown her in the flood.[76]

> Heed this, heaven and earth! Now fear.
> The seas of the abyss all move together.
> And you fast flowing Jordan, return.
> Arrive soon John, to baptize Christ.
>
> Bright and pretty are the forests; open the trails.
> Allow the Baptizer John to approach Christ.
> The nations of the earth, and all of us, rejoice.
> The Angelic choirs in heaven celebrate.
>
> The Savior descended into the Jordan, standing in deep water.
> Behold the Holy Spirit descended on him appearing as a dove.
> "This is my beloved son," the father proclaimed from a cloud.
> This Messiah will restore the substance of us all.
>
> Sanctify the current for us. Crush the head of the snake.
> Give to us, Christ, your spirit, the dew and your glory,
> So the snake will not drown us.

---

[76] Rev 12:15

And all of us from the edge of the earth
Will fly unto your paradise and there rest.

The Restoration of the World

The 7 heads are Satan and are as one. The head is like the setting sun, distorted by gloom. Soon then the world is covered by the nighttime darkness. Innumerable bats and night birds, flying in the darkness, pronounce unnecessary blasphemy and slander against the glory of the supreme. A large Angelic host then appeared, as many as stars in the night sky but mild in comparison. The Archangels, fulfilling what is written, "At that time knowledge will cease,"[77] and captivated by the heavenly Susanna, the more beautiful of all earth's daughters with her heavenly beauty, endured and resided in prayer, reciting, "Lord, our God! Your truth lives in the sun, and the sun stands upon your truth. This sign is yours, from you and to you among us. From you is the spoken word about you. You alone have created it. Behold the seven-stair ladder installed for us to attain you. And behold, Satan has pushed it down! He has created from it the gates of hell, calling what is necessary – difficult, and calling sweet – bitterness. And these gates of hell catch your people. Stand, Lord! Stand, our glory! Arise early. You lie down, you rest in your overwhelming sorrow, like a lion sleeping for many years. Awaken, as did Samson. Touch the mountains and they will smoke; shine with lightning and scatter the enemies, and let us see the new light in your light. And you will renew the face of the earth. You and yesterday and today and forever; the one who was and is and will be. Amen!"

Having prayed, all of them in a most joyous voice shouted, "Let the new light appear."

The new light appeared. Suddenly a joyous morning penetrated. The sun shined and lighted the skies, proclaiming God's glory and the face of the earth was renewed. And the Angels called the previous day darkness, while that day they called light. And there was an old light, and now there is a new, but the day and the world are the same. God created the world in ancient times in 7 days for people, but at this final age for the sake of the

---

[77] 1 Cor 13:8

Angels he renewed it in one day, since one day is like a thousand years. Let the prophecy of the supreme Peter be fulfilled, "Repent! So that times of refreshment come from the person of the Lord. The day of the Lord will arrive like a thief at night, and then the heavens will depart in a thunderous noise. New heavens and a new earth we await."[78] And also what John said, "Children! The final era has arrived and the world is departing and its lust, but who observes God's will live forever."[79] "They will not hunger and not thirst. The sun will not scorch them nor any intense heat. He will shepherd them like the lamb in the presence of God's throne, and he will lead them to living fountains of water, and God will remove every tear from their eye."[80]

As soon as the ancient world passed and departed, Noah's world appeared and a new time and a new year. At the twinkling of an eye and at the last trumpet, all the night birds, all the poisonous reptiles, all fierce animals, every labor and illness, and all the legions of evil spirits, all the innumerable books that vomit blasphemy against the Supreme, will be swept from the face of the earth and vanish. And behold, Singing. The Archangels and the entire Angelic host began to sing Psalms and hymns, and the spiritual songs of victory.

Song of Victory

Sing and continue to sing of how good God is!
Stretch your hand out,
Arise for the day of battle.
Your enemies and foes, chase them, defeat them.
Glorify, O, strong arm.
Ascend, O, messiah.
Marvelous in victory, upon the backs of the disobedient.

---

[78] Acts 3:19, 2 Pet 3:8, 10-13.
[79] 1 John 2:16-17
[80] Rev 7:15-17

Anthem

Unto You God, I dedicate this new song.
The song of Moses, the song of Christ.
I sing in spiritual lyrics,
On a 10-stringed harp.
Every king in battle against You,
Against You and David, the sword will not defeat.

You have permitted me to uproot them,
Not allowing the alien enemy to conquer us.
From their lips, the sword of death is ready to devour me,
And the evil of their right arm will not retain virtue.
Among the regiments of Angels such words were heard.

Let us sing to the Lord!
O, God omnipotent!
Again You have accepted our meek wail and cry.
Again You have spared judgment against us.
You have gained the victory!
Our fierce enemy has fallen.
And the antichrist has been executed,
The great enemy of our households.

Return to us, the joyous world is near.
It brings wellness and health with it.
Day and night it is painted with the best colors of goodness,
And the sun releases its majestic rays.
And its face radiates in its most beautiful color.

The winter has passed.
The sun had unveiled its red face to the world.
Flowers appear from their underground cavity,
Earlier defeated by the frost.

All the birds of paradise
Are released from their cages.
They everywhere fly, sweetly singing.
Filled with joy.

The green fields filled with grass,
The oak trees filled with leaves,
They rise, are clothed, looking, laughing.
O, how sweet it is to behold all this!

Life-giving fountains of water now appear in the dry fields and deserts. Cities and residences surface. "How beautiful are your homes, Jacob." The crooked mountains opened their roads, decorated with many flowers. "I am the flower of the fields and lily of the valley."[81]

The wild and inhospitable Caucasus Mountains have opened its doors to pilgrims. The sea has shown a route for all the floating ships. Productive islands, mountains, cliffs, harbors and capes now can be seen. A beneficial hope. Safe harbors for all those who sail the seas are now available.

They see the glorious kingdom and the holy land, "There your mother gave me birth. You will see the king in his glory and your eyes will see the land from the distance."[82] You will recline in green pastures and in blessed meadows. From here radiant crowns will shine upon the heads of all holy people who are surrounded with a diamond glory. It is easy to be good. Then an imperishable crown will be placed upon my head.

The Archangels, having sung the song of victory, flew high into the skies and descended on the 7 pyramids called the great Sabbaths who observe the wisdom of the glory of the Father and Son and the Holy Spirit yesterday, today and forever.

I, elder Daniel Barsabbas, truly saw this vision, and I wrote it for the enlightenment of the blessed uneducated people seeking a means of acquiring wisdom.

The end.

---

[81] Song 2:1
[82] Song 8:2, Is 33:17

NARCISSUS:

A DISCUSSION ON THE TOPIC OF COMPREHENDING YOURSELF

Prologue:

This is my first-born son. He was born in the 7th decade of this century.[83] A certain flower and a certain youth are both called a Narcissus. The youth Narcissus was a person who saw his reflection in clear water at a fountain and so fell fatally in love with himself; this incident is an introductory parable from obsolete theology, which is the Hebrew mother. Narcissus's image proclaims this, "Comprehend yourself!" It was as if he said, "Do you want to be content with yourself and fall in love with yourself? Then comprehend yourself! Test yourself firmly. Right! How can you fall in love with something you know nothing about? Straw will not burn until a flame touches it. A heart will not love until it sees beauty. It is obvious that love is Sophia's daughter.[84] Where wisdom ripens there love burns. Truly blessed is Narcissus if it is holy; and it is holy if it is true. Yes, I say, it is true if it has acquired and seen its sole beauty and truth, "In the midst of you stands a person whom you know not."[85]

Gracious is the man who acquires in his home a fountain of comfort and does not chase the winds with Esau, hunting in desolate environs. Michal the daughter of Saul scattered her gazes from her father's home

---

[83] Referring to its composition in 1766.
[84] Sophia is Greek for wisdom.
[85] John 1:26

through a window; she is the mother and queen of all who wander in desolate environs chasing after some wayward and lost gigolo who like a wild bull, after being cornered, is chased into the house of our shepherd. Where is the demon chasing you? "Return to your home."[86]

These are Narcissus' gang of rebels. But my wise Narcissus loves his home, as Solomon's proverb, "A virtuous person's intellect will be a friend to him."

Whoever looks at the decay of his beauty in the waters will not fall in love with his superficial appearance or what he sees in the waters, but with himself and his internal appearance. "You will rest in your paths in the midst of you."

My Narcissus, it is right that you be fervent, you are aflame with the coals of love; you cry, you wander and you turmoil and caress and have concern. You repeat rumors, but not many, and not of some futile subject, but of yourself, about yourself and within yourself. Finally it is like ice that melts from the flame of ambition and transforms into a fountain. Right? Right! In whatever a person falls in love, into that he will be transformed. Every person is what his heart is within him. Every person is where his heart is.

O, my dearest mercy, Narcissus. Today from a crawling worm a winged moth has appeared. Behold today's resurrection! Why have you not changed into a creek or stream? Why not into a river or sea? Tell me? Narcissus responds, Do not harm me, for I have done a good work. The sea evolves from a river, the river from streams, the streams from springs, the springs from dew, and dew always near the fountain is its strength and offspring, its spirit and heart. This is love! I love the source and head, spring and origin, the eternal trickles seeping from the dew of the heart. The sea is puss; the rivers flow by; the streams dry; the springs vanish. The fountain eternally breathes its mist, enlivening and cooling. I love only the spring and yet it will still go dry. The balance of it all is passing away for me, a shadow, shade, chaff. O, the sea's heart! A chaste abyss! Holy fountain! You alone I love. I vanish into you and am transformed. Do you hear? Behold what the eagle's chicks sing, the eagle mother and the wisdoms of Thebes.

Hypocrites and superstitious, you hear this and go astray and revile it. Will you be transformed into a spring? How can this occur? Don't

---

[86] 1 Kings 1:53

complain! It is extremely easy for a believer, and I will say it more clearly, for the person who recognizes this beauty in himself. Mist is the strength of God and what flows is the pure glory of the Almighty.

It would be better for him to be transformed into gold or into a jewel, or... Wait! He has found the best. He is being transformed into the sovereign of all creatures, into the sun. Is the sun and spring the same? Yes! The sun is the source of light. The springs trickle water, providing drink, cooling, washing dirt. The fiery spring radiates rays of light, enlightens, warms, disperses darkness. The water spring is the beginning of the water sea. The sun is the head of the fiery sea. But how can all of this be, for a person to be transformed into a sun? If this is impossible, then why are the following words proclaimed? "You are the light of the world, that is, a sun."[87]

O, hypocrites! Do not judge by the appearance, but by the heart. Yes! The sun is the source. So how can the man of God not be a sun? The sun is not what it is based on the face, but because of the strength emanating from it, it is the source. So it is with the person of God who emanates life-providing trickles and releases rays of deity, and so is the sun not because of its sun-like appearance, but due to its heart. Every person is what his heart is in him. Having a wolf's heart makes him a wolf, even thought it has the face of a person. Having the heart of a beaver makes it a beaver, although it has the appearance of a wolf. Having the heart of a wild boar makes it a wild boar, although it looks like a beaver. Everything is what its heart is in it. But the hypocrites arrogantly push with their horns. Let them sleep deep! However for a person to be transformed into the face of the sun is impossible. The face and heart are different. Rightly judge; rightly! And I ascertain: It is impossible. So what use is this? Having the appearance of a beaver does not make the wolf a beaver. O, deaf people who love such ostentation. Heed the shout. "The flesh is nothing; it is spirit that livens."[88]

And you do not know that the appearance, face, flesh, image is all the same and nothing? Do you not know that this world is the idol of the field of Dura?[89] The sun is the face of this statue, and Narcissus does not like him. The world is the street of Michal,[90] the prostitute of Babylon, the demonic sea, while Daniel and Narcissus in these hot infernal waters have

---

[87] Matt 5:14
[88] John 6:63
[89] Dan 3:1
[90] Saul's daughter and later wife of David.

seen their beloved mercy. Which? The dew carrying spring and devout sun. Where are you resting? Unveil to me you appearance. O, wisdom is more blessed than those who see the sun.

Gratitude to the blessed God. This is his inexpressible mercy and authority, creating what is useless to be impossible, while creating what is useful to be possible. Now my Narcissus has been transformed into truth and not into an empty sun. A question of the hypocrites: What is this? Can there exist 2 suns in one sun? Answer: So where are your ears when the heavenly trumpets thunderously declare, "Place your settlement in the sun."[91]

Notice that in the gold head of your idol – this world – and in the oven of Babylon resides and Sabbath-rests our un-attainable light, and not your darkness. But our sun is glorified in the following trumpet song, "The spring flows and satiates all."

So let us leave this behind, so the hypocrites will be tormented in their fiery lake. Ourselves with Israel will cross to the other side of sea, according to the counsel of Baruch, "Who shall cross to the other side of the sea and acquire wisdom? The paradise is there."[92] The Narcissuses all recognize each other there. Behold the first who meets us is the beloved David singing his song, "In you is the fountain of life. In your light we will see light."[93]

Remain hypocrites with your personal sun. We in our foolish sun will acquire what is new and beautiful, "Let there be light! Let the sun rise! And the sun was confirmed."

Behold behind the wall and our property it meets us, having clothed itself in its light as clothes. Behold it shouts to us, "Greetings! Be bold! Peace unto you! Fear not! I am light! I am the light of the sun-shining idol and its world. Who is thirsty come to me and drink."

---

[91] Ps 19:4 in the LXX.
[92] Baruch 3:30
[93] Ps 36:9

The miracle that occurred in the waters of Narcissus.

Tell me beautiful Narcissus, what did you see in the waters? Who appeared to you there?

Answer. Upon the waters floated Elisha's iron.[94] I saw on the smooth panel my disintegrating flesh the un-manufactured image that is the radiance of the Father's glory. Place me as a seal upon your arm. The light reflects upon us. I see Peter your haven. The land in the midst of waters was installed by the word of God. I see my friend, Isaiah's friend, You will see the king in his glory, and your eyes will see the land from afar.[95] O, wizard – my flesh unveiled to me my Samuel. This is the only one I love, for whom I melt, disappear and am transformed. Nonetheless, from the Egyptian we will look at the Hebrew Narcissus. Here is the first who greets us. Being zealous, I became zealous in the Lord God. Here is the 2nd. My soul enters your word, that is, it is transformed. Here is another Narcissus for you. Behold we have left all and follow you. And is not David the true Narcissus? My heart and my flesh vanish. My eyes vanish in your salvation. When will I arrived and appear in your presence? And it not this exactly Narcissus? The world is crucified to me and I to the world. It is not I who live, but Christ who lives in me.[96] Until this humble body is transformed. I desire to be separated. For me to live is Christ, and to die is acquisition.[97]

Just as a person's face was in the spring, so in Isaiah's words. Narcissus' love was seen as though a rainbow in the cloud. God will be with you always, and He will fill you full to the extent your soul desires, and your bones will become fat and will be as juicy ripe grapes, and like a spring with plenty of water, and your bones will grow as does plant life, and become healthy and the generations of generations will inherit. And your eternal desolations will be rebuilt and the generations of generations will be your eternal foundations, and you will be called the builders of walls, and you will rest upon your paths.[98]

---

[94] 2 King 6:6
[95] Is 33:17
[96] Gal 6:14, 2:20
[97] Phil 3:21 1:23
[98] Is 61:4

First Discussion Regarding Comprehending Yourself

Persons: Luke, his Friend[99] and a Neighbor

Luke: Yesterday we were dining at my brother's house, myself and my neighbor, and especially because it was a Sunday and we wanted to discuss something from God's word. The table was set in the garden. What motivated the conversation were the specific words written upon the arbor, "Whose heel you preserve will smash your head."[100]

During dinner 2 scholars showed up: Nabal and Shebna. They discussed and interpreted this passage considerably at the request of my bother. I have absolute faith that Sacred Scripture is the food of paradise and the healer of all my thoughts. For this reason I sighed since they could not see any taste in these sweetest words.

Friend: Why do you call them sweetest words when you are not able to taste any flavor in them?

Luke: In the same manner as a person looks from afar at flowers in paradise, not hearing their perfume, but only believing that they exude some marvelous fragrance.

Friend: Listen, brother. Even if they were to exude fragrance right under our nose, it is impossible for us to taste their smell.

Luke: How is this? Do we not have a head and nostrils?

Friend: Head and nostrils? Know that we complete humans have shortcomings and must say, "Lord, as people we have not."

Luke: Since when we as people cannot possess and see these members?

Friend: What is the use if we have and do not understand? Not to recognize taste and smell? And if you want to know, then know that this is how we see other people, it is as if someone should show you a person's foot or heel while hiding the balance of the body and head. Without the balance it is impossible to fathom a person. You even look right at

---

[99] Shebna
[100] Gen 3:15

yourself, but not comprehend and not understand yourself. And not to comprehend yourself, word for word, is one and the same as to lose yourself. If your treasure is buried in your home and you are not aware of it, word for word, it is as if it does not exist. And so, you need to comprehend yourself, and search for yourself, and find that person: this all means the same. But you do not comprehend yourself and are not a person having eyes and nostrils and hearing and the other senses. So how can you comprehend and fathom your friend. "If you do not comprehend yourself, O, the best among women, follows the tracks of the flock and shepherd your goats at the shepherd's tents."[101]

Luke: How? But I see my hands, feet and my entire body.

Friend: You do not see anything and know completely nothing about yourself.

Luke: Your thoughts are cruel and very stinging. In no manner can I swallow them.

Friend: I did say to you that you cannot hear taste.

Luke: You have confused me. How is it that I cannot see anything in myself?

Friend: You see in yourself only earth. But even then you do not see anything because earth is nothing; earth and nothing is one and the same. One person sees the shadow of an oak tree, while another sees specifically the tree. When you see your shadow, plainly said, it is your emptiness and nothing more. You do not see yourself restored to life.

Luke: My God! Where are such alien thoughts coming from? You have spoken much, saying I have not ears and eyes.

Friend: And yes, I said this a while back that you have none of these.

Luke: How can this be? Are not my eyes – eyes, and are not my ears – ears?

Friend: I will ask this of you. Tell me: your heel and your body, are they the same?

Luke: My heel is the final part of my body while my head is the beginning.

---

[101] Song 1:8

Friend:	So do I answer you with your own answer, that this eye of yours is a heel or tail in your eye.
Luke:	But where is this specific or exact eye, the primary and original eye?
Friend:	I just said that you only see your own tail, but know nothing about your head. So how can you know someone based on only his heel? But since you do not see your eye, except for its final member, so you have not seen the ear, or your tongue, or hand, or your feet, or any of your other members, your entire body except for its final member, which is called the heel or tail or shadow. How can you say that you have comprehended yourself? You have only lost yourself. You have no ears, no nostrils, no eyes, none of any of what you are, except for just your shadow.
Luke:	Why are you calling me a shadow?
Friend:	Because you have lost the truth of your essence, and of your entire body you preserve the heel or tail, bypassing what you exactly are and so you have lost what is primary.
Luke:	So why do you call my members a tail?
Friend:	Because the tail is the final member; it follows the head, while itself cannot begin anything.
Luke:	You are tormenting me, my beloved. Maybe it is like you say. But you, having destroyed my opinions, do not provide me your own.
Friend:	Listen, my soul! I recognize the fact that I do not know this exactly. But if you are interested in my thoughts, then we will discuss this more openly. You know without a doubt, that what we call an eye, ear, tongue, hands, feet and our entire outer body does not operate at all in any manner on its own. But all of it is enslaved to our thoughts. Thought, the body's sovereign, is day and night in a consistent state of agitation. It ascertains, counsels, decides, compels. But our extreme flesh, as an unrestrained bull or tail, follows it against its will. So you see that thought is our primary point and the middle. And for this reason it is only called the middle. And so it is not our superficial flesh, but our thought is our primary person. Of it we are composed, and it is us.

Luke:	Well, this I can believe. I noticed that when I (and I will call myself Thought from this point on) swayed over to the side, then I notice that the eye is not able to see anything and even the closest object. So what good is an eye if it is unable to see? You did right by calling it not an eye, but a shadow of the actual eye or tail. I thank you for having found me. Glory to God. I have now eyes, ears, a tongue, hands and feet. I have lost the old and found the new. Farewell, my shadow. Welcome, desired truth. You will be for me the promised land. Enough for me to always be a laborer. And never did I even think about this matter. Where is this going? I love this opinion. Please confirm it for me. I want it to be steadfast.
Friend:	Please do not hurry. If a person clings too quickly to some new opinion, he will just as quickly depart from it. Do not be windy. Ascertain to a safe conclusion every word, and then at that time give it a place in your heart. I myself inexpressibly like this opinion, and I would like it to also be yours forever, so that in the both of us there would be one heart and mind. And there is nothing that can be sweeter than this. But please first masticate it well, and then swallow it in the joy and simplicity of your heart. Be plain, but in the meanwhile also be careful. If my opinion interests you, then know that it is not my personal thought. Look at Jeremiah, chapter 17, verse 9.
Luke:	My God! I will look up this exact verse of Jeremiah's and see if I can fathom his thought. But please, what are his exact words?
Friend:	Here they are, "Profound is the heard of a person, worse than all in a person, and who can fathom it?" And so if you have eyes and ears, take note! Can you feel this?
Luke:	I feel it, my friend. The prophet calls the human a heart.
Friend:	And what else do you notice other than this?
Luke:	This, that our hidden thoughts are an abyss and with a profound heart are one and the same. This is remarkable! As impossible as this is to accept, that a person is not the ostensive self or the superficial flesh, as people in general feel, but his deep heart or thought. This is exactly what a

	person is and his head, while his external appearance is nothing else but a shadow, heel and tail.
Friend:	So do you see? You are already beginning to fall behind. How easy it was for you to believe at the beginning, and this is why your faith is quickly reducing: as fast as you are ignited, just as fast you are extinguished. But a firm attitude with stagnation will strengthen, because counsel does not exist without slowness. O, how contagious is the earth. A person cannot quickly tear his foot from some sticky carnal opinions once they become rooted in us and we call them dogmas. The carnal thought is the beginning and source of our carnal life style; it slithers along the ground seeking flesh, looking for some dirty heel, while our eye is safeguarding ourselves from it, and this is our counsel. But who will crush the head of the snake for us? Who will prick the raven's eye once the night descends? Who will mortify our flesh? Where is Phinehas who pierced the prostitute?[102] Where are you Jeremiah, who desolates the land?[103] But God has sought for the wise to place against the wise, snake against snake, family against family, land against land, paradise in place of hell, the living in place of the dead, rectitude in place of falsity. Behold your savior comes bringing with him compensation.
Luke:	Please speak more clearly. I do not understand any of this.
Friend:	But who can hear taste not having faith? Faith is light seen in darkness, the fear of God, the penetration of the flesh; God's love is as strong as death: this is the sole door to possessing a paradisiacal taste. Can you believe that the most chaste spirit has the ability to maintain all the dust of your body?
Luke:	I believe it, but I myself also feel the weakness of my faith. Help me if you can to extract me from the mud of unbelief. I recognize that this word of faith in my dirty lips dreams for only one habit, but I do not hear any taste at all in it.
Friend:	Do you at least know where faith is looking?
Luke:	I know that I must believe in God, but I will not tell you about anything else.

---

[102] Num 25:8
[103] Jer 1:10

Friend:	O, destitute and fruitless person! Know that faith can look at what your empty eye cannot see.
Luke:	So what is it about an empty eye?
Friend:	This was already discussed, that all flesh is emptiness.
Luke:	And yes! In the entirely of what is under heaven I see nothing else other than the visible, or as you say it, the bodily or fleshly.
Friend:	Then this makes you an unbelieving pagan and idolater.
Luke:	How can I be an idolater if I believe in one God?
Friend:	How can you believe if you see nothing except for the visible? True belief disdains visible emptiness, but depends on that located inside a barren head, which is strength and fortitude and this will never perish.
Luke:	This is why another eye is needed in order to view the invisible.
Friend:	Say it better in these terms, that it is better for you to have a true eye so you can discern the truth in barrenness. But this old eye of your is good for nothing. But if you possessed within yourself the true person, then using his eye you would be able to watch for truth in everything.
Luke:	So how is this person to acquire this?
Friend:	If you can recognize it, then you will attain it.
Luke:	Then where is it? But first answer. Why did you first speak of faith, and now about the eye?
Friend:	The true eye and faith is all the same.
Luke:	How is this?
Friend:	So the true person has a true eye that – since it circumvents the visible – watches newness beneath it and rests upon it, and so it is called faith. And to believe and to depend on something as a firm foundation is all the same.
Luke:	If you find in me 2 eyes then also 2 persons.
Friend:	This way of course.
Luke:	But if one is sufficient, why should there be 2?
Friend:	Look at that tree. If there is no oak tree, can there be a shadow?
Luke:	I am not a shadow. I possess a firm body.

Friend:	You are shadow and darkness and decay. You are just a dream of a true person. You are a piece of clothing, while he is the body. You are a hallucination, but he within you is truth. You are a void, but he within you is a substance. You are mud, but he is your beauty, image and plan. You are not your image and not your beauty, since this depends not on you, but is just dust, while the real person is within you. And you have not recognized him up to this time, and will not until you realize with Abraham that you are just dirt and dust. And so you eat the dirt, love your heel, slither along the ground. O, seed of the snake and non-existent shadow! The day promised of God will soon arrive promising blessing for the chaste soul and will destroy your evil counsel with the word, "He will smash your head."

Second Discussion Regarding Comprehending Yourself

        Persons: Cleopas, Luke, and a Friend

Cleopas:	You say the truth. However as eloquent as Shebna is, I do not hear any taste in him. Let us go again to our friend. His words are edible, but I do not know how pleasant they are.
Luke:	And he is arriving just in time.
Friend:	Dead shadow! Welcome!
Luke:	Welcome, Thought! Spirit! Heart! Is this really your person? We repeated your thoughts while reading books. They say that you must show us your opinion in nature.
Friend:	What does this mean: To show in nature?
Luke:	I don't know.
Cleopas:	How can you not know this? You must disclose what is not only residing solely in a person, the invisible that has the supremacy, but in other creatures.
Luke:	So exactly. This is reason to come to you.
Friend:	Up to now you do not know?
Luke:	Of course, and you must prove it.
Friend:	Do you believe there is a God?

Luke:	His invisible power governs all and possesses all.
Friend:	So what more do you need? You have proved it yourself.
Luke:	How have I proved it?
Friend:	When you say that the invisible power governs and possesses all, is not this the same as saying that what is invisible has the supremacy in creatures? You have already called the invisible the head, while the visible is the tail in all the world.
Luke:	So take something out of all the world as an example of explanation.
Friend:	I present to you all under heaven and the entire Copernican universe. Select whatever you want. But what you are saying – to show it in nature – it should have been stated in this manner: Explain to us in parables or example and similitudes that a person does not consist of his external flesh and blood, but of his mind and heart: this is the true person. Look at that wall. What do you see on it?
Luke:	I see a person pictured. He stands on a snake, crushing the snake's head with his foot.
Friend:	Do you see the artist?
Luke:	I see him.
Friend:	Tell me, what is it that the artist is attempting to magnify: The painted colors or the drawing within the painted colors?
Luke:	The painted colors are nothing else than dust and emptiness; the drawing or the proportions and arrangement of the drawing is its strength. And if this was not there then the paint is just mud and emptiness.
Friend:	So what do you see with this work of art?
Luke:	I see words copied from the Bible. Listen, I will read them, "The eyes of a wise man are in his head. The eyes of a fool are at the ends of the world."[104]
Friend:	Well! If someone sees paint on words, while cannot read letters, what does this seem to you? Does such a person even see letters?
Luke:	He sees with his fleshly eyes solely the final emptiness or paint in words, but does not comprehend the figure in the letter. He sees the heel but not the head.

---

[104] Eccl 2:14

Friend:	You have correctly ascertained. This is why if you see bricks and plaster in an old church, but do not understand its plan, what do you think? Have you viewed it and know it?
Luke:	No way! In such a manner all you see is the least and superficial appearance, which even cattle see, while its symmetry or proportions or size you do not see, or its material that ties all of it together. So it is not comprehended since you do not see its head.
Friend:	Your basis is a good one. Now remove from my account the entire balance.
Luke:	How?
Friend:	This is how! As paint is in the picture, so is a figure in letters, but it is a plan for a building. But do you sense that all of these heads as pictures as well as the figure and plan and symmetry and size is nothing but thoughts?
Luke:	It seems to be this way.
Friend:	Why can you not fathom that even in other creatures the invisible has the supremacy and not only in a person? This you can recognize in grasses and trees and other growth. The spirit penetrates all and everything. The spirit sustains all of it. But our eye observes the heel and the superficial outer appearance, circumventing the strength, beginning and head. And so, although we are just a body if we have no soul, then we recognize the fact that we are not satisfied with the amount that we know about ourselves.
Luke:	For what reason?
Friend:	In order that, while honoring the superficial dust of our body, we do not ascend in our minds into the plan that sustains our weak figure of dust. And we never sense any taste in these words of God as we slither along the dirt of our understanding toward our true body as it is being exalted, and namely, "Fear not Jacob! Behold, upon My hands I have written your walls." So let us ascend higher.
Cleopas:	We do not yet want to ascend higher due to our doubt, and prefer to know what you call a true body. This amazes us.
Friend:	What is so amazing? Does not God sustain all? Is He not the head and all in all? Is He not truth in emptiness; the true and

primary foundation in our negligible dust? And how do you doubt an exact, eternal and new body? Do you think to find something other than this, where God does not govern as the head and beginning? Is it possible that something could have existence outside of Him? Is He not the existence of all? In a tree He is the true tree; in grass He is the true grass; in music, music; in a house, the house; in our body of dirt there exists a new body and He is its definition and head. He is the omnipresent in the ubiquitous, because the Lord is truth. The Lord, spirit and God are one. He alone is marvelous in everything and He makes anything new that He wants, and His truth reside in everything forever. The balance such as the ostensive superficiality is nothing but His shadow and His heel and underneath and a dilapidating garment. But the eyes of the wise person are in his head, while the eyes of the foolish are at the ends of the world.

Third Discussion Regarding Comprehending Yourself

Persons: Cleopas, Luke, and Filon

Cleopas: Stop, please! Do not doubt. He is a good person and in no manner does he disdain our friendship. I know well about your good heart, and he seeks nothing except what we discuss.
Filon: I know many scholars and they are arrogant. They do not want to speak with villagers.
Cleopas: Please believe me.
Friend: What are you arguing about?
Cleopas: Bah! We are doing this purposely. This is my friend. Please do not get angry.
Friend: Why should I? A person looks at the appearance, but God looks at the heart. And Luke is not here?
Cleopas: He cannot understand your speeches. He clung to Shebna during yesterday's conversation, but your innovations are interesting.

Friend:	So what was his speech about?
Cleopas:	Do you remember, Filon?
Filon:	I remember. The speech was about the abyss.
Cleopas:	Ah! Here are the words, "And darkness was over the abyss."[105]
Filon:	Then the argument was about some kind of old and new bags and about wine.
Cleopas:	One argued that the abyss is called heaven, upon which planets swim, while Mr. Nabal cried that the specific abyss is a great ocean. Another swore that it signifies a woman, while another interpreted it as teaching, and on and on.
Friend:	If we want to measure heaven, earth and sea, we must first measure ourselves with Paul using our personal measure. And if we do not find this measure within us then how can we measure anything? And not measuring ourselves earlier what advantage it is to know the measure of other creatures? So can this be done? Can a person who is blind in his home also be perspicacious at the open market? Can he grasp measurement not comprehending what is a measurement? Can he measure, not seeing the ground? Can he view the head and its strength, not having found and not having comprehended the same in himself?
Cleopas:	Can you not explain this more simply?
Friend:	To measure and to know the measure is the same. If you were to measure the length and width of a church with a yardstick or tape, what do you think, would you know its dimensions?
Cleopas:	Not necessarily. I would only know the expansion of its inside dimensions, but its specific measure sustained by its materials I would only know when I understand its plan.
Friend:	So then if you were to measure the entire Copernican universe and not having known its plan, which sustains the entire superficial vastness, then nothing of any of this would exist.
Cleopas:	I think that as the vastness is emptiness, so is its measurement.
Friend:	So who can find the plan in earth's and heaven's expansive vastness that adheres to its eternal symmetry, if you first cannot view it in the emptiness of your flesh? All and

---

[105] Gen 1:2

everything is created and woven using this plan, and nothing can be sustained without it. It is the chain and rope for all the materials. It is the right hand, the dust that sustains all dust, and the hand of God having measured the entire perishable vastness and including our empty composition. God's word, counsel and His thought are this plan by which the material in all the universe is insensibly enlarged, entirely sustained and consummated. This is the depth of wealth and His wisdom, and who can further spread these thoughts? O, heart, the immense abyss of all waters and heavens. How deep you are! You encompass and sustain all, and nothing interferes with you.

Cleopas: It is right to say this remembering the words of Jeremiah, "Profound is the heart of a person, worse than all what is within a person."

Friend: This is definitely a person who can retain a lot. He confirms your fleshly hands and feet. He is a keystone and strength and eyes and ears. But if you can believe Him, "You eyes will not fade and your lips will not desist for ever and ever."

Cleopas: I believe and compel my heart toward obedience of belief. But can you in the least strengthen me? Do not be angry with me. The higher I ascend in understanding the invisible, the stronger my faith.

Friend: You are right is requiring God not to be able to accept prayers or sacrifices from us if we have not comprehended Him. Love Him and become close to Him always; come close to Him in your heart and knowledge, and not with just your feet and statutes. Your heart is the head of your superficial nature, and when it is the head then you have become your own heart. But if you do not come near and not cling with the entity that is the head of your head, then you will remain a dead shadow and corpse. If there is a body over your body, then there is a head over your head and a new heart higher than the old one. Ah! Is it not shameful for us and not pitiful that God asks us to reflect on ourselves and yet does not receive it?

Cleopas: Is it possible? How?

Friend:	Its adversaries are idols and idol temples. But we justify these at every judgment.
Cleopas:	What a horrible offence! And this I do not understand.
Friend:	You do not understand? Now at this moment you will be a judge against it.
Cleopas:	I fear. But please, strengthen for me my disbelief in the immortal body. These words of yours I like, "You eyes will not fade."
Friend:	Well tell me, if your external or animal body would last 1000 years undamaged, would you love your flesh?
Cleopas:	For this to happen is impossible. But were it possible then how can I not love it.
Friend:	Know that you have acquired so little knowledge about yourself.
Cleopas:	At least I know that my body is founded upon an eternal plan, and I believe this promise of God, "Behold upon my hands I have inscribed your walls."[106]
Friend:	If in the construction of some house you knew the structure of its walls, is this sufficient to knowing completely the entire house?
Cleopas:	I think not. It is needful, it seems, to also know for which reasons or activities the house was built: is its purpose to bring sacrifices to demons or to the invisible God? Is it to be a haunt of criminals or a settlement of Angels?
Friend:	And it seems to me that you do not understand this sufficiently. For example a clay pot, if you comprehend solely the figure that is depicted on its dirt surface, how do you know whether it is clean or dirty inside, or whether it is filled with liquor or water?
Cleopas:	Now I understand that my body is exactly like the walls of a temple or like a piece of a pot. While my heart and thoughts are like the gifts offered in the temple, or like the water in the pot. And as the walls are cheaper than sacrifices – because they are for the sacrifice and not the sacrifice for the walls and likewise the water is not for the pot – so it is that my soul, thoughts and heart are superior to my body.

---

[106] Is 49:16

Friend:	But tell me: suppose these beautiful walls were to collapse, would they be destroyed? Would this pot be ruined if the figure on its surface was removed?
Cleopas:	Blah! Even a child can comprehend this.
Friend:	Do not rejoice my Israel and do not be happy. You have gone astray from God your master. Have you never heard from the prophets that God has a judgment with His adversary the land?
Cleopas:	So who is it that can judge it?
Friend:	You have already pronounced your judgment upon it, destroying that facet of it.
Cleopas:	In what manner?
Friend:	Who judges corruptly has without doubt insulted the innocent. But there is no way to justify them both. Such a judge was like you Ephraim, whom one of the prophets called a foolish dove deprived of a heart. And it is not surprising because according to this prophet's parable, it is just like an oven hot from its fire that all of these judges have been consumed from the heat, that all their instructors have vanished from the land, and there was not even one who was acceptable to God.[107]
Cleopas:	Have a kind heart. Tell me what judgment I have stated against God?
Friend:	In this way! You loving the land imposed on it your judgment, which solely belongs to God.
Cleopas:	I do not understand.
Friend:	Listen, you half-blind dove! Does not power belong to God? And is not fortitude the Lord's?
Cleopas:	So who is arguing with you over this point?
Friend:	So what gave you the boldness to say that because the crock is broken the pot is ruined? Can you establish a pot on dust and not on God? What fortitude can you assign something that is every minute subject to possible ruin and change? Is it not God's invisible finger that sustains the dust in the walls? Is He not the keystone in the walls? Is not the wall eternal if its principle design is eternal? So what gave you the right to destroy the head, magnify the tail, sentence harmlessness to

---

[107] Hosea 7:7, 11

	decay, fortitude to dust, deity to an idol, light to darkness, life to death? Here is an iniquitous judgment and counsel against God. Here is the evil eye of the evil snake, loving the heel and not the head Jesus Christ. "He is everything possible in all."[108] Did you not say that it is impossible not to love the decaying body if it was to remain undamaged over a 1,000 years? And so how can you say that you at the least measure possible have comprehended your body? So why do you boast of these divine merciful words? "Behold on my hands I have inscribed your walls and they will be in My presence forever." Can the consumable exist always, that is forever? Can the unworthy exist as honorable, or the darkness as light or evil as goodness? Is not this all the same: to believe in the dust of your feet and depend on a silver idol? All that is visible is an idol. All that is consumable is dishonorable. All that is temporal is darkness and death. Look at the earthiness of your flesh. Do you believe that in this dust of your composition there is buried a treasure, meaning that there is hidden in it the invisibility and finger of God, which sustains your dust and your earthiness?
Cleopas:	I believe.
Friend:	Do you believe that he is the head and original basis and eternal plan of your flesh?
Cleopas:	I believe.
Friend:	Ah! When you would have believed, you would never have said that your body collapses at the dissolution of your dust. You only see the animal in your body. You do not see the spiritual body. You do not have the staff and spirit for the mutual division. You do not sense the taste in these divine words, "If the honorable departs from the unworthy, then what will my lips declare?"
Cleopas:	It is not understandable to me how you can possibly attribute deity to an idol, and life to something that is dead. Did I hear you say that the perishing is the one who calls light – darkness, and bitter – sweet.

---

[108] 1 Cor 15:28

Friend: Do not be surprised my soul! All of us cling to dust. Whoever is in love with his tangible body cannot but chase after the visible in all the expanse of heaven and earth. But for what reason does he love it? Is it not because he views in it brightness and pleasure, life, picture and merit?

Cleopas: Of course, this is why.

Friend: So is not all of this the same – to consider an idol living and to attribute life to it, while it must die. It seems to me this way: to consider bitter as sweet and attribute the sweetness of honey to gall. But would this not be an insult to honey if you were to call gall – sweet? In this manner do all people gather against the Lord and His Christ! They cry, "My fortitude and my strength. I am the way, truth and life." But we judge that all of this pertains to the external flesh and the bodily appearance. And our judgment we unalterably affirm with the conduct of our life in the presence of other people.

Cleopas: I now recognize your guilt and I am terribly amazed at how the darkness has settled over your eyes. How much the prophets cry, "Spirit, spirit! God, God!" All the superficial is grass, shadow, nothing, while we complain and grieve when our flesh fades, weakens and the dust returns to dust. Is it even possible to find a worse and crueler disaster?

Friend: I am often astonished at this also. Now I think you understand what the judgment is that God so jealously demands from His prophets. And how can we provide a good judgment to our lesser brethren having insulted their firstborn brother Jesus Christ?[109] He was the foremost orphan since all abandoned him; he was the first destitute since everything was taken from him. They went, they ran after darkness, leaving the light.

Cleopas: So where among us is this cursed seed born? If the ground is cursed so is love towards it.

Friend: It is well that a thought is considered a seed. A seed is the beginning of a fruit. Counsel in the heart is the principle of all our activities. But since the heart is the essential person, then it is apparent whom God's wisdom calls His seed and whom it

---

[109] referring indirectly to anti-Semitism.

calls the snake's progeny. These people love the ground, but it is the heel and nether-region and shadow. For this reason they will never be satisfied with what they find. Gracious is the person in whose heart this cursed head has been crushed. Otherwise it would lead us into sorrow and others into an imaginary sweetness. But what is the origin of the snake being born in the heart? Do you ever ask this of yourself?

Cleopas: I want to know.

Friend: What is the source of the evil seed along the garden beds? They seem to be filled with counsel of every type. You cannot safeguard it so that none of this will grow. So what should be done? Son! Preserve your heart! Stand on guard with Habakkuk.[110] Comprehend yourself. Watch yourself. Reside in your home. Care for yourself. Listen! Care for your heart.

Cleopas: So how should I care for myself?

Friend: In the same manner as a field. Remove and uproot and tear out every evil counsel, all evil seed of the serpent.

Cleopas: What exactly is the wicked counsel and seed of the serpent?

Friend: To love and justify at every occasion futile superficiality or the heel.

Cleopas: Say this in more simple terms.

Friend: Do not believe that your arm will become crooked, but instead that it is eternal in God.

Cleopas: Such thoughts are astonishing.

Friend: Of course they are novel. If the content of your arm is sentenced to be part of flesh's decay, then you will be an old bag filled with the air of an abyss of thoughts, unenlightened until the time should come for you to say, "God who commanded the light to shine from darkness has shined in our hearts.[111] And this occurs at the creation of a new heaven and earth. Behold I create all anew, says the Lord.[112]

---

[110] Hab 2:1
[111] 2 Cor 4:6
[112] Is 65:17

Forth Discussion Regarding Comprehending Yourself

Persons: Luke, Cleopas, Filon, Friend

Luke: So this is not a trivial matter to know your personal self.

Friend: There is one difficulty in both of these matters, to know your personal self and to comprehend God. To know and comprehend a specific person is difficult because its deception evolves from its shadow, upon which all of him is based. But it seems the same applies to a true person and God. And never has it been that something visible is truth, but truth is always invisible. But always the unseen truth in everything has been a mystery, because it pertains to the Lord. But the Lord and Spirit do not possess flesh and bones, and with God it is all one. I am sure you have heard the speeches regarding the true person. If you were to fathom yourself regarding the good wife, then pasture your goats near the shepherd's huts. I am not a husband unto you, not a shepherd and not a master. You do not see me because you do not know yourself. Depart from my eyes' sight and appear not in my sight! And you cannot be in my presence until you finally comprehend yourself. Who knows himself can alone start to sing the song, "The Lord shepherds me."[113]

Cleopas: But we from the previous discussion have some doubts.

Friend: When the conversation turns toward some important issue, this is not astonishing. So what are the doubts?

Cleopas: Well first you said that a person who falls in love with his visible flesh everywhere chases after what is visible, until he notices in it radiance and comfort, life, beauty and strength.

Friend: But what do you think?

Cleopas: It seems to me that if a person cannot believe in the existence of invisibility and thinks that he possesses only his own personal existence, it is only what his fleshly hands can touch and what he dreams in his decaying eyes. Nonetheless he does have the ability to understand and fully knows that all that he

---

[113] Ps 23:1

	loves elapses. For this reason he weeps when this leaves him, concluding that all of it has fallen to the wayside, just as a child weeps over a broken walnut, not understanding that the essence of a walnut consists not in its shell, but in its kernel that is hidden by the shell and upon which the kernel is dependant for preservation.
Friend:	This is so correct, and the farmer would be so stupid if he was to agonize over the husk holding the kernels of wheat in his field if it should dry and whither in the month of August, not ascertaining that there is hidden in the husk the small kernel which will appear in autumn, but what is invisibly hidden in the kernel is the eternal and true essence of its existence. But is not all of this the same, to ascribe power to the husk and rather not to the seed and not to believe or recall the existence of the seed? For example, it is like the judge who assigns his blood-related cousin authority and power in an inheritance, since he is assured that no closer blood relatives are alive. And this is that dishonorable judge of whom the previous discussion we had was about.
Cleopas:	Another doubt. I actually said it this way. I remember this word of Jeremiah, "Profound is the heart of a person, more than all; and it is the true person." But you affixed the following words to it, "This is the very person who will sustain all things."
Friend:	So what do you doubt in?
Cleopas:	I without doubt understand that all our outer members have their hidden essence in the heart just as wheat husk contains within itself a kernel. Once it has dried and withered it bends due to the weight of the kernels. A seed then has the capacity to again sprout and be green, as though it does not die, but is renovated and as if exchanges its garment. But since all we see without exception is that people are their external members, which witness of their seed, meaning that all of them have a heart, which – as God's prophet teaches – is definitely a person and true. And this is a great matter, but will it ever occur? Will every person become true? And what is the difference between the good man and the bad?

Friend:	It is not this way at all! Take away your thoughts from a person for a short time and watch strong nature. Each one is not a walnut and not husk with a wheat kernel.
Cleopas:	What an awesome spectacle!
Friend:	Fear not! I know. But you do see that what exists in nature is not new. Enough of this is to be found in produce from the ground and from trees. But it is nowhere as much to be found as in people. It is very rare for a person to preserve his heart, or as commonly said, to save your soul. And this is what Jeremiah taught us, and we believe him, that the true person in the heart within that person. The heart is profound and can only be comprehended by God in the form of our thoughts, which are an unlimited abyss, or to say it plainly, the soul is a true substance and existing substance, and the very essence – as they say – and it is our seed and strength, and of which our life and our health is solely composed. And without it we are just a dead shadow, and so it is very apparent how incomparably futile you become when you lose yourself, even though you may gain the entire Copernican universe. But this would never occur if people would strive to recognize what a person is and what it means to be a person, that is, if they were to comprehend themselves.
Cleopas:	Ah! I cannot fathom this because every person has their own thoughts and unlimited drives, just as with lightning, which penetrates an immeasurable distance, and that any such immense expanse does not interfere and is not subject to the progress of time. Such is comprehended only by God.
Friend:	Stop! It is not this way. You are correct that it is difficult to explain that evil people have their own heart, meaning that they have lost themselves. And although in our initial conversation someone said that if a person does not recognize himself, then he has just lost himself, nonetheless for better assurance, here is for you God's voice, "Listen to me, those who destroy the heart, who reside far from justice."
Cleopas:	Ah, we already believe this. But how have they lost themselves? Do they not have thoughts likewise that produce and develop? What do they not imagine? What do they not

deceive? The entire world cannot fit them. Nothing is sufficient for them. They consume one another, swallow and still are not satisfied. So is not the abyss of their heart bottomless? You said that the heart, thoughts and soul are all the same. How can they get lost?

Friend: We do not ascertain what we cannot attain. You must compel yourself and give some place in your heart to the memory of God's word. If someone should spread his grace on us then all will seem to us to be simple and direct. Often the simplest items seem to not be very simple to us. But a person is a small world, and it is so difficult to grasp its capabilities, as hard as finding the principle by which the universe operates. The hardening of our insensibility and accustoming ourselves to the taste of justification is the basis of our destitution. You can place stuff in front of a blind person all you want and how much you want, but for him it is completely futile. He can touch, but without approaching it he will understand nothing. How many times do we hear of water and spirit?

Is it not on the wind that birds depend? It is stronger than iron. It even has the capability to knock over a wood fence. But the air is considered as nothing. Why? Because air is hardly noticeable. A fence you can feel. You can quickly view many colors. But air is not very heavy, although firmer than rock or iron. And it is absolutely necessary since you will die without it. So it seemed that we make mistakes in our attitude toward the most menial of items and should consider it as the most active. Why? Because a fence is rough and in our eyes are strong blocks, as I already mentioned, but the air is hidden and it seems there is no strength in it, although it can drive ships and agitate the sea, break trees, ruin mountains, penetrating everything and devouring everything, and still remains whole. You can see that nature is not just what it is you discern it to be. It also contains what is stronger and not seen.

And if something is entirely enclosed, then with none of your senses are you able to touch it, then the item has strength. But if you cannot be completely assured with the strength of air and consider it as nothing, as if it does not exist in nature, although it shouts, shakes, agitates and in this manner lets its presence be known, then how can we dirty what has already been cleansed from every material dirt hidden from all our senses, freed from all noises, crashes and changes, existing in eternal rest and residing in the blessed tranquility of eternity.

Ruining our mind's eye from the very beginning, we cannot in any way penetrate to that point of something that is the pinnacle of our worth, what deserves our honor and love for ever and ever. Let your mind excite you! And if God's spirit has blown upon your heart then you must now look at what you have not yet seen from birth. You saw during this time only that a fence is built from wood planks on the outside. Now raise your eyes – if they are enlightened with the spirit of truth – and look on it. Now you see light. Now you see things in double: 2 waters, 2 earths. And all creation is now for you divided into 2 parts. Who divided it for you? God. He has divided everything for you in 2, so you would not mix any darkness with light, or any falseness with veracity. But since you have not seen anything except lies, as if it were a fence hiding the truth, this is the reason he has now created for you a new heaven, new earth. He alone creates marvelous truth. When you have looked and seen God with your new and true eye, then you have become full in Him, as if in a fountain, as in a mirror, you have seen what has always resided in Him, but which you have never seen. And what is the most ancient has become for you, the new viewer, something new, because it has never yet entered your heart. And it is as if all is new, because it is all of what you have never seen in the past, but perhaps only heard of. So now you see 2: the old and new, the obvious and the secret. Now gaze at yourself. How did you previously see yourself?

Cleopas: I saw and recognized one obvious part in me, but have never thought about the secret. And even if someone was to remind me – and this has occurred on occasion – of the secret, nonetheless it would seem to me amazing to consider

	something that does not exist as existing and as truth. I for example see my hands, but it has never entered my mind that within these hands there are hidden other hands.
Friend:	So all you saw in yourself is solely dirt and dust. And you up to this time have been just dirt and dust. To say this concisely, you were never in the light, because dirt, dust, shadow and empty futility is all the same.
Luke:	You proved from Jeremiah that a person exists not as external dust, but as a heart. How could Cleopas not exist on earth? Will not Cleopas' heart always be with him and now is?
Friend:	Stop, stop! How you have soon forgotten – 2, 2! There is an earthly body and there is a celestial body that is secret, hidden, eternal. So why should there not be 2 hearts? You have seen and loved the block and idol in your body, but not the true body that is hid in Christ. You loved yourself, that is, your dust, and not the hidden truth of God in you, which you have never seen or even recognized as existing. And which you cannot touch, and so is the reason you did not believe in its existence. And when your body felt such pain that it brought you to a point of danger, you immediately fell into despair. So what is happening here? Are you not the old Adam, which is the old bag with the obsolete heart? You are just a shadow, emptiness and nothing with this particular heart and which is the same as your body. Soil returns back to soil, death to death, but emptiness loves emptiness. The gaunt and famished soul is dust, not true bread, and so it eats and drinks outside of paradise sharing its sorrow.

Listen to what God says of this to Isaiah, "O, Isaiah, know that their heart is dust. And they are deceived, and not one of them can deliver their soul. Remember this, Jacob and Israel, because you are My slave. Behold I have removed like a cloud your crimes and like a hallucination your sins. Turn to Me and I will deliver you."[114]

A certain artist of ages past depicted on a wall some types of berries that appeared so real that hungry birds beat themselves against the wall considering them real berries, all |

---

[114] Is 44:22

	as a result of their keen eyesight inherited from nature. This is what such hearts swallow but are never satisfied. Show me even one of such dust-lovers that actually has a satisfaction in his soul. Love for a shadow is the mother of hunger, and the daughter of such a father is death. What is this drive in such a heart? It drives it in order to distress it. Have you seen any big, round arbors and birdcages in large gardens?
Luke:	I have seen some in royal gardens.
Friend:	They are fabricated from gold-plated steel wires. A large number of birds – siskins and goldfinches – chirp incessantly inside of them, flying from one side to the other, but cannot seem to be able to fly much of anywhere. This is the exact situation of the hearts of which you spoke above, that they dream and hurt themselves flying side to side, like lightning confined by the lattice. What is so narrow and tight as visibility? For this reason it is called a pit. Why does the figure seem to fly through the net to the freedom of the spirit? But how are we again to fly there, to acquire what we do not consider to be existence? We have for a long time, from earliest childhood, been drunk with this evil spirit, the seed sown by the snake, occupied with the poison inserted into our heart, so that only this coarse visible entity – having the heel as its end – loves only the external darkness, pursues and has pleasures always and in every item. It is this way? Yes! Always and in all things. Ah! Where are you, Jeremiah's sword desolating the land? Paul's sword? Phinehas' sword? We have gone astray in the land and become encompassed by it, but who will deliver us from it? Will you fly like a bird – our heart – from its cage? Ah, you will not fly out of it, because its heart has become our heart. And when your heart, our head and we in it only pretend, then our hope is only dust. Can dust that lies in the coffin arise and stand and recognize that invisibility exists, that there exists spirit? It cannot. Why not? It cannot arise and stand before the Lord. Why is this? Because this dust cannot accept within itself this seed. Whose? In order to believe what still transcends it and what we cannot feel and measure with a yardstick. O, blessed seed!

O, beginning of our salvation! We can accept you but it will be within us unproductive. Why is this? Because we love the superficial; we have accustomed ourselves to it. And we will not allow the entire superficial observable to be able to bend to the seed, but allow its sole strength to remain in it invisible. And without this any new fruit cannot exist or be produced.

So did our teachers direct us to learn. "I will feed them with wormwood, and give them water as bitter as gall to drink. From Jerusalem's prophets there will proceed defilement on the entire land."[115]

Fifth Discussion Regarding Comprehending yourself

Persons: the same

Filon: Based on this I think of the ancient proverb, "He is so stupid that even 2 people could not assess the amount." And we have by this time become the only people in the entire world to assess what no others have seen any of.

Cleopas: Would it not be better to tell you that only to us this shadow is visible? There is nothing that is not visible to us. We grasp after water like some empty shadow. Now we look like the residents of the faraway Norway, who because of their 6-month winter darkness hardly see any morning dawn and all creation begins to somewhat solidify.

Friend: If you will not close tight and turn away your eyes, then you will see all creation radiantly. You will not be like a mole, who loves to reside in the ground. But as soon as he breaks the surface and enters free air – alas! – it is so repulsive to him. Raise high your eyes and straighten them to watch that of which is said, "I am the world's light."

All that we have seen to this point is what? Ground, flesh, sand, wormwood, gall, death, darkness, malice, poison, and etc. Now the morning of the resurrection has begun to shine. We must stop looking at what we have been looking at,

---

[115] Jer 23:15

considering all the visible as nothing, but rather direct our eyes at what has been formerly closed to us and due to our negligence. Up to this time we have not felt the insubstantial invisibilities sufficiently worthy to number them with objects, and thought that they were just dreams and emptiness. But with us now, on the contrary, the visibilities are grass, deceit, dream and vanishing colors; but the eternal invisibilities find for itself a head, strength, rock of foundation and our prosperity. Let's listen to what the new and true person says and what he promises, "I will give to you," he says, "the treasures hidden in deep darkness, what is invisible I will disclose to you, and you will see that I, the Lord your God, calling your name, am the God of Israel."[116]

Now reason. Does this transition interest you? Or do you prefer to be as you were formerly residing in your visible ground? Or should you cleanse your heart in order to accept the new spirit? Whoever discards the old heart has become a new person. Woe to obstinate hearts.

Luke: This is the reason why it is difficult to soften the heart and grieve. The deeply rooted opinion is just like a child that has grown into a giant. Of course, it is difficult to fight with him.

Friend: But what is prohibiting you in life to reason this matter and discuss, and instead want to apply to it some supernumerary time? The new spirit can just like lightning suddenly enlighten your heart. Some 600,000 were summoned to enter the promised land on foot, but why only 2 entered it?

Luke: Two. The son of Nun and Caleb.

Friend: And this is why. Why should something happen if there is no need to watch it? Why such emptiness. "Why," they complained, "is the Lord leading us into this land? For us to fall in battle? So if we should lose our hands and feet, what will happen to us? We do not want this. This is only leading us someplace that is stronger than us and what we cannot even see from here. Let us return to our old land. We no longer like this person who is leading us into emptiness."[117] Do you hear

---

[116] Is 45:3
[117] Num 14:3

the thoughts of these Old Believers?[118] Here we have 600,00 idiots! Imagine for yourselves old bags filled with rotten kvas.[119] Is there any way to inspire such cattle? So according to their opinion, their existence does not need a god, if they want to be clean from all visibilities. If what they do not see does not exist, then god would have vanished a long time ago. The water of contention![120] The seed of the snake! The unbelieving heart! Evil counsel!

Learn the manner to confess the Lord and call upon His name. Was this not in the heart of the 2 prosperous heirs? "And the Lord gave Caleb strength, and resided with him even to his old age, placing him on the heights of the land. And his posterity held the inheritance, so that all the children of Israel could see what benefit it is to walk after the Lord. All those that were angered will not see it," says the Lord, "My servant Caleb had My spirit residing in him and has followed Me, and his posterity will inherit it."[121]

Cleopas: Now all strength resides in God, and not in some external visibility.

Friend: So what is idolatry, if not to attribute strength to statues? You do not want the arm of innocence. It is apparent that you attribute your strength to and venerate the visibility. But will this visibility of yours endure long? What do you base this on? What is the visible flesh, if not death? And upon it you have founded your heart and love. All superficiality is a river circumventing as it flows. Is it not upon a block of ice that you have raised your tent and placed your hut? Please move it to someplace firm. Move it into the courts of the Lord; raise it on a new land. But otherwise what will you have left for joy? Or rest? Will you not always be fearing that the ice at some time or other will eventually melt? It may be good at some time or other to leave the mortal body. O, you the most destitute, honoring your perishable body and not believing in

---

[118] Staro-Veri, dissenters from the Russian Orthodox Church, who held to the ancient traditions when the church was modernized under Patriarch Nikon.
[119] A mildly alcohol beverage made from old bread.
[120] Ex 17:7
[121] Num 14:24, Josh 14:9

	the new! Such people are in constant agitation and have no ability to rest. Do not rejoice in criminality, says the Lord.[122]
Filon:	What is the crime?
Friend:	Honoring what can decay.
Filon:	How?
Friend:	Honoring it in this manner: thinking that even if you remove the condition of decay, that your existence is still not possible in any manner. Is this not a great manner of honoring dust?
Filon:	It seems this is not a trifling matter, because a person deifies his dust in this manner, ascribing to it the actuality of his life.
Friend:	So now I think you can grasp these words, "I am the Lord God! This is My name – not some foreign one. I will not give My glory to something else, and not My virtue to statues."[123] That which we call reality is here called virtue, that is, strength and fortitude, which God for His own supremacy has appropriated and applied to Himself, removing it from all decomposable. What is a horrible evil is for someone to have the boldness even in the least to apply it to some creation or statue, which items God from the beginning of time has always incurred a zealous struggle. All of us horribly insult Him in this matter, always and everywhere.
Filon:	How?
Friend:	This is how! The entire world consists of 2 natures: one is seen, the other is unseen. The seen is called the created, while the unseen is the divine. This invisible nature or the divine penetrates and sustains all the created, is everywhere, and has always been and is and will be. Is it not insulting to Him if we, watching the changes in the decomposable nature, are afraid? Yet we ascribe to it importance by offering sacrifice to it, which we should not do, since we are removing this importance from God, to Whom it belongs along with strength and existence and name. He alone is the fullness of all in all and acquired this without participation of any other entity. Ascertain if he is able to lose anything that is in existence or all that He fills? Whatever you have, He is

---

[122] Ps 37:1
[123] Is 42:8

likewise all that you have. Nothing that you have will ever be lost because God has no shortcomings. What remains for you is the school of faith, or as David says, instruction in eternity. Persevere for a while in it, until your old-believing and dust-made heart will be somewhat cleansed from its present secular inherent stains.

Sixth Discussion Regarding Comprehending Yourself

Persons: the same

Friend: Land! Land! Land! Listen to the Lord's word!
Filon: I hear nothing.
Friend: Why not?
Luke: Who can ascend into heaven, except him who descended from the heavens? Who can listen to God's word unless God reside in him? Light is seen when light resides in the eyes. A person can crawl through a wall when God is the leader. But when the eye's strength is diminished, or better said, when the eye loses its strength and cannot focus on the object any longer, now the eye has no ability remaining to distinguish between light and dark.
Cleopas: But can God not make the dead alive, and the invisible to be visible? Yes! At a specific time they will resurrect. A spark of God can fall on the dark abyss of the heart and immediately illuminate it. We must only be assured that God resides in the human flesh. He is genuinely in our visible flesh – the non-material in the material; the eternal in the temporal; the One in each of us and His entirety in all things; God in the flesh and the flesh in God. But the flesh is not God! And God is not the flesh. Ah, the mustard seed! Belief! Fear and God's love. The seed of virtue and His kingdom! I feel that the secret falls upon the soil of my heart just as the rain upon the fleece.[124] O, that the birds of the air would not peck at you.[125]

---

[124] Judges 6:37
[125] Matt 13:4

Filon:	Now remember with David the eternal years and learn from them.
Cleopa:	What to learn or whom to learn about?
Filon:	We will learn of eternity. To whom in the flesh can the eternal person – our Lord – be compared?
Friend:	He is comparable to a good and ripe wheat kernel. Now discern: does the stem have blades? Stop! The kernel contains everything. Husk covers the kernel, but the husk is not the kernel and the kernel is not the husk. What is the kernel? The kernel is the strength within which the stem with its blades and the husk reside. Is not all of this contained in the kernel, and does it not become ripe in the autumn, changing from green to yellow and its obsolete cover? Is not the strength of the kernel unseen?
	So it is. It is active at this time, when its entire cover bends it over, so that someone will not ascribe some new production from the dead and insensitive soil, which is the decaying external. But that all the glory be given to the invisible God, who in the secret of his right hand is effective in all areas, so that He alone would be the head, while the external would be the heel and tail.
Filon:	Now I see in the ear that which was not apparent to me earlier.
Cleopas:	Better said that you in Him have seen only the tail.
Friend:	Why don't we call what is new in the ear – growth. The Lord God causes it to increase for our sake.
Luke:	But as we have passed from the field to the garden, look at what this person is bringing to us from the arbor.
Filon:	This icon was painted by my friend, the artist.
Cleopas:	How this does please me! From behind a black cloud a ray is directed to his head. So what are the words on the ray? They together with the ray descend upon his head enveloped with light. Read it Luke. You are a book reader.
Luke:	It is the image of Isaiah the prophet. In the ray the words are written, "Cry out."
Cleopas:	So what are the words emanating from his lips?

Luke:	I know these words. "All flesh is straw, and all human merit like a flower in the grass."
Filon:	So what is written on the paper he is holding in his hands?
Luke:	I know them, "Our God's word resides forever."[126]
Filon:	Do you see the paper with writing on it?
Cleopas:	The 2 of us – myself and Filon – have worked several years near a farmer, but only recently have we actually looked close at wheat. But as far as the paper is concerned it is prophetic. Ask Luke, it is his responsibility.
Luke:	You see in his hands a prophetic paper. But know that what you see is a matter very small and very great. This blessed elder easily holds in his right hand this matter, within which everything everywhere is all sustained. Discern of what the very revelations enlightened by light held in the elder's hands consist: he carries what is to be carried and he holds close what is to be held. Did you look at the ear? Look now at the person and recognize him. You saw in the ear a kernel, and now look at the seed of Abraham, right here and in 2 areas. Did you see in the ear the husk and stem? Now look at the grass of your perishable flesh with your deliberations made of dust, up to now filled with empty light. Have you seen in the ear what you previously have not seen? Now comprehend in a person what was unseen in him earlier. Seeing the ear you still do not see it, and knowing him you still do not know him. But what was finally disclosed to you in the ear was not of the flesh but of God.

Raise your thoughts above the earth and comprehend a person, the one in you born of God and not created in the recent period of your life. You saw in the ear a new growth that is so strong that for all the husk and stem it has become the head and refuge. Recognize within yourself the new Jacob – meaning growth – your new shepherd, father and nurse. In the ear of wheat you have noticed a fragile external, where the secret activity of the invisible God is encased.

Look now at the spoken word of God, the prophetic word, as a fragile cloud that covers. With your intelligent eye you

---

[126] Is 40:6, 8

have seen the strength of the kernel. Open the eye of belief and you will also see in yourself the divine strength, God's right hand, God's law, God's spoken word, God's written word, God's kingdom and authority, the secret and invisible. And having known the son you will also get to know the Father. The worthless husk over the kernel does not fear removal. Why are you agitated, grass and flesh? Be bold! Fear not! You shall yet see within yourself God's right hand, which protects you just as the husk over the kernel. Or do you not believe this? If this is so, then fear. There is no hope; all flesh perishes. To where can you escape? Flee with David to the Lord's house, or go with Jeremiah to the gates. Open your heart to accept belief and for the residence of that person whom the Father will install as His right hand and His strength for ever and ever. Listen, know that the Father is through him and in him and speaks to us. Listen, "I will put My words in his lips and will shelter you under the shade of My hand." And what hand? With the one that I installed heaven and established the earth. Are you listening? How strong is the kernel in you. This heaven is visible and the earth in enveloped in it. And will it not be difficult for you to preserve the seed in you? O, please be assured that even the insensate hair of your head, part of your superficial appearance soon to perish, will be protected without harm and be preserved, blessed.

Say with Paul, "I know a person." I found a person. I acquired a Messiah, not a statue of flesh, but a true person who is the incarnation of God in my flesh. With effort I found him, in the grass and in my flesh and in the remnant of my days. The blessed seed! The salvation of myself as an individual! The light of revelation to the blind nations.[127] To this point I resided in darkness and lived in mud, that is my heart, where I ate and devoured the dirt. But now you have released me from my chains, you have killed the seed within me, preserving me with an empty heel. And in place of it you are reigning in me for ever, you have unveiled for me a new

---

[127] Luke 2:32

heaven and yourself sitting at the right of the heavenly Father. Be for me now peace in my strength and calm! Be for me now the blessed Sabbath! Carry me away from the earth's abyss with the wings of a dove and I will rest. Why should you sorrow any longer my soul? Why should you further discomfort me? Have you recognized that person within you and his endless strength? Rely upon him if you have recognized him, and immediately you will know him. He is your husband. He is the head upon you under the guise of your flesh and blood: your God and the salvation of your entire self.

Seventh Discussion Regarding the True Person or the Resurrection.

Persons: Elder Pamba, Anton, Kvadrat, a Friend and Others.

Friend: Listen Pamba. Why do you study so much? Have you already learned all David's Psalms?
Pamba: I have only learned one Psalm.
Friend: Just one?
Pamba: One, meaning one.
Friend: Which Psalm?
Pamba: This is it, "I said, I will preserve my path."[128] I do not need any others. I have sought a gate for my lips and have installed it.
Anton: This is so true. It is the tongue that turns the body and is the actual head.
Kvadrat: O, Pamba! Blessed are you if you do not sin using your tongue. David and the son of Sirach fervently beg for the same from God.
Luke: But what did you speak of earlier, Pamba? Did you not have a tongue earlier?
Pamba: I have set a seal on my tongue from ancient times.
Anton: So who sealed it for you?

---

[128] Ps 39

Pamba:	Who can seal the abyss except God?
Luke:	It is not a bad idea to call the tongue an abyss because David gives the deceiving tongue a name using flooding words; the flood and abyss are the same.
Kvadrat:	I heard that the mind of the wise is called a flood by the son of Sirach.
Friend:	A speech of some type or other is just like a river, and the tongue is its source. But if the Lord has already delivered you Pamba from the cursed tongue, then it is apparent that in place of the deceiving tongue you have been gifted the tongue of David, learning all the day God's virtue, proclaiming His strength to the entire coming generation.
Kvadrat:	This is so true. Who can speak of whiteness if he is not familiar with blackness? One taste senses both bitter and sweet. If the Lord gifted somebody the ability to recognize the deceiving tongue, the same can also recognize virtuous lips that teach wisdom.
Anton:	What is this? You have babbled some outlandish statements. Will the person who does not know the new tongue be able to grasp the old?
Pamba:	Without doubt. At the time you grasp the new the old will be disclosed. Have you ever seen a person grasping darkness not having ever seen light? Can the mole, for example, please, tell you where the day is and where the night is?
Anton:	If the mole cannot, then a person can.
Pamba:	Can a blind person recognize and show you white paint on a portrait?
Anton:	He cannot.
Pamba:	Why?
Anton:	He has not seen and cannot distinguish even the black. And if he were even able to distinguish one of the opposite colors, then he would be able to distinguish the others.
Pamba:	So the same applies here. The person who understands maturity can understand youth.
Anton:	I cannot be astonished enough at this that it is possible for a person to be born and not be able to grasp the concept of

youth and maturity, if he will not be a second time born from above.

Pamba: The light unveils all that is blocked to us by darkness. So does God alone shine upon us with His truth. At this time we are able to recognize the empty dream, having seen truth; and grasping youth we can understand maturity. The earthly person thinks of himself, as if he actually understands. A child can see little gazing in darkness. But the shining light causes all hallucinations to vanish. Are not all the following words familiar to us: time, life, death, love, thought, soul, passion, conscience, grace, eternity? It seems that we grasp it all. But if someone asks for an explanation, then everyone starts to think. Who can explain the meaning of time if he does not penetrate into the divine heights? Time, life and all else is retained in God. Who can grasp something from all the visible and invisible creation, not grasping what is the head and basis of everything? The beginning of wisdom is to comprehend the Lord. If someone does not know the Lord, he is like an inmate thrown into a prison. What will he ever understand sitting in darkness? The most principle and fundamental point of wisdom is knowledge of God. I do not see Him, but I know and believe that He exists. And if I believe, then I fear; I fear lest I should anger Him; I seek what is pleasing unto Him. Herein is love! Knowledge of God, belief, fear and loving the Lord is the same with one goal. Knowledge resides in belief; belief in fear; fear in love; love in the fulfillment of the commandments, and the fulfillment of commandments, are love to associate. Love never envies.

And so if you want to understand and grasp something you must first enter the mountains of divine knowledge. It is there that you, once enlightened with the secret rays of deity, will comprehend – if you want – not only the eagle's youth who is shedding the aged garments, but also the old of the old and the heaven of heavens. But who shall lead us from the pit of the nether-region? Who shall lead us to the Lord's mountain? Where are you Jesus Christ, our light? You alone speak the truth in our heart. Your word is truth. The gospel is a lighted lamp and you are the light in it. This is the sole means to escaping deceit and the darkness of unknowing. Here is the house of David, where the judge's throne resolves and rends all falsity.

What is it Anton, that you want to know? Go to this beloved village. If you do not find the entrance into one chamber, then knock at another, at 10, at 100, at a 1,000, at 10,000. This divine house from the outside seems to be nothing more than a cave for cattle, but inside the virgin is giving birth to him of whom the Angels sing incessantly.[129] In comparison to this wisdom all the wisdom of the world is nothing else but a slave's conniving. The image of a thief will not enter this house. Find the door and knock and until it opens. You will not be worthy of the entrance if there is something in the world you prefer more than this divine mountain. No one with just half a heart is allowed to enter here. And if you should force your way in, then you will be discarded to the darkness outside.

How David did burn in love toward his house! He desired and insisted on wanting to stand at the Lord's doors. He knew that it was not possible in any manner to escape the fundamental insanity of human darkness except through these doors. He knew that all had gone astray from even their mother's womb. And although they said, "Behold the door! Here is the way!" Nonetheless they all lied. He knew that no bird of any kind – as fast as it may fly – and no human wisdom was strong enough to carry him from the abyss, except this immaculate dove. For this reason he cried in his impatience, "Who will give me wings?" And that they would be of the type that a dove has, that is, silver, and that gold would glisten between the wing's flapping. And if it is not this way, if they cannot fly very fast, then there is no reason for me to do any flying. This immaculate dove got so much pleasure, was so captivated that it sat at the window of its beloved, just as did Magdalena at [Jesus'] sepulcher. He asked and begged that they open the door for him, so his suffering

---

[129] Referring to the Catholic tradition that Jesus was born in a cave.

would end, so the coal-black darkness and the inner revolt would scatter, calling it its comfort. "Arise," it speaks while weeping, "My glory. Arise you my sweetest ten-stringed Psalter and pleasantly-sounding harp. If you only will arise then I will likewise immediately arise and ascend into the light. Why should I reside in darkness any further?"

When should I arrive and appear before God's face? Who will lead me into the established city if not you, the most beautiful girl of all the world's daughters. It is only through your door and only through your path that the virgins can be brought to the heavenly king, as long as they have your friendship. It was not in vain that David labored, and with what celebration did he cry, "Open to me the gates of virtue. I confess You so that You would hear me. This day we will rejoice and be happy. God the Lord has appeared to us. I called upon the Lord and He heard me in His expanse. What will any person do to me? I fear nothing."[130] David expanded wide and flew from the trap and the nether-region to the freedom of the spirit. All darkness suddenly disappeared; wherever he walked light was everywhere. "Where can I go from Your spirit?"[131] The winged David fears, loves, is amazed as he flies from place to place. He sees all, comprehends all; and he sees in whose hands are light and darkness.

Kvadrat: It is true that faithfully and zealously the beloved David loves his beloved. I think he calls her his mother, Zion, daughter, queen, clothed in gold and decorated like a divine chariot, the kingdom of living people, the residence of all who rejoice, and etc.

He asked for one thing from the Lord, to live in this house of God, at the place of shelter beyond marvelous, where the voice of joy and the noise of celebration is heard.[132]

And other than this he wants nothing else in the heavens or on earth, except for this cup filled with divine prosperity,

---

[130] Ps 118:19, 24
[131] Ps 139:7
[132] Ps 27:4

except for the royal daughter where her entire beauty is concealed and hidden within her. And how much he loved these gates of Zion and its path that leads to the knowledge of the Lord; he took so much consolation in it just as a person would having great wealth. Whatever was said there was called marvelous and sublime, completely distinct from any opinion of the general public. Here is his sacrifice, song and intrinsic comfort, the sanctuary of all desires. O, the intrinsic tranquility. How rare you are, how valuable! This is the very place he conceals God's face in secret away from the revolt of humanity and from the discredit of the nations which evolves from all secular opinions opposing divine wisdom, which he also called the beauty of the Lord's house, the rock of refuge for relocated sinners, of which is written, "The wicked flees even though not pursued."

Anton: Without doubt it is to these rocky mountains that he raises his eyes relying upon them for help.

Kvadrat: It is well known that as soon as a sinner senses danger on the path he is traveling he runs like a pursued rabbit to those mountains found in the confusion of his destitute reasoning, which in the past seemed to him very correct. But when the sun shining upon his person from the divine mountains discloses to him the deceit, at that time his entire road is destroyed on its own, just as it occurred to Paul when on the road to Damascus. It is in this strength that David says, "You marvelously shine from the eternal mountains. All foolish hearts are confused." For whom has this light not been kind, even if you only had a little of it to taste?

O, icon-frame of light, the holy glory of the heavenly Father! Of course your radiance is intolerable to our eyes if they are not accustomed to the light. Otherwise we would have not under any conditions given sleep to our eyes until the door opened in order to see where God had located His settlement, where the kingdom and its virtue are located, so that it can also be said of us, "He opened our eyes and we comprehended him, and then we saw him not."[133] Or the

---

[133] Luke 24:31

	following, "We came and saw where he lived, and resided with him that day."[134]
Anton:	Why did you say earlier that Sacred Scripture raises divine knowledge to the summit of the mountains, and now you are calling this the mountain?
Kvadrat:	David calls it the divine mountain. Does this astonish you that we ascend the mountain via a mountain? If the path leads from a hole to the mountain, then of course its initial portion is low, and the latter portion is so high, as high as the mountain to which the end of the road ascends. You can compare this to a ladder leaning against some tall place. The initial rungs are nearest the bottom, but those that wish to climb higher can do so to the top, to the celestial. For this reason it is also called wings and doors and boundaries or limits, a harbor, sand or the shore, the enclosed sea and a wall.
Anton:	So why it is called a wall and a boundary?
Kvadrat:	In addition to this the wall also serves as a border to separate what is personal to us from the foreign. But how can this wall created of God not be called a boundary when it serves as a limit between the light and the foreign darkness? This wall has a dark side that faces toward the darkness. But its side that is turned toward the east is gilded internally with all the light of the supreme God, such that if a resident of the dark side walks to its gates and he is dark from the outside he does not see any colors and departs back, wandering in the darkness. But should we believe and due to utter despair the doors are opened, and at that time with the light of radiant resurrection he cries with David, "I confess You, for You are awesome and amazing. This is not anything else but the house of God and these are the gates of heaven."[135]
Anton:	So it must be like the moon, when the moon is directly between the sun and earth. At this time one side of it is dark while the side facing the sun is bright.
Kvadrat:	This intermediary is like a bridge that allows association between God and the dead.

---

[134] John 1:39
[135] Gen 28:17

Anton: If this marvelous bridge transfers the dead into life, then it is deservedly and correctly to call it resurrection.

Kvadrat: Yes this dove is specifically the resurrection of dead people. It places us – those who have fallen from the mountain and onto the field – again on this very mountain.

Luke: And I agree with this. This word – resurrection – in the Greek and Latin languages signifies, it seams, to place a fallen person back on his feet. And God clearly says to Jeremiah that He will again place him on his feet if he will be obedient to Him. And just as in Sacred Scripture the word sit signifies an extremely destitute condition, so on the contrary the word *stand* signifies to be in considerable prosperity. And just as it is an unfortunate matter to sit and be an inmate in a prison, it is even worse to be in the company of those whom Paul must stimulate, "Stand, sleeper and resurrect from the dead."[136] Break the sleep of your eyes, O, unfortunate corpse. Rise to your feet! Now comprehend how Christ is the light of the world!

Friend: I cannot keep silent any further, having heard the most gracious and sweetest name of the radiant resurrection. I rightly so sit among others in a cold fatal darkness. But I sense in me a secret ray, secretly warming my soul. Ah, Pamba. We must preserve his divine spark in our heart. We must protect it so the dust and ashes of our coffins do not suffocate it. What will we become like when this time comes? Will we remain as solely dust and death? We are unable to annihilate the fire; I cannot contend with this. But what are we to do without fire? What benefit is there for us if we consist solely of flesh and blood? Know that this must be released to decay. So when this time arrives will we perish without an end in sight? And are we nothing else but a fantasy, dream, death and vanity? Our substance is so overwhelmed with disaster if all in all it is solely nothing more than decomposable material of a temporary nature. And if we have nothing secret within us – outside of the ostensive – that would serve as our composition, as upon a firm basis, then

---

[136] Eph 5:14

every living person is solely and in every respect vanity of vanities.

This is an actual fact if your kingdom is really so strong. O, bitter death, your victory is undefeatable. O, grave! Who or what can oppose the law of decomposition, once turning into dust without any reconstitution? Ah, what disaster! Annihilation! Illness! Sorrow! Revolt! Do you hear? Do you understand? In what language are we speaking?

Pamba: Lord, deliver my soul from the lips of the wicked, from the tongue of the sacrilegious, from the unjust person. Their tongue is a sharp sword, an open coffin.[137]

Friend: This is definitely the poison of asps, the sting of sin, the snake's tongue, which brought Adam down to labor and illness! What have you whispered to us, O, ancient malice and deceit? Why do you exalt so very highly the dying corpse and ageing old age and decaying decomposition? Is it only death that reigns? And is there no life? Deceit survives in the absence of virtue and malice exists without goodness, and old age without youth, and darkness without light, and flood without dryness. May the Lord rebuke you, O, tongue of the flood vomiting a river of mendacious water, drowning the children of Zion's mother, covered with gloom and a black cloud, descending into hell away from the Lord whom they discredit in their pride, destroying his kingdom and virtue, youth and eternity, the new land and the living generation! Listen here you deaf daemon, dumb and empty tongue! Since you do not recognize the Lord's residence, confessing that only death occupies everything and is dragging all in all into the hell of decomposition, for this reason know that the new and imperishable person will not only trample your laws inducing decay, but is arming itself to take complete vengeance to destroy you to the very end, to overthrown you from your throne having made you into the head of a vacant mistake.

Pamba, listen! Pamba! Why are you silent? Know that you have already recognized your path. No longer does the

---

[137] Rom 3:13, Ps 52:2

evil tongue whisper into your heart, now having become dumb. Or has it again become live? Has the illness of the sinful tongue been renewed in your womb? Does the sword again penetrate your soul? It is apparent this is why you are silent, having become dumb and contrite. You speak nothing good, and you do not ask about the peace of Jerusalem.

Pamba: A long time ago in my heart I secretly cursed this tongue.

Friend: So why are you not publicly singing? If you have genuinely learned this Psalm of David, why do you not propagate all the day long the song with Isaiah to his beloved?[138] If the Lord gave you new lips, why do you not say with Jeremiah? "And my opened lips will not close to this matter." If your heart is warmed within you, you must in your instruction enlarge this crowned spark of the resurrection, until the wrath of this virtuous flame becomes an inferno and consumes all of the contradictory decay that is held against you, until the fiery river of God is filled with those drowning. The warm heart is a fiery tongue of the holy spirit, a new one in heaven and on earth singing the miracle of the resurrection. Do you not see that all people still retain an obsolete heart, an earthly language? All the cowards, sorrowful, unsatisfied, despairing, are deprived of the paraclete's heavenly comfort.

But on the opposite side there are few of whom the following is said, "On your walls Jerusalem I have installed guards day and night who will not cease to remind us of the Lord."[139] Few are the sons of Amos whose purpose is the comfort of God's people. There are few Habakkuks who stand on divine watch.[140] Of all of them may be said: You are the dead with your dead heart. The iron will penetrate your soul. You sit in darkness, lying in a coffin. O, divine spark! The seed of the mustard and the wheat! The family of Abraham! The son of David! Christ Jesus! The heavenly and new person! The head and heart, and light of all creation! The focal point of the universe! The strength, law and kingdom of

---

[138] Is 5:1
[139] Is 62:6
[140] Hab 2:1

peace! The right side of God! Our resurrection! When will we comprehend you? You are the true person from true flesh. But we do not know of such a person, but those whom we know all die. Ah, the true person never dies.

It is apparent that we have never seen the true person, but those whom we know have hands and feet and an entire body that will return to dust. But what does the rock of Sacred Scripture witness? "His eyes will not darken and his lips will not fail." But where is such a person to be found? We have not seen him and do not know who he is. We have not comprehended eyes or ears or the tongue. All that we know is that we are not like him. It speaks here of an immortal person and imperishable body, while we are but dirt to this time. We have not seen such a person, who is not flawed. So then sit in the mud and depend on it, those just like it and we have become the same. We have eyes that see nothing, and feet unable to walk, and the same type of hand unable to touch, and tongue and ears of the same design. This is how we can grasp what a person actually is. Who among the resurrected will say that we are not just a dead shadow? That we are not just dust blown away by the wind? Can the insensitive soil recognize the invisible?

Pamba: It is better to say it as did David. "Does the dirt confess you?"[141] Soil and water that is flowing by is the composition of every flesh created of the elements. It is a den of suffering and pit of darkness. "Save me," cries David, "from decay. Let me not drown from the many and deep waters.[142] For not the dead praise you."[143]

Friend: From this dirt the memory arises of David's royal daughter, the immaculate dove and most beautiful girl, decorated not in anything perishable but gilded on her breasts and having wings of silver of God's spirit. Winged in this manner we fly with David and rest. Leaving behind the earthly Adam and his bread, we migrate by flying to the man Paul, to the unseen, to

---

[141] Ps 88:10
[142] Ps 69:14
[143] Ps 115:17

the heavenly, to our world; not beyond the sea and forests, not above the clouds, not in other places and centuries – since he is for ever – but we penetrate into the very center of our heart and our soul and, bypassing all decaying and flooded thoughts with all the extreme superficiality of our flesh, leaving behind all storm and gloom under his feet, we ascend by the above-mentioned ladder to the supreme entrance and exit, to life and our head, to the true person in the un-manufactured tabernacle[144] and to his imperishable and immaculate flesh which is our earthly temple – the weak shadow and appearance – and after deliberating the matter, is the true hypostasis integrated into one, without having blended the divine and decaying natures. This is specifically the true person, an entity existing from before the beginning of time with the Father, and who is equal in strength, is one with all of us and is complete in all of us, and of His kingdom there is no end.

This very person – if anyone was able to notice – is the one who loves us, and himself has become mutually beloved, and we are one with him just as dirt that sticks to us, although we are dirt ourselves and will return to dirt. But the one who comprehends the imperishable and true person does not die, and death cannot possess him, but with his master the faithful servant reigns eternally, having removed his garment, his earthly flesh, just as a worn does and having clothed himself in a new one, a flesh comparable to his flesh but which will not sleep but will change, having accepted in place of earthly hands those that are imperishable, in place of animal ears, eyes, tongue and other members those that are true, hidden in God, as Isaiah says, "Behold your savior comes, having with him compensation and reward, giving silver in place of iron, and gold in place of copper, placing as your foundation the jewel sapphire, that is, the heavenly, un-manufactured temple."[145] May God may be everything in all that is yours, and not a dead land and soil.

---

[144] Heb 9:11
[145] Is 60:17

Who is willing to acquire this true life during these gracious days? Right now and immediately like lightning it will be provided you. Just restrain your tongue from evil and your lips. O, evil tongue! O, snake's head! The beginning of sorrowful days! You lead all away from paradise, and drown them all in the abyss. Who will place these wounds on the heart and the punishments of wisdom on our meditations? Otherwise it will be impossible for us not to fall.

We flee to you, O, mountain of God, the inconsumable burning bush, the golden candlestick, the holy of holies, the ark of the covenant, the immaculate girl who continued such after your birth. You alone gave birth as a virgin. Your only most holy child, your one son, died outwardly, and in the same manner was the one who resurrected and now reigns, can smash the snake's head, the tongue discrediting the Lord.

Anton: If Sacred Scripture is the sweet harp of God, it would not be bad if someone would provide our company with some joy, playing a little something on a musical instrument.

Luke: I am in complete agreement with Anton and ask the same.

Kvadrat: I will not interfere with your good agreement and ask for the same.

Friend: Do you hear this, Pamba? Get your harp. You have long been learning David's song. After 10 years I am sure you have learned more than just a little.

Pamba: Ah! What in life is more pleasant for me than to sing to my beloved person? I do not fear ruining the tune. What causes me fear are these words of the son of Sirach, "Speak elder and do not forbid music."[146]

Friend: Sing and sing more! Fear not! Be assured that our conversation will be just as sweet to him.

Pamba: But how can I make it more pleasing if I have no artistic talent?

Friend: To make it more pleasing? This only applies to a young son who tries to do something pleasing for his father but it turns to become some incorrect nonsense in his talk or poor performance on a harp. Have you forgotten that artistic talent

---

[146] Sirach 32:3

in any sacred instrument is not worth one cent without love? Do you not hear David? "Love the Lord." And then what? "And confess and praise and exalt Him."

To love the Lord is the most sublime head of wisdom. What need is there in anything else? Sing boldly! But just as in secular music one voice without another cannot indicate harmony, and with even a 3rd voice music is perfected, now consisting of 3 voices all harmonic, so it is exactly with David's harp, that if one string is out of tune it is not in harmony with the others. But all 3 strings in harmony are like witnesses that fully testify every word.

Let us shout, friends, in the harp's song. Let us be armed in agreement against the cursed tongue, the enemy of our divine person. At least we will banish this unclean spirit from our company.

A BOOKLET PERTAINING TO READING SACRED SCRIPTURE ENTITLED LOT'S WIFE.

Prologue

My beloved Mikhail.[147]

Near the region of Kharkov, during a time of incessant autumn rain and wanting to banish my boredom, I wrote this booklet while at the Sennyanski Monastery. The holy Justin, Metropolitan of Belgorod, gifted this monastery to Pecher Monastery complex, a place where he often isolated himself among the mountain gardens and bright sky. My brother, Justin Zveryaka, who was at the time Father Superior, could not make sense of my treatise on Lot's wife, even though he was a printer and dabbled in Greek and Latin texts. But you, my beloved friend, have a sense of taste that is not animalistic. Am I permitted to say this about you? You have appeared unto Abraham, disclosing to him an immaculate portion of theology.

All theologize, but not in the manner of Abraham. All eat and chew, but not in the manner of Jacob's son. "Judah my son, your brothers will praise you. Your teeth are whiter than milk."[148] "Sing to the Lord all His saints and profess the memory of His shrine."

Do you not see that holiness and memory are indivisible friends? Holiness and memory as a double ray emanate from the sun before its sunset. Holiness sees belief, and hope hopes, love encompasses the heart, while the memory remembers. These 4 spirits are one in eternity, with the abyss of imperishability, with the hail of the apocalypse, with the sun never setting. Do you see the smoke?

---

[147] This composition was dedicated and written to Mikhail Kovalinski.
[148] Gen 49:12

Remember the fire. Do you see this world? Remember eternity. What is this world? It is the smoke of eternity. Eternity is a fire all-consuming.

The foolish hunter gazes at the tracks but the thought of a deer never enters his mind, yet the tracks lead to the deer. The foolish scholar looks at the idiot but the thought of eternity never enters his mind. But the paths lead to it. "Your paths are among many waters."

The Bible is its path and you have delved deeply into the paths. But awaken and remember. Where do these tracks lead? Where will these feet take me? Here is where! Nahum sings, Behold the feet upon the mountains. Whose feet? The person who evangelizes and proclaims peace.[149]

Do you see? Upon the mountains is your deer and these tracks lead to it and these feet will carry you there. Raise your memory to the mountains. From there comes help.

What is Lot's wife? The track. Where will it lead you? Where it is going? You can see where it is going. Where you are looking is where its idea is to be found. She looked back at Sodom. The wife and Sodom are the same. Sodom signifies what is secret. This is where the wife was brought, to Sodom. But where will Sodom lead you? There, where the smoke rises and its smoke rises to the sky. Its smoke rises high. Smoke, offspring, spirit, thought, interpretation is all the same. Do you see? Where does Sodom lead you? The wife and Sodom are feet. Do you see them ascending the mountain? Behold the feet upon the mountains.

But the tracks on the mountain are God's, and to where do they ascend? Leading to Mount Zion. But Zion is an earthly mountain, although it rises to the sky. You can see Zion from the mountain; the entire world from the heavenly mountain. There your Lot resides. Mount Zion is your residence. Where is our heavenly Zion? The sun shines upon all the world; here is your heavenly mountain. The sun is the true Sodom. Lot's wife is the sun. Lot hid in this stupidity. It sees his pure memory. It watches his holy belief. The sun is Sodom, but he is Zoar. The sum is brimstone, he is incense. The sun is hell, and he is dew. The sun descends below the earth. Lot will remain in eternal memory. He is father and groom unto you; Cupid and the Ancient of Days.

---

[149] actually Isaiah, Is 52:7

First Sign: Regarding the Preceptor

The sea draws near, large and expansive, seeking the guidance of God's Angels. So was Raphael a guide to Tobias. The Angel, apostle and true theologian are all the same. But how can you know whom God sends? Listen to Jeremiah 23:22. "But if they had stood in My counsel to listen and observed My words and My people turned away from their criminal paths and from undertaking evil."

Do you see that the messenger of God's counsel is the one who interprets this tending more toward morality and less toward belief, since without [morality] virtue is not virtue. Such were Basil the Great, John Chrysostom, Gregory Nazianzen, Ambrose, Jerome, Augustine, Pope Gregory the Great, and those similar to them. These were able to say with Paul, "We have the mind of Christ."

The theologian teaches or values the most secret undertakings of the soul, counsel and thought. "They have become dissipated and vile in their undertakings." Undertaking, beginning, counsel, logos and God are all the same. Just as from a fountain, all of our superficial actions evolve from counsel or the head. If there is good counsel there are good fruits produced.

And so theology is nothing else but the removal of evil thoughts, or as Paul says, principles and authorities. If we can identify the 2 as persons, one earthly and the other heavenly, although residing in one person, then there are 2 principles, one of the serpent, or of the flesh, and the other of God. This one will remove bad thoughts and in its place plant God's word, the seed of all good activities, of which can be said, "Jesus began to teach and heal."

Only love can make the Angelic language effective.

Second Sign: Regarding Sympathy or Compassion between the Reader and the Preceptor

The origin of all and taste is love. As with food so scholarship is ineffective if unloved. So you must select for yourself one of the angels mentioned above, one that will be more conducive to you than the others.

Eat a little of all of them or some of them. At this time you will suddenly sense a special inclination to one of them. They all eat of the same manna and the taste is pleasant to all of them, but it varies.

Third Sign: Regarding Rejection of Secular Opinions

Approaching this heavenly writer, a person must first take cleansing pills and all of the old opinions instilled from association with foolish society must be vomited, just as Israel took nothing from the destroyed Jericho, and if someone did retain something he was executed. If people go to the sea to wash themselves, then what is the reason to retain secular dirt? A deceitful man is an adversary, a prying spirit, crippled in both legs, not hot and not cold. A neutral man is an enemy to effectiveness, and the Bible becomes God's contentious case against the dead. This type of people inquire of God, "Are the sparrows in my hands alive?" "They are alive if you do not squash them," answers God. "Do not tempt the Lord your God."

Fourth Sign: Regarding the Awesome Danger in Reading

Since according to Augustine's statement that not only in secular matters but likewise pertaining to paradise itself, God's words if hidden become a diabolic web, and so a person must conduct himself with great safety lest during reading and instruction in the supreme law he gets tangled in the wicked web as did Judas, "With the bread Satan entered into him."

And these are the webs: love of money, ambition, promiscuity, vanity. All of these spirits return to the ground, that is, to the stomach and to the flesh, the place from which God's word intends to lead us.

So many have been destroyed by the dirt of Lot's drunkenness. An innumerable amount have been corrupted by the poison of David's adultery, and while in his old age it was as if he just imagined the rape. No less is this poison narrated pertaining to his son [Solomon]. We read of the zeal of Elijah and the sharp sword turned against his associate. We have heard of Ezekiel's illness, threatening him with death and our superstition. The wealth of Job was envied by those greedy, while the gratitude of

Abraham makes us vain. Lazarus' resurrection, return of sight to the blind, liberation of those possessed by demons, entirely converts us into animals whose intelligence is in their flesh. This very seed of God, also known as the word of faith, deceives us, causing us to depend on the elements of the superficial world. As a result we depend on the flesh and blood of the saints: our hope is on what disintegrates and is cursed. We deify the substance in incense, candles, art, images and ceremonies, forgetting that no one is good except God and that every superficial item can disintegrate and is cursed. To say this in short, the entire Bible is overly filled with abysses and deceits. "This lies for the falling."[150] And its entire road is like the one to Jericho besieged with criminals. We will say with David, "Upon this road did they lay a trap for me."

Have your heard of the tax collection system? So here they are. Nonetheless, they are actually non-existing. Remember that the Bible is a Hebrew sphinx, and do not think that this is as if written about something else, "Like a lion roaring, walking, seeking whom he can devour."[151]

Remember that it is a dangerous situation to meet with Goliath. Fortunate who has the opportunity to severe apart this lion and find in the hard something soft;[152] in the bitter something sweet; in the ferocity some mercy; in the poison something edible; in the rage something pleasant; in death some life; in dishonor some credit. But as the proverb states, not all is according to Jacob, some of it following the pattern of Samson.

Fifth Sign: Regarding Reading in Moderation

We really need to remember the admonishment of the son of Sirach, "Many have died from overeating." As a result as much as possible strive to eat in moderation, not overloading the stomach with thoughts. Only a little healthy and clean food is satisfactory, while the defiled throat devours without measure and without taste. This is the reason God does not allow any cattle that do not chew the cub to be sanctified unto Him. To eat much and chew little is unhealthy. Those many that think differently and reading the same books will not evolve as properly educated.

---

[150] Luke 2:34
[151] 1 Pet 5:8
[152] Judges 14:6-8

When our age or our country has a number of wise men considerably less than there were in previous ages and regions, then the blame is because we bounce back and forth in innumerable and diverse books of various topics, not selective as to what we read and without a haven. A sick person will annoy various creatures, but a healthy person is satisfied eating the same food. He eats the same with a sense of taste and this is satisfactory. There is nothing more harmful than different and innumerable dishes. Pythagoras, having chewed the cud just on the triangle, was he not completely satiated? David, having tasted the experience of standing in the shadow of the ark, how full he was. He even skipped and danced. Chew just one piece of magnificent glory and an entrance and exit will be provided you in God's labyrinth winding through many residences. Magnificent glory, word of God and His thoughts are one and the same. Eat just one morsel, for example, of this glory:

The magnificent was spoken in you, city of God.
Throughout all the land is your glory.
When the corpse is, the vultures gather.
Or this one, Birds shall increase in number in the land.
Or this one, Birds flew upon the slaughtered bodies.
Or this one, Seven young men among the people's men.
Or this one, Your eyes are as those of a dove.
Or this one, I know not the eagle that soars toward the sun.
Or this one, Is it due to Your command that the eagle rises?
You have raised us, as if on the wings of an eagle.
God shall call a bird or prey from the east.
The voice of doves is heard in our land.
Let the sun stand still! And the sun stood still.
When he arrived he went up where the young man was.
Samson will carry the city gates to the top of the mountain.
Princes, take your gates.
These gates will be closed.
Her husband will be praised at the gates
Behold the ladder established in the land.
The iron rod will not rise above my head.
The iron gets hot.
What is a person that You remember him?

His life shall be exalted above the land.
I am alone until I cross.
Let us cross to Bethlehem.
You, God, will not depart from our strength.
Wisdom was proclaimed in their exodus.
Rejoice, barren who gave birth.
Your eternal deserts will be developed.
Your daughters will be raised upon your shoulders.
Kings will become their butlers.
Let those devastated in heart draw near to me.
I was behind their backs and above them.
You will see My past.
Remember your earlier years.
They will lick the dirt like snakes.
I will sing just like the sparrow.
Ephraim was as a senseless dove, not having wisdom; or
Who shall travel to the other side of the sea and obtain wisdom.
Stars now shine in their chambers.
They shall dream dreams.
They will travel to their possessions.
Profound is a person's heart and who can fathom it.
As deep is water so is counsel in a man's heart.
Man, plant a vineyard.
It is necessary for a person to be born from above.
I would then give you living water.
The Angel of the Lord agitated the water.
Who climbs in first would regain health.
They recognized him in the breaking of bread.
They will pick up snakes; they will speak in new languages.
Arise and walk. And jumping he stood and walked.
Arise sleeper and resurrect from the dead.
Two wings similar to a large eagle's were given to the woman.
Whoever even ties one sheaf, the eye of Israel will shine in him.

The person who is wise will preserve this, or stated in other words, observe, attain and meditate. When you hear the words, "Remember Lot's wife," it will not just remind you to remember this one item, that Lot had a wife. Such food is dry, gaunt, without nourishment, poor quality, or in short, an empty ear of corn. Such is the famished cows of Pharaoh's dream and secular vanity. So should we not decipher and remember where the figure of salt of our minds can lead us? With what do these bland and dumb cows inspire us? Do not turn your hearts to Sodom in decaying hunger and vanity, do not rest here in the shadow of death, but in the future struggle to ascend the mountain with Lot and moving in this manner you will attain the salt that is the imperishable strength of our decay and the glory of its resurrection. What is sown in decay will rise in imperishability, and then you will sing, "Arise, my glory." I am alone until I cross. And you will become that blessed wanderer and migrant of which the perspicacious Baruch proposes, "Who will cross to the other side of the sea and possess it?"[153]

This is what it means to remember, "Remember Lot's wife." Or stated in another manner: Chew, taste, interpret; destroy and shatter this idol; rend the lion, this devil, and search inside of him for the hidden food and sweet sleep of eternity, the undeclared and secret wisdom of God, of which Isaiah spoke, "Our salvation is in treasures." The word of God consists of 2 essences: one that speaks of God and the other that hears Him twice.

Two countries possess the Biblical sea. One is our country, the second is God's. On our shore the ears of corn are empty and the cows gaunt; but on the other side of the sea the ears are healthy and the calves are the best quality. Our shore is destitute and dry, but the one beyond the sea is a Haven of Good Hope, the bosom or the bay of Abraham, a green area, where the entirety of Israel pastures and rests, having abandoned the famine-stricken region of the people of Sodom. "Who shall cross to this side of the sea?" This is who: I will fly and then rest. I fell asleep and slept and arose. And so the young girl spoke, I wanted to be under his shade and there I sat. Rest my soul, wise virgin. Do not fear, if you oversleep, your sleep will be sweet.

O, paradise, my paradise. We honor you but cannot fathom you. With elucidation you must eat God's word, chew with the teeth of Jacob's son, Judah. Laying down, you fall asleep as a lion. And this is not surprising: he can chew and obtain for himself a sweet rest. The land before you is like a paradise of sweetness.

---

[153] Baruch 3:30

And all of them have Jacob's teeth, of which it is written: Like the morning dawn multitudes of people spill over the mountains, they are strong and none like them since the beginning of time. The righteous person is bold like a lion. Remember Lot's wife.

All created items are like a ghostly shadow, but God is a spirit of vision. I present to you the 2 shores of the Caspian Sea: the northern and the southern.

Remember Lot's wife.

Do you hear the dark illusion? Remember the light of vision through this darkness. You will touch the intangible statue of salt. So think this subject through, why should the salt of imperishability and taste of eternity not enter your soul? Do you see the northern shore? Also bring to memory the southern, unseen shore. God shall arrive from the south. Prepare the Passover. This is not a place to make a profit. You will not cross on foot, or by ship or with wings The Lord Himself will steal your heart and transfer it from death to life, from rebellion to intellect and justice. The Lord's path is justice and mercy. If you gaze upon this woman, why do you commit adultery in your heart? Why do you rest on her flesh and think about her blood? Why do you not prefer to meditate that flesh and blood is not the heavenly kingdom, is not rest and consolation, but a dead wood block, shadow and ghost. This topic leads you to your mark, to your husband, so you will with him – and not with Lot's wife – find rest and consolation. You have annihilated all traces of promiscuity residing in you.

Was her husband Lot great in some manner? O, my friend! When the descendant of Abraham became the great person Christ, then this nephew of Abraham could likewise make himself into something highly considered. Regarding this type of people we can boldly state, "As for his generation of people, who considered it?"[154]

Lot is a different type of person, as it states regarding him, "You flow in the fragrance of this world." Undefiled girls follow after him from the northern shore to the mountains of the Caucasus, so they may drink and rest. They feast on the abundance of your house.[155] Lot is part of the same generation as the humble, which is the abundance, or the secretions of aromatic trees. Behold the wisdom of Boaz. You provide a fragrance like myrrh; myrrh and drops of perfume and cinnamon upon your clothing. In

---

[154] Is 53:8
[155] Ps 36:8

the language of the Greeks it is drops of perfume, but in Hebrew it is Lot. Are not these drops a kindly spirit? And is not a kindly spirit the same as God? Sabbath! Here we will rest. "And I will fly and I will rest." The Lord provides me a pasture. He leads me to a green place. Remember Lot's wife.

O, wife, wife! You are both my sorrow and my delight. You live and you die. If they did love you so much, as they did your husband Lot, just as Christ loves his church, then we would never have separated, those whom God had united. This mystery is great. But now your love is cold and senseless, and I absent-mindedly and unconsciously remember you who forgot about your husband who shared your indivisible paired unity and forgot God's counsel, "O, human, do not create children after the flesh."

And it was impossible for this Eve not to have eaten the fatal fruit and not given birth to children for ruin when base and carnivorous men and the descendents of Ham made love to your heart. Of them it is written thus, "They will eat the dirt like snakes that slither upon the ground."

Know that their hearts are but dust and they deceive. His enemies will lick the dirt and death is their only deliverance. The poison of asps is under their lips. Their throat is an open coffin. Take me away Lord from the evil person. In their heart and again in their heart they speak evil. How is this? This is how! They bring with themselves malice in their hearts, and so could not find any goodness in the heart of Lot's wife, except words that flood and a deceiving tongue that they bring with themselves. They have not been able to attain to the goodness that is hidden from them. All the glory of the king's daughters is within.

And these are the men of Sodom who lurk along the city street. "Glorious will be spoken of you city of God."[156] "Mary preserved all the words in her heart." But how are we to find them, knowing that a profound heart resides in each person. "And his life will ascend from the ground." But their fate is to slither along and eat dirt all the days of their life. Their death is their bread and their mother is the night. They hunger when the wind blows and encompass the city. You are cursed above all animals; cursed is the young son of Ham. O, foolish and dull of heart.[157]

Remember Lot's wife.

---

[156] Ps 87:3
[157] Luke 24:25

Among women is my beautiful and blessed one who has not birthed children. I cannot think of you enough to satisfy myself, so sweet is your memory, the memory of Lot. Seven husbands and you could have had even 7,000, but all of them would be adulterous, except for the son of Tobit, and Raphael was the friend of Tobias. He accompanied the groom and provided incense and perfume for his bed chamber. The offspring born of him provides a sweet memory of Tobias, being righteous in eternity, properly and prudently taking Sarah as his wife, without the shame of idolatrous or demonic defilement, filled with perfume and myrrh in her clothing. Children grew not in servitude, but in freedom, who were born not of the lust of the man or the lust of the woman, but born of God as one prophet stated, "Lord of my salvation, I will from this time have children who will proclaim your righteousness. Tell me who among you is a man that fears the Lord? Who? Not the young son of Ham, but an upright man, The Lord is with you, man of strength."

Is there such a man among you? Husbands, love your wives. I speak in regard to Christ and the church. Likewise love with me also the woman who never gives birth. Rejoice barren one, who has never given birth.[158]

If this one does not appeal to you, then there are many royal daughters in place of her. Who? And here they are: Judith, Ruth, Rachel, Rebecca, Sarah, Hannah the mother of Samuel, Tamar, Abigail the beloved of David, Samson's Delilah, Esther. But have you forgotten Eve? Have you never read that God's Angels had love affairs with the daughters of humans? Such women kept David warm in his old age and his son also had love affairs with many of them, and even boasts of one in the last chapter of his proverbs.[159] All of these wives from their love affairs had offspring not in the distant northern shores, but in secure regions of Paradise. God approaches Job with a question, "Have you comprehended the time of the birth of goats living in the mountain rocks?"[160]

There David renews his young strength as the eagle.[161] He grows new horns just as with the goats. So are the Evangelic deer, Elizabeth and Mary who ascended into the heavens.[162] There where Peter raised Tabitha, who

---

[158] Eph 5:25, Gal 4:27
[159] Pr 31:10
[160] Job 39:1
[161] Ps 103:5
[162] referring to the ascension of Mary

was also a gazelle or antelope.[163] The Angel and Peacemaker is sent there. To say of them all, Let their virginity not be violated. And there was given to the woman 2 wings like those of a great eagle.[164]

Remember Lot's wife.

What are you thinking, my lover? Are not my counsels the same as your counsels? Know my friend that the Bible is the new world and people of God, the land of the living, the region and kingdom of love, the celestial Jerusalem and, transcending all Asiatic iniquity, is supreme. No animosity or strife will be found there. In this republic old age will not exist, neither will prejudice due to gender or nationality. All will be communal: a society residing in love, love residing in God, and God residing in the society. Here we have an eternal ring. With people this is impossible.[165]

Banish the thought that Eve is an old woman or strange woman. Such thoughts derive from the shores of Sodom. Their clusters are clusters of gall.[166] Such a root will grow extending upward, defiling many. And were not many defiled having read of Lot's drunkenness? To the pure all thing are pure, but their mind and conscience is defiled.

Spit at old wives' and children's fables, untrue tales and lies regurgitated by carnivorous snakes, such as the one that violated Eve, turning its evil eye again toward Sodom, to its own vomit. Hungry like a dog.

But you my friend, hurry forward and look not at the right or at the left, but travel to the celestial with diligence, to where you are summoned and not by the deceiver snake, but as the perspicacious Zechariah states, "O, O, run from the land of the north."[167] And so does Isaiah, "Depart, depart, leave from there.[168] Come, I will show you the judgment upon the great whore, for she has made all the nations drink from the wine of her promiscuity.[169] O, city of blood, completely false, full of crime. The crack of whips and sound of wheels, and a galloping horse, and noisy chariots."[170] I will unveil your past right to your face and disclose to the

---

[163] Acts 9:36-41
[164] Rev 12:14
[165] Matt 19:36
[166] Deut 32:32
[167] Zech 2:6
[168] Is 48:20
[169] Rev 17:1
[170] Nahum 3:1-2

nations your shame and the kingdoms your dishonor.[171] I shall make you a joke. I will cast you down and silence you because of your filthiness. Falling, falling is Sodom. Remember Lot's wife.

Anyway you, my friend! First arrange your affairs and prepare for Mount Sinai, smoking with the sweet smoke of our Lot. We are the fragrance of Christ.[172] Please be a wise virgin if you want to be in Cana of Galilee and to be transformed from one of these vile dogs who urinate against city walls to rejoice drinking wine sweetened by Moses' rod. Begin to wail as did Jeremiah for the destitution of good young girls.[173] But you must joyfully sing as did Isaiah, "Shine, shine, celestial city."[174] Look with your eyes about you and see, behold, your daughters will be raised upon their shoulders.[175] Which are these? They fly like clouds and like doves with their nestlings to me. Your gates will be opened forever, and the wealth of the nations will be supplied to you.[176] Rejoice desert.[177] Who shall give unto me wings and I will fly.[178]

So how are you in such joy and in such a celestial location to arrive at the wedding? How are you to approach the untouchable Caucasus and fly to its summits? I will revert what is difficult into the easy. I will give them a new path by which they will travel. What path. You will never know it. Why is this? I will tell you. If a person's nature is not reborn from above at this new region, he cannot find this path to ascend to the celestial. Do not bore me with the foolish questions of Nicodemus. The flesh, even if born 3 times, is still dirt and one and the same soil of the ground. The necessity is for your clay nature to conceive, accept and install a seed as though in a field, conceiving a celestial nation and seed of a new type of people. Listen, see, sow of your own species. Listen according to your nobility. Who shall comprehend his generation?[179] So now what is born of the spirit is the second, new and other-birth transcending the birth of the flesh. Or said in the Mosaic style, "A person is a person," since for many the idea of something else than material – such as spiritual – is not comprehendible. "I

---

[171] Nahum 3:5
[172] 2 Cor 2:15
[173] Jer 9:1
[174] Is 60:1
[175] Is 49:22
[176] Is 60:11
[177] Is 35:1
[178] Ps 55:6
[179] Is 53:1

who speak to you are from above, while you are from below."[180] What I repeat to you is what is necessary, so that a diamond would shine from this pile of dung of which you consist, and from your sandy mountain a cornerstone would roll down. So that blades of grass would grow from the swamp and mud of your corpse, and provide seed after the divine species. So that the field lilies and oaks and fragrant bushes grow from the ground and above your ground. So that your dead bones would sprout as grass and your walls will be erected and your deserts transformed forever for generations and generations. This is the second birth or in other words, the birth from above. And you must acquire the sense that existence has never had a beginning, but you deafly only heard of it and without any taste, but it did not enter your heart, but you did not await it or think about it, and even if you did think about it, your thought was similar to a toothless child attempting to put into its mouth the best walnuts of Solomon's groves, but not having any teeth. The walnut's fruit is inside of it.

Then your heart becomes a fertile field, seeds falling into it for eternity and accepting them, but the flesh like the flowers of the field sprouting its autumn branches and like a dry plough lying in the bushes. I am the bread of life. I am the flower of the field and the lily of the valley.[181] The ground sprouts blades of grass. Flowers appear in the soil.

At the moment of his second birth from above he becomes a virgin, newly conceived and inherently holy. Behold the slave of the Lord.[182] The Lord caused conception and she travailed and the spirit of Your salvation was born. The word became flesh and resided among us.[183]

Comprehend me and remember this, the theological creation of a person, "God created the human."[184]

In the celestial republic all is new: new people, new creation, new creatures – not as those that now reside under the sun, all of which are the oldest rag of rags[185] and vanity of vanities.[186] All of His activities were

---

[180] John 3:31
[181] Song 2:1-2
[182] Luke 1:38
[183] John 1:14
[184] Gen 2:7
[185] Is 64:6
[186] Eccl 1:1

completed in faith. He learned from observing the works of Your hands.[187] He makes His Angels spirits.[188] I create and who will repel it?

Listen! Let this be written with the finger of God on the heart! The creation of the person is that second birth. It occurs not when the person of Sodom made of flesh and blood and dirt and the mud of clay is created, intermixed, formed, sculptured; and stands, walks, sits and waves; and possesses eyes, ears and nostrils; and maneuvers and flaunts his presence as does a monkey; babbles and articulates as does a Roman Caesar; has feelings to the extent of a statue; wisdom to the extent of a idol; touches as does the underground mole; feels his way as does a blind person; is proud as an insane; changes as does the moon; is disturbed as is Satan; attracting as a spider web; hungry as a dog; malicious as a snake; friendly as a crocodile; steady as the sea; consistent as the direction of the wind; dependable as ice; bulky as dust; and disappearing as a dream. So is every false person: a shadow, darkness, steam, mold, dream.

When does the direct creation of a person occur? With the second birth. Do not be astounded of such a glory and this statement, "You must be born from above."[189]

A statue made from soil is limited, just compressed matter. The spiritual person is liberated. In the heights, in the depths, in the widths he flies limitless. Not mountains, not rivers, not seas, not deserts bother him. He sees into the distance; views the hidden; reviews the past; infiltrates the future; soars over the face of the ocean; enters locked doors. His eyes are dove-like; wings are eagle-like; agile as the deer; bold as the lion; reliable as the pigeon; gentle as a lamb; grateful as the stork; swift as the hawk; vigilant as a crane. His body is diamond, emerald, sapphire, jasper, crystal and onyx. Over his head flies a group of 7 divine birds: the spirit of taste, spirit of faith, spirit of hope, spirit of kindheartedness, spirit of counsel, spirit of premonition, spirit of clean-heartedness. His voice is as the sound of thunder. It is unexpected as lightning and echoes the sound of the storm. "It breathes where it wants."[190]

---

[187] John 5:19
[188] Ps 104:4
[189] John 3:6
[190] John 3:8

Lord, this is the type of person that You will remember and place over the work of Your hands.[191] The memory of a virtuous person is pleasing unto You. We must remember this person.

Do you want to place his name and his memory upon our heart? This is the reason You brought him into our eyesight, clothed like a statue in our skin, that the son and this brother of Yours would be glorified among us, who descended for our salvation. But we did not recognize him and in place of him divided for ourselves his garments, in the fashion of Potiphar's wife.[192] From where is this fashion derived? And the people of Sodom only touch the tangible, deprived of Isaac's guess who smelled from his son the garments of Lot's fragrance. We are deceived by this fashion: not Lot or his wife could recognize him. For this reason the unproductive blade of grass was unproductive for us as when we played on Sodom's field with Isaac, and not on the mountain with Jacob. I looked and beheld one man. His majesty will ascend far beyond the heavens. The thoughts of his heart will pass generation to generation.

Here for you is the second birth and direct creation. "The Holy Spirit will descend upon you,"[193] referring to something intangible, second, new, eternal, or said in other words, "The final Adam is a life-providing spirit."[194]

When all of his activities are conducted in faith, then the person created of God is intangible. Spirit creates spirit. "What is born of the Spirit is spirit."[195] Sodom's blindness is unique born of the flesh, touchable, and cannot extend into the distance. But Isaac's faith, touching his son's garment, discloses what is invisible but touchable above and brings the dove's eye to see something transcending and lofty and perspicacious, satiating thoughts of the heart against the base and vile, and then as if higher and higher transcending the wandering celestial heavens, alluring eagles, hawks, ravens and falcons to the discarded carrion so it would not devour, as it occurred in Pharaoh's dream, select calves and the virgins of God's wisdom. But in place of this dead cattle and putrefied food of Sodom let there be devoured the imperishable glory, the power of resurrection and supreme eternal thoughts, as if they were brought to us by

---

[191] Ps 8:6
[192] Gen 39:12
[193] Luke 1:35
[194] 1 Cor 15:45
[195] John 3:6

eagles flying down from above. Behold! The eagles will gather where the corpse is.[196] The signet ring! Here it is! Birds shall increase in the land.

Will you understand this? "He shall call a bird of prey from the east."[197] Or the following from Solomon, "May the ravens and vultures peck at the eye discrediting and vexing mother in her old age."[198] She has covered her nest as an eagle and covets her nestlings.

This celestial eagle provides us a new birth, creating from our flesh its spirit: something existing from what does not exist, humans from animals and beasts. Conceived in this wood block that we are, as in the walnut and husk of grain, while the juice of grapes is sweet when unfermented. Your law resides within my chest. You do not know the person standing in the midst of you. Behold the virgin will conceive in her womb.

He will not arrive from the edge of society and not from fleshly web, but woven into an eternal and complete entity, in our very body as if a radiant spark hidden in a piece of flint finally at its opportune time appears, just as a lily in a field and a spring in a waterless desert. The fountain of paradise clearly portrays this, "A spring appeared and provided water to all of them."[199]

Isaiah releases his arrow at this very target in the following statement, "Your bones will become fattened and become a watered garden and as a spring never to lack in water.[200] Your bones will flourish like grass and enlarge and have an inheritance unto the generations of generations. And your deserts will develop to last eternity. And you will be nicknamed the builder of walls and you will rest in your paths."[201]

The Samaritan woman was astonished hearing about this water. She asks for it of the Teacher, just like David's deer wanting it.[202] "Who shall give me water to drink?"[203] Not the water of Sodom, but from the cave of Bethlehem, from the dew of the heights and beauty of Joseph,[204] from the mountains of Hermon that flowed upon Aaron's beard[205] and upon all the

---

[196] Matt 24:28
[197] Is 46:11
[198] Pr 30:17
[199] Ex 15:27
[200] Is 58:11
[201] Is 61:4
[202] Ps 42:1
[203] 1 Chron 11:17
[204] Gen 49:22
[205] Ps 133:2

world's rabble, as the words be put to goodness, "Rivers will flow from his entrails."[206]

In the presence of this person blindness and cold will vanish while his nose, smelling and satisfying the senses of Jacob, can smell Lot's incense burner and becomes great, as great as Solomon's pyramid, or said in simply terms, the Bible. And where he states himself as to his relative, "Enter my garden my sister, my bride."[207] Who is this that hides counsel from Me, retaining the word in his heart? Does he think to hide from Me?[208]

This person born of you – a chaste virgin – was born without a husband, but was not created of God without a mother: spirit from spirit, light from light, he leaves you – his parents – and clings to his wife. This existent Lot cried from joy, "Now you are flesh of my flesh, and as if wine is poured into a bowl, the 2 shall become one."[209] Open to me my sister.[210] These gates will be locked and to no one else other than him will they be opened on penalty of death. Here is the one who opens to us the path to the celestial regions. "I know a person who traversed the heavens."[211]

He is not only traveling on the inaccessible paths directly on the summit of the Caucasus Mountains, but in heaven, even as far as Saturn and to the place where the sun rises and sets. Do not think, "How can he say that he descended from heaven?"[212] Do not grumble among yourselves. I am the door. Remember Lot's wife.

But when this beautiful Hebrew child suffocates or drowns in a flood of the snake's vomit, or from the malice of Herod, then not only Rachel and Judith will remain widows, but all Jerusalem's daughters wail, deprived of a husband and wedding clothes. Do no think that as if Jeremiah's lamentation viewed the city beneath, and not the city above, the Biblical one, upon our mother. Let me weep day and night.[213] So was all the beauty of Zion's daughters removed from it. All have committed adultery. Then the beautiful bride grieves, dreams, runs, and sees him. I have sought him but could not fine him. The men of Sodom have attacked

---

[206] John 7:38
[207] Song 5:1
[208] Job 38:1
[209] Gen 2:24
[210] Song 5:2
[211] 2 Cor 12:2
[212] John 6:38
[213] Jer 9:1

me, a shadow that can be felt, they beat me, poisoned me. A sufficient number of criminals and worthless rabble who stole from me my clothing, dividing my garments among themselves, but they did not smell the sweetness and my desire: the lilies, my garments, the fragrant peace of my groom, Lot!

Depart from me you adulterers to the fire and brimstone of your passion of Sodom. Flee from me you dirt-eating snakes, dogs that wet the city walls, carnivorous beasts, wild boars of the oak forest. Eat tumbleweeds and sagebrush. This will be salad for your lips. The bushes of paradise are not for your nostrils. Your teeth are like those of Hagar's sons, eyes like that of Leah,[214] ears like that of the asp, nose and nostrils like that of a pig and distorted, unable to hear God's spirit neither among the flowers of paradise, nor in the holy of holes, nor in the pillar of fire, not in the pillar of salt, not in the pyramid of Lebanon. I gazed to the right at those staring at me and none were recognizable to me. I looked and behold there was no person, and I saw no man, since all of them departed to Sodom; every one of them was unnecessary.

Where are you, O, person, person? Disclose to me your appearance and I will hear your voice, for I am infected with love that is pure, imperishable and prudent. Lead me from this prison of Sodom. Faithful man Abraham, liberate your nephew from captivity, let us depart to the celestial regions with diligence and there at the celestial region we will be joyful as new people with new wine and we will rest. Remember Lot's wife.

Have the ability my friends to remember Lot's wife. When you read in the divine books about alcoholism, concubinage, incest, illicit love, and the like, do not wander about Sodom's streets, but proceed directly, not considering any of such items, and do not stop in the street of sin. The Bible has no association with the activities of these streets, but will lead you through them to the celestial country and chaste region; not in carnal sophistication, but what will lead to eternity. The stomach needs not the Bible, neither does the inferior god, or some genealogical king. It is only to reside in the supreme God. Have you never heard the taste of the words, "Wisdom is sung in the exits."[215] Do not be drunk, but discuss matters in the highways, as also during Passover. Yes! Lot's fable from ancient times

---

[214] Gen 29:17
[215] Pr 8:1-2

ruins the readers with their unwashed hands and feet, motivating them to satisfying the flesh. Paul pointed his finger at them, that they should not drink wine, but under the designation of wine they should drink God's spirit and the New Testament wine; and not that of Sodom. Here is the reason for washing feet at the Lord's supper. So did Moses prepare Israel to eating the Passover, so that wearing their traveling masquerade, with their waists girded, standing and wearing their hats and holding their staves, they would eat the Passover. But what does this ceremony signify? That the Bible is the Passover, the passage, transfer, exit and entrance.

What more is there? That the Bible is the book and word bequeathed of God. Is it? Yes it is, you tell me and so does your grandmother. Is it so? Exactly so. Even every fool knows this. So now I judge you by what proceeds from your lips. Why do you not sit at home when this day is not the day for you to work, but is a Sabbath unto the Lord and your God? Why do you drag on the Sabbath, the rest day, trash and stuff from your vile little home to some other room or building or residence of God? Why are you a busy-body attempting to move your poverty and stench to the city above? Did you forget that even grandmothers know this? Do you not remember that the Bible is the temple of eternal glory, and not your body's trash? Why are you bothering to find there drunkenness and people gone astray and illicit love? Is not all of this defiling the Sabbath, the Sabbath of the greatest blessing? Yes, you defile it when you introduce the yoke of slavery and heavy labor into the country of consummate peace and freedom. Please, be prudent. Untie your shoes at home, wash your hands and feet, abandon all that you have perishable and migrate to the divine. Passover! The Bible is unto you a bridge and ladder for this passage. Passover! There you will be provided imperishability in place of decomposition. Passover! You will taste what your eye has not seen and what has never entered your heart.[216] Passover! If it should strike you on the cheek, turn towards it with the other southern region of the sea. Passover!

If you were to repay goodness in return for goodness, the grace residing in you would be small and the lost reader does the same. But if someone imposes a wrong upon you, and you in place of it impose some goodness, then you become a son of the Supreme and this is the Passover.

---

[216] 1 Cor 2:9

When you deal with Lot do you praise him for his drunkenness? Remember that our drunkenness is wrong, but God's is good.

Passover! Your mother the Bible blasphemes nothing, and praises nothing except what is God's. Passover! Should I praise the snake? "Be wise as snakes." Remember Christ's wisdom, who was like a snake himself.[217] Passover! He counsels you to sell all you have and to purchase a knife.[218]

O, child! Do not remember this knife. This is the same dagger that Aaron's grandson Phinehas used to stab the Israelite through the stomach who was promiscuous with the Midianite woman: with one stroke both he and her.[219]

O, my readers, readers! May the Lord give you my dagger so that you and the many curious would stop the poison and malice of Lot's wife. Let it spear the adulteress as she lies on her bed asleep, and even penetrate her bones and brain, and with the slender and sharp strength and Spirit of God. Passover! Does it magnify in your presence the sun, moon, stars, rainbow, flowers, grasses, trees, birds, fish, the person – the sovereign of all these creatures – in the radiant heptad created by the Lord? Please halt the Copernican system for a short while with its vile world and all of its dead writers. Abandon this physical pus and scab and leave it for the foolish and drooling virgins. But yourself eat from Ezekiel's fragrant unleavened bread and satisfying manna of the sacred Passover of God, traveling from the earth to heaven, from the tangible to the intangible, from the lower, decaying world to the firstborn world. Passover! Command as did Joshua son of Nun as command the sun. "Remain in your place. Now I need you not. I go toward the sun that is better than you. You feed, light and warm my servant, the bodily system. But this sun that will never see the night is mine, my center, my thoughts, the abyss of my heart, and in no manner is it visible or touchable, not attainable and unstoppable in its agitating and wild thirst, wider than all the Copernican world it satisfies, charms, consoles, and comforts in full.

Passover! May the sun remain in the west. May your heart see the new light summoned from darkness and gloom, from yesterday's sun shining over the heavenly expanse and the abyss of your heart. May your memory

---

[217] John 3:14
[218] Luke 22:36
[219] Num 25:7-8

remember your heart that the eyes of your body cannot see. Lord! What is this light of yours that we remember as a monument of the western sun? Tell me. "Tell me Lord, my end and the number of my days, that I may understand."[220] Disclose to me: To what end does this pass lead us, and where is this day of ours and this sun of ours? Untie for me the significance of the number of my days, the number of heptads, whether the heptad of my days will be poor. "And it was night and then day."[221]

O, senseless people! How we are so dull and inert in understanding prophetic songs! But is this a sacred pattern in order for us to imagine the sacred person, and to place the world-wide eye as a monument of the eye that never rests? This is the other man, "Lord, what is a human that You remember him?"[222]

The prophets compared him to our sun. "The person has reverted to vanity." But is not the Biblical kingdom celestial? Is He not the authority in the heavens and on earth? Is He not the judge over the work of God's hands? Is He not the beginning and end of the entire Bible? Did He not place his residence in the sun,[223] being clothed with his light as with a garment?[224] Did He not measure with his palm the extent of our days? Is He not wisdom who built for itself a home that is a seven-story pyramid? Does not the sun sing a song on his behalf in the words, "He shall reside with the sun."? The heavens proclaim him,[225] and to him is attributed supreme glory in these figures. He is the day, the source of eternity, beyond the heights, the depths, and immeasurable expanse, filling all and carrying all to the final tendon and hair. To him belongs the day, the great and marvelous day, while we ruminate on the word during our day and this word is beneficial. Our day is an icon and picture and an image of what is to come, just as was the sea to Jonah and the whale that regurgitated him.

Here is a sign unto you. You will find the child dressed in sun-filled clothes, although in a shroud and swaddling cloths, the most beautiful of all the sons, himself the son. "When I arrived I stood high, where the young man was." "Behold I proclaim to you a great joy.[226] I proclaim from

---

[220] Ps 90:12
[221] Gen 1:3
[222] Ps 8:4
[223] Ps 19:4
[224] Ps 104:2
[225] Ps 19:1
[226] Luke 2:10

the ancient times what is new, from sorrow an eternal joy. Trumpet heavens! Evangelize, you my friends, evangelize day to day."

We will rejoice and celebrate this day. O, our sun, I have not led you to some bad place. O, you fiery Cherubim, the chariot of our new person. O, chariot of God, you have carried us to the same place as did the star of the Magi.

Others sitting in the chariot had nothing to seek except some physical swamp and their flesh. They sat in it themselves and upon its horses as if upon a firm something. For this reason they dirtied the sun with their sea of fire and with the fire and brimstone of Sodom. We however having called upon God's name and speak as did the person Isaiah, "You will see the king in his glory and your eyes will see the land from a distance."[227] Israel finally arrived at the haven, to the firm haven at the southern edge, leaving behind the pursuer's chariots and their riders in a massive flood, singing unto our Lord a song of victory over those on chariots and some on horses.[228] They have become dirty as tin in water.[229]

Abandon yourself, chariot! You are no longer needed now that you have delivered us to Him whose name is The East, and arrived at the place where the child resides. He commands you, May the sun stand in its place. And the sun stood still.[230]

This is the manner for the Passover to be eaten and be filled with wisdom during the exodus: to converse during the passage.

Passover! In this manner greet it with the moon and with all the manufactured products and trash that you are dragging along with you for the week. Do not touch the curse of Jericho.[231] Hew with the son of Nun every godless foreigner and even to the extent of his property. The curse pertains to every foreigner, the flesh is this curse, and flesh is but a shadow, a sign, a figure or boundary. Listen! Hew and spare none. Butcher with Peter everything breathing, discard the dead, eat the living, defile the defiled, and sanctify the sacred. There is one who is holy and one who is the Lord. "In the morning he slaughtered all the sinful of the land."[232]

---

[227] Is 33:17
[228] Ex 15:1
[229] Eze 22:20
[230] Josh 10:12-13
[231] Josh 6:18
[232] Gen 34:25

A criminal act is to convert the spiritual into fleshly, and God's activity into a human's and a physical web. This ruins our common mother Eve who is the Bible, and our life then follows the deception of the snake. God has sanctified all things for Himself, so why do you slither towards Him, O, snake? Why do you destroy what has been created, O, murderer? The flesh is useless and all fleshly is an idol and worthless. Commit to what is spiritual! Here is truth. This is the issue. Here is the creation! He created his Angels to be spirit and not flesh. Whoever serves God is an Angel and every person who serves is praised, and every person praised will be gathered, developed and sanctified. Listen to me and be creative, then you are unto me a wise man who founds his temple on a rock and not on sand. This is solidity. Passover! Do you hear the resurrection? Do not be narrow minded. Do you hear the birth? Forget your possessions. Do you hear of Lot's daughters? Do not remember your people and your father's house.[233] Progress further. O, my daughter, bend your ear closer. Prophets speak to you in your language, but not in your vile and obsolete language, but in a new and wisdom-filled. Transcend yours and migrate to the good one. This is the significance: Wisdom is sung in processions, and my processions are the procession of life.

Approach even the sun as an eagle and the sun is just decaying and trash, but you nonetheless are still soaring through the air. This eagle disdains Solomon, "I do not recognize the eagle soaring through the air." But not only everything under the sun, but even the sun is trash and vanity. The entire secular system is the idol of the plain of Dura.[234] Its gold head is the sun. As long as you are in the world, you reside in vanity and not in God's procession with the perspicacious-eyed and confidant eagle. And so does God inquire of his beloved Job, "Does the eagle fly at your command?"[235]

All is malicious and all is base except for God and is unable to give credit with Paul, "Not observing the flow." You are abhorrent to Solomon as long as you slither with a snake along rocks and the physical elements. But if you are with the eagle having an owl's eyesight you will fly through the tangible atmosphere. "All flesh is grass."[236]

---

[233] Ps 45:10
[234] Dan 3:1
[235] Job 39:26
[236] Is 40:6

Fly beyond the elements, soar through the entire airy abyss, fly away from all decay to the firm solidity of eternity. Then you will find yourself at Israel's exodus, now from physical slavery, the destitute and distressed. At this time sing with Habakkuk this song, "The Lord is my God, my strength and will make my feet firm in the summit, and he raises me to his heights above which will gain me the victory, as I sing in my song."[237] In other words, enter where God's muse leads. So did the Romans speak, "Arise, ascend to the mountain." This means that the mountains must be located so that the physical shadow of Lot's daughters would not interfere, so not to obscure faith which with its eagle eye – as if through a telescope – penetrating the distant and high but omnipresent light that shines in darkness above the hills and appears from the midst of the flood; the land and haven of Israel; the promised, high pinnacle and bay and womb and chest of Abraham; the rock and house of the wise person; the nest of the dove; the beloved settlement of the Lord of hosts; the Sabbath and rest of exhausted swimming; the conclusion of days and consummation of wailing that tells you your entrance and exit; and Passover that was the center of sweet conversations between the 3 conversationalists: Christ, Moses and Elijah on Mount Tabor. Come and we will ascend the Lord's mountain.

However, O, Lord! You will not ever lead us upon Your mountain with our strength and sophistication, unless You do it alone for us. You will not find this, God, in our strengths. You alone are our assistance. Your processions above trend toward life, while we are all made of physical clods of dirt, flesh and blood, spirit, and wander about dead elements, not turning toward the celestial, but rather toward Sodom. So who will enter? The desire to do so is prepared of the Lord and His eagle ascends at His command. Where can we get a second will, a second soul, heart and eye? Here is where, "It is necessary for a person to be born from above." Then you will be able to taste the flavor in the words, "Wisdom is sung in processions."

Remember Lot's wife.

If you my friend, are already born from above and possess a special substance, then long live the daughter of Lot. Greetings, bride who is not a bride. Listen, daughter. Do not forget that in the country, in the kingdom of the living, there is no bias due to maturity or gender or other different. All who are there are in God, and God resides all in all. Your daughter is then

---

[237] Hab 3:19

also a bride and mother and sister, while Lot unto you is father and groom and son and brother, and so the opposite also. Isaiah is likewise a bride and the groom is disclosed as God. "As upon a groom you have placed upon me a crown. As a bride you have decorated me with beauty."[238]

Christ calls his friends altogether his mother and brother and sister. Although the Bible applies to you, you are still its daughter and father, and brother to a brother and friend to a friend and sister to a sister. Solomon is also a wife and sister and brother, and a brother's keeper, and this is also called God's wisdom. Someplace in the Gospel a neighbor-friend helps a friend with bread for guests.[239] Is this not the same as when the beloved Abigail brought to David as a gift some baskets filled with figs and clusters of raisins and fresh baked bread?[240] And did not Melchizedek do the same to Abraham,[241] and Abraham the same to his guests?[242] And did not the same occur with David who together with Abraham defeated the entire Sodomic rabble – as related by Habakkuk – in God's Song of Songs and transcended all the elements and resolving all death entered Zion – as related by Paul – to the prepared dinner on a table, which the tangible people of Sodom have no right to eat, but still they did not just satisfy themselves, but even to hunters having nothing he distributed just one pancake in a frying pan?[243] "You ascended above and took captivity captive."[244]

To say it in short, all praise that can be said about friendship, relatives, hospitality, bread, food, clothing, home and all its furnishings, gifts, grapes, wine and produce is just like the provisions that Joseph provided his brothers and like the gold that was placed in their bags.[245] The queen of Sheba visits Solomon and was treated hospitably.[246] Bread was distributed in the desert for a hungry 5,000.[247] Gifts from magi are brought.[248] The

---

[238] Is 61:10
[239] Luke 11:5
[240] 1 Sam 25:18
[241] Gen 14:18
[242] Gen 18:6-7
[243] This is a play on words using Skovoroda, which means skillet or frying pan in Russian. The pancake is a crepe that is made in a *skovoroda*.
[244] Eph 4:8
[245] Gen 42:28
[246] 1 Kings 10:1
[247] John 6:10
[248] Matt 2:10

royal feast is being prepared.[249] Know that all of this pertains to Lot's daughters feasting and can be compared like the root to the branch or the spring to the stream. They will drink of the fat of your house.[250] Blessed is the person who has relatives in Zion. Blessed who will eat this dinner.[251] Wisdom has created for itself a house.[252] They drank and were satisfied with him. Drink of it all of you.[253] He became known to them in the breaking of bread.[254] Place it in the apples. He rested in its shade. Brother helps brother as a strong city.[255] I am a brother to him and he is a brother to me.

Who is mortal and not born from above is not relative to the Bible. A mortal heart cannot be united with a divine heart. There exists a great resistance or an antipathy between the sky and the ground, and the birds of the day and those of the night, and between the destroyable and the eternal. Mind or heart is that spirit which is the master of the house, meaning, controls the body. This is precisely the person. And the body? It is just an oyster shell. If the physical thoughts and the heart is crushed, then the person dissolves into lifeless elements, dust and a shadow and nothing more. O, Isaiah! Know that dust is their heart.

How right it is for the Bible to refer to such people as dead. They will be reconstructed and resurrect when an eternal heart will be conceived in a crushed heart and the sun of truth will shine over the dark abyss of night thoughts. Let there be light. He has shined in our hearts.[256] The Bible is God's thinking and here can be found an eternal heart, and an eternal heart is an eternal person. The thoughts of his heart migrate generation to generation.

By the way, is it not the prophets who are the visionaries with living and divine hearts? From physical mud developing a god-person as a portrait of the shining sun also known as divine thoughts and the source of eternal rays to become the heart arising over the dark abyss of infernal hearts and providing light to the daylight. These are the hearts that will enjoy the Bible! It is their blood relative, the eternal loving the eternal; the

---

[249] Matt 22:4
[250] Ps 36:8
[251] Luke 14:15
[252] Pr 9:1
[253] Matt 26:27
[254] Luke 24:30-31
[255] Pr 18:19
[256] Eph 5:8

spirit knowing the spirit. The spirit tests all things, even the depths of God. An immaculate spirit composed the Bible and not any other. And it is this same immaculate spirit and heart that will unbind it and say, "And am I supposed to hide this?" I disclosed this to my brother, and my brother will pass. I have found a man after My heart.

And just as the chaste and radiant heart – as during the mid-day sun – is true God, so the elements and dust is the unclean spirit. It is subtle but airy, and if it is airy then it is elemental, and so it is coarse and spurious. This airy spirit reigns among all the dead, even if such are just born, and just as he is so are his subjects and his household – all enemies of our person. This is the king of Sodom, the blind spirit, elemental, fleshly, physical. For this reason the people of Sodom roam in darkness, beating themselves against the walls, touching doors and pushing with their strength to enter some feast. They are unsteady and possessed, they stand at the doors but they are excluded. But Lot has no kindness for their hungry heart that eats dust and air their entire life; he wants not to satisfy their vain soul and their hungry soul, and prefers to dine and treat his beloved family consisting of Angels, guests, those born from above, and divine people who descended from above. This is what David was viewing when he said, "Who do the heathen rage? The kings of the earth have gathered."[257] They seek flesh to fornicate. The divine spirit does not reside in their hearts and they will never taste the Lord's supper. "Blessed is he who dines in God's Kingdom."

Remember Lot's wife.

Let us further philosophize my friend, regarding these empty heads. The teacher did not say, "Touch," but said, "Remember." Let us not be adulterous. The flesh touches, but the spirit remembers. Dust is touchable, but eternity is believable. The hand feels a rock, but our heart with its eternal memory smells the myrrh of imperishability. In a special word, with a special divine sensation, the essence that is special in us is sensed with a special sense, as though viewing the rainbow. At that very minute behind our back our memory sees the sun displayed as in a mirror, in the most chaste of the heavenly waters and when our eyes see shadow cast by the sun, then the heart, the master of the eyes, will act as a lamp for the world in peace. O, Lot! Our Passover! O, our sweetest Lot! Lead us, lead us unto your mountain. We will look upon your wife as upon a rainbow

---

[257] Ps 2:1

and remember you – the light never of the night – shining upon the abyss of our hearts! We remember with a clean memory and faithful heart, singing to you with our Isaiah, "The path of the Lord is justice. I relied on His name and memory, for whom my soul desires."

You have seated yourself above your wife just as a vulture over some carrion, just as a judge sitting over a rainbow delivering justice, and preaching peace upon peace for those near and far. You are flesh and spirit. You are the rainbow and our sun. The rainbow displayed by the sun as an immaterial image of the hypostasis of Your father. The sun is the rays and radiance of His glory. "You will see the king in his glory, and your eyes will see the distant land."

Our corpse sits and rests while our hearts flow forward. It migrates from the corpse to God, from the insane to the wise. It flies as does Noah's dove high above the flood's waters over the elements so it can rest on the hills of eternity. The Lord's Passover is that judgment when the heart flies from darkness to light, from foolishness to intellect and justice. The wicked will not arise to acquittal.

Tell me my brethren, to what can our Passover be compared? It is like a ship floating toward an ancient harbor on the island of Rhodes. The gates of this harbor are an idol temple. Its feet are the pedestals of the gates, while the top of the gates are his waist. All the ships enter the harbor through these silly gates between the knees of his giant.

O, my friends! The awesome and shameful meets you. This is the vile idol – Lot's wife. Do not fear this Goliath, you can defeat him with a dagger. Beloved prophet Nahum! Come and show us what this great prostitute is. Here is the prophet! I will unveil the past to your face.

Fear not. A fatal poison will not harm your chaste heart. This basilisk in person will kill the asp. So is a lion dangerous when standing at the threshold, but behind his back is peace and friendship. There the wolf rests with the lamp without any danger, and the leopard with the kid, and the lion with the calf, and the bear is friends with the bull, while a young child sits next to an asp's nest. There you will boldly trample upon the asp and basilisk, over the lion and snake, and not to be poisoned, but as an amusement.[258]

Be bold! A child is born unto us, a never-aging Cupid. He leads us, although we walk along the shadow of death, although between the knees

---

[258] Is 11:6-8

of this giant of Dura. Do not fear, God is with us. Let us go now into the harbor. Let us pass to Bethlehem. Not in the storms of the sea, and not in the wild waves or rivers, and not in the fast currents of flowing elements do they give birth, but in the celestial mountains and productive regions, and so are the goats and deer productive and clean. There your mother was born. Let us pass to Bethlehem.

Farewell, pillar of salt! Farewell, vile and stupid person! Farewell, adulterer and murderer of souls and bodies! Remain a numb statue!

Open for us gates of virtue, the doors of the chaste virgins, the doors of the good wife, the praiseworthy wife and brother, and her husband is at her sealed and locked gates. Behold our new Nahum is unveiling for us the final divine Passover! He leads our new heart to a new justice and mind, behind the adulterous person who stands behind the walls. Behold he stands behind our walls.

For our personal history that transcends old wives' tales and other than fatal juices he opens for us a second, pure, imperishable deliverance, immune to poison, beyond the mountain ridge, final, eternal and divine. Yes, he does not look upon the person, the existing one, but is tested with what is hidden behind the curtain and locked behind the door. And if he should drink something fatal our faithful heart will not be harmed. So death, now where is your sting? Where now is your victory, you infernal giant? We have passed through the fire and water. I will disclose your past to your face and show the heathen your shame and the kingdoms your dishonor. I will make you a joke and will vomit upon you revulsion due to your promiscuities.

This imprudent fable regarding Lot is a parable and figure developing a pure pearl of God's Kingdom inside a filthy rag, and enclosing a seed as if inside the hard shell of a walnut. These walnuts are the Biblical paradise, the produce of the gardens of Rhodes, filled and overfilled. I descended into the walnut grove.[259]

The specially born person is so delighted with this garden. Just as in a mirror Solomon's Song of Songs is visible. O, most admired affection! O, the sweetest eternity and insatiable candy! Who eats of you will still be hungry and who drinks of you will still be thirsty. God is love. He who devotes his soul and meditates on the law of the supreme wisdom of all the ancients and seeks the meaning of prophesies will be learned. He will

---

[259] Song 6:11

preserve the narratives of famous men and delve into the meaning of parables. The hidden parables he will seek and sustain himself with the inquest of proverbs.[260]

Sixth Sign: Regarding Study that is a Benefit to the Soul

Do you see my friend that one word pressed will produce much juice. The Bible is a mature walnut tree; take one walnut from it, but only one walnut. Break it apart and chew on it. Now you have chewed the entire Bible.

Even a small broken piece of glass will reflect your entire face. But the multifarious wisdom of God can be viewed from a 100 facets, or like the thousands of garments among the royal and the villagers, in the past and the present, on the rich and on the destitute and on the basest and mixed of people, like a lily in the brush is still very beautiful and stands out among it. Yes! This is the exact and right Morpheus.

The educated will chew thoroughly. The wise person eats little that is tasteful. The true taste occurs if a person is healthy, while upright wisdom is useful. There is nothing better than truth that is useful, and there is no better use than what is useful for the soul. Inherent usefulness is medicine, food and well-being for the heart. Health is happiness. What can be more valuable than this? All is vain other than this. Live your life as long as the world: all of it is still vanity without joy. Health is different from gluttony just as wisdom is different from education. Gluttony breeds illness, while a moderate diet strengthens. If you read you will increase vice; if you read you will defeat vice! If you love badness, you will hate your soul. Love your soul and you will be a gracious narcissist. The beloved Solomon sung about this, "The prudent and virtuous person is a friend to himself."

But this only occurs when we have no other undermining or pretentious intentions, but we only read in order to cleanse, enlighten and strengthen our soul; to cleanse ourselves from popular opinions; to be satiated with the divine and to strengthen ourselves against the passions of the soul, against envy, hate, anger, sorrow and agitation; and in place of all of their inner tyrants to install within ourselves God's kingdom, which is also the spirits of salvation, peace and joy. This is that virtuous scribe and scholar whom Christ, praising, equates him with the master. Every scribe

---

[260] Sirach 39:1

who learns of God's Kingdom brings out of his treasury what is new and what is old.[261]

A squanderer chases after the wind, vanity, but the Kingdom is useful. Simon the Magician here seeks for gold; but the scribe seeks the Holy Spirit. Truly, no one who believes Paul will ever consume prophetic mysteries, because such mysteries are not worth 2 cents if God's love will not be his guide. Its foundation transcends everything. It begins with a bitter cross to carry but concludes with Christ who is our peace, love and virtue.

Seventh Sign: Regarding the Trustworthy Leader

What I have at the first and so must I also say altogether at the end, so that we do not select a guide for ourselves from the number of those who are lovers not of the spirit, of the husk, the literal darkness, or the fables of grandmothers that only kill us. These are the tales that Paul calls vain genealogies,[262] Jewish and old wives' fables that do not satisfy the soul. Such leaders love the external shadow and completely rest upon it, not raising their eyes with David to the spiritual mountain to the dinner of God's Kingdom, and it is only those who have transcended the flesh of their haughty minds that will be filled, as was Tobit's guide Raphael. Paul brags of this table in this manner, "We have an altar from which those who serve the shadow must not eat."[263]

Calling themselves servants not led by the letter but of the spirit, and they know Christ but not from following the historical record. Christ calls them his slaves who reside in his house, but they do not know the master's secrets. The confidant says, "They evolved from us, but they were not of us."[264]

Joshua son on Nun curses such in the 9th chapter.[265] Therefore you are cursed and we will never be lacking in slaves because of you. And how could he not curse them, having interfered with the posterity of Isaac? These young men with their master solely labor to dig a well of clean

---

[261] Matt 13:52
[262] 1 Tim 1:4
[263] Heb 13:10
[264] 1 John 2:19
[265] Josh 9:23

water, that is, a fountain that transcends digging. They dig as if in the ground, into physical history, discarding it to the side, as Moses diverted the rock from a spring in order to quench the thirst of his father-in-law's destitute sheep.[266] But the Philistines interfered everywhere, everywhere filling the wells and crying, "This land is ours."[267] This should be understood bodily, but it is also foreknowledge, like a dream. But the children of Isaac's spirit rest in the truth and consider all flesh as vanity and will not cease to remove the dirt from the old wells and dig new wells in their place, crying with their master, "The flesh avails nothing."

Of what good is the historical genealogy? What use is it? Why do we need to know the physical location of a perishable paradise? What benefit to our soul is the form and measurements of the ark? Why does the body need a physical healing? What good if the resurrection is only a physical that returns to a perishable condition? Then again we become slaves to the vile flesh and its passions. Yes! Only the spirit is tasteful and useful to us, cleansing, healing, penetrating into the secret evolutions of our soul and causing peace to be born in us.

But it seems the holy apostle Jude cruelly values them. "Waterless clouds, of the flesh, not possessing the spirit."[268] These sow dissension in all the world. They argue over the procession of the spirit,[269] over sacraments, over belief, over ceremonies, over Angels, over torments, over bliss, and other matters. They are enemies of the cross of Christ and his life-providing commandments.

The end and glory to God.

---

[266] Ex 2:16
[267] Gen 26:18
[268] Jude 12
[269] the filoque

GRIGORI SAVVICH SKOVORODA

DIALOG NAMED THE SERPENT'S FLOOD[270]

The soul and imperishable spirit converse. August 16, 1791.

My beloved Mikhail.[271]

The ancient monk Eriratyus[272] brought notes to his friend and master Patriarch Sophronius,[273] and so I do to you. In our friendship you are to me a master, and in our rank you are to me a friend.

I wrote this booklet while in Burluk, to escape my boredom. It was stolen, but then I, depending on notes, was able to restore, increase and finish it.

The flood of the serpent, Noah and the Bible are all the same. If it is the sea, then how can it not be a flood. Look at the portrait of Naso's flood.[274] The wolf swims among the lamb. Is not the entire world overwhelmed with this sea? Yes, it is. Yes, all of it. They have sullied it as tin tarnished in water. It is only Israel that has flown over this crevasse and crossed it. Only it has caught the sorrowful zeal of Baruch. "Who shall cross to the other side of the sea and find wisdom?"[275]

What in the Bible is not peace? What is peace if not the idol of Dura?[276] What is its head if not the sun? What is the sun if not the fiery sea? Did it not intervene into our harbor for us? Behold it stands at our walls and speaks, Hypocrite! Why are you sleeping?

---

[270] Rev 12:15
[271] Referring to Mikhail Kovalinski
[272] This name means emasculate in Latin.
[273] Patriarch of Jerusalem 634-638 AD.
[274] A section in the Metamorphoses of Publius Ovid Naso.
[275] Baruch 3:30
[276] Dan 3:1

Are not all those who were unable to swim across suffering torment in the fiery abyss? Are they not complaining about hell fire? And who understands hell fire? Is it not funny that all of them are in hell fire, but are afraid to fall into it?

This is exactly the Sphinx, tormenting those who have not solved the riddle. They are agitated and cannot rest, walking in the flame of your fire.

But my Noah sees the rainbow and the flood receding. What is the beautiful rainbow? Is not the rainbow happiness? Does not the sun see its reflection in the mirror of the cloud's water? Does not the sun look at the sun, upon a second sun? On the image that is portrayed, on the joy and on the firm peace? Does not our leader look in that direction? Do not the magi lead us there?

Remain, sun and moon! Farewell, fiery abyss. Forgive, western sun. We will create a better light. We will create a happier day. Let there be light, and behold there was light. Let the sun and moon arise! Let it be established! Let it shine for ever and ever. And behold the sun and moon appeared! A new sun and moon from the divine God.

Sing of this, Isaiah! Sing to us a song of victory. Behold, Israel will cross the sea! The sun will not set on you and you will not be deprived of the moon. Your lord will be your light. And you will fulfill your days, the days of your wailing. And I will also sing with you, my beloved Isaiah. I will place my rainbow in the clouds. This means: I will establish peace within you. The sun views all creation. Its gaze comforts the rainbow. The heart is an abyss. O, awaken! Be a friend to yourself and be in love. Then the entire flood will vanish. The rainbow will shine forever. Only once will you need to wipe the tears. Inwardly all the parts will be at rest.

Be yourself a rainbow.
And you will depart from anguish.
Behold the creation will not satisfy all.
The abyss catches the abyss. [277]

This is the following. "The intelligent and virtuous person will be a friend to himself."

---

[277] These 4 lines rhyme in the original Russian.

Chapter 1: A Parable of the Blind and the Seeing

Two strangers entered Solomon's temple: one blind and the other having his sight. The blind uselessly raised his eyes and aimed his eyelids toward the temple walls. But the seeing person, gazing at the walls saw the portrayed people, animals, birds, mountains, rivers, forests, fields, flowers, sun, stars and jewels, and staring at the immeasurable size of the artists pictures he was filled with a joy that could not be satisfied. And even more was the curious pupil [of his eye] staring at the seven-lamp candlestick and the shadow of the Cherubim.

The blind says, "I do not see any joy in this temple."

The sight-filled person cried, "O, destitute. Go home and dig out your eyeball buried in an old sack. Bring it here. And at that moment this temple will be renewed and you will feel the bliss that will provide you delight."

Chapter 2: Dialog or Verbiage

The persons in the conversation: Soul and Imperishable Spirit

Soul: If something has no taste then it causes me to secret saliva. If you will be so kind, Imperishable Spirit, tell me what the 2 strangers signify.

Spirit: Every person born in this world is a stranger, blind, or enlightened. Is not the beautiful temple of the wise God this world? There are 3 worlds. The first is the universal and the inhabitable world, where all that is born reside. It is composed of an infinite number of worlds upon worlds and is a great world. The other 2 are the private and the small worlds. The first of these is the microscopic, also known as the tiny world or puny world, or the person. The second of these is symbolic, also known as the Bible. The sun is the eye in the world that is inhabitable by anybody and this eye is the sun. And just as the sun is the head of the world then it is not astonishing that a person is called a microcosm, which is a small world. While the Bible is the symbolic world, because in it are the heavenly, earthly and subterranean creatures gathered as figures, in order for them to be monumental, leading our thoughts in the understanding of the eternal nature, concealed in something perishable just as a painting is concealed in its colors.

Soul: What does it mean to dig the eyeball out from the old bag?

Spirit: The beginning of eternal feeling depends on the ability to recognize yourself, to vision your eternity that is decaying in the body, and as if to dig out the spark in the dirt. This spark is the other worlds and this thinking eyeball can envision eternity in them.

Soul: Is not eternity and God the same?

Spirit: Of course, eternity is a firmament, everywhere, always, in all things standing firm, and all perishable creation like the clothing we wear, and all division and foreign sensations. This is truth and imperishability. Do you see that the light of wisdom then enters the soul when the person of 2 natures recognizes the perishable and the eternal. There is a proverb regarding the uncomprehending, "They have problems adding to 2."

Soul: But tell me, what use is it to see everywhere 2 natures, and rather just one? And what comfort is there in this?

Spirit: Let me picture for you this similarity. The talented artist inscribed on the wall a deer and peacock very artistically. His son, a child, was inexpressibly joyful over the images. And the older son looked with astonishment. The artist in time washed the paint and the animals disappeared from view. The child wailed with no manner of consolation, while the older son laughed. Now tell me, the reason for the laughter and wail.

Soul: O, I cannot say, but I thirst to hear it from you.

Spirit: Of course, the child thinks that the animals have perished. For this reason he wails.

Soul: If they disappeared, did they not perish?

Spirit: Oh, do not call paint the image. It is only one shade in the image, while the strength and heart is the picture, which is also the immaterial thought and secret inscriptions, to which clings paints, or else the paint is removed. And so paint is like the flesh, while the picture is like the bones in a body. For this reason the person not understanding a picture can never add paint. This the elder brother understands and so laughs. Even the best of all images before they appeared on walls were earlier retained in the mind of the artist. They were not born and will not perish. But once paint is applied then the retained mental image is not in a tangible view, and if it should disappear its eternal existence still does not disappear.

Soul: I believe that your word is not false, but for me it is somewhat vague.

Spirit: Attend to the second similarity. Draw a circle, make it of wood or of clay. Then erase it or remove the materials from which it was made. Now tell me: Was the circle destroyed?

Soul: The drawing, wood and clay perished.

Spirit: Your conclusion is correct. What perished is obvious, it is the visible, but the intangible and existent circle resides in the treasures of the mind. Since it is something un-manufactured, then it cannot perish. The material circle can, but to say it directly, it is just a shadow of the true circle and causes it to materialize.

Soul: What is the vein of your speech?

Spirit: In order to understand in every manner the 2 essences: the divine and the material.

Soul: And to where will these understandings lead us?

Spirit: There, to the place where nothing can perish, but only where the shadow can be lost.

Soul: Where will this further take us?

Spirit: Nowhere! Except to fearlessness, contentment, hope, ambiance, joy and a clear sky to enjoy that heartfelt peace that Paul says transcends every mind. Ponder in your body what we discussed about the images and circle. Count all the world's nature as paint. But the eternal measure and omnipresent hands of God support the entire wall, like the flesh that is clinging to bones, and He resides as the head, while beyond His inconsistent shade is the tree of eternal life.

It is not regarding the actual – the apparent – bones and hands that the Bible is looking at in the words, "Not a bone of his will be broken."[278] "Do not fear, Jacob. Behold on my palms I have inscribed your walls."[279] And the ancient Plato was able to guess this when he said, "God measures the earth." My soul, do not be of the number of those who consider their substance as perfect. They do not confess the substance of God. They remove the strength and honor, existence and glory from the immaterial and good spirit, and in its place venerate the dead and coarse elements. This is what this signifies: to condemn and sentence to death the author of eternal life and the provider of the life of all creation in general. God – it is apparent – cannot be killed. But their iniquitous thought places God's virtue as their personal issue. Then they have removed life and strength from God, and have assigned Him to a state of decay. And when they have assigned life to decay so they have removed it from God. Here is the judgment where the slave now reigns over the master. Just ask the murderer Barabbas about himself.

Plato calls vile and sitting in a dark pit and hell such patricides and blind people who sense the shades, seeing only a dark shadow and not considering anything as essential truth, except what they can feel and can grab into their hands. This is the source of godlessness and the ruin of the heart's city. The vileness that slithers along and eats the dirt that sticks to its stomach has become mud itself and dust that is scattered by wind. The person whose heart clings to the Lord is one with Him in spirit and can boast with Isaiah, "I am God's. The portion of the pious is the right one. We will not fall, but all those living on earth will fall."

All 3 worlds consist of solely 2 essential substances that are called material and form. Plato calls these forms ideas, which are also visions, apparitions and images. They are the original worlds, the un-manufactured secret ties, the passing shadow, or material, the containment. In the large and in the

---

[278] John 19:36
[279] Is 49:16

	small worlds the substantial view provides knowledge about the forms that are hidden beneath him, or the eternal images. So it is in the symbolic or Biblical world, the gathering of creatures is composed of material. But the substance of God, wherever it leads creation with its banner, is a form. Because in this world there is material and form, which is also flesh and spirit, shadow and truth, death and life. For example, the figure cast by the sun is material or a shadow. But since it signifies placing your residence in the sun,[280] for this reason the second thought is form and spirit, as if a second sun in the sun. Just as 2 fragrances evolve from 2 flowers, so from 2 substances are 2 thoughts and 2 hearts: the perishable and imperishable, the clean and unclean, the dead and the alive. O, my soul! Can we boast of this and sing, "We are the fragrance of Christ."[281]

Soul: O, my spirit. Gracious is the soul. At least they can say this about us, "We flow in the vein of the myrrh's aroma." Finally, teach me, what does the seven-candle lamp signify?

Spirit: This signifies the Biblical heptad, within which the entire symbolic world is created.

Soul: What is it that I am hearing? You have related something to me marvelous and unknown.

Spirit: I already said that the figure caused by the sun is material and shadow: 7 days and 7 suns. An eyeball resides in each sun: the second is a beautiful little sun. These little suns from behind their shadows shine with eternal light, just as burning oil shines from its lamps.

Soul: O, the divine! O, the beloved! O, the sweetest little sun! Also tell me: what are the Cherubim?

Spirit: The heptad and Cherubim are the chariots and thrones: all the same.

Soul: Why are the Cherubim – thrones?

Spirit: The sun is the temple and eternal chamber, while in the rooms are chairs where they rest. The chariot is the movable house. Know that the sun is a fiery sphere and does not stand on

---

[280] Ps 19:4 according to the LXX.
[281] 2 Cor 2:15

something, but the sphere consists of many circles as if from wheels. For the sun is not only a chamber and eternally-migrating Abrahamic tent, but a chariot serving our imperishable Elijah who can carry our eternal little sun. These sun-filled rests,[282] also known as chambers and eternal rests, are also named a heptad of cows or calves, and a heptad of ears of wheat,[283] while with Zechariah they are a heptad of eyes.[284] He opens these blind and guessing eyes sitting on the Cherubim when from the eternal pupils [of their eyes], a shine begins with the imperishable light of the resurrection, just as little suns do from suns.

Soul: Another item: the Cherubim's shadow, what is it?

Spirit: Shadow, shade, paint, outline, clothes, mask dragging after itself its form. Its idea, its picture, is its eternity; all of this is the Cherubim and shadow together, which is the superficial dead.

Soul: Why did Ezekiel attribute to all of them wings, so they would fly through the sky above the eagles, bulls and cows?

Spirit: So that the cart would fly toward one principle, meaning, toward the little sun. He did not assign this attribute, but noticed that they were all winged.

Soul: What do the wings signify?

Spirit: The second and eternal thoughts flying from death to life, from material to form. This is for you the Passover, meaning the transfer. O, my soul! Can you from dead creation and from the Cherubim's shadows be transferred to your Lord and to the materialization of your form? Love is as strong as death. Its wings are the wings of fire.

Soul: O, my father! It is difficult to tear the heart from the gummy mud of the elements. Yes, difficult. I saw a drawn image of a winged young man. He is attempting to fly into heaven but his foot is secured with a chain to the earth's sphere and it interferes. Who shall give to me wings?[285] My heavenly father, to ameliorate my sorrow continue with your delightful

---

[282] that is, Sabbaths.
[283] Gen 41:2, 5
[284] Zech 4:10
[285] Ps 55:6

	conversation. Disclose to me why David wanted these wings. Did you not say that only the Cherubim are the sun?
Spirit:	The sun is the archetype, meaning the initial and primary figure, while its copies and reproductions are innumerable, filling the entire Bible. Such a figure is called an antitype or pre-figure, meaning something installed in place of the primary figure. But all of them, as if to their source, flow toward the sun. Such pre-figures are for example: the prison and Joseph; the basket and Moses; the den and Daniel; Delilah and Samson, meaning the sun; skin and Job; manger and child; coffin and resurrection; chains and Peter; basket and Paul; wife and family; Goliath and David; Eve and Adam; Abraham's shade and the guests; the ark and Noah; the well and Jeremiah; the sea and Israel. All of these are like the sun and little sun, like the snake and God. More beautiful than all of them and mother of others is the figure of the sun. It is first blessed and sanctified on the rest of God. "And God blessed the 7th day." For this reason other creatures that serve as a pre-figure are placed in relation to the sun; all of its existence developed during the days of the radiant heptad, since all creation was born during it, although [the heptad] was created before any of it.

Let there be light, and there was light. Light, morning, day, always near the rays, while the rays are near the sun. And so it is not amazing that David, discovering the Cherubim as a copy, wants wings, having the same strength and thoughts with the heptad. He meditated on the initial days and remembered the eternal years and learned from them.

He provides an interpretation applying to all created beings and the bright light of the heptad. These are the 7 eyes of the Lord that watch over all the earth. When they are blind, then the entire Bible is darkness and Sodom. David learned from it. Seven suns are there while David has the eyes. A sun travels while resting upon another sun. And so with David, he endured patiently; rising he arose. "I will exalt you Lord, just as you have raised me." The sun is a setting shadow, but its strength and existence resides in its little sun. And David's eyes are a vanishing dust, but its shadow flows there, so it can be transformed into an eternal pupil of the eye, into the second reason and into the life-providing word of God. My eyes have vanished in your word.

The Cherubim are Zechariah. And he views the heptad and what it signifies, thinking, "He remembered the eternal years. He saw it," cries Zechariah, "and behold a lamp entirely of gold." What direction a person looks, there he goes. To the eternal years! The road for him is in that direction! He flies toward the bright heptad, soaring with eagle's wings. And where are his wings? Here they are, said the Angel to me, who was speaking with me. His wings are within him. His heart has wings. Love is strong like death. Its wings are the wings of fire.

The Cherubim are predecessors. He was a bright and burning lamp.[286] 'Was' does not signify that he 'was' but that he was made and created to be a lamp. Some stars are attractive and a pseudo-dawn, but do not shine. John was the true dawn.

Soul: Please heavenly father, tell me what the pseudo-dawn signifies. I burn and am fervent to know.

Spirit: The pseudo-dawns are the same as pseudo-cherubim.

Soul: So where are they to be found? I do not understand this at all. Disclose it!

Spirit: My beloved friend. The apostle Jude, he is the one to disclose it to you. Here are your pseudo-cherubim, here are your pseudo-dawns. Angels that did not preserve their dignity, wandering stars, bodily people, that is egoistic or bestial, not possessing the imperishable spirit.[287] To say this in short, they have gone astray from the radiant heptad, which is the harbor for all, and which is also the meaning of 'not preserving their dignity.' God, principle, eternity, light, is all the same. This light lighted its residence during the heptad; the heptad is the scroll of the book. "In the scroll of the book it is written of

---

[286] John 5:35
[287] Jude 6, 13

me," says Christ.[288] The principle and the scroll are the same. My Jude shines with his word in this place, "Angels not preserving their dignity, wandering stars for whom the gloom and darkness is reserved forever." These are the 7 Lucifers who were thrown from heaven. Dawn – in Latin, Lucifer – is the light bearer, or the one who leads the day after him. The dawn is the predecessor of the sun and the harbinger of the day. Look! Behold the beauty of the dawn. In the morning John saw Jesus walking toward him and said, "Behold God's lamb."[289] O, our beloved dawn, where is your day for us? Give it to us! Know that you are not an enchanting star fallen in love with the darkness. The abominable night has already died for us.

This is the person who is to follow me, who was ahead of me. And so the son of Zechariah is a lamp a candle burning and shining, filled with holy oil and created as a eye having a pupil encased within it. Among the ancient people, a candle, lamp and eye of the world was called the sun. But he was not that light, but testified to the light. My daughter, here is the true Cherubim for you. And this is why you see its winged image in the temples.

Soul: O, my most valuable Cherubim John [the Baptizer]. I thank you heavenly Father for him. Are Luke and Cleopas not also Cherubim? I heard yesterday in the temple about their travel and much enjoyed it. If they were not also Cherubim, then what are Cherubim? I was very happy.

Spirit: It is because they were on a Sabbath day's journey. It is only obvious that these travelers already had on their mind the radiant Sabbath heptad. On the Sabbath they broke their bread for themselves the hungry, opened their sightless eyes, or to say more correctly, taking their Sabbath rest in the sun who is exiting its chamber. Their eyes were opened. This groom assigned them other wings. Its wings are wings of fire. He gave food and taste to these tasteless blockheads, but it occurred along the road and by understanding the Sabbath.

---

[288] Heb 10:7
[289] John 1:29

	But my foot travelers, attaching wings to themselves and transforming themselves from slithering and dirt-eating snakes into winged eagles, follow Isaiah's words, "They who are patient for the Lord will renew in strength and accept wings like the eagle."[290] They cried with immense joy, "Did not our hearts burn within us when he spoke to us on the road?"[291] This actual means that he fervently motivated them to fly into heaven, from death to life, instilling in them taste and the light of the radiant heptad.
Soul:	Now I have understood. The little such, as though from its most radiant chamber, shining from the grave, provided them wings and opened for them their eyes, so that the Cherubim's shadow would not shade them on the road of sinners, but bypassing this shadow, they would be exalted to their sole invisible form. And then he became invisible to them.
Spirit:	O, my soul. This mercy did not only pertain to Cleopas. The radiant heptad is the mountain of God where He is pleased to reside. Mary is arriving here with diligence and greets Elizabeth.[292] All the families and tribes of Israel ascend there.[293] The blind, crippled and dumb run here. Here friendship and company invite the wolf and the lamb, and the lynx and the kid, the lion and the calf, the asp with a child; and they create seeing wings just as those of the Cherubim,[294] flying toward their ruler, and there is only one, the King. All will arise and he will be God in every manner for all of them. It will only be difficult for these mountains to play, to skip along, to scoop sweetness, to rise and breed as healthy calves. Arise, let us go unto the mountain of the Lord.
Soul:	I read at some time that deer and mountain goats cannot breed on these mountains.
Spirit:	This, my soul, can be concluded with a discussion on God, but it is insufficient with the nature of creatures. In the symbolic world, in which the Bible appears, where the word

---

[290] Is 40:31
[291] Luke 24:32
[292] Luke 1:39-40
[293] Ps 122:4
[294] Rev 4:6

is located regarding the sole God, it leads us to understand this; but this matter in our great world is just a fable. All is possible in God and from God; but not from creation or in creation. These figurative mountains are the suns. They are the refuge for such deer as was David, and of him was the word spoken, "The crippled will skip like a deer."[295]

David discards his old horns on these mountains, and new ones grow in their place, "There I will return the horn of David."[296] This is where the crippled person healed by Peter skips,[297] and the inspired word that proceeded from him, Tabitha, meaning a mountain goat.[298] Upon these hills the young deer skips and runs, the brother and groom of Solomon's bride. Here she and her brother come, "Unveil to me your face, where it is you rest." The answer, "In midday, in the sun." The entire host of Angels also sings that only the eternal thoughts and glory of God reside in these high places and the celestial mountains. Glory to God in the highest! And then the entire promised Biblical land – the world – will be in calm and eternal friendship. Just as it says in the book of [Joshua son of] Nun, The land rested from war.[299] The shepherds hurry here. Let us cross to Bethlehem. There your mother gave birth to you.[300]

The magi travel here following the star. They saw, they saw his star in the east. They cry with Zechariah, Behold I saw a lamp. But the east without a sun is nowhere to be found. I stood high where the child was standing.

There is no rest, not only for deer, but all for stars, except for this mountain. All creation sighs wanting to be clothed in the heavenly residence. Magdalena also, seeking her joy and comfort, very early arrives at the sepulcher. It is impossible for the rock over this sepulcher to be the same one that Jacob rested on when he saw his ladder. Heed and notice, my

---

[295] Is 35:6
[296] Amos 9:11
[297] Acts 3:8
[298] Acts 9:36
[299] Josh 11:23
[300] Gen 48:7

daughter, that with Magdalena the sunrise and profound morning is remembered, while with Jacob it is the sun. Do you sense that this rock, as if it was morning, even just a little bit penetrates from the darkness? It enigmatically portrays the rocky mountain of God and His most radiant chamber – the sun. You are very much in error my little dove when you do not think that this sepulcher is anything else other than only that cave that is hewn into the womb of the rocky mountain where wisdom rests.

Now learn and believe and know that the land is the Lord's and all that resides in it, and all of it travels to the mountain of God, in whose womb is found the sweet paradise and eternal life that is heretofore hidden, while the day breathes and the Cherubim's shadow stirs. One light and day. He breathed on them and said, "Accept the Holy Spirit."[301] They all ascend to God through this divine mountain, as if by a ladder. This is none other than the house of God and these are the gates of heaven.[302]

Soul: Enoch was no longer found among the living. Elijah was taken by a whirlwind. The prophet Habakkuk was taken by the hair by an Angel,[303] and Phillip likewise disappeared. Paul as a person was raptured to the 3rd heaven. And all of this seems to me to be hard and hungry. Now in this hardness I have found with Samuel some delightful and sweet food. Your speech regarding the Cherubim and the marvelous mountain has sweetened me. Not only the miracle-working mountain, not only Elijah, but the oxen and the skipping mountain, and the mountains possessing wings, and the trees. Is not all of this our mother Zion and does not Isaiah's song pertain to her? "God will provide rest on this mountain, they will drink wine, joy will overflow on this mountain, they will smear myrrh on this mountain."[304]

Spirit: Have you guessed with Samson his riddle? This is the capital city Zion, who is the mother of us all, crying to all of us, "I

---

[301] John 20:22
[302] Gen 28:17
[303] Bel and the Dragon 36 (Dan 14:36, LXX)
[304] Is 25:6

will give to you my breasts." Watch her, my sister. Where are the 12 disciples going? Is not their brother and friend the beautiful Jacob leading them upon the mountain of Galilee, after leaving the prison as if from a bright hall? Upon the mountain with his brother he rejoices, exults, blesses and comforts with the hope of the Holy Spirit that wants to comfort them. In this chamber are the sacraments and fragrance of the dinner that is breathing with immortality and assurance of Thomas. In this room is the wind and noise from the wings of the paraclete. In this temple foreign languages and the hope of perfection are poured. Children of Zion rejoice, for I have provided you the food of virtue. And Stephan, is he not a Cherubim? Does he not gaze at the mountains? Behold I see the heavens opening! And Paul? Does he not raise his eyes to the mountains with David? I raised my eyes to the mountains and looked and behold a man. His body was like the [gold of] Tarshish. And was not Paul the same? "I know a man.[305] Meditate on the celestial."[306] How his beauty will be exalted. This is just a small number of Cherubim that surround the Lord of glory. And does not the wind and noise of eagle's wings breathe into your ears my beloved, those that carry the woman of the Apocalypse with her beautiful son?[307] Its silver wings soar high! And it desires to hide from the pursuing snake in the holy mountains. And I will fly and I will rest. O, prudent mother, the un-brided bride, there is no peace for you on earth. I beseech you, hurry with your beloved child, to the mountains of your eternal Sabbath. Assuredly you will be satisfied with a resting place on the 7 hills, as Noah's dove or as the swallow fleeing the winter frost, flying from the northern regions through the Black Sea to the Pontus to the south, singing this song, "There is no rest for me here." Who shall cross to the other side of the sea and acquire wisdom? It is only I until I cross.

---

[305] 2 Cor 12:2
[306] Phil 3:1
[307] Rev 12:14

The radiant heptad is the day of the Lord, a calm mid-day, a flowering spring, eternal summer, a good era, for all a resurrection, enlightenment and sanctification. "All eyes depend upon You and You give them food at the proper time.[308] Receive the Holy Spirit."

Chapter 3: God's Power is Tested in Certain Places in the Bible

Soul: O, beloved father, I cannot remove from my memory the radiant heptad and the Cherubim's shade. Light, warmth, cool shade, food, juice that will satisfy to eternity, living involvements, a firm hope of comfort – all of this I find for myself in its radiant chambers and upon the beautiful mountains. I love Israel as it sucks on the rock of this mountain. And is this not the manner to learn of the divine shrine? But this spectacle is dear to me and also pitiful: a woman with her beautiful son soaring through the air, fleeing from a pursuing snake. O, abomination! Right behind the divine bride the vile thing vomits bitter waters consisting of its vomit.[309] Tell me my father, what use is it for the dragon to drown the child?

Spirit: The advantage is that having drowned this bride with her child, then it will be easy to cover the entire world with a flood, while God will cleanse it from the water.

Soul: From where did he acquire this malicious and arrogant attitude toward the Supreme?

Spirit: Why are you asking this? The flesh by nature is hostile toward the spirit.

Soul: So does this Satan reject the flood that occurred during Noah's days.

Spirit: Without doubt, that which occurred during Noah's era.

Soul: What is this wife clothed in the sun?

Spirit: I am sure you can guess that it stands over the figure of the sun and is a copy of it.

---

[308] Ps 145:15
[309] Rev 12:15

Soul:	Of course. This snake is the one who whispered to Eve, that as if the fatal tree had good fruit.
Spirit:	This is the very one. Then when he squashed the seed of the woman and drowned the heir of these promises, "I will give to you and to your seed another land." Then it was easy to bring a curse upon the land and its containments, and subsequently it was covered with its bitter waters, but it is easier said with David, it is a flood of the snake's words and flattering tongue. Then everywhere began an evil era, foreign darkness, decay and vomit, the growth of his fatal fruit, which are only to him tasteful. The beautiful radiant rainbow was not visible any more in the clouds, neither any happy or enjoyable scene in the sky, or the pleasant eternal opportue year of which the un-brided bride speaks.
	Winter has passed, the rain has ended, flowers have appeared in the ground, it is the time to cut the ripe clusters off the vine.
Soul:	I would like to know my heavenly father, and ask that you open this to me – I am not apologizing – what does this snake directly and exactly signify? If in the figurative Bible every breathing entity and all creation of this world is gathered for the composition of its system, to be found in its figure, for this reason it must be a figure that signifies something distinctly. So it is written in this sacred world that with other creatures the reptiles also laud the Lord. But how can a voiceless creature give praise to Him? He is only able to gesture with his body and for you to guess since he is silent, and wearing colors, to try to convey a meaning of God to you. In no other manner can the voiceless heavens declare the glory of God, since they are silent. However, His most kind-hearted providence as a trumpet preaches it in His world in a clandestine manner. Teach me holy Sovereign, what this snake signifies. And this seems to me ignorant nonsense, to consider both floods as the same: the snake's and God's. My heart cannot contain all of this.
Spirit:	Well my soul, arise! Let us teach and together we will learn. What is sweeter, except to follow the counsel of the son of

Sirach, to learn holiness in your intellect. "Blessed is the man who dies in wisdom and who has learned holiness in his intellect." But do not hurry my beloved. Do not be naive and do not consider it enough when you reach what is not understandable to you. Remember that the figurative world is woven from riddles and sealed as mysteries in a book. Your thoughts need to be involved in this mental paradise. But do not discern this manner naively in any place. Have you ever heard that the verifiers existing from antiquity eternally in the past created the snake as a figure? The snake was a subtle icon regarding the knowledge of God.

Soul: I have heard. It is written that he slithers, and sometimes will bite his tail and rolls in a circle.[310] But why is such a figure created?

Spirit: Because the subtle one becomes a ring, so that you cannot decipher the location of his head when you think about it. So does eternity exist everywhere, but at the same time it is nowhere, because it is invisible, sealing its hypostasis. Similar to it is the lesson regarding it. So its convolution and ring are the icons of eternity and the mysterious hoops of the divine lessons. Other than this he has a perspicacious stare that is apparent from his name. The Greek work *derko* means to see; so dragon means to see; the dragon had the ability to see beforehand, meaning a prognosticator. There is nothing more difficult than to perceive the future having your eye dirtied with mud. If you have chewed and felt taste in the following words, "The word was toward God and God was the word,"[311] then understand that the Bible – all of its figurative word in its vision of eternal expansion – has become God Himself. "And God was the word," in the same manner that an image on a gold coin also becomes golden. Now no longer hesitating I will say that the Bible is God and is the snake.

Soul: O, father. What I hear is strange and unexpected.

---

[310] during his era, people believed this.
[311] John 1:2

Spirit:	Its head is a heptad. Here for you is Daniel's seven-headed dragon.[312] Stop being amazed at the flood mentioned above and do not say, "My heart cannot contain all of this."
Soul:	So is the sun the snake?
Spirit:	Of course. It has the head of a snake, while the face of God.
Soul:	And all the other archetypes are snakes?
Spirit:	Without doubt. They are the trunk of its body and its tail, while having divine feet and footstool. Its throne is heaven and the sun.
Soul:	Now I see many snakes everywhere.
Spirit:	For God, a 1,000 years is as one day, and 1,000 prefigures fit into one day's sun, while one [sun] represents a 1,000 of them. Just as the snake weaves itself into various hoops in the same place, and it appears there was a change, so does the Bible present various narratives and sermons, but all of them rotate around one focal point, just as a wheel rotates around its center. "The snake was the subtlest." The figure of the snake was made as the wisest of all beasts, which is very proper of the life-providing book of eternity and power of God. This snake you created so you can revile it.
Soul:	How is this? The Bible is both God and the snake.
Spirit:	And why not? It is definitely flesh and spirit, rebellion and wisdom, sea and haven, flood and ark. Do not be stupid and inert! Think agilely. And it is obvious that you already heard that all worlds consist of 2 substances: badness and goodness. Why is this snake extremely frightening to you? It is not always harmful and detrimental, but on occasion is attractive and useful. If it whispered to Eve in a satanic manner, perhaps it heralded good news to Mary in an archangelic manner.
Soul:	Why then all these ages and in nations is the snake discredited, spit upon and disdained?
Spirit:	Not amazing. It threatens them with a flood. It was created to be discredited and is worthy of it.
Soul:	So it is worthy of this?

---

[312] Dan 7:6

Spirit:	Because in many places it conducts itself shamefully and harmfully, and lies without any feelings of guilt. It also spreads false gossip and fables and defames people.
Soul:	So where does it lie? Show me even one place.
Spirit:	I will show you. And if I were to number all of its lies it would take me 6 months to do it. It is a plague upon you standing at the very threshold lying. In the beginning God created heaven and earth.
Soul:	My God! Is this also a lie?
Spirit:	It is the greatest Creatian[313] and Scythian lie. As long as there is an apple tree, so long will there be its shadow. The shadow signifies a small area, as large as the shadow from the sun on the apple tree. But the tree of eternity is always green, and its shade is not limited by time or by place. This world and all world, if there are an infinite number of them, are the shadow of God. It disappears from view in part, does not remain constantly and in various forms changes appearance, however it never is distinct from the tree of life. And enlightened people have long ago stated such news. The thing exists forever, meaning that it fills all place and time. Only an infantile mind can say that the world, as great as the idol or Goliath, did not exist at some time or cannot exist. This infantile falsity entered during the 10th century after Christ and shook the Christian world so hard that everybody felt the catastrophe, just as do those escaping a shipwreck after a terrible storm.
	Just imagine my soul, the state of the Christian soul in ancient time due to the snake's torture. It did not just last for 7 days, as a storm at sea, but continued and discarded Christ's philosophy into extreme contempt and discredit, until finally it was revealed that all the gentiles are worthy and right. They ridiculed this Christian insanity and now continue to do so. Even the first day was inconsistent, "Let there be light."
	Where did this light appear if the heavenly lights did not appear until the 4th day? And how can day exist without a sun? Blessed is the continuous nature. All that does exist right

---

[313] Titus 1:12

now was not always sufficient. Such nonsense is vomited through the entire week, as if there was some ecumenical spectator of this miracle-working theater and whether it was light or mushrooms that first were born.[314] Finally the entirety of the divine fabrication of this coarse imbecility is sealed in the words, "He rested from all His works."

As if exhausted he is not capable of creating anything more. And if this statement was not included in the text, then absolutely there would exist among us lions without tails, winged turtles and pigs, rabbits with long tails, cattle with one horn, beautifully voiced quails, smooth hedgehogs, 4-eyed and 4-eared people, virtuous slanderers and instigators, smart idiots and other monsters and retarded, and subsequently Elisha's iron rod floating away, and the philosophical swamp of Europe would be transformed into gold. At the present all of this has settled into God's abyss.

Listen, my soul! Jacob fled from these lies contained in the flood waters of a vomiting spring, as it writes, "Jacob left the cursed well and went to Haran."[315] He went to the place where eternal friendship and virtue sits and judges. Just as God removed His divine indefatigability, so did he adopt what was alien and unrelated, meaning in a human language, "The snake said to the woman."

Soul: I also began to decipher nonsense in this world, "Rested. There was light." This signifies the bright and sunny time. Then as though unconsciously it relates about the sun, that as if it did not earlier exist, but is created anew. If the first day was created clear and bright without a sun, then what need was there to create a sun? This is not a complex lie.

Spirit: O, my soul! Know that to read the Bible literally will lead to a false understanding of it. "The Lord God planted a paradise[316] in Eden in the east." What a mess! So He planted a garden inside a garden? The Hebrew word Eden is the same as garden. So how is a person supposed to be in this garden and

---

[314] The irony is that mushrooms can grow in the absence of light.
[315] Gen 35:27
[316] The Hebrew words rendered as Eden and paradise mean garden.

then look at it to locate it in the east? But it is apparent that just as it has a sun, so it also has an east.

"Cain knew his wife." O, shameless futility! He has forgotten his own tale that only 4 people existed in the world at this time. Where did he acquire a wife for himself, with his mother the only female?

Soul: This also seems like nonsense to me. "God was walking in paradise." How can an entity who is omnipresent change his location?

Spirit: But this slanderer will whisper to you my little dove, that God weeps, angers, sleeps, repents. "God thought and reconsidered creating humans."[317] Then he will tell you that people are converted into a salt pillar, ascend to planets, ride on chariots at the bottom of the sea and in the air; that the sun is like a carriage that can stop and reverse its course; that steel floats; rivers reverse their course; city walls collapse from a trumpet sound; mountains skip like lambs; rivers clap their hands; oak trees and fields rejoice; wolves are friends with sheep; dead bones arise; heavenly lights fall like apples from a tree; while buckwheat porridge[318] and quails fall from the clouds; water becomes wine; while the dumb speak after drinking wine and sing beautifully; and other matters. The leopard will lie with the kid, and an ox and bear with them.[319] "O! I know not the snake slithering in the rocks!" cries Solomon.[320] Do you notice that the snake slithers in lies, eats lies, vomits lies. It is obvious that you my soul cannot recognize him. What solidity exists in the following statements of his? "Do not eat any fat or any blood." Then forgetting what was said he says, He fed them with the fat. Drink all that is in it, this is my blood. There is not much flavor in these words: Let the priest remove its memory from the sacrifice. Let the priest remember it on the altar. Let every sacrifice be salted with salt. What flavor is to be found in these unsalted words?

---

[317] Gen 6:6
[318] referring to Manna
[319] Is 11:6-7
[320] Pr 30:19

Churn the milk and butter will surface. If you pick your nose it will bleed. Give to her from the fruit of the lips and her husband will be praised at the city gates. What can be more lean, thin and tasteless than this, "He drinks from the stream along the road: for this reason he will lift your head." What is more shameful and harmful than what occurred with Lot in the cave during his escape? And the following statement is a lie beyond all lies, "You subjected all creation under his feet." Other than a few animals and reptiles how many thousands of tiny insects fly and crawl that suck human blood and eat what people have gained by their sweat and blood. Finally, look my soul! Have pity and sorrow over the infinite number of martyrs deprived of a crown, the unfortunate sufferers who have removed the eye that led them astray, circumcised their foreskins for the heavenly kingdom,[321] voluntarily emasculated themselves,[322] or in great numbers cremated themselves,[323] all because of accepting the deceit caused by the great deceiver. God uses superstition and beliefs to catch these people in secret.

It was superstition that aggravated the kind-hearted Caesar Titus, hearing that it was the Bible that did not allow these people to subject themselves to kings, and so as a result he leveled the walls of Jerusalem with the ground. Look please at the entire earthly sphere and at the entire destitute humanity. Do you see how agonizing and destitute these heresies, arguments, and superstitions are with their diverse and many facets and interpretations acting like floodwaters with its agitation, storm and drowning. But this specific flood is not bestowed upon us from above, but released from the jaws of the infernal snake, vomiting and regurgitating, just as it is written, "The deceitful tongue are the words that drown." Protect me Lord from the wicked person.

---

[321] referring to Jews
[322] referring to the Russian sect of the Skoptzi
[323] referring to Staroveri (Russian Old Believers) who cremated themselves rather than submit to the Imperial government, which they considered antichrist.

Now tell me, my little soul, is not the snake worthy to accept torture, loathe, abuse and worldwide ridicule for such blasphemies, nonsense, plagues? You created it for it to discredit You.

Chapter 6: Regarding the Transformation

Pour upon me Lord, dew from heaven.
Beautiful fruit will I bring to you, as the rose,
The apple of Paradise
From the garden of the Transformation.
The motivated saw Your glory.[324]

All the world sleeps. But yet it does not sleep in such a manner since it says regarding the virtuous. "He shall fall but not be broken." He sleeps deeply, stretched out, as though dead on the ground. But the preceptors who shepherd Israel not only do not awaken him, but caress him, "Sleep, do not fear. This is a good place. What is there to fear?" Saying, Peace, when there is none. O, blessed Peter with your friends! The Lord himself awakens them, "Arise and do not fear!" Peter and those with him were overwhelmed with sleep.

"Arise," he says to them, "Stand from the ground! Then you will no longer fear." Paul in the same manner beats on these dead people, "Arise, sleeper! Stand, you corpse! Resurrect from the dead and Christ will provide you light. As long as you are part of the dirt and not transformed in Christ, you will not see the bright heavenly person." Regarding him the following statement applies, "Awakened they saw his glory."[325]

Tamar, the daughter-in-law of Judah son of Jacob, appeared to him as a prostitute. He did not recognize her because her face was covered. After investigating the situation, he discovered what had occurred and said, "She is more justified than I am."[326] In this manner the sons of Israel were not able to look upon the shining glory of the face of Moses, the man of God. But upon what were they looking? Only upon the veil which shaded the

---

[324] This poem rhymes in the original Russia.
[325] Like 9:32
[326] Gen 38:26

brightness of his eyes. What are you Israel? Truly despicable. You are circumcised in the flesh, but not circumcised in the heart. Darkness has descended upon your eye, and you cannot tolerate looking at the truth. You lie on the ground. You rock with your prostitute and she satisfies you. You turn your eye away from your father – the eye that discredits father and aggravates the old age of your mother. But the eagle's chicks are not seen, so that they can pick from you your unfortunate eye just as Solomon wanted.[327]

So the present contemptible Christianity and with exactly such an eye looks on its leader Christ. Where was he born? Who were his parents? How long did he live in the world? To what age and date? Is it about 2,000 years ago since he departed? O, Christian! You are baptized in the flesh, but your minds are unwashed. Why did you instill your curiosity into such gossip? Why do you not attempt to raise yourself higher? Here you wonder and then fall asleep. You want to build a hut here with Peter? Not knowing what you are saying. Do you not hear what your Moses is saying about this, "The shame of my face was covered, and this is why my brethren cannot see me."[328] I was a stranger to the sons of my mother. Up to this time have you still not guessed that all of this is flesh and gossip and a shade that covers the supreme wisdom of the mountain? Know that at the right time this veil must be all torn. Is this not hypocrisy, attempting to discern the face of the heavens?[329] Here is an evil and promiscuous generation seeking a bodily sign. This is the kvass[330] of the Pharisee's teaching.

So let us listen! Is this what Christ is teaching his beloved disciples in private? How to understand? What is a true person? "What do people consider me to be? Listen Peter! Tell me, what does the riff-raff think about this person? I know that they err. But what do you think?" "You are Christ, son of the living God." Rightly did Peter answer. It is obvious that he was able to penetrate further through the empty bodily veil with his dove's eye. So why did the true son of humanity say to him? "Blessed are you Simon, with this eye you have. It is not looking at flesh and blood, like the understanding of the riff-raff, but circumventing flesh and blood it has

---

[327] Pr 30:17
[328] 2 Cor 3:15
[329] Luke 12:56
[330] A Russian drink made from dry bread, slightly fermented and sometimes mildly alcoholic.

found a different generation, a true generation, Israel's generation, my father's generation which is not dependant on blood or on the lust of the flesh." Listen Christian! Listen with your gentile heart. Will you lie on the ground forever? Will you ever become a man? You will not? Why? Because you are staring at a veil covering the carnal face, while in no manner are you able with your impatient eye to look at the face of the true man of God. You will not be transformed my friend, from the earthly and into the heavenly until you see Christ, until you recognize that he is a true man. Your vision will not penetrate your eye as long as flesh and blood possess your heart. So will it possess it for a long time? Until you recognize that your flesh and blood is dust and futility. This is where your personal opinion has brought you. It is so? Exactly. He will be discarded from his glory.[331]

Deprived of God's glory we have learned to judge our brethren based on the flesh. In the same manner do we look upon Christ. It seems we only notice irrelevant or trivial items concerning him, but do not view his specific person and his glory. It is right what Paul relates, "He will transform our humble body for it to be identical to his body of flesh."[332] I argue not, but do you look upon Christ as does Paul? He boasts, "I no longer know Christ according to the flesh.[333] I know a person who transcended the heavens, created after the likeness of God in virtue and sanctification and truth."[334] Truth was never flesh at any time. Flesh and falsity are one and the same, and the person loving this idol is himself the same. And when flesh is falsity and a vacuum, then it is not a person. Have you heard the book of the generations of the true man, the son of David, the son of Abraham?

Jacob birthed Judah; Judah birthed Perez from Tamar, and etc. Know that this book is an eternal book, God's book, a heavenly book and does not contain anybody in it except for the generations of Israel. "I will not gather their counsels based on blood and will not remember their names."[335] Our Christ was of this generation. Nonetheless, the generation of Israel will not die, just listen to Joel, "When it is morning people strong and many will overflow mountains. There are none similar to them from

---

[331] Is 14:19
[332] Phil 3:21
[333] 2 Cor 5:16
[334] Col 3:10
[335] Ps 16:4

the beginning of time, and there will be none like them for generations of generations until the final years."³³⁶

If it were possible to add something during these future years then they would have their end, but now they are to themselves their own demise in the end. Not an end so that nothing will occur after them, but there will be an end for this entire generation. The remnant does not reside among the gentiles and is not the backbone among creatures. The backbone is God's and the remnant is Israel, and it is only the remnant that will be saved, while the balance will just by-pass all of this. The gentiles will disappear as water that passes along. The remnants of evil will be annihilated.

But listen to Moses the man of God regarding what Joel exactly sings about the generation of Israel. He is a relative of Christ and was with Christ on Tabor discussing the events of his exit, meaning the remnant, discussing, "Blessed are you Israel. Who is like unto you, the generation saved of the Lord? He shall defend his helper. And the sword is your praise." Your enemies will lie to you (meaning they will err and not recognize it), and you will step on their neck.

Do you see that the person who judges Israel by the flesh, looking at the ostensive humility of Christ – not comprehending how his humility raised him supremely high – is an enemy of Christ from the number of those whom Paul calls enemies of Christ's cross. In Moses' words it is called a sword, "The sword is your praise." This is comparable to Jeremiah's flesh that hews, kills and murders, just as a cross does.

Let us retain our eyes discussing the dead and immaterial shadow, and adapt our eyes to the darkness of the flesh, while we raise them slowly to the celestial regions. Let us learn to look upon Israel, that is, upon the true person, circumventing the body's cover. Here we are sleeping on the ground, and Paul awakens us, "Seek what is above you! Philosophize about celestial matters! When Christ appears – your life – the true living person, then you will appear in glory." Also Jeremiah awakens in this manner, "Why are we sitting? Assemble and we will enter the strong cities and prostrate ourselves before the Lord who created us. There and not here, in the elements we looked for peace and no good came."³³⁷

O, true, imperishable God of Israel! Shine with Your light upon us as much as is possible for our eye to tolerate. Let Your face proceed in the

---

³³⁶ Joel 2:2
³³⁷ Jer 8:14-15

light and sensitively be transformed into something new, we will attain supreme joy and even the last hair on our head will attain the resurrection. To You be the glory, and with Your man and with Your holy spirit. Amen.

"Having awakened they saw his glory." So did the raven chirp ascending the mountain, but did not depart, fulfilling what is written, "Where the corpse, there the vultures gather." Birds increase in the land.

Chapter 7: Regarding the Resurrection

> Pour upon me Lord, dew from heaven,
> A beautiful cluster will I bring to you, like the rose.
> Clusters of Paradise,
> From the Garden of Resurrection.[338]
> Let him kiss me with the kisses of his lips.[339]

Beloved students, do not fear! Raise yourself boldly to that face upon which you could not stare on Tabor due to fright. Listen to what is said, "Be courageous. Peace to you. Rejoice."

There you were unable to endure his gaze, but now you will listen to his sweetest words and with his kiss he will confirm with you eternal friendship! Only be capable of drawing near to him. Do not ever forget the person instructing you, the words enlightened by an Angel, "He is not here, he has risen!" These words will easily lead you to this glorious true person. This is your resurrection and life. "Let him kiss me with the kisses of his lips."

Abraham's son Isaac became old and he wanted to die. This is not unusual. His eyes had lost their sight; his eyes vanished as David's into God's word. He could no longer see anything here, in our futile world, preparing for his blessed death, "Blessed are the dead who die in the Lord."[340] He wanted food. His second son satisfied his soul. "Thank you my son! Come close to me," he said. And coming close he kissed him.[341] The fortunate Isaac, under the guise of Esau he found Jacob. And we contrary to this under the diapers of the child of Israel, under the shroud of

---

[338] A poem that rhymes in Russian.
[339] Song 1:2
[340] Rev 14:13
[341] Gen 27:27

Christ, we often find the enemy of Israel – Esau. He is the one who welcomes us and kisses us! What is the reason? We do not think about the manner of searching this and so foolishly seek. Many seek him in the autocratic Caesar Augustus during the era of Tiberius in the possessions of Pilate, and other places. But they continue to seek. Where? Here!

In this world! Among the dead! Please seek more professionally, "He is not here!" Many wander about Jerusalem, the Jordan, Bethlehem, the mountains of Carmel, on Tabor, the hills of Sinai and Athens, smell the regions between the Tigris and Euphrates Rivers. Here he is, of course, they think, "Here, here! Here is Christ! Here! We have found him." They cry to others, "Here is Christ." "I know," cried the Angel, "the crucified Jesus is the Christ. He is not here. No!" Many seek him at the highest reaches of the earth, in majestic homes, with ceremonial pillars, and other places. Many seek with their mouth wide open viewing the clear blue starry outer space, the sun, the moon, the entire Copernican universe. "He is not here!" They seek him in long prayers and liturgies, in fasts, in sacred rites. They seek him in money, in a hundred-year healthy life, in a physical resurrection, in a physical healing of the eyes. "He is not here!" What is the problem? So where is he? Of course he is here. If we were to orate our sermons, learn all the prophetic mysteries, relocated mountains, resurrect the dead, distribute our possessions, torture our bodies with bitter cold, and etc, but the Angel appearing as lightning only cries to them, "He is not here." Of course, he is nowhere to be found if he is not here. So what? Of course my friend, for you he is not here. You do not know him and so cannot see him. Take off your shoes with Moses and discard your stupid Here. Yes! On behalf of the Angel I say to you, "You will find him in the blink of an eye." What remains to be done?

Passover! "Arise Lord, let your enemies be scattered and may all those that hate you flee."[342]

After the defeat of the Amorites the sons of Israel arose against the west. This is not conducive to King Balak. "Behold," he says, " what new and amazing people have migrated here from Egypt, and they overflow the mountains, and even higher than the mountains. What kind of miracle is this?" He sends messengers to the wizard Balaam for him to destroy God's

---

[342] Num 10:35

generation. The messengers arrive and announce the king's will. "Good," says Balaam, "Spend the night here."[343]

Not in vain, my friend, does the Angel not command you to seek here. Do you see that the enemies of God's generation rest in this nest?

Passover! The descendents of Ruben and Gad come to Moses.[344] They ask of him, they do not want him to take them to the other side of the Jordan for settlement. Their side is good ground for cattle grazing, and they have much cattle. Moses yells at them, "Your brethren will go to battle and you will sit here? Now you will change the hearts of the sons of Israel so they will themselves not migrate to the land which the Lord gives them." Because they wanted to remain here the Lord angered at them and swore that they would not enter the land promised to Israel, except Caleb and Joshua son of Nun, calling the people who preferred to remain there those who knew good and evil, as was obviously also the reason Adam was banished from paradise. This is what the cursed nest caused with its Here.

Passover! "If your Lord leads you," says God's man Moses, "into a new location beyond the Jordan, the road to the west of it, a land that is completely different from Egypt, because it is mountainous and level, and what is best of all about it is that the eyes of the Lord your God are upon it from the beginning of the year to the end of the year. So want it! Want it! With destruction destroy all that is pagan and perishable, even to the last hair, except for the first fruits and firstborn of your cattle and sheep. Do not do there," he says, "what you are doing here now. Every person whatever he wants. Otherwise you will not ever enter the rest."

So please, my friend, listen to Moses. My beloved person, true man, friend, brother and close associate, do not seek him here, meaning in the perishing pagan decay. Seek him there on the other side of the Jordan, toward the west, the road toward the sunset. Not here, not today, not now. He is there! There are the first fruits of the dead and all that has decayed.[345] Otherwise you will be kissing some pagan.

Passover! The foolish scribe Shebna sought a person on this side of the Jordan.[346] What did Isaiah the Lord's Angel say to him? This is what. "What are you here, and what do you have here? You have carved for

---

[343] Num 22:19
[344] Num 32
[345] 1 Cor 15:20
[346] Is 22:15-16

yourself a coffin and hewn a tomb for yourself in the heights. Behold the Lord Sabaoth will discard you and erase you and remove your possessions from you and your glorious throne, and will hurl you into a large and immeasurable land and there you will die." Unfortunate scribe. He read the prophets, sought a person, and then he tripped over a corpse and fell himself. Of course he sought a person along with King Balak's messengers, the counsel of destroyers and physical wizards, all of whom were turning to flesh and blood. This is the reason that the blessed Job speaks about such people. "They say to the Lord, Depart from us. We do not want to know your path. Let them be like chaff before the wind or as dust. Let their own eyes watch their own demise. So he is taken away in his coffin and people watch over their graves. The pebbles of the creek become sweet to him."[347] And another Angel wails over them, Micah, "Arise and go, for there is no rest for you here, because the place is unclean. It is decaying."[348] The Lord says to a 3rd Angel, Ezekiel, "Do you see, do you see what they are doing? The crimes of the great house of Israel are conducted here, having departed from my sanctuaries.[349] O, criminal, are you here? What have you done? You have led us away from the living person to dead corpses; from the holy man to perishable wood forms and scarecrows." He pitifully says, "The crimes of my feet will by-pass me." O, his cursed heel has fallen upon us, and not his blessed head so he could kiss us. We only see his heel, the posterity of vipers, the wandering heel.

The person says, "They will settle and hide." So tell me, who will hide you, your treasure? O! Will it be you, he answers, but you do not see how many there are in the house of Israel? In the Sacred Scripture? And what are they creating? They are themselves here, in their coffins, they sit and attempt to drag me and you there; but I have never coexisted with corpses, except my heel. Many are there that fight with me from the heights. My enemies have trampled me. They will protect my heel. They will settle here and hide my resurrection.

Passover! Arise, arise Jerusalem! I am! I am the one who comforts you. Recognize who it is that is Existent.

---

[347] Job 21:14, 18, 32
[348] Micah 2:10
[349] Eze 8:6

Walk through My gates and create a path for My people, and remove the rocks on My roads.[350] And there was a great earthquake. The Angel of the Lord, descending from heaven, approached and pushed the stone aside.[351] Why are you here? You are seeking someone? He is not here! He has risen. Tell us kindly, where is he? The answer: He is not in the realm of the dead. He is always living. You must seek him there, in the realm of the living. And now, why are you here?

Passover! Arise! Arise! Resurrect, Jerusalem! And so it was when Joshua was at Jericho he raised his eyes and saw a person standing in front of him.[352]

So see him! Not in vain does the Angel say, "There you will see him." So where is this? On the other side of the Jordan, at the holy place, and not at a perishable place. In the mountain region, the high, the promised. That is to where he lifted his eyes and saw the man. He recognized him and fell at his master's feet.

Passover! Arise! Arise, Zion. Shake the dust! Abraham lifted his eyes and saw the place from a distance and said to his young men, "Remain here with the donkeys. I and the child will go there."[353] Do you see that even Abraham, having discarded all that is local, found a true person on the mountain? This is what occurred there, "And he saw his day and rejoiced."[354] It is not possible to have any better eyes than Abraham. They alone saw the ram caught by the horns in the garden of Savek.[355]

Passover! Caught by the horns in the garden of Savek. What does Savek signify? Savek signifies brush. But can brush grow on both sides of the Jordan in the presence of the Lord? It alone is consumed entirely by fire and reduces to nothing. But the person Isaac is whole and alive. Yes, and how can he not be whole when God himself defends him? "Do not do anything to him."

It is obvious that it is not brush that remained behind his shoulders. As Isaiah spoke, "Behold all will be consumed by fire as brush."[356] While this will occur to people that are opposite to the brush, "As the new heaven and

---

[350] Is 62:10
[351] Matt 28:2
[352] Josh 5:13
[353] Gen 22:4-5
[354] John 8:56
[355] as in the Hebrew, translated as thicket in English versions, or brush by Skovoroda.
[356] Is 33:12

new earth that I create will continue in My presence, so shall your seed and your name."

This is the person whom the son of Nun saw standing – not falling – but residing eternally in the presence of the Lord. Passover! Arise, arise Jerusalem. The Lord gave a miracle-working iron staff to Moses and sends him to liberate his brethren from Egypt. He orders Aaron to greet Moses. Where does he greet him? Here is where, "Where he met him at the mountain of God. And the 2 kissed."[357]

After the liberation of the Israelite brethren from Egypt Jethro the father-in-law of Moses wanted to see him.[358] He took his daughter the wife of Moses with their 2 sons and traveled to the desert. They arrived and it was reported to Moses.

O, generation blessed by the supreme God. They arrived directly at Mount Horeb. "Moses went to meet his father-in-law and bowed to him and kissed him and they greeted each other and Moses brought them into his tent." Passover! The most cautious Moses would not allow any brush to be brought in from those arriving from the desert land, referring to it as cursed, idolatrous and deceitful for their royal journey. Heed this firmly, firmly, that you eat no blood! Do not eat it! Then matters will go well with you and your offspring forever.[359]

However the present Israel as foolish as was the ancient continues to complain to the Lord. They wanted to eat Egyptian meat, "And the Lord heard and his wrath was provoked, and a fire was incited within him." They said matters went well with them in Egypt.[360] And the Lord said to Moses, "Why are you entangled in this issue? Does not the Lord have meat to provide you other than pagan? When will the hand of the Lord be insufficient? Today you will ascertain if My word will be accomplished or not."

Often due to our senseless stagnation our heart will speak and complain to the Lord. Blah! Is it possible for a person to exist with body, flesh and bones? Blah! What is this! Here is arrogant and insensible brush!

Arise, awaken Zion! What are you weaving? Who is touching your land? Leave it alone the way it is! Just let the Lord give to you His blessed blessing, as Isaiah says, "While your land will be settled anew with many."

---

[357] Ex 4:27
[358] Ex 18:1
[359] Lev 7:26
[360] Ex 16:3

However you need to know this, that any lie or superstition or vanity taken from the land in which you are now residing will not be accepted in the foundation of God's land. This is why there it is written, "You will not see anything like this, resolved and created, Jerusalem to be a praise in the earth."[361] You must only strive for God's virtue to shine out of your fraudulent land. Pray so you will be able to attain the blessed 3rd day, the radiant resurrection, when God's land will produce blades of grass. Do you really think that it is only your land alone, and it is impossible for another to replace it? If so, then remain here with your own! Eat it with the cursed snake, chew it all the days of your life, without the life of God, without eternal life. If you opinionate and say in your heart that the Lord does not have His own, whether it be land or flesh or blood or bones, or anything, you will not hear the most blessed voice, "Behold, now this is bone of my bones."[362]

Arise! Arise Jerusalem! Listen with your other ears regarding the other flesh! Do you hear this? "And my flesh will flourish."[363] Do you hear about other bones? "The humble bones will rejoice.[364] My bones will not be hid from You, which You have created in secret."[365] Listen to Solomon, "Healing for your bones."[366] In the Hebrew Bible, "Understand the attachment of the new to the old." Listen to Isaiah, "Your bones will grow like the grass and fatten and inherit the generation of generations."[367] Do you see this? These bones are not those that will decay in the grave. They are in the presence of God. And those are there.

"And I heard a voice," cries Ezekiel, "When I was to prophesy. And behold quaking! And bones assembled: bones to bone, each to its ligament. And I saw and behold there appeared tendons and flesh covered them."[368] So what is this new generation upon Your mountains? Beyond the sorrow of any decay. Is not this an attachment? Cannot life become attached to something that is dead? And resurrection attached to your grave? Is this not a new creation? "I create and who will revert it?"

---

[361] Is 62:7
[362] Gen 2:23
[363] Ps 72:7 in the Russian (71:7): My righteous person will flourish.
[364] Ps 51:8
[365] Ps 139:15
[366] Pr 15:24
[367] Is 66:14
[368] Exe 37

Is not this a confirmation? "Behold I prepare for you the carbuncle, jewels, and sapphire as your foundation, and will reward you using virtue."[369]

Listen and understand this today that Joel is not weaving some nonsense for you, but is evangelizing this Orpheus, the resurrection. Here, "When it is morning people strong and many will overflow mountains. There are none similar to them from the beginning of time. The land ahead of them is like the paradise of sweetness, but what is behind them is a field of ruin. They appeared as horses, as the sound of chariots, they descended from the mountains tops. As warriors they charge and as valiant men they scale the walls. And not one of them will slow before his brother. The cities are taken, they run on the walls, and enter the houses, and crawl through the windows as thieves. Blow the trumpet! Preach healing."[370]

So are you afraid of medicine? Just allow God's generation to enter your land. Do not be a Balak! Pease do not be afraid! Every one will take half an apartment from their brother, and without any offence. "The Lord's spirit is upon me. To give glory in Zion to the weeping instead of ashes."[371] Is any offense to be taken here? Accept, you destitute person, glory instead of mud!

"And the sons of foreigners will build your walls, and in place of copper they will bring you gold. In place of iron they will bring you silver. And in place of wood they will bring you copper. And in place of stones, iron.[372] I will open your graves and lead you out.[373] So you will inherit the land a second time and eternal joy will rest over your heads.[374] Shine, shine, Jerusalem. Behold darkness covers the land and gloom over the gentiles. Upon you the Lord has appeared and His glory upon you is visible.[375] Let him kiss me with the kisses of his lips."

---

[369] Is 54:12
[370] Joel 2:2-9
[371] Is 61:1
[372] Is 60:17
[373] Eze 37:13
[374] Is 61:7 as in the LXX.
[375] Is 60:1-2

Erodi,[376] having evangelized regarding the resurrection at the conclusion of autumn, has arisen and together with a raven has not ceased to sign this song, "Behold I am with you all the days, to the end of time."[377]

Leave and depart, sorrowful night! The sun is rising, bringing light, bringing light, birthing joy. Depart away flooding night, far away.

End.

---

[376] A word formed by Skovoroda from the Greek meaning Beloved of God.
[377] Matt 28:20

A SYMPHONY CALLED THE BOOK ACHSAH, REGARDING COMPREHENDING YOUR PERSONAL SELF

Born the year 1767.

My beloved Mikhail [Kovalinski]!

About 7 miles from the city Kharkov I wrote this book in the forests of Zembrovski. The spirit ordered me, "Let it be called Achsah." Achsah, meaning beautiful, was the daughter of Caleb, who entered the promised land. He gives her as a wife to his nephew, because he acquired the city Arba.[378] This city, which is otherwise called Hebron, also means friendship and the literary city. This is God's wisdom hidden in the depths of the Bible. All that seek its wisdom are the same as having joy with their bride, as Isaiah's words, "Just as a groom rejoices over his bride, so will the Lord rejoice over you."[379]

Our heart that recognizes this is like the dove. This dove evolves from Noah's ark, from the Bible, pure – as a chaste dove. Here is the bride. Here is the most pleasant and sole sacrifice to God! Here is the pair of doves! This is the fragrant smell unto the Lord! Here is the pinnacle of bliss! This fragrance will conclude this book. What does it mean to break the wings of a dove? The same as breaking horns. "I will break the horns of the sinful." Horns, nails, hair, wings, all evolve from the body, as all of them are in the body. Is there is difference between being in the body and from the body? What is it? Thought! A pure thought is the hair upon the imperishable head, the horn and rays upon Moses' head. The horn and Jeremiah's nail

---

[378] Josh 14:16-17
[379] Is 61:10

like diamond are the same, that is, pure thought. The dove's wings, easily floating in eternity, are here, "The thoughts of his heart endure for generations and generations." Break the wings – comprehend: rend your hearts. Then you will break the bad wings and your dove – the Bible. Here is the pair! Let them sever the head of the dove. Let them separate the throat with the wings. This is what it is, "God separated the water from the water." What is this water if not a river, speech, thought, word, throat, heart, feathers? Every figure, and much more the sun, is a thought; it is something that is preached to us. If the sun exists then there is a thought! It is the dove. Where is it flying? To eternity. "I will fly and rest." Here eternity is called the east. What is above it? East is its name. Cast it here! Cast the throat and feathers to the east. Meditate on the celestial! Ascend high. Sacrifice the feathers to God. Flap above the dust and in place of dust.

In place of the flesh turn your sorrows to the Lord, and your decay, your flesh, something that is not yours. Let your eyes as the dove's be above the dust in another place far from the dust, because all is dust except eternity. So then you will squeeze blood from the sun. Once knowing the truth the sun will turn into blood for you. What if all of this if not flesh, blood and dust? And just as you remove bloody wings from your heart, so should you separate your cattle. Your body is your sorrowful portion – this is you! Give place for something in place of your dust. Listen! In every place give a place to your God! In your hair – His hair; in your stomach– His stomach; in your bones – His bones. Share with Him the last of your crumbs, as did the King of Sodom with Abraham. Then the following will occur, "Your wife – wisdom – will be as a fruitful vine, in all the corners of your house."[380] So will your years grow, your children! New veins! New flesh and bone! While your supreme dining table is your heart.

Grigori Skovoroda

---

[380] Ps 128:3

Prologue to this book:

The earth was unseen and darkness was over the abyss.[381]

When you will be known in the ten-thousands of your miracles and your virtue in the forgotten land.[382]

His miracles will be remembered, that is, the resolutions of His lips.[383]

My bones are not hidden from you, which you created in secret.[384]

The spirit tests all things, even the depths of God.[385]

Symphony:

With the following verse: If you do not know this yet, good wife, go to the flocks and feed your goats at the huts of the shepherds. Song of Songs.[386]

Persons in the discussion:
Pamba, Anton, Luke, Konon, Filon, Kvadrat, Friend.

Pamba: What a beautiful morning, what a bright Sunday. This is a joyful garden, with new leaves appearing. We can have here a heavenly discussion with the presence of the Sacred Bible, one that is sanctified and decorated with its pictures. Does not all of this excite us to have a discussion? Listen you gathered here, the new Israel, beloved brethren! Your presence is enlivening for me. I find myself surrounded by how many honorable and considerate hearts. I can say with the beloved David, that my heart is warmed within me.

Anton: But what is this picture you speak of? Listen, Luke![387]

Luke: The royal daughter with her maids – do you see this – have found a child floating in a box.

---
[381] Gen 1:2
[382] Ps 88:12
[383] Ps 105:5
[384] Ps 139:15
[385] 1 Cor 2:10
[386] Song 1:8
[387] The conversation starts with the persons looking at 2 pictures in the Bible: Moses found in the Nile River, and Joshua, Caleb and Achsah near Hebron.

Anton:	Yes, yes, yes. The man of God Moses. But I do not understand these 2 pictures.
Luke:	I do not know what the 2 cities are atop the highest mountains.
Pamba:	Here is the city Hebron,
Anton:	What is Hebron?
Pamba:	Joshua son of Nun blessed Caleb using it, having given it to him as an inheritance. He otherwise called it Arba, while the other was Debir. From ancient times it was called the city of teaching, or the literary city.
Luke:	And who are these 2 armed men and between them a woman is standing?
Pamba:	This is the man of God Caleb. He is giving his daughter, the beautiful Achsah, as a wife to his nephew because he was able to conquer the city Debir. This entire history is noted in Joshua son of Nun chapters 14 and 15.
Anton:	What a beautiful picture!
Pamba:	But you are only looking at its surface. But if you were to see the hidden thoughts inside of it and if you were of the number of God's holy people, examples of those who can view events and comprehend the strength in such pictures – the intent, end and limits – of course you would not hesitate to say with David in the presence of the ark, and there would occur with you the very same as with the queen who is mentioned in Kings, "The queen of Sheba came and saw all the wisdom of Solomon, and the house that he built, the food of Solomon's table and the residence of his servants and those that served him, and his decoration, and his cup-bearers, and his offerings which were brought into the Lord's house, and she could not retain it all. And she said to Solomon, True are the words which I heard in my land about your affairs and your wisdom and I did not believe what was told me until I came here and saw with my own eyes. And this is not even half of what was told me; your wisdom is beyond any reports I heard."[388]
Luke:	This is so familiar to us.
Anton:	What is?

---

[388] 1 King 10:4-7

Luke:	The birth of Christ.
Luke:	How is that? Are we not all Christians?
Pamba:	If this picture is yours, then the first is yours, otherwise none of them are yours.
Luke:	No way! There is Moses, and here is Christ. He was Jewish, while we have a Christian leader.
Pamba:	Was not Moses Christian?
Luke:	No way.
Pamba:	So why do Christians in church read this, "Opening it they saw the child crying in the basket, and Pharaoh's daughter had compassion on him and said, This is a Hebrew child."[389]
Luke:	It is read because Moses was a figure of Christ, God's son.
Pamba:	Do you fully comprehend what you are saying yourself? What does it mean to be a figure?
Luke:	What does it mean to be a figure?
Pamba:	Yes.
Luke:	What does this mean?
Pamba:	I do not know.
Luke:	Busybody! How can you not know this? He was an image and one shadow of God's son.
Pamba:	How was he a shadow? God Himself testifies that he was a man of God. And divine and veracity are the same. The man of God and son of God are the same. For this reason Paul calls the man of God being created after God in virtue and sanctity of truth.[390] And this is the person he praises.
Luke:	However, Moses was perishable as we are people, but he was called God's by grace.
Pamba:	So you have found a way out. Please, stop your However! Don't give me any more vain scholastic theological leaven. Listen to what God's word has to say about Moses, "His eyes were not darkened and his lips were not weakened."[391]
Luke:	However Moses was one thing and Christ was another.
Pamba:	Listen so I can guide you! The wisdom of the Gospels say this, "If you would have believed Moses then you would have

---

[389] Ex 2:6
[390] Eph 4:24
[391] Deut 34:7

	believed me without doubt." Do you see that to comprehend Moses means to comprehend Christ, and Moses is included in the Gospels in the manner that all of Moses' books are absorbed into the Gospels, much like a chronicle.
Luke:	Yes, and the following words are also noted, "Of me it was written."[392] This you did not mention.
Pamba:	Of course he would not have written this if he did not see him. And what is eternal life if not knowing God? This is what it is to be alive, eternal and imperishable person and to be transformed into deity, while God and life and unity is all one. Beyond this note that the 2 of them are very similar one to another. In one place the Israelite child lies wrapped in a diaper, and there it is a Hebrew child. One is placed by the mother in a manger, while the other is in a basket. Here the mother watches over him, while in the other the sister from a distance. Here came shepherds and magi, while there the royal daughter with her pagan maids. Among the ancient people kings were also called shepherds, for example, "Shepherd of Israel, take heed."[393] This is referring to the shepherd and king of Israel.

Nonetheless, that the people of Israel will not die, listen to the prophet Joel, "In the morning people many and strong will pour over the mountains. There has never been any similar to them from the beginning of time, and not for the generations of generations in years ahead will there be anything like them."[394] If during these future years a greater could have occurred then this would indicate their demise. But there is to be found a different end for them, which will be endless. Israel is itself a remnant from all the nations of the earth that have demised. So what did Moses say about the Hebrew people, "Blessed are you Israel! Who is like unto you?" |
| Luke: | However Moses is one thing, and Christ is another. |

---

[392] John 5:39
[393] Ps 80:1
[394] Joel 2:2

Pamba:	How can one be different from the other when one spoke with the other on Mount Tabor? Have you heard of the genealogy of Christ?
Luke:	I have heard it. "The book of the genealogy of Jesus Christ." And etc.
Pamba:	What do you think? What type of book is this? This book is not a plain one. It is a divine book and this book does not include anything that is of the flesh. Listen to David, "I will not gather their council from blood." And those that are inscribed are only not from blood, not from the lust of the flesh, but are born of God.[395]

And when Moses – whom God's word calls a man of God – is commanded to record in the Book of Numbers, to place these among the most fortunate number and record, how can you dare to want to delete this book? Learn! Are you not understanding this? The names of Christ's disciples are inscribed here. "Rejoice," he said, "For your names are written."[396] Yes, he commands us to rejoice over this. In this book the entirety of the genealogy of Christ is recorded, but not of the flesh – are you listening? – but of the spirit. And here it is, his relatives, "Who is my mother or my brethren? The person who performs God's will is my brother and my sister and my mother."[397]

This seems to amaze you, that Moses and Christ are one. But do you not hear what Christ says about his relatives when speaking to his immortal father? "Let them be one as we are one."[398] "There is no Jew, no Greek, no slave, no free, no male gender, no female gender. You are all one." Says the Apostle Paul in Christ and Christ in you.[399] The family of God is the consummation and so it has no division.

Luke:	How can they be one when they are not one?
Pamba:	Let me ask this of you. How is it possible for 12 to depart in different directions and in various languages have the New

---

[395] John 1:13
[396] Luke 10:20
[397] Matt 12:49
[398] John 17:21
[399] Gal 3:28

	Testament printed and it become one book? If just one of them was to know, then all of them would know. If you would know Moses you would know Christ, or if you were to know Christ you would know Moses, Elijah, Abraham, David, Isaiah, and the others.
Luke:	I know Christ, but I do not know Moses.
Pamba:	You know Christ in the manner certain stupid people know him having only heard fables about him. A rich father had 8 sons. They were educated as far as what was bad and what was good, but were not submissive to there father and vexed him greatly. Among the father's family was one son who was deaf and dumb, but he was a fervent supporter of his father's will.

As he was dying the father ordered all of them to come to him, and blessed each of them, finding something good to say based on the nature of each of them. Then he turned his attention to the idiot and said, "I know that your brothers will offend you in the inheritance. As a result I will double my blessing upon you. Here is my staff for you as a testimony. Take it and protect it. You will sense your prosperity when these words are fulfilled upon you, God's principle will shelter you."

After his death the sons squandered all of his property they inherited. Only the youngest survived with a small house and garden. Here he led a plain life along, lonesome for his father. One Sunday morning 7 years later in the autumn, while walking in the hills above his little paradise, he almost stepped on a snake. He smashed its head with his staff and struck him so hard that part of the staff broke off, like a shedding. He sensed in his ears an unheard noise in front of him and an amazing voice saying, "Fool! Why are you weeping? Whom are you seeking? I am always with you." An inexpressible joy overwhelmed him and he regained his hearing. And then he looked and noticed that his staff was of 2 materials. He removed the outer bark and underneath was a new gold staff, with jewels embedded in it from top to bottom. The head of the staff was made of one large deep blue sapphire, while on the top of the stone was an image of his father painted with eternal colors, while surrounding the image were the words, "God's principle will shelter you."

And the same way for you, listen! You know Christ just as this person did who was deaf and dumb knew his father's staff. These words seem unbelievable to you, that knowing Moses you will know at one glance Christ, and you will hear another marvelous word. Not only when you are led to recognize Adam or Abel or Noah or Joshua son of Nun or Caleb or Job or Solomon or Jeremiah or Paul, or when you even get to comprehend yourself well, and then at one glace you will know also Christ. There is only one generation of Abraham – as mentioned above – and having no number, no beginning, and no end, and fulfilling all 4 sides. "If a person can," says God to Abraham, "Count the grains of sand on the land, then he can count your posterity."

Nonetheless this is not the end, and there is something yet to be said later. All perishes from God's fire, and only the ashes of the evil will remain, and even then their remains will be no more. The fiery person of God will tolerate nothing. All is burned as straw, except for the kernels, as Isaiah wrote, "Just as the new heaven and new earth which I create will exist in My presence, says the Lord, so shall your posterity and name."[400] And the same with Jeremiah, "Rejoice in happiness. Proclaim to the heads of the gentiles. Perform what is heard and give praise. Say, The Lord will save his people, the remnant of Israel."[401] These are the generations that seek the Lord, seek the presence of Jacob's God, before whom no nation can endure, "Just as fire exits from His person." From this nation saved of God, even if just one should know Him, all will know Him. From among all of them is one new person, and they are in him and he is in his father. But since not one of them can know Him, then at least we will strive to know ourselves. In this manner we can recognize the true person created after the image of God in virtue and sanctity of

---

[400] Is 65:17
[401] Jer 31:7

truth. And this is the very thing that is eternal life. Having known Him, in a twinkle of the eye we will be transformed into Him, and our entire deathly nature will be swallowed by His life.

Listen to what he said to his beloved who in his generation was born of Him and wants to be one with Him, "If you have not known this, O, benevolent wife, follow the tracks of the flock and pasture your kids at the shepherd's tents."[402] Write these words with eternal paint on your hearts and on your thoughts. Pass this voice of God to your posterity as a legacy, so that their remnants would be blessed and be happy in the good land and be satiated with bread, wine and oil, and pasture at still waters, and become fat with the bread of God's word, and so inherit the land a second time, and may eternal joy rest over their heads.

And if someone does not recognize himself, he cannot audibly hear the voice of the Lord his God, so that the Lord would open to him his benevolent treasure – heaven. And he will not receive it, not see it, not comprehend these sweetest words of God's promise in Isaiah, "Then early will your light be unveiled, and your healing will quickly shine, and your virtue will pass ahead of you, and God's glory will encompass you. Then you will call and God will hear you, and he who is speaking to you will say, 'Behold, he has arrived.' And God will be with you always, and you will be satisfied as much as your soul desires. And your bones will become fat and be like a watered garden and like a fountain where water will never be lacking.[403] And your bones will grow like the grass and increase in size, and the generations of generations will inherit all this."[404]

"O, humbled and agitated, you have not had any comfort. Behold I prepare for you onyx, your jewel, and sapphire for your foundation, and I will place jasper as your pinnacle and crystal will be upon your gates, and as your walls there will be

---

[402] Song 1:8
[403] Is 58:11
[404] Is 66:14

select jewels. Behold, I will send foreigners unto you and they will rejoice in you and run to you. Behold I have created you, but not as a smith who blows upon coals and forms a tool for a certain use. I have created you not for ruin, but to heal."[405]

Who are these foreigners?

"Raise your eyes around yourself and look. All your sons are gathered and come to you. I live, says the Lord, and so shall they. You shall adorn yourself and be clothed in beauty, with all of them surrounding you, as the decor upon a bride."[406]

Friend: You argue, Luke, and then boast as if you are Christ. Do you understand what you are boasting about. Fear these words of Jeremiah, "You are near to them, Lord, with their lips, but far from their inner person." And David's, "They have placed in heaven their lips, while their tongue slithers about the ground." And Moses', "Do not mention the name of the Lord in vain." And Christ's, "The flesh is nothing; the spirit provides life." It was easy for the sons of Israel to look at the outside of Moses' veil, but they were afraid to look at the appearance of his face – glorified of God. Do you see the dual nature of Moses? In one Moses there is a decaying and a glorifying. The same occurred on Tabor. One Christ was endurable to the eyes of Peter, but the other was awesome. The first was seen by many, the second by no one except the disciples, and it was not until later that their minds were opened to understanding the Scriptures. The decaying and dying they all saw, but the living not one could endure to see and hear. It took effort for the disciples to believe and watch and see. Paul did not want to know or see the first dying Christ, and which was different an attitude than others. Listen to what he says, "From this time we do not know anyone according to the flesh. If we did recognize Christ according to the flesh, but now we do not recognize him in this manner."[407]

---

[405] Is 54:11-12, 16
[406] Is 49:18
[407] 2 Cor 5:16

Tell me now, what do you understand with this appellation Christ? If you understand some entity of decay, then without doubt, through the appellation Christ you understand emptiness. And so to accept his name in such a manner is vain! And what is not futile and false if it is not what decays? And this is not life, but only views its future ruin, "Let his eyes watch his own murder." Job cries, "You will not be saved of the Lord." This very decay is specifically the field of perdition, and upon it is whatever meanders into it, whether a person or cattle. The Lord's fire with thunder and hail destroyed all and everything in the land of Egypt, except for the land where the generation of God, the sons of Israel, lived. This is the place to go to seek knowledge of Christ, to the land of Goshen. All of them are of the same generation, "The generation saved of the Lord."

But meanwhile learn what David says, "Arise from sitting, you that eat the bread of illness. How long will you depend on a person? And you are always killing people. They have decided to reject my values, and have descended into greed. With their lips they bless and with their hearts they curse. I have heard the both of them as though they were one, says the Lord."[408] And take heed to what Micah again sings, "And you tower of the dark flock, the daughter of Zion will come to you, the initial authority will enter, the kingdom from Babylon, the daughters of Jerusalem. And so now why have you recognized evil? Did you not have a king? Or has your counsel perished? And pains have overwhelmed you as a woman giving birth. Suffer and take courage and draw near, daughter of Zion, as a woman giving birth. Because now you will leave the city and rejoice in the field and will reach Babylon. But the Lord God will remove you from there and will deliver you from there."[409]

You cannot see Christ, Luke. It is an embarrassment: his face is covered and you only see his behind. And as Joel says, "The land behind you, the field of ruin and those that have

---

[408] Ps 62:3-4
[409] Micah 4:8-10

fallen, is what you see."[410] And fear that such an attack will not happen to you, and having looked at his shoulders, you would not by-pass the Christ that was recognized by Paul, yesterday and today and forever existing. And the one who was seen by Isaiah, who said to you, "I am, I am the one who comforts you."[411] Grasp who it is that exists?

You did fear the dying person and his son who are dried like grass and have forgotten God who created you and created heaven and established the earth. This is a divine person if you will recognize him, of whom you boast. At this time boldly cry with Isaiah, "And I myself am God's."[412] But now know this that you will never get to know even one person from the divine generation until first you comprehend yourself. You will not ever become a nomad with Abraham. You will not ever place your tents with Jacob. You will not ever settle in a green pasture with David. You will not ever be numbered with Moses and others of God's people. You will not ever await the promised kings with Isaiah, who will be your providers. This generation is the royal priesthoods and holy nation: kings, priests, providers and prophets, and this is what God says of all of them, "He has raised you as if on eagle's wings, and brought you to Himself."[413] If you will not ever comprehend yourself, your king will be Balak and your providers will be his messengers, the enemies of the generation of Israel, who rest in the evening in the presence of Balaam. These are false providers and prophets of whom Micah sang, "The gentiles will see and be ashamed of all your fortresses. They will place their hands over their lips, and their ears will become deaf, they will crawl upon the ground like snakes slithering on the ground, disturbed from their lairs. They will be afraid of the Lord our God and fear him because of you. Who is God like you?"[414] And of whom Zechariah speaks, "O, you worthless shepherds who abandoned the

---

[410] Joel 2:3
[411] Is 40:1
[412] Is 61:1
[413] Ex 19:4
[414] Micah 7:16-17

sheep! A sword attacking his arm and his right eye! His arm is drying and becoming gaunt, and his right eye is failing and becoming blind."[415] And of whom Isaiah spoke, "Now listen to this, the young sitting daughter of Zion hoping in her heart, I am yet speaking and there is no other. I will not sit as a widow and will never incur being an orphan. Now there will suddenly overtake you both of these in one day: childlessness and orphanage will suddenly occur to you. Regarding your sorcerers and your magicians in your fortresses, behold the fire will consume all of them like straw and they will not be able to deliver their souls from the flames."[416]

Behold, these are the shepherd's tents to which the person of God is sending you if you are not able to grasp yourself. These tents are completely repulsive to Moses and the burning bush and to the tabernacle that is described in Numbers. "How beautiful are your houses, Jacob and your tents, Israel, as shading oak trees and as gardens planted beside rivers and as tents that the Lord erected, and as cedar tress along the waters."[417]

Anton: Of course, what is most necessary is this work, for a person to comprehend himself. What is more necessary than to see God? Hosea cries, "There is no truth, no mercy, no vision of God on earth. Swearing, lying and murder and theft and immorality spill over the land, and blood is mixed with blood. Since you have rejected knowledge, so will I reject you. I will no longer be a priest unto you, and you have forgotten the law of your God, and so will I forget your children. And this will effect the priest as well as the people."[418] And also, "I observe Ephraim and Israel has become defiled. They have not abandoned their intentions to return to their God, because the spirit of adultery resides in them and the Lord they have not seen."[419] So they are not able to observe anything because they have not known the Lord.

---

[415] Zech 11:17
[416] Is 47:8-9
[417] Num 24:5-6
[418] Hosea 4:6, 9
[419] Hosea 5:4

O, you who vex education. There is no room for you on earth in these dust-filled hearts. O, supreme governing science, how appropriate, but where are you now? The sword of your concubine has struck you, meaning, the earth and flesh and blood. Her lovers have increased everywhere. They are not able in any manner at all to know the Lord, not having known themselves. It is true that we see ourselves and each other and we know ourselves, but how do we know ourselves? And how do we see each other? Is not this in a pagan manner? Is not all that we have comprehended in ourselves perishable? What we see is our spine and not our face upon us. We only seen the falsity of our flesh, but not the truth in it. So how are we to find truth?

Isaiah cries, "O, ferocious one. The multitude of many nations, agitated like the sea, so shall the spine of the nations crumble; they roar like the waters and like many waters, many nations, like the roar of many waters, carried by its demands and he will toss it and drive it far away like the dust of the field in the face of the wind and like the dust from chariot wheels in the approaching and turbulent storm."[420]

Is this sufficient when we see only ourselves decaying away like water flowing by? Why do we not penetrate into what sustains it? Jeremiah cries, "O, false city! Why do you boast in your valleys? Your valley will flow away O, shameless daughter depending on your riches, saying, What can happen to me? Behold I will bring terror on you, says the Lord Almighty."[421] Ezekiel echoes the same, "O, ferocious city of blood. Poison is in you and the poison will not leave you. For this reason Adonai Lord says, Behold I will judge you for your blood spilt and for your intentions. I will judge you the unclean, notorious and great, and pour My wrath upon you."[422]

It is not enough for us to only see our land in us, but we must rise and look beyond our land and to the Lord's land, of

---

[420] Is 17:12-13
[421] Jer 49:4-5
[422] Eze 24:6-8

which Isaiah says, "With joy enter and learn in happiness."[423] And Joel follows after, "The land before his presence is like the paradise of sweetness, but while behind him it is a field of ruin, and none will be saved upon it."[424] It is not enough for us to see only our decaying person, but to penetrate through our shadow in order to see them, the faces of the persons who have evolved from the divine nation, of whom Joel speaks, "And the Lord will shout in the presence of his strength, for immensely great is His army and firm are the works of His words."[425] And describing this imperishable generation, the following is sung, "As the appearance of horses is their appearance, and as steeds they chase. As the sound of chariots they pour over the summits of the mountains, and as the sound of a burning fire consuming reeds, and as many and strong people armed for battle, from their presence many are shattered. Every person is like a scorched pot. Like soldiers they flow and like valiant men they climb over the walls. Each marches on his own path and they do not depart from their path, and not one will stray from his brother. Loaded with their weapons they proceed and are shot down with arrows but they do not die. They occupy the cities and spill over the houses and climb into the temple and enter through the windows like thieves."[426]

And here is another generation! One generation and another generation: the pagan and Israelite; one has a beginning and the other begins; one has an end and the other ends; one has a middle, the other has a beginning and end. Divide! Do not mix the elect people with the rejected. Do not spill innocent blood on the ground. There is criminal blood and there is righteous; there is a perishable flesh and emaciated bones, and there is a flourishing and unbreakable; there is a darkened eye and there is a radiant. "His eyes were not darkened and his lips did not weaken." So why should all of this not exist if there is a new land in his presence? Why

---
[423] Is 57:2
[424] Joel 2:3
[425] Joel 2:11
[426] Joel 2:6-9

should there not be a new land if the entire world will be recreated anew?

There is a beginning of a beginning, but this is not the beginning because there is another one that is before this beginning. And there is a beginning without a beginning, of which the Lord says, "I will provide Zion a beginning. Zion is with me." And this is the true beginning what has no beginning. "And without it there was nothing made of what was made."[427] The endless beginning and the end of all things, meaning, the end of all that can end: as with the commencement so with the remnant. You will reach the Lord and the beginning will greet you. Seek the Lord and you will acquire the remnant. You will acquire the remnant. Provide to the Lord the first fruits, since all that is first produced belongs to Him. Dedicate to Him whatever you have that is pleasing to your hearts, whatever you see, since His is the heaven and earth. Gift the firstborn of your sons and daughters and all that is born. Gift the first produce of your barns and of your cattle, and of all that is yours. Give the first produce and carry it into the house of the Lord your God. The Lord's acquisition is the vision of first fruits. The vision of the first fruits is the knowledge of yourself in yourself. Let this comprehension that is in your heart increase. Dedicate of yourself the participation unto the Lord. Dedicate this if you gain knowledge of yourself.

Luke: If this word is so necessary in order to discover yourself, and without it and the Lord nothing can be understood, then I think that this should not just be indicated in only one place in the divine books. I remember Moses cleansing the people of Israel for the descent of God on the 3rd day upon Mount Sinai, so how can we better prepare ourselves for this meeting? As it says, "Take heed that you do not enter the mountain."[428] Of course, all of them that did approach the mountain did die, not heeding what was said.

---

[427] John 1:3
[428] Ex 19:12

The principle point to be made is, "Take heed." And this is fully compatible with the statement, "Comprehend yourself." It is apparent the reason for them not to approach the mountain was because it was reserved for the place God was to provide them with his rules and regulations. Nonetheless, to walk with the Lord, observe his commandments, accept him as leader and your shepherd, is all the same. And so, "Take heed that you do not approach the mountain," seems completely compatible with these words, "If you do not know your personal self, follow the flocks' paths."[429] Whoever will approach the mountain will die, meaning, they will not be directed by the kingdom of the Lord's commandments.

Of this very item David asks, "Make me alive upon your path."[430] Because it is not the dead who can praise Him,[431] and so the warning is stated at the beginning, "Take heed for yourself." And this is inherent in the following words, "If you have not known." If you are not able to comprehend your personal self, then I am not your king, says the Lord. Now depart and leave my green pastures! Pasture along with the flock of the false shepherds. The criminal heel, mountain, flesh, falsity, earth, are all the same. To say this in short, "Death is your only deliverance." And of course, the person who dies approaching this mountain is nothing but falsity and flesh. But how is it able to kill? But just as Moses gives the order not to approach it, so does Isaiah banish from it the scribe Shebna, shouting at him, "Why are you here? And what have you here? How you have hewn for yourself a sepulcher, and made for yourself a coffin, and have carved a place for it among the rocks. Behold, now the Lord discards you."[432]

How high many have risen in the wisdom of the divine writings! They exalt themselves calling themselves historians, geographers, mathematicians, but this is all carnal. We will say with Isaiah that this is what the highly-placed coffin

---

[429] Song 1:8
[430] Ps 119:40
[431] Ps 115:17
[432] Is 22:16

signifies. As Obadiah cries, "The pride of your heart has moved you living in the caves of the rocks, you who have raised your residence saying in your heart, Who will throw me down to the ground? Though you soar like the eagle, and if you will place your nest among the stars, and even from there I will cast you down, says the Lord."[433]

It is apparent that this type of mountain is not Jacob's, or his vine or Bethel's, but is Isaac's Seir. Amos cries, "Evil people destroying Zion and relying on Mount Samaria. They have accepted the rules of the pagans and entered the house of Israel."[434]

But in regard to what this mountain in its high and material meaning signifies, listen to what Obadiah says, "On that day, says the Lord, I will destroy the wise from Idumea and knowledge from mount Esau; let every man be removed from mount Esau; and those saved shall enter mount Zion in order to take vengeance on mount Esau, and the kingdom will be the Lord's."[435] The Lord burns, shakes and agitates these mountains; but faith will endure, while the senseless will futilely wail, "Cover us."[436] The letter kills while the spirit provides life.[437]

Kvadrat: This is what I remember in the second book of Moses, "Behold I send my Angel before your presence, so he may preserve you on the path and may lead you into the land which I have prepared for you."[438] And so they would not be deprived of a leader at the very beginning, he tells them as an absolute order, "Take heed and listen to him and do not disobey him, because my name is in him." It is apparent nothing is capable of being done without "Taking heed," and then saying, "And obey him." From a knowledge of yourself an obedience unto God is born, and this is what obedience causes, "You will be my elect people from among all the

---

[433] Obadiah 3-4
[434] Amos 6:1
[435] Obadiah 8, 9, 21
[436] Hosea 10:8
[437] 2 Cor 3:6
[438] Ex 23:20-21

pagans, for all the earth is mine; and you will be to me a royal priesthood and holy nation.[439] Blessed are those who listen to the word of this angel."[440] This Angel there has the appellation of fear, "And I will send fear; while leading you I will terrify all the nations."[441] This is exactly the same terror that Jacob imposed on the region of Bethel.[442] And does not Moses thunder the same in the 5th book, chapter 20? "Do not follow after other deities, the deities of the pagans who surround you, since I am a jealous deity, the Lord your God who is among you.[443] And does he not stand among you as a person whom you do not know, but do know?[444] Blessed is the person who has ears to hear and does hear." Little by little I will banish the pagans from you, until you grow and inherit the land.

But the following words are the entrance and door, "Take heed to yourself."

Pamba: Without doubt this one entrance does not allow us to incline to another side and directs us to walk straight to the door, which cries itself, "I am the door. Take heed to yourself – said the Lord to Moses – all that I command you. Behold I banish before your presence the Amorites and all others." But so that Moses would not blemish the people with idolatry, he stated this, "Take heed to yourself, so that your children at some time in the future will inherit the covenant of the land into which you enter."[445] Moses, having comprehended himself, destroyed, and hewed and burnt all that was idolatrous. Then he descended from the mountain from God having a glorified appearance on the body of his flesh. And every person will remain false and flesh or a primary idolater, and this applies to any person, if they will not attain a comprehension of themselves.

---

[439] Ex 1:6
[440] Rev 1:1, 3
[441] Ex 23:27
[442] Gen 35:5
[443] Deut 20:18
[444] John 1:31, 33
[445] Deut 31:13

Friend: Moses in his final book in some places repeats the phrase "Take heed to yourself," as something absolutely necessary. Let's listen to them:

1

And now Israel, listen! Behold I have given to you statutes and ordinances, so preserve them and observe them, because this is your wisdom and your knowledge in the presence of all the nations, and they will say, "What wise and capable people! What a great nation they are." And so do not forget these ordinances and do this, "Take heed to yourself and diligently provide for your soul."[446]

2

The Lord your God leads you into a good and large land, where there are brooks filled with water and fountains from the deep, and fields and mountains, a land of wheat and barley, a land of olive oil and honey, a land where even the most destitute will have bread to eat, and you will lack nothing on it.[447] And what more? Take heed to yourself. And why? Lest you heart be lifted up and you will forget the Lord your God; lest you say in your heart, It was my effort and the strength of my hands have acquired me this great wealth.[448]

3

And the Lord will give rain at its proper season, the early and the latter, and you will gather your harvest and your wine and your oil and you will have food in your villages for your cattle. And what further? And who has eaten and become filled, take heed to yourself. And why? So your heart will not be deceived and you proceed to serve other gods.[449]

4

Do not do there all the things that you have done here today, each person whatever he wants. But where is there? It is astonishing that you do not know. Bring your burnt sacrifices here and your offerings and your tithes and the first produce of your effort. Here is there! Take heed to yourself,

---

[446] Deut 4:6-9
[447] Deut 8:7-8
[448] Deut 8:14, 17
[449] Deut 11:14-16

lest you bring your burnt sacrifice in any place.[450] My God! If you will not comprehend yourself, then you will not obey God, or bring Him sacrifices, or know where to bring them; you will not know anything at all, or what to do.

5

Regarding sacrifices the following is commanded, Only do not eat the blood; spill it on the ground as water. Do not eat the blood. Then of course, eat [the sacrifice] in the presence of your God; He will himself select a place for you. And eat it, and your son and your daughter and male slave and female slave.[451] Also do not banish the Levite. He has no portion of his own; his portion is the Lord. Accept the migrant.[452] So what is the Levite? It is astonishing: take need to yourself and at that time you will not abandon the Levite, and you will know where is there.

6

Do not eat [blood], and it will go well with you and your sons with you forever if you perform this and all will be good and pleasing with you in the presence of the Lord your God. Who would envision that happiness would evolve from not eating blood? One person cries, Take heed seriously not to eat blood. Because blood is the soul of the animal. Spill the blood on the ground.[453]

Do not bring blood, because blood destroys. But so you do not become a pagan by bringing a sacrifice of blood, Take heed to yourself, so he does you will not seek after them, that is, the pagans. The pagan brings flesh and blood to God.

7

In the seventh year you will perform an emancipation. And this is the law of the emancipation. Every person will renounce the debt that your associate is indebted to you, and you will not require it of your brother. So how will you perform emancipation for the Lord your God? If your brother or brethren will be insufficient in one of the city in the land that the Lord your God gives you, do not turn your heart away from him and do not

---

[450] Deut 12:8, 13-14
[451] Deut 12:23, 28
[452] Deut 12:12
[453] Deut 12:24-25, 17

clasp your hands, but open your hand to him and lend to him, as much as he asks and as much as he needs. And so that the emancipation and kindness will be performed for your brother he adds this at the end, Take heed to yourself. Do not allow a hidden word of crime reside in your heart so that your brother cries out to God against you.[454]

8

There is so much commanded in the Third Book of Moses about leprosy. And if anyone wants to be cleansed of it, this is how, Take heed to yourself in the illness of leprosy, it says in Deuteronomy.[455]

9

Finally, Moses as he was gifting the Lord's commandments stopped to add this phrase that served in the place of a key, Take heed to yourself. He sought another key in its place, and namely, Destroy the evil among you. Where it was formerly said, Take heed, there is now says, Destroy the evil among you. He commands to kill the prophet who philosophizes about secular matters and provides carnal miracles, and then adds, Destroy the evil yourselves among you. He commands to execute by stoning the Israelite who swears by the sun or moon and adds, Destroy the evil among you. He commands to execute the person who is a disobedient priest who is a priest by the flesh and not by the spirit, So that the evil will be removed from Israel. He commands the false-witness made toward an innocent person to be returned upon his own head and adding, Remove the evil from among you. He commands to execute a son rebellious to his parents and says, And so shall you remove evil from among you. He commands the execution of an adulterous couple and then adds the same words; and this continues and continues.[456]

Friend: It seems to me that this phrase is compatible with the topic of comprehending yourself. And no person can destroy within himself malice if he earlier does not discover what it is that resides within him: what is bad and what is good. And if he

---

[454] Deut 15:7-9
[455] Deut 24:8
[456] Deut 21, 22.

	does not comprehend himself, how can he comprehend and banish what is inside others?
Anton:	And the elder admonishing his son Tobias, says to him discontentedly, "All your days son, remember the Lord your God and so you will not want to sin or violate his commandments."[457] And here is more where he as if entrusts him with a key, "Take heed son of all immorality. Do not take a foreign woman who is not of the tribe of your father, since we are the sons of prophets: Noah, Abraham, Isaac, Jacob – our fathers from the beginning of this era. They all took wives from among their brethren."[458] And at the end he attaches a seal, "Take heed son in all your activities." So if Tobias would not have obeyed his father, he would have been punished all his life; he would not have found a person – the angel Raphael – to accompany him, not have escaped death from Asmodeus the evil angel in his bridal chamber, or rejoiced with his beloved Sarah, but would have become a complainer and abuser, and would have strived to first comprehend himself well. Solomon says this, "Evil with vexation propagates evil; but you should know wisdom." He gutted himself out like a fish, as Habakkuk said, "You created the person like a fish of the sea."[459] He removed from inside of him the stone heart and the liver of carnal lust, and the gall bladder, of which is written in the Fifth Book of Moses, "If there is a man or woman or family or tribe among you whose heart departs from the Lord your God in order to serve the other gods of the pagans…"[460] What root is growing upon the mountain in bile and sorrow? Their grapevines are the grapevines of Sodom and their branches are from Gomorrah; their clusters are clusters of poison, clusters of sorrow.[461] And now regarding the source, "Honey drips from the lips of the

---

[457] Tobit 4:5
[458] Tobit 4:12
[459] Habakkuk 1:14
[460] Deut 14:6
[461] Deut 32:32

woman-prostitute who for a while will sweeten your throat, but afterward she is more bitter than bile."[462]

Uproot all of this evil from yourself and burn it with the Lord's fire. Then safely settle in your beloved residence, of which Solomon says, "I have searched for my beloved in my youth, and I desired to take a bride for myself, and I was in love with her beauty."[463]

Pamba: To the extent of the difference these words are externally, to the same extent they are compatible internally, "Heed yourself; and Seek first of all God's Kingdom and its virtue." God's Kingdom does not arrive as a guest to a guest's house, as if it is greeting someone arriving from behind a mountain, from beyond the sea, from beyond the clouds. It is not far from us. It is within us. "The commandment that I command you today, says Moses, is not difficult and not far from you. It is not in the heavens so that you would say, Who among us will go to heaven and take it to bring to us. It is in your lips, in your heart, and I require it from your hands to perform it." This very word of the Kingdom was envisioned by the prophets, sown by Christ, preached by Paul. Who understands himself has found the Kingdom.

Kvadrat: Now I am beginning to comprehend Solomon, "The wise heart will understand what is spoken by his lips, because the lips carry wisdom."[464] The word of God's Kingdom is hidden within our heart, as though a fountain in the concealed land. Who has understood himself has acquired the desired treasure of God. He has acquired the source and its fulfillment within himself, understanding his inner self, as Solomon stated, "Deep waters are the word in a man's heart; a flowing river is the fountain of life and the wise man scoops it."[465] Who has scooped this vision has the wings desired by David, and eyes that praised his son. "His eyes are like the doves over the overflowing waters, washed in milk, sitting in the filled

---

[462] Pr 5:3-4
[463] Wisdom of Solomon 8:2
[464] Ps 16:23
[465] Pr 18:4

waters."[466] This is what an understanding brother and his friend says to such a person, "Turn away your eyes for wings have been given me."[467] But this person, having understood himself, that is, having understood him, does not remove his eyes from him, and friend delivers friend, praising, "I am my brother's and my brother is mine, pasturing me in the fields."[468]

Luke: To understand this fulfillment Paul also desires for the Ephesians, "May he give you strength according to the wealth of his glory, and his spirit to strengthen your inner person. May Christ reside by faith in your hearts, rooted and founded in love, so that you can comprehend with all the saints what are the width and depth and length and height, to comprehend the transcending intellect of Christ's love, so you may be filled with the complete fullness of God."[469] The same for the Colossians, "Beware that no one from among you be deceived by philosophy and futile flattery, according to people's traditions, according to the elements of this world, and not Christ, since in him bodily lives the complete fullness of the deity."[470]

Every person is soil, field and garden, but this land is filled with God's water. "And he made him to be the head of all, the church, which is his body, by whose filling is the fullness of everything in all things."[471] A field can grow bushes, but a garden requires seeds or else it will be empty until, as Isaiah writes, "The spirit will descend upon you from above and the desert will be converted into Carmel."[472]

Friend: Jesus the man of God, having freed a man of the land of the Gadarenes from legions of demons, in the end tells him, "Return to your home."[473] And he also sends home the

---

[466] Song 5:12
[467] Song 6:5
[468] Song 2:16
[469] Eph 3:16-19
[470] Col 2:8-9
[471] Eph 1:22-23
[472] Is 32:15
[473] Mark 5:19

crippled.[474] He sends also the blind who in the end gained his sight,[475] indicating that all people are like wood or brush. But another blind person, after gaining his sight, is not found in the streets, but in the temple.[476] But what is our house if it is not as Paul says, "You are the temple of the living God."[477] And who can comprehend what is living within us, not having inspired himself and not having understood himself? All of our health and enlightenment depends on this. The son of Nun invites Israel to this temple, "Approach here, he says, and hear the word of the Lord your God."[478] This is where you will understand that the Lord lives within you. And so he promises you that the tribe of Ham will be destroyed through destruction with all of their enemy family.

The wise wife searches this temple to find the piece of money, utilizing the lamp of God's scriptures, the word, saying, "I am the light of the world.[479] Your law is a lamp unto my feet."[480] David swears that he will not give sleep to his eyes until he acquires a place for the Lord, until he finds a residence for the God of his ancestor Jacob.[481] And then he cries, "Let us enter his villages. I rejoiced when they said to me, Let us go into the Lord's house."[482] I will provide you my prayers in the midst of you Jerusalem and in your gates. And where exactly is this? In the midst of the church I will sing to you. So where do you sing to your Lord? Answer: In the sincerity of my heart in the middle of my house. State this more clearly, David! Here it is. In order to perform your will as my God wanted, and your law is not in the heavens, not beyond the seas, but in your inner person. I sought and dug as a fountain of living water your virtue and kingdom within me, in my decaying earth, I have not hid or mixed it as the

---

[474] Matt 9:6
[475] Mark 8:23, 26
[476] John 5:14
[477] I Cor 3:16
[478] Josh 5:14
[479] John 8:12
[480] Ps 119:105
[481] Ps 132:4-5
[482] Ps 122:1

Philistines with the earth. I have dug my hidden treasure out of its hole in my field.

I recognize with Abraham that I am dust and ashes, but in the midst of my boundaries I sought salvation, which you have provided in the midst of my land. This truth and salvation of yours I have told to others and have not hid it from the people. Now I will says, "Discard, O, my friends, the desires of the nations! Return to your home, to your father. Will you not grasp that Christ is leading the blind person out of the village, and at this time is opening his eyes.[483] Do you not hear that the demon-possessed was not earlier residing in the temple, deprived of decaying garments? So then where was he residing? The unclean spirit pursued him through the deserts and he was living among the graves.[484] Our lust's desires are our graves. We are pursued through the desolate places of the world, there seeking desirable bliss and contentment.

But listen to what the captive bride says, "I will arise and walk around the city. I sought him and did not find him."[485] And for what? Because I was seeking him in the market places and in the streets.[486] These streets are nothing else other than the path or counsel of the godless who understand nothing other than decaying visible items and depend on them, and they seek the earthly elements outside of themselves. These very ones are agitated and are unable to rest, like dust thrown up by chariot wheels, carried away by storms, of which was said, "I will lay them flat like the dirt of the roads."

Outside the house of God they seek those of whom David spoke, "There will always be plenty of recklessness and deceit in the streets." So why do you walk about the city, as it is written, "The criminals walk about." Why do you not enter inside? You want to get your fill of wandering about. But do you not hear that this is recklessness and something

---

[483] Mark 8:23
[484] Mark 5:5
[485] Song 3:2
[486] Luke 14:21

unessential, deceitful, and not truth? Do you not hear that such wisdom is a sword in the lips of your heart? Believe that you hunger and will do so as long as you wander about. It is out of this village, from these streets, that the heavenly teacher leads the blind person.

Let us return with him to our home. Not to our existing home, but to God's house. Our body contains 2 temples: one is earthly, the second is heavenly or un-manufactured, which is imbedded in our earthly temple. Not remaining in ours, we pass through it to God's with David, "I will enter God's house to God who provides joy in my youth."[487] While we sit in our external composition we will stupidly and rudely seek with the bride. She sought on his bed but was not able to find.[488] But this is what Jeremiah cries, "Why do we sit? Let us gather together and enter the fortified cities and reside there."[489] So where is there? In the presence of the Lord who created us. There where Paul says, "Seek the celestial."[490] There, up high! There! On that side of the Jordan, in the new mountainous land. There where Christ is at the right of God. While on the streets he is not to be heard. If our body is darkness, then its surrounding material is extremely thicker than darkness.

So this we will strive to find. But the bride has been seeking at night, but did not find. So what is she doing? Do not fear! She did not stop on the paths of sin, upon which travelers in terror cry, "O, you who have abandoned the paths of righteousness; you walk on the paths of darkness." And Jeremiah says of them, "I will desolate from the cities of Judah and from the roads of Jerusalem the voices of joy and the voices of happiness, the voice of the groom and the voice of the bride."[491]

This is why the unfortunate Magdalena weeps, wandering about the crooked surroundings, she seeks among the corpses

---

[487] Ps 5:7
[488] Song 3:1
[489] Jer 8:14
[490] Col 3:1
[491] Jer 7:34

in their graves, while it was still dark. Please, even though you will search for a thousand years or centuries you will not find. It is really that up to this time you have no ears? And you do not hear what the Angel appearing as lightning cries, "He is not here!" So meanwhile her path is cleansed, the stone is thrown to the side, a signal is made.[492] And what type? "There you will see him." As Isaiah, "Enter through my gates and create a path for my people, and remove the rocks on the roads, raise a banner over the nations."[493] And so that Magdalena would not take the path of idolaters to seek, it is raised in the mountains of Galilee. So where is Galilee? "Go to the mountain of myrrh and to the hill of Lebanon."[494] So where is Galilee? "Run my brother, be like the gazelle or the young deer, upon the mountains of aromas."[495] So tell me, where is Galilee? You will be in error if you begin to search outside yourself to find it.

Listen! The Angel to Isaiah did not divide mountain from the house. "The word that came from the Lord to Isaiah son of Amos. In the final days the Lord's mountain and God's house on the summit of mountains will be disclosed, and it will rise higher than the hills, and all the nations will come to it."[496] Know that Abraham ascended where he could ascend high! He was there with Isaac. Where is there? "I will acquire you outside, and kiss you, and none will stop me." Where is there? "I will take you and lead you in to the house of my mother and into the bed where she conceived you; there you will teach me, and there I will give you my breasts."[497] Where is there? "Under the apple tree I awakened you, there your mother gave you birth, there she was in pain because of giving you birth." Where is there? "Place me like a seal upon your heart, as a brand upon your arm. Because love is as

---

[492] Matt 28:1-7
[493] Is 62:10
[494] Song 4:6, 8
[495] Song 2:9
[496] Is 2:1-2
[497] Song 8:1-2

strong as death."[498] Wait! Its wings are as wings of fire. Wait! The many waters cannot extinguish love.

Please wait, I do not understand. Where is there? In the green pastures, There, under the apple tree. He who turns the ocean into dry land, they will cross with their feet, there they will rejoice. In the churches bless the Lord. There is Benjamin.[499] There the Lord revealed himself to Jacob. There enter the tribes of Israel. Do not do there all of what you have been doing here today, every person according to whatever he wants. This is Mount Zion upon which you have made your residence. Do you comprehend the mountain? I do not comprehend.

"Your rectitude is as the mountains of God; your judgments are a great abyss."[500] Do you want to attain the mountain? Learn of rectitude. Your rectitude is as the mountains of God. Do you want to attain rectitude? Learn of God's Kingdom. Do you want to attain the Kingdom? Learn of yourself. If the mountain is in you then God's is in you also. Divide yourself entirely: your entire animal body in 2. Divide at the tail and at the head. Pummel your entire body, beat at all of your members as a certain prophet commanded, "Do not even spare one hair."

Here is how God is angered at those who mix, "And the word of the Lord came to me, cries Ezekiel, saying, Son of humanity. Behold, the house of Israel was mine, mixed entirely of copper and iron, and with pure tin and with lead. Say it for this reason! Thus says the Lord Adonai. Just as all of this was mixed together, for this reason I will gather you just as silver and copper and iron and lead and pure tin is gathered together in a furnace. And I will blow on you in the fire of My anger and all of this will be fused together.[501] And the priests have rejected My law and have defiled My shrines, and have not made a distinction between the holy and the defiled, and have not made a division between the clean and

---

[498] Song 8:5-6
[499] Ps 68:27
[500] Ps 36:6
[501] Eze 22:20-21

the unclean, and they have allowed Jerusalem to be filled with thieves on my Sabbaths. And they grease their prophet-magicians who speak vain lies saying that this is what God requires, even though such has never come into the mind of the Lord."[502]

So this is how it is. Divide my friend, the Church of God into 2. Do you have a staff? Leave it here. Sell all you have and buy Ezekiel's sword, "Thus says Adonai Lord, Say! Sword! Sword! Be sharpened, destroy, overthrow every tree.[503] To divide, hew and cut is all the same. And this is the sole judgment that God requires of you. And He seeks this, wanting to make you virtuous. "For the word of God is living and sharper than every sword."[504] Seek, knock at the door, sweep the house well, dig out what is in the floor, sort all you have. Ask among the back alleys, ascertain all rumors, test and overhear, seeking for the wisest, sweetest and most friendly of curiosities. Such science is the most profound and novel, and because it is something that is nowhere to be learned. But it is the entrance because it is the most needful. Where have you seen or read or heard about some type of prosperity that is not a treasure you are carrying within yourself?

There is no need to search outside of yourself. True prosperity is within you. Consistently meditate on understanding yourself. And this is a prayer, that is, an ignition of your thoughts toward this matter. This wail of yours, a secret wail, alone enters the ears of the Lord Sabbaoth and is just like fragrant sacrificial smoke that emanates from the blessed Arabia, ascending and delighting the nostrils of God. This is not the only reason that the Lord speaks this to Jeremiah, "Cry to me and I will answer you, and I will proclaim to you the great and strong, what you have not yet comprehended."[505]

---

[502] Eze 20:26-27
[503] Eze 21:9
[504] Heb 4:12
[505] Jer 33:3

But what benefit to us is there from this? So now listen, "Behold I will bring upon them horrible plagues and healing; and I will cure them and appear to them if they will hear me and I will heal them and perform for them peace and provide faith"[506] All of this the Lord says regarding the houses of Israel. And is it not the house? The land and darkness are the same, and no light of any type shines in your darkness. It was only David who said, "He shines in my darkness."[507] But you do not penetrate anything in your house except the darkness. You see only sand. Only the flesh and blood. O, destitute city! What peace do you have here? And have you any faith? Have you founded your temple using the sand as a foundation with the fool of the Gospels.[508] Hurry, please, seek in your house what the Lord has promised in Isaiah, "A hidden treasure I will open to you." Isaiah found this and said, "Your treasures are my salvation." And you during the night are not able to find the morning?

But there came the word of the Lord to Abraham in a vision at night, saying, "Fear not, Abraham! I will protect you. A great reward is awaiting you."[509] Here is true peace! His type of peace cannot be given. Here is faith! Your security can be based on this. The blessed Abraham found light in darkness, and a rock in the sand, and life in decay, the imperishable in death, the healing of a plague in ruin. He did not seek anything else, but only as if began to remember much of this in a dream. From a distance the word of the Lord began to touch his thoughts: something else is there to be found where the darkness is. Through the abyss of this darkness the Lord wants to relocate him and settle him in another place, if only Abraham will obey him. He promises him a new land as a reward in place of the old. And this means that your reward will be very great. Of which Isaiah, "Behold your God! Behold the Lord! The Lord comes with

---

[506] Is 19:22
[507] Ps 18:28
[508] Matt 7:26
[509] Gen 15:1-2

fortitude and his arm with authority. Behold his compensation is with him! And his work is ahead of him."[510]

But in order to better understand that this compensation of his exactly pertains to the non-manufactured temple, know that here we have the dust and decay of our hidden tabernacle. No one can reach unto this if his heart like tin has been made dirty while building his personal house. A little bit further above the following was said, "Cry! And I said, What shall I cry? This is what. Every flesh is straw and the glory of humans is like a flower in the grass. While the word of our God resides forever."[511] Isaiah sought within himself the 2: the external and the inner. In this straw the word of God speaks of finding the kingdom in our midst. For this reason he cries also to us, "All flesh is straw." He orders the straw to be discarded, and seek beyond the straw what is concealed inside the husk. He placed his secret in darkness. It lies on our straw and in our dark shadow, in our temple, but no one, except kings and shepherds, can worship him. Why is this? Apparently because they do not see him. Why? Because they did not find king or kingdom. What is the reason? They did not comprehend themselves. Here is plenty of wine for you! They sought, yes and outside themselves, in the market places and streets. But kings arrived from a distant to the city of David at night and sought for it in the secret dens. There you can se it, whoever is seeking! "And the word became flesh." There is David, "You law is inside of me."

A kingdom does not exist without laws. And Abraham said, "Since you have not provided me with offspring, a home-born servant will be my heir." And Abraham erred again. And immediately the voice of the Lord came to him saying, "He will not be your heir, but one will be born of you who will be your heir." Seek, Abraham, another heir within yourself. Exit at the time when you recognize him. You are nothing else but a dry and dead stick, but from the midst of you an unfading flower can grow. Our crooked glance as soon

---

[510] Is 40:9-10
[511] Is 40:6, 8

as possible needs to be raised unto heaven, although immersed in the dust of our body. Abraham slowly said, "I am soil and dust." But now he says, "Lord sovereign! How will I know that I must inherit a new land with a new heir?" What did the Lord say to him? He ordered him to cut in half a bull. "And he divided it in half, and placed the halves opposite one another."[512]

Behold! At this very moment at the division there began his obsolete earthly opinion that enters beneath the surface of the earth, as the suns sets and vanishes and hides. "And behold He ordered a dark fear to descend on them." Do not seek, please, outside of yourself either kingdom or cattle. Listen to what Malachi cries, "The sun of virtue will shine upon you who fear my name and there is healing in its wings. And you will exit and begin to play as do calves freed from their chains, and you will tread on the criminals and they will be dust beneath your feet on the day that I create this to be."[513] Watch how Paul divides a person, like cattle in 2, "There exists a material body and there is an immaterial body."[514] And that he through the material understands an animal flesh and blood is apparent from Deuteronomy, "If you butcher one of your bulls or sheep, then take this seriously, to not eat the blood." And why? Because the blood is the soul. Do not eat the soul with the meat, do not eat this. Spill it on the ground like water."[515] It is amazing how strict this is forbidden. "Do not eat it, so it will be well with you and your children after you forever, if you do what is good and pleasing before the Lord your God, since you are my holy people." Tell me, where is he who has the spirit of division or the spiritual sword? Only he can bring himself as a sacrifice to the Lord. But can such a sacrificed be sanctified? It can be, if you comprehend yourself.

At this time a person will find what is holy and divine within himself, bypassing what is flesh and blood. And the

---

[512] Gen 15:10
[513] Mal 4:2-3
[514] I Cor 15:44
[515] Lev 7:26-27

person who, having watched closed with his serpent's eye at his criminal heels, at the filth of his flesh and blood, will never inherit God's Kingdom, and even Ishmael, and his children will be destroyed in a land not theirs. Listen to how Jeremiah awesomely thunders at these blood-thirsty people, "Cursed is the person who depends upon another person and establishes his reliance on someone's strong arm of flesh and whose heart departs from the Lord. And he will be like a wild olive tree in the desert, in a brackish and desolate land."[516] Is it not upon the ground that these snakes slither upon their belly? Do not the whales play in the water? But what does Isaiah say about such snakes? "On that day, he says, the Lord will bring his holy and great and firm sword on the dragon, the snake that attacks the dragon, the evil snake, and will kill the dragon which lives in the sea."[517] Tell me, why have you been watching your blood? What is the benefit that you tend to it and protect it? Why do you, O, whales, not seek Jonah among yourselves? "O, shepherds, Zechariah cries at you, futility! And you have abandoned the sheep! Here is the Lord's sword against your arm and against your right eye!"[518]

What is your flesh if not an empty land, brackish and desolate? Here you sit and watch it, upon the spine of your flesh, completely transformed into a pillar of salt. What is your blood if not some useless liquid just flowing by? You have sunk your entire mind into what is the word, and you swim it in, satisfied with it and assured of it. Is it not written about you in Job? "The darkness shall be light unto you, the sleeping water will cover you."[519] Do not these words pertain to you? "The flowing river is their foundation. While saying, what will the Lord do to us?"[520]

This is what you have been watching! Listen to Job himself, "Let his eye see his own murder! Let him find no salvation from the Lord! He dies in his sorrow, not tasting

---

[516] Jer 17:5-6
[517] Is 27:1
[518] Zech 11:17
[519] Job 22:11
[520] Job 22:16-17

anything from the good; while they sleep on the ground, decay covers them. The wicked person is kept for the day of his destruction, and he will be taken away and suddenly carried off in his coffin, and there is a vigil at the cemetery. He is delighted with a stream of broken rocks, and every person attending will wander away, while an innumerable amount will follow him."[521] Arise, unfortunate corpse! Raise your eyes and understand yourself! Do you really think that your essence consists of this vile decay? Comprehend yourself and understand that profit from usury is not true conduct. Your shadow is not the strength of the oak of Mamre, but dishonor, the actual value of what is hidden within you. O, a person wants to live in honor but does not understand himself. He considered himself an animal and so became one. His coffin in the ground has become his village. And why? "They promoted their names in the land."[522]

Blood and flesh is what I am, they say to my heart, and what is it, if not this? What are you saying, foolish person? Is this the reason there is no God? It is better to say that yourself as something existing does not exist. How can something occur to you if not ever written in the heavens? You say that they do not exist, except for your earth. You cannot be Israel. You will never think of an ability to divide because the 2 do not understand you. One is completely sealed by your thoughts. One is decay and is inscribed on your forehead, on your dust-made heart, as Jeremiah says, "The sin of Judah is inscribed with an iron pen, with the nail of a diamond carved on the stone plates of their hearts and on the horns of their altars."[523] And a little further down he cries against them, "O, mountain resident, your fortress and your treasury I will give to plunder, and your high places also, because of your sins which pervade all your areas. You alone will remain of your heritage that I gave you, and I will cause you to serve your

---

[521] Job 21:21-25, 30-33
[522] Ps 49:11
[523] Jer 17:1

enemies in a land which you do not know. For you have lit the fire of my wrath and it will even burn for ages."[524]

So says Habakkuk, "In malice does he build a city with blood and he prepares the city using crime." And again, "Woe to him the greedy, who uses evil greed for his house! And he has built his nest very high, and withdrawn from the reach of evil people. You have devised shame for your house, killed many people, and your soul has sinned much."[525] If you had within yourself the ability to distinguish the honorable from the unworthy, Habakkuk would never have cried against you, "You have drunk to the full contempt instead of honor, and you, the heart, shake and shudder." And why? "The cup of the Lord's right hand will not by-pass you and dishonor has been gathered on his head."[526]

No doubt you have heard of the cup of salvation and that salvation is in the strength of his right hand, and not in the abomination of your dust. So listen further to the song of Habakkuk, "In malice he speaks to wood, Have courage, arise! And to a rock, Be erect! These are but dreams, and this is the inclusion of gold and silver, and there is no spirit of any type in them. The Lord resides in his holy temple."[527]

Hear! Do you hear that an idolater is only the person who understands the visible in himself and honors this? So what should be done? Gather what is scattered upon the secular deserts due to ambition, due to love of money, due to the passion of your mind, and then enter within yourself. Circumvent the walls and the veil of your dead temple. What benefit is it for you to bounce about desolate areas, forgetting your house, the Lord's temple. Listen, listen to Isaiah, what benefit and peace to acquire from this, "They broke open asp's eggs and weave a spider's web." And so what will come of this? "And wanting to eat of their eggs, forgetting that the eggs are harmful, he finds inside of them a snake. A spider's web does not serve as clothing and neither will their efforts

---

[524] Jer 17:3-4
[525] Hab 2:9-10, 12
[526] Hab 2:16
[527] Hab 2:19-20

clothe them, because their works are crimes. Their feet flow toward evil and are quick to spill blood. Their thoughts are thoughts of murder. Destruction and destitution are their paths, and the way of peace they have not recognized, and there is no justice in their paths."[528] It is possible to more vividly display the results of secular activities?

Now I think that you understand this well, what insanity signifies, of which Luke writes, "He possessed demons for many years and did not wear clothing; he did not live in a house but in the cemetery." And lower, "He was driven by the demons through the desert."[529] Christ sends this person to his home in order to seek at his home God's kingdom, that is, his personal welfare, and having comprehended himself he would see what he had not been able to up to that time. Habakkuk comprehended himself and this is what he sings, "Lord, I heard your voice and was alarmed. Lord, I comprehended your works and became afraid."[530] "The fear of the Lord," says the son of Sirach, "brings gladness to the heart and provides joy and happiness and longevity. How great is that person who acquires wisdom! But there is no greater than the person who fears the Lord."[531]

But you must also know that everybody would fear the Lord if they would only comprehend themselves. How long did Paul not understand himself? Finally, after paying attention to himself and hearing the voice of the Lord he said, "Lord, who are you? What do you command me to do?" And it responded. "Arise and enter the city."[532] It was as if Paul was not content with entering the city, nonetheless this means nothing. But it is not that city of which the gate-keeper says, "When brother helps brother the city is firm and high and is strengthened like an established kingdom."[533] Who does not know that Christ calls his brethren those who do the will of

---

[528] Is 59:5-8
[529] Luke 8:27, 29
[530] Habakkuk 3:2
[531] Sirach 1:12, 20
[532] Acts 9:5-6
[533] Pr 18:19

God? There in the city it will be told you what to do. So what is God's will if not the law? And what is the law if not authority and the kingdom? And if Paul says, "You are the temple of the living God," then why should someone not say, "You are the city of the living God." David places the city of God and his mountain as the same, "In the city of our God, in his holy mountain."[534]

But if God says that Zion is with me, then his city is with him and his house and temple. "And you will be called," says Isaiah, "the city of the Lord, the Zion of the holy Israel."[535] It is astonishing that God does not call those who love his will his city, but instead Isaiah calls them a new heaven and a new earth. All of this is the residence of God.

But you strive for one thing: to comprehend yourself. How can you become God's place, not hearing His intangible voice? How can you hear, not comprehending God? How can you comprehend, not having sought for Him? How can you find him, not having grasped yourself? It is true that Paul boasts of a certain person, but he sought for this person within himself, "It is not I who live, but it is Christ who lives in me."[536] So in what manner do we comprehend ourselves?

This has already been stated and Habakkuk there suddenly mentions this, "In the middle of the 2 animals you will be known." Do you see what God says to Abraham, "Take a 3-year old calf." Abraham grasped what he meant and severed it in half. Many would have thought that Abraham was weaving nonsense and futility. Not at all! Abraham was very perspicacious. He heard what God wanted in dedication. "Sanctify them in your truth; your word is truth."[537] Who can say in regard to a person's sanctification, that is, your comprehension of truth, that the Lord required of his Abraham – ox, sheep, calves, goats? Is this not just futility? So what is the difference between a person and animal and beast, if the person does not comprehend himself? Listening

---

[534] Ps 48:1
[535] Is 60:14
[536] Gal 2:20
[537] John 17:17

to David that a person who is found indubitably in honor but does not understand the majestic beauty of God's kingdom within himself has become just like an animal, not grasping the Lord's truth. A lamb, for example, barbecued and eaten in an assembly of people who love the truth and a group of friends tied in a unity of blessed love can be part of ceremonial performance, that is, to secretly indicate and lead our intellect to guessing that a person for the sake of his welfare must dedicate himself to God, that is, to give himself to the search and mastication of the exact truth.

But this is only a ceremony, that is, a bundle and secret badge. If we do not penetrate through the peel or crust by guessing and not understanding, subsequently not fulfilling, at this time it is just a ceremony, like a walnut without a kernel, empty. And why? So as not to bring your thoughts to this center, to show you why it was born. If a person is called a goat, and no one knows this, then to call him a goat at this time is a futile act, because the thoughts of the hearer remain with the goat and never reach the person. Every country and age have their ceremonies, all of them bundles, all of them secret images in print and signs of the center or conclusion, how all of this should end. So what type of person is this? Whatever he is: by act, by activity, by word, all of this is empty nonsense if it does not receive materialization in this person. Is not every breath and is not every creature inscribed on the picture of the Holy Bible: heaven, earth, sea and all that fills it?

But all of this flesh is from different aspects, and all of this immeasurable innumerability and visibility flows into a person and is consumed in the person and like an expansive tree grows old as time passes and decays and vanishes, but in it are seeds where its branches, leaves and fruit is safety hid as if in a small dot. All that is named there, even to the final character, to the smallest comma, all is necessarily obligated for all of this to enter a person.

But in regard to this Paul, remembering the sun, moon, stars, sees all of this in the resurrection, that is, in a person.

And can the resurrection occur in some other place when this very person resides in that person who says regarding itself, "I am the resurrection."[538] And of this Paul says, "The second person is the Lord from the heavens."[539] So and only Paul accepts this fact that all of this returns to the center of its own self, as if solid food that is chewed with strong teeth.

So it was with Abraham. He knew that it took little wisdom and no holiness to kill a ram, and that God is not a hunter to eat the meat of a calf and drink the blood of goats, And against those who cannot fathom (and maybe it transcends their comprehension) to what this is leading them, and what the secret matter that this ceremony signifies is, he formidably thunders at them, "What use to me is the multitude of your sacrifices? I want charity from you."[540]

Listen, Ephraim and Judah! This ceremony provides you a small path so you would strive to know God. Seek and provide for me charity, and having dedicated it to me, take some of it for yourselves. Your verdict and understanding of me, and your present charity, never and nowhere is of any worth. I do love ceremony, it is not repulsive to me. It can advise a good and intelligent soul. I do not argue this. But know that charity is most of all beloved to me – it is justice or the vision of God. This is the goal of all your sacrifices and sacraments of all sorts. But now that you have gone astray from the subject and point of all ceremonies, will you say, "What use is it to me, or subsequently to you? What good are they?" Why should you have them if you do not want to resolve the riddle? What is harmful to you is not of any good to me. How many ages have you been philosophizing about ceremonies, and has anything productive – other than schisms, superstitions and hypocrisy – been produced? Busybodies use them as leaves to cover their nakedness. Fools base their happiness in their shade? Ignorant zealots birth the arguments of sectarians and the international community of

---

[538] John 11:25
[539] I Cor 15:47
[540] Micah 6:6-8

the world's residents. My temple is incompatible with the babble of demolishers who want to introduce what I have never desired, that is, that all ceremonies would be woven in the same extent and forms to all the ends of the world. From this point there occurs irreconcilable enmity and hate and often bloodshed in neighboring lands. What is this occurring, such perversion? This labyrinth that was supposed to be for you a guide to charitable conduct actually leads you away from it.

So do I say to you, Discard it! It is nothing else but emptiness and abomination in my presence. Accept directly justice and charity and truth. Ask my David and he will tell you what it is. But better to ask yourself. You are not alone within yourself, but I am also within you. Comprehend and take heed to yourself. Listen furtively to my voice vocally crying. And my word and truth, fate and charity and my name, is all the same.

The supreme heart of the man Abraham understood all of this. His zeal burned for visions of God, while his high soul rose hour to hour like an eagle. "Sovereign Lord, how am I to comprehend the new land?" Listen, Abraham! Get for me a 3-year old calf, and 3-year old goat, and 3-year old ram, and a dove and pigeon, and at that time you will comprehend." Abraham with all his soul and all his gathered thoughts without faltering began to ascertain, not allowing his intelligent eye to slumber, "What need does God have in an animal? And considering this further, why should they be 3-years old? What is occurring here? It seems like a lot of babble." But God says, "Ah, but it is not babble." It is indeed a mystery, but who shall instruct me? Open my eyes, enlighten me! At that time I will learn. Abraham in time proved with this very act what the gatekeeper said, "He who seeks the Lord will acquire knowledge and virtue; he who seeks his justice will acquire peace." And so does Solomon say, "All creation in all of its species was formed from above, serving your personal commands. Let all of your young men be preserved without harm. A cloud overshadowing their regiment that appeared ahead of the flooding waters caused the dry land to surface, and did not impede their path through the Red Sea. Out of the violent stream a green field appeared and their entire nation passed while seeing the astonishing miracle accomplished by your hidden hands. They were satisfied as steeds and played as do lambs, praising you Lord who delivered them."[541]

Abraham had his path in this direction, the beginning without a beginning, having as if an iron staff in his hands, and namely, "Abraham believed God." He guessed correctly that the matter was not about animals, but referring to that calf of which his spiritual posterity, the prophet Hosea, said, "Ephraim, a calf, trained to love argument. I will find her pretty neck and crush Ephraim."[542] The same is said of his posterity by Jeremiah, "Hearing, the weeping Ephraim has heard. You have punished me Lord and I was punished. Like a calf I have not learned."[543] This appellation designates the entire pagan heart of people, containing nothing within it except the dust of decay, not understanding and getting muddy in the water and not moving to dry ground.

Jeremiah calls all of them Egypt and calls them a calf. "Egypt is a select and decorated calf, but its destruction will occur at midnight, and also its workers living in its midst like fat calves fed there."[544] Having placed trust in their dust as if it was something reliable, the justice of God in the same manner will destroy these and hide them in the dust. Not understanding and not having found it, they become obstinate as cattle with their decaying horns. Jeremiah pertains to this, "The horns of Moab are cut off and his right arm is shattered."[545] And David, "I will break all the horns of the sinful."[546] So and what need is there for God who has called you to the comprehension of yourself to demand of you cattle

---

[541] Wisdom of Solomon 19:6-9
[542] Hosea 10:11
[543] Jer 31:18
[544] Jer 46:20-21
[545] Jer 48:25
[546] Ps 75:10

and to remind you of this? You are yourself a calf and goat and sheep and deer and all. And otherwise what need was there for Daniel to philosophize about a goat defeating a ram? "And it struck the ram and broke both its horns and no strength remained in the ram to withstand him and he cast him to the ground and trampled him, and there was no more ram that could deliver itself from his hands."[547] What need was there for God to threaten the shepherds through Zechariah? "My anger is inflamed and I will visit the lambs, and the Lord God Almighty will visit his flock the house of Judah and will transform it as a decorated steed for battle."[548] The ram that has no testicles is not dedicated to God, and so with other disfigured animals.[549] In Deuteronomy God does not allow a eunuch or emasculated man into the Lord's temple.[550]

My friend, all of this directly applies to you, whoever you are as long as you are a lover of truth. If you would comprehend yourself at such a time, you become God's and God becomes yours; you would reside in the midst of His house not as a eunuch, just as He mentions in Numbers and in His heavenly compositions, but as a man who knows his Lord as God himself, just as did Moses who testified. "Moses in my entire house is faithful. I speak mouth to mouth to him openly and not in riddles, and he sees the Lord's glory. So why have you dared to speak against My servant Moses?"[551]

Listen! Here is how wisely the situation and subject of other cattle and eunuchs who have not comprehended the truth is vividly described by Solomon! "The woman meets him and she appears to be a prostitute and causes the young man's heart to beat fast. She is an undercover prostitute and her feet cannot remain at home."[552] So here we have this young man. This young man is not identified in the Book of Numbers among the number of God's men, even though they

---

[547] Dan 8:7
[548] Zech 10:3
[549] Lev 22:24
[550] Deut 23:1
[551] Num 12:7-8
[552] Pr 7:10-11

are adults. And where does she meet him? Of course, in the streets. You heard that her feet do not rest at home. And listen further, "And she flatters him with much conversation, with the snare of her lips she draws him into immorality and he immediately follows her having gone insane and is led like a bull to be butchered, or like a dog on a chain, or like a deer whose entrails have been wounded with an arrow, and he hurries as a bird in a cage, not knowing to what he is leading his soul."[553]

Here are your cattle and animals and birds! Now somehow be informed about all cattle not sanctified unto God, and you will see that all of such decay pertains to your comprehension. For example, "The blind or crushed or having his tongue[554] severed, and others such, will not be brought to the Lord."[555]

So now listen to what was said above about the person, "Every person who is blind or crippled or snub-nosed or without an ear, or with crushed hands or feet, or hunchbacked, and others, will not be allow to bring an offering." What does this mean? Discard ceremonial prattle and listen to what Hosea says, "Just as you have rejected knowledge, so will I reject you lest you continue to sacrifice to me. And just as you have forgotten the law of your God, so will I forget your offspring."[556] These are the people whom God does not want to provide sacrifices. Their knowledge he interprets above in this manner, "Hear the word of the Lord, sons of Israel, as the Lord's judgment on the living of the earth, for there is no truth, no charity, no vision of God in the land."[557] So what is the blind or crippled or snub-nosed? Listen to David, "They have eyes but do not see, have ears but do not hear, nostrils but do not smell." What is further? "So those who make them are like them."[558]

---

[553] Pr 7:21-23
[554] referring to the penis
[555] Deut 23:1
[556] Hosea 4:6
[557] Hosea 4:1
[558] Ps 115:5-6, 8

Do you sense that the mother of all of such shame is ignorance of God? She is the one called a prostitute by Solomon, who is away from her husband's house, and so has departed from knowledge and leads others away. So Isaiah refers to them, "Touching the wall as the blind do."[559] And David, "They have withered and become lame because of their ways." These are the asps of which Isaiah says, "The deaf shall hear and the blind shall see. But who is blind? Except my servants. Who is deaf? Except those who govern, and God's servants have all become blind."[560] These are those who have lost their tongue, "My tongue will learn your righteousness. Lord, the Lord, gives me a language of knowledge."[561] These are the hunchbacked of which is said, "The hunched will not be healed. Let their eyes be darkened so they will not see and their spine be weakened when I remove the cord inside."[562] "And the land is filled with abomination, the works of their hands. And they worship what their fingers have created, and a person is brought low and man is humbled, and I will no longer tolerate them."[563]

Who is the snub-nosed? The person who is deprived of this nose, "And Isaac his father said to him, Come to me child and kiss me. And he came near and kissed him, and he smelled the odor of his clothes, and blessed him and said, Behold the odor of my son, the odor of a grown field that the Lord has blessed."[564] The nose of Isaac was precise, and filled with sharp senses. Everywhere he senses the sweetest spirit and the fragrant smoke of God's presence everywhere.

Such a nose did Job have, "The spirit of God is in my nostrils."[565] Such a nose the unwedded girls also had, those who said, "Lead me after you. In the fragrant of your peace

---

[559] Is 59:10
[560] Is 42:18-19
[561] Ps 119:171-172
[562] Ps 69:22
[563] Is 2:8-9
[564] Gen 27:27
[565] Job 27:3

we flow."[566] These girls followed after the one of whom we heard, "I am a flower of the field and a lily of the valley."[567] And one of them said, "My nard emitted its fragrance, the ripening grapes provided their pleasant odor."[568] And what is the vineyard? Listen to Isaiah, "The vineyard of the Lord Sabaoth is the house of Israel."[569]

Do you see that all of this comes to you, to your very home: you and land and animals and cattle and trees and vineyards and houses. It was in this very house that the bride found her brother. In this very vineyard she sensed the sweetest aromas of the trees and aromas of the herbs with that smell that her beloved friend brags of her having. "Who is she, pressing upon us as the morning? Your eyes are as the lakes in Heshbon. You nose is as the pillar of Lebanon viewing the face of Damascus."[570] But at what time did she receive such sharp vision and sense of smell? At the time she began friendship with her brother. "My brother is mine and I am his, shepherding in the lilies."[571] So why was she not sent to the shepherds huts? Here again is our haven.

Pamba: O, no. I cannot endure this any longer! Here is another virgin for you. "To God be the gratitude who has always made us victors regarding Christ Jesus, and the fragrance of his intellect is unveiled unto us in every place, and we are unto God as the fragrance of Christ among the saved and the ruined."[572]

Kvadrat: Why have you become quiet, Pamba? This is what follows, "We are not like the many who insincerely preach God's word, but sincerely and from God, and before God in Christ do we preach."[573] Take notice, does not complete agreement exist here? Do not the shepherd's tents preach insincerely? It is apparent that these have not comprehended themselves. But

---

[566] Song 1:3-4
[567] Song 2:1
[568] Song 1:11
[569] Is 5:7
[570] Song 7:4
[571] Song 6:3
[572] 2 Cor 2:14-15
[573] 2 Cor 17

just as these who have not comprehended themselves, and even do not sense within themselves the fragrance of God as they associate with each other in friendship, so it is stated in the holy house of the Bible. One spirit breathes in both these churches. And how are you supposed to obey and observe outside of yourself all that is written on paper, if you disdain within yourself your noisy house? And Paul speaks of these 2 houses. "Who from among people know what is within a person? Only the spirit living in him. Likewise no one knows what is God's except God's spirit."[574] Are you not listening to the inner person? Who will send you to the Siloam of the most sacred and living Biblical waters? Will you not go voluntarily? Listen to Isaiah, "And in place of fragrance there will be stench, and in place of a waistband you will gird yourself with sackcloth, and in place of a gold decoration upon your head, you will be bald."[575] Why is this? For the sake of your actions. Your criminality interferes with the secret voice of God's spirit living within you. Of this voice Paul states, "The law is spiritual."[576] This law thundered at him, "Saul! Saul."

Then the obedient servant turns to the Bible. So it is, "Take food and be strengthened."[577] The law sent him to the law, brother to brother, friend to friend, relative to relative, Jacob to Joseph, Tobit to Raguel, king to king. And so the proverb teller relates, "The brother who assists his brother is like a firm and high city, fortified like an established sovereignty." For this reason Paul says that he was not sent by some person, but by God,[578] and that he was not of the number mentioned by Jeremiah, "I did not send the prophets, but they flowed; I did not speak to them, but they prophesied." And God continues to speak to them in the same place, "If they were sent from my parliament and with my counsel, then would My words have been heard. And which

---

[574] 1 Cor 1:11
[575] Is 3:24
[576] Rom 7:14
[577] Acts 9:4, 19
[578] Gal 1:1

ones? They would have turned My people from their evil paths and their criminal activities. But who can fathom this?"[579] As Jesus Sirach says, "Only those who know their soul will meditate on the supreme law. He will seek the wisdom of all the ancients and study prophecies."[580]

Anton: So here you are with your nose full of God's fragrance, only a virgin girl, breathing the sweetest odor of Isaiah, "The spirit of the Lord is upon me." O, Isaiah! And was it your nard that provided you your fragrance? Evangelizing to the destitute, it seems that he very much sings in agreement with the son of Sirach, "Listen to me, holy children and flourish as the rose and provide a fragrance as frankincense, a pleasant aroma."[581] Having recognized your brother, they lead others to him following themselves. "They brought the girls to the king."[582] "We have not accepted the spirit of this world, but the spirit from God, and so we know that this was provided us from God. So do we speak not in words of human wisdom, but in the instructions of the holy Spirit; discerning spiritual matters in spiritual terms."[583]

Luke: How far away has the blind and deaf and crooked-nosed led us! Reap, Israel, and bring this into the house of the Lord your God. Reap with joy, saying with the beloved sister, "Let my brother descend into his garden and let him eat his fruits and vegetables." Your Bible is your very vineyard! If this is your vineyard, then why should we defile it with a bodily harvest?

Let us gather the produce from you, through you and for you. But not all of this is yours: what is defiled; all that is defiled, which is the land, flesh and blood. You sow the land, you also reap the land, but not the land itself. It is of the land, but the land is not yours. There is earthly land and mountainous land, promised, heavenly, spiritual, the Lord's. You planted upon the land your paradise, so gather its produce. If you were its beginning, then also be its end. What

---

[579] Jer 23:21-22
[580] Sirach 39:1
[581] Sirach 39:13-14
[582] Ps 45:14
[583] 1 Cor 2:12-13

are you saying to us, Paul? He says, "The person who sows into his flesh will reap the decaying; but the person who sows into the spirit will from the spirit reap eternal life."[584] Up to this time I have sown upon the divine field but I have comprehended it according to the flesh. And so what did I reap? Dead sheaves and solely poison.

But now I understand well what Hosea instructs me, "Sow unto yourself virtue, gather the produce of life, enlighten yourself with the light of vision. While there is time, seek the Lord, until the harvest of virtue arrives."[585] Blessed are you the Lord my God. Behold I begin to sense your life-providing spirit, the sweetest fragrance poured upon us without limit, as a sweet-smelling incense ready to follow its flow. Write me including me in the number and incline me to follow you with those girls of whom Amos spoke, "On that day there will be a dearth of good girls."[586] And Zechariah, rejoicing, cries, "Wheat for the young men and fragrant wine for the young women. Reap, friends, reap."[587]

Pamba: If those who are blind, crippled, crooked-nosed or whose members are crushed, or having some disfigurement cannot participate in the Lord's temple, then it is useless to bring as a sacrifice such cattle or unclean animals as the counsel of God defines them, and such cannot be dedicated unto Him. On the other hand, clean animals, birds, signify people whose heart is capable of envisioning God. Discern this please: God only permits such animals and cattle that have a split-hoof to be dedicated to Him. But this is not all. He seeks beyond this the requirement of animals to chew their cud, meaning that food must be chewed twice before it is digested through the stomach. Such for example are the cow, goat and deer.

Is not such wisdom just a joke? But of course this is divine wisdom, which is true and supremely blessed if you were to chew it twice and well. It is possible for a person to become happy after a thorough search into the matter of food?

---

[584] Gal 6:8
[585] Hosea 10:12
[586] Amos 8:13
[587] Zech 9:17

Is this the sole conclusion of God's wisdom? What dissonance! "My son, give to me your heart. Dedicate to me your soul. So it will be the same to you."[588] But here it seems that God has forgotten something. "Give unto Me the ox, goat, sheep." All of these daily ceremonies exist as though presented on a theater stage, they are a secret gesture provided to allow people to grasp having to heed their inner self, and so in time this will allow them to attain envisioning God. Such ceremonies were serving as a guide by a relative. All of this is summarized clearly and precisely by Paul who said, "The law was a teacher to bring us to Christ."[589]

However all the ages and nations are everywhere full of such people who are residing in the shadow that the law cast, and not finding themselves acclimated to chewing the cud they colonized and settled. Of such people Hosea writes, "With sheep and calves they will go to seek the Lord and will not find Him, because He has declined from them."[590] And for what reason? Because they did not consider the mysteries of the sacrifice the means of leading them to that something that was secret and, not being able to chew on it, they were alienated from this conclusion that their ceremony, as a definitive trail, had the ability to lead them. This is the entire reason!

Hosea continues, "Just as they have abandoned the Lord, they have begotten alien children for themselves, and now rust will devour them." Such senseless cattle are admonished very clearly by Micah, "How will I attain unto the Lord? How will I find my supreme Lord? Will I find Him in burnt offerings? In one-year old calves? Will the Lord accept thousands of rams and ten-thousands of fatted goats? Will I offer him my first-born – the produce of my loins – for my dishonesties, for my sins? Has not what is good already been proclaimed to you, man? This is only to practice virtue and

---

[588] Sirach 16:24
[589] Gal 3:24
[590] Hosea 5:6-7

love mercy and be prepared to walk with the Lord your God."[591]

This is the conclusion of every and all ceremony and rite: mercy and justice. And how can mercy and justice be defined? Listen to David, "Provide me life according to your mercy and according to my destiny. Mercy and truth have greeted. Your justice is forever justice, and your law is truth. Much peace be unto those who love your law. Virtue and peace will kiss."[592] Seek first God's kingdom and its virtue. God's kingdom is within you.

So how am I to attain the Lord? The first chew consists in removing the crust or the historical, ceremonial and parabolic husk, or to say it concisely, the flesh. But since flesh and blood is not and in no manner this divine kingdom and is not divine virtue, then our virtue is unclean, like the cloths of an unclean woman.[593] This is why we must proceed further to another manner of mastication and find that something which is hidden beyond the useless walnut shell, the taste conforming to the kernel inside, hidden inside its shell, just as it was written to the Corinthians, "The spirit puts all to trial and even the profound matters of God."[594] Behold the cattle with its mastication! Listen! "I consider all to be futile in comparison with the supreme comprehension of Christ Jesus my lord. For his sake I have abandon all and consider all I have as nothing, in order to be able to acquire Christ and for him to acquire me, not possessing my own personal virtue which is from the law, but that which is the belief in Jesus Christ, the virtue evolving from God in belief." So this is how it is chewed again. "In order to grasp him and the power of his resurrection and participation in his passions. My God! To be conforming to his death."[595] Perhaps it would be possible for me also to attain to the resurrection of the dead.

---

[591] Micah 6:6-8
[592] Ps 85:10
[593] Is 64:6
[594] 1 Cor 2:10
[595] Phil 3:8-10

Is it possible to select a better animal for God? He has abandoned all – he is chewing. And what he has chewed he is chewing again. He is humbling himself as though he has not already attained, in order to motivate others to want to do the same. It is as if he was deceiving, but in a truthful manner. Here for you is another animal beloved of God and which is also chewing. "For this reason the deer desires a spring of water. When will I arrive and appear before the presence of God?"[596] Here is an animal worthy to be dedicated unto God, appropriate for the search of divine virtue, and there is nothing that is sweeter than this. Of this the son of human beings prays, "Sanctify them in your truth."[597] This is the one who will attain the mountain of divine virtue. The mountains are high for the deer. "Enter the high mountain, evangelizing to Zion."[598]

There! Look! The deer prances in the Acts [of the Apostles]; he is healed by Peter. "Leaping, he stands and walks. He walks and leaps and glorifies God."[599] Of such animals God asks Job with great importance, "Have you grasped the time of a goat's birth, those living in the rocks of the mountains? Have you seen the pain of deer when they give birth?"[600] Here is the deer! "Tabitha! Arise!"[601] Here it is! Look at the deer giving birth, at Isaiah, "Due to fear of you Lord, they conceived in the womb and it was painful when they gave birth to the spirit of your salvation. This you performed in the land. And all such living people who do not find it will perish in the land." From such animals divine truth was born and it resides with humans. They chewed on it for their own benefit and so gave birth in the land to prosperity for others. This is another example for you of a clean animal with good teeth. Listen to what Jacob says to his son Judah, whose family name is the source of all the cattle and animals

---

[596] Ps 42:1
[597] John 17:17
[598] Is 52:7
[599] Acts 3:8
[600] Job 39:1-3
[601] Acts 9:40

that are provided for chewing by those gifted with good teeth. "Judah, your brothers will praise you. There will be no dearth of princes from Judah or leaders from his loins. His happily-oriented eyes surpass wine and his white teeth transcend milk."[602] David encourages the posterity of Judah, "Taste and you will see how good the Lord is."[603]

Paul from his early years had poor and weak teeth. "When I was a child I philosophized as a child."[604] He says to his friends who had not yet attained maturity in the fullness of Christ, "I nurtured you with milk, and not with flour."[605] Wheat is called flour with which Joseph furnished his brothers and of which Zechariah speaks, "Wheat is for the young." This is the seed of resurrection, the seed of the word and divine wisdom buried in the dirt of flesh and blood, of which it is said, "Who will comprehend the Lord's mind?"[606] Such food made of wheat is for the immature having the teeth of Judah, which is just a little above children's milk. A child's chewing is unable to masticate the outer shell of the walnut confining the kernel. He says this only regarding himself and those like him, "We have Christ's mind."[607] And it is surprising how he has the ability to chew this well. Is it not possible to have better teeth than with the following, "He knows the books, never having been educated."[608] Even with a little reading there is much to chew. O, what a tasteful flavor! Those who have no capacity of attaining such an ability to taste have the following cried to them, "Is not this the reason you go astray, not knowing the scriptures or the power of God?"[609]

O, my Lord! Why do they not know this? From an early age they have begun to babble Your Bible, upon which they were nurtured; not allowing even one verse or passage not to

---

[602] Gen 49:8, 12
[603] Ps 38:8
[604] 1 Cor 13:11
[605] 1 Cor 3:2
[606] Rom 11:34
[607] 1 Cor 2:16
[608] John 7:15
[609] Matt 22:29

avoid being debated. Your name, Your cross always hangs upon their chests, on their lips, upon their clothes, on their walls, on their plates, in their ceremonies. But they do not perceive the benefit of chewing and tasting. It is for this reason that he sends away such toothless cattle, "Go and learn what this means: I want charity and not offerings!"[610] Even the chosen Paul does not like such animals that are useless to God. "Led by diverse lusts, they are always learning but never able to attain the comprehension of truth."[611] Calling them enemies of the cross of Christ,[612] while David calls them men of blood and flattery.[613] And why is this? Concentrating on ceremonies and sitting at feasts with meat on the tables, they could not orient their mind to seek divine truth. Leaving its light they have returned to their darkness, to which their ceremonies have led them, to their flesh and lies, and then returning to their festivities.

And so, deceived by dinners of meat dishes, they deprived themselves of that food of which the son of Sirach writes, "There is a stomach for every bread; but there is a bread better than another bread."[614] So to what does this pertain? "Blessed is the person who dines in God's kingdom."[615] So what is the flour? "Blessed are they who hunger and thirst for virtue."[616] Now listen, "There exists an inherent body, and there exists a spiritual body."[617] So what is this body? "This is the bread that descends from heaven." What is this bread? "It is the spirit that provides life, the flesh is of no benefit."[618] David sings regarding this life-giving truth, "The Lord's truth resides forever. Let your word provide me life."[619] Departing from it they have turned to

---

[610] Matt 9:13
[611] 2 Tim 3:6-7
[612] Phil 3:18
[613] Ps 5:9
[614] Sirach 45:26
[615] Luke 14:15
[616] Matt 5:6
[617] 1 Cor 15:40
[618] John 6:33, 63
[619] Ps 117:2

their sorrowful evening dinner, not wanting to pursue truth with Paul. "Brethren, I do not consider myself having attained it, but only placing the past behind me I strive toward the future, I drive to the goal ahead of me."[620] While the son of Sirach writes of stupid people who, having heard the good word, discard it over their shoulders. Such are mentioned in the Psalm, "Let them turn back and be ashamed."[621] And by Isaiah, "O, you sinful tongue! Sons of crime! People saturated with sins! The seed of wickedness! Return, you who have abandoned the Lord and angered the Holy one of Israel."[622] This is the family of Ham, "Cursed is the young Canaan,[623] and the angels who did not observe their office."

Jude the servant of Christ thunders horribly and threateningly at them, calling them, among other things, devious stars for whom the gloom of darkness is reserved forever, and also carnal creatures devoid of spirit.[624] These senseless descendents of Ham have completely stripped God their father of all his actions. Finding any residing in belief or spirit they, having destroyed them, seek to install in their place their own hands and feet and body and decay, and while at the same time they philosophize that the terrible curses of Deuteronomy would overtake them. "Since you did not serve the Lord your God with joy and goodness of heart and instead served your enemies, the Lord will bring upon you a nation from a distant place, from the end of the earth, and He will crush you in all your cities, and until all of your high and strong walls are destroyed, those upon which you depended. And you will eat the children of your womb, the flesh of your sons and daughters which the Lord your God gives to you."[625]

This is the type of annihilation that will occur to those who have weak teeth. Let us also listen to what Job says about

---

[620] Phil 3:13
[621] Ps 6:10
[622] Is 55:6-7
[623] Gen 9:25
[624] Jude 6, 13, 19
[625] Deut 28:47-53

them, "Even their demise perishes."[626] Now notice this, that they do not reach their designated place with Paul. And what does it further say? "In scarcity and waterless famine." And why? "They fled to yesterday's waterless oppression and destitution."[627] It is not surprising that they have fallen into despair. It was not necessary for them to flee to yesterday's oppression, the evening is always full of hunger. They hunger at night.

This is what should have been sought! "It is spirit that provides life." Apparently they did not understand what is spirit. This is what is so pathetic, they have a difficult time chewing. And so Job relates further, "They sought for herbs in the forests, and these herbs served them as food, dishonorable and destitute people, deprived of all goodness. They chewed the roots of trees due to their great hunger."[628] It is possible to have worse teeth than these? Tell me, please! Do not these retarded people seem to be related to the horrible beast of Daniel, all of which devoured and broke and then even worse he trampled on the remains with his feet.[629] Take note that the one that trampled the remains is the same type of people of whom Job spoke, "Even their demise perishes." What a marvel! They tore, devoured and swallowed with the steel teeth inherited from their father, and with nothing remaining. Where are the remains? You trampled the remains! O, you sinful tongue! The snake's progeny! You have trampled the person who complains in David, "My enemies have trampled me."[630] And also, "I am the beginning and the end."

Only Israel pursued and attempted to attain its all-encompassing prosperity, that of which Moses said to Asher while blessing them, "The divine principle will shelter you."[631] Only one remnant attempted to attain this, "There

---

[626] Job 8:18
[627] Job 30:3
[628] Job 30:4, 8
[629] Dan 7:7
[630] Ps 7:5
[631] Gen 33:27

remains a remnant in Israel."[632] It alone devours all, destroys, tramples, if only to somehow arrive at and preserve for itself what is written, "Blessed are you in the city and blessed are you in the village, blessed are your offspring, and the produce of your land, and your herds of cattle and flocks of sheep; blessed are your barns and your remains."[633] There is nothing anywhere comparable to your teeth, the generation saved of the Lord! Their difference from the cursed steel teeth is like the distance of the sky from the ground.

Let us listen to what the beloved David attained in mastication: The Beginning. But now tell us what is this beginning? "The beginning of your statements is truth." Then subsequently David knew also the end. Of course. The beginning and end are both the same. Your meal is even better if you do not discard the remains. And how are you supposed to trample it if you ask yourself, "Tell me Lord my end."? It is sweeter than honey and juice for you. I have already received this from the Lord, "The end has seen every other conclusion." But what is this end? O, how wide is his commandment. "They like garments become old.[634] Heaven and earth will pass away."[635] In reality David, your teeth are white and your eyes are joyful appearing and your feet are beautiful! You have tasted of the Lord, saw him, attained truth, virtue and God's kingdom. Here are the cattle and animal for you that chews the cud.

Konon: This animal is definitely clean. Not crippled, not blind, not to be said that it possesses any blemish. For all good reason it is beloved of God. It is worthy of the Lord, and the Lord is worthy of it. Now it seems, and I am an uneducated person, I am beginning to understand what we and Filon often hear read in church, "The teeth of the sons of humans are weapons and arrows. God will shatter their teeth."[636]

---

[632] Rom 11:5
[633] Deut 28:3-4
[634] Is 34:4
[635] Matt 24:35
[636] Ps 57:4, 58:6

Filon: O, Konon. It would be better for us to just keep silent and listen. But for your sake I cannot retain my silence. Us simple people are referred to as cattle. But if only God would grant me to have a few blemishes. At least then we would be unpretentious. What I love doing is to chew on something I enjoy from my past memory. "He considered himself a lamb destined for slaughter."[637] Blessed is the Lord who has not given us to be spoils for their teeth."[638]

Kvadrat: Pamba, the words of Job that were told you, "They chewed the roots of trees due to great hunger," brought to my memory the parable of the son gone astray, the destitute shepherd of swine.[639] He is himself gaunt from hunger while he feeds swine. It is apparent that the shepherd and his herd have the same type of teeth and the same taste. This is what occurs with a person who is not knowledgeable of himself! He left his home, the house of his father; he squandered his thoughts in alien distance regions; his soul he discarded from his inner treasury just like a cluster of grapes cut from the vine, like an uprooted willow previously planted along living waters. He wants to be fed but yet his life is spent feeding others. And his herd is never to be oxen or goats or sheep or deer, until he returns to his father at his home.

It is true that a pig has a split hoof, but it cannot be dedicated to God at his place of offering because it does not chew the cud. Yes and how can God live in this herd when demons are dispersed there to reside.[640] Other than this, swine love mud and not springs with deer; they prefer swampy and dirty water. And this cannot mean anything else than the soul that possesses such a taste and teeth, of which the Book of Numbers mentions. The Jews complained and wailed in tears, "Who will give us meat for food? Give us meat to eat." O, how difficult it is to comprehend yourself. What is the same and identical mastication if a person cannot comprehend the physical substance residing in himself? We can attain to

---

[637] Is 53:7
[638] Ps 124:6
[639] Luke 15:11-32
[640] Matt 8:31

eating the meat of Egypt, but not penetrating with our teeth into the flood of divine fulfillment, as Job states, "From the fragrance of the waters the newly-planted will flourish and create an abundant harvest"[641]

But so how are we to comprehend ourselves as we philosophize with our brethren regarding Sacred Scripture? Already the Lord has given us quails, the new food He acquired for us from the sea. We emaciated ourselves on animal fodder and now tasted the spirit, however as it says, "The meat was still between their teeth and before they swallowed it."[642] Enough of this meat that the rulers eat, let them chew their own meat in their teeth.

This is how difficult it is for our intellect to gnaw a second time as we chew! And all of our misfortune resides in this matter. "And the Lord was much angered at the people, and the Lord inflicted the people with a very infectious plague. And the name of the place was called Graves of Lust." Take heed to yourselves, unfortunate interpreters! Chew the information more firmly! Do not remember the first and do not think about the olden! Devour the olden of all the olden! The Lord says, "Behold I have make all new." So if heaven is sewn closed for you, then will this occur? For you will never be able to arise from the sleep of your coffins. We chew meat, but we ourselves personally consume our own dead flesh with our teeth. But for our second dinner, give me these teeth, "Your teeth are like a shorn flock of lambs that have left the washing, all of them expecting twins and giving birth to twins."[643] Give me please, Paul's teeth. "We have an altar from which those who serve the shadow have not received authority to eat."[644] Give David's teeth to them, "You have prepared me a dinner table in my presence."[645] I do not want

---

[641] Job 5:10
[642] Num 11:33-34
[643] Song 4:2
[644] Heb 13:10
[645] Ps 23:5

the teeth of those stupid animals that say, "These words are extreme and who can grasp them."[646]

Such swine's teeth eats the same Pharisaic leaven, and it is not in the bread of Angels but in the animal, not in the real flesh but in the Lord's flesh that descends from heaven to which David encourages us, "Taste and you will see." It is the spirit that provides life. Do you think that you alone consist solely of flesh, and that God has never possessed anything like it? Other than yourselves, is there nothing divine? Why do you spill upon your ground righteous blood, true blood, the Lord's blood, the non-decaying blood? These are the people who eat the bread of affliction and the defilement of their corpses. These are the beasts of Daniel that trample on the Lord's remains.

These are the Arabian wolves of which Zephaniah says, "Their princes among them are like roaring lions. Their judges are Arabian wolves who leave nothing behind for the morning."[647] Are they cursed with gluttony? During the night they devour all they possibly can, not leaving any for the morning, for the beautiful morning, as Isaiah states, "Install for me the morning, yes, the morning,"[648]

You kill your inner heavenly person with the sword of your thoughts, not recognizing it in the midst of your darkness, concluding that the essence of your spark consists in only decaying darkness. Know this you Arabian wolves that I am a prophet unto you and the terrifying will overwhelm you. "And they will look upon him whom they have pierced, and weep over him with tears as though over a beloved son, and they will feel the pain of him with illness as though over their firstborn."[649] And also, "Your life will hang before your eyes, and you will be afraid during the day and during the night and you will not believe your own household. In the morning you will say, Where is the night? And in the evening you will say, When will it be morning? This will evolve from the fear in

---

[646] John 6:60
[647] Zeph 3:3
[648] Is 28:19
[649] Zech 12:10

your heart, and you will be afraid, and from the sight of your eyes, because you will see what is occurring."[650]

Now listen to what Zephaniah has to say about the reason for all of this disaster, "O, radiant and delivered city of doves! Not having heard the voice, not having accepted punishment, not relying on the Lord, and not getting near to your God." And then he says, "Its prophets are full of hot air, men of insight; its priests defile the holy and the law has no affect on them."[651] So where was it that they heard the voice of God? Herein lies their entire desolation: they did not realize what it was that would surely follow, "The Lord is just among them."[652] These are the consequences! I have said enough, my friends, regarding the many cattle and animals unacceptable to God because of their poor chewing development.

Anton: Just as their chewing the cud, so does their cloven hoof together apply as instruction for us. Paul, interpreting the words, "Do not muzzle the mouth of the threshing ox," says, "Do you really think that God's concern here in these words deals with oxen?"[653] My friend, he is admonishing you and you personally toward knowledge of truth. Leave your oxen for economic and physical researchers. What use is it for you to be knowledgeable in oxen, while blind in the comprehension of yourself? Chewing the cud is eating the Lord's truth, and a cloven hoof follows the same thought likewise. Peter says, "Where will we go and to whom? You possess the words of eternal life."[654] To divide the hoof is to divide your foot and path with David, "Guide my steps according to your word." Listen to Micah, "Person! What is good has been proclaimed to you." Here is the truth for you. You have already eaten it. What else other than this does the Lord require of you? This is what, "To do justice and love mercy and be prepared and to walk with the Lord your

---

[650] Deut 28:67
[651] Zeph 3:1-2, 4
[652] Zeph 3:5
[653] 1 Cor 9:9
[654] John 6:68

God."[655] Are you beginning to recognize truth? Love it and conform to it accordingly, otherwise without such an attitude you are worthless as a dedication to it. Up to now you have wandered in your own direction leading you into the pit of passions, but now having recognized truth recognize it with David, "I have professed my ways and you have heard me."

For this new path you need to acquire new feet. One of your feet will be following just one path, as thought it was cloven or separated. The journey of God your king is distinct. Raise yourself from base servilities and onto the mountain of virtue and its kingdom until your feet develop into those of the deer, until you are able to say, "My feet stand on virtue." And is this not what it means to be an ox thresher? The ox tramples the sheaves, removes the husk, separates the grain.

You following the Lord's path must do the same. What else is the entirety of human decay if not husk and the floor? "All flesh is grass, just like dust," cries Isaiah. But you seek and try to find the word of your God, the seed of the word and his endless kingdom, in this husk and the dust of the floor. Circumvent all that is pagan. The speech of Micah is directed toward you, "They have not comprehended the Lord's thoughts and have not attained understanding his counsel when he gathered them as sheaves into the barn. Arise and thresh them, daughter of Zion."[656]

At this time you become a lamb, saying with David, "I have walked in my virtuousness. The Lord shepherds me." As a result your feet do not flow toward crime. But then Isaiah prophesies regarding such oxen and lambs, "They will not find fear there. Bushes and thorns will become pasture for my flocks of sheep and to be trampled by the ox."[657] The same applies to goats, "Run my brother and be like the gazelle or young deer on the aromatic mountains."[658] O, how beautiful are the feet of those upon the mountains evangelizing peace! They will acquire wings like those of the eagle, will proceed

---

[655] Micah 6:8
[656] Micah 4:12-13
[657] Is 32:13-14
[658] Song 2:17

and not hunger, run and not tire. They will grow from strength to strength until the following is fulfilled upon them.[659] My people will recognize My name on that day, for I am the very one who is saying, Here I am. On that day they will sing this song in the land of Judah saying, Behold the city is firm. And our salvation will be the walls and enclosure. Open the gates that the people may enter, those who observe virtue and observe truth, who possess truth and observe peace. And upon You is the reliance of those who possessed hope, the Lord forever, the great and eternal God who has humbled and brought down those living high, has destroyed the strong cities and leveled then even with the ground, and the feet of the humble and contrite will walk upon them. The path of the virtuous is the right one, and this path of the virtuous is prepared, for the path of the Lord is justice.[660]

So does Amos state, "On that day I will reestablish the tabernacle of David that has fallen, the harvest will arrive, the gathering of grapes, and the clusters will ripen for the picking, and the mountains will drip with sweetness. I will return the captivity of my people. I will replant them in their land and no one will ever uproot them from their land again, from the land that I have given them, says the Lord."[661]

Now do you see or do you not see the significance of the split or cloven hoof? And to where should this clean animal dedicated to God proceed? Figure this for yourself what the bull of Isaiah means, "On that day your cattle will graze in a fertile and immense place, your calves and oxen with which you plow the ground will eat grass mixed with barley." But listen, my friend, I hope you will figure out whom Isaiah is identifying by using the term cattle that chew the cud and possess a divided hoof. "May all the desert places of Jerusalem masticate in joy because the Lord has pardoned his people." [662] If during this time these herds of cattle ramble in your head, and are unable to chew, then all of this seems to

---

[659] Is 52:7, 40:31
[660] Is 26:1, 60:18
[661] Amos 9:11, 13-15
[662] Is 52:9

you like the words of David in his later years, "My heart rejoiced in the good word. My lips rejoiced in song." But what pertains to clean hooves is mentioned by Isaiah, "Depart, depart, leave this place and do not touch what is unclean."[663] So with what type of water does the Lord wash the feet of these animals? Isaiah speaks, "The Lord will wash the defilement of the sons and daughters of Zion and will cleanse the blood of Jerusalem from them with the spirit of judgment."[664]

Is it not possible that the divine word is weakened? It is what provides them a new taste and clean feet. It is what turns Zephaniah's lions into sheep and calves, while his wolves that do not chew the cud and do not leave anything to be eaten by the morning are transformed into lambs; and the mountain lion into a goat. These are the very animals earlier indicated but now with the several stomachs of a sheep and with deer's feet. They ruminate with joy and skip on the mountains of aromas. My God! Is not this a new creation and new creature? What a miracle! The fierce leopard and kid together both loving creatures; the ravenous wolf and gentle lamb; the formidably roaring lion and the calf lowing for its mother. O, most beloved Isaiah. This very truth is what you sing, "The wolf will graze together with a lamb, and the leopard will rest with the kids, and the calf and sheep and lion together will graze together."[665] When will this occur? It will, do not worry! Just allow God to cause the shoot from the root of Jesse to flower.

Luke: Sacred Scripture is a lamp, shining for our sake with the divine light, for us travelers. I believe it is this way and I am surprised that its speech flows in an excellent manner, not compatible with other writers. The Biblical speech is similar to the Asiatic river called the Meandr.[666] They say that this river flows through the most beautiful of all places, but its course is serpentine, and it changes its direction regularly like

---

[663] Is 52:11
[664] Is 4:4
[665] Is 11:6
[666] The Buyuk Menderes River in southwestern Turkey

a labyrinth. And this is actually a good thing, that the person seeking God's kingdom is distinct from other people and like an animal that chews its cud, and this is different from other animals. So it is! I hope this can be understood as a parable! Let the cloven hoof signify a special journey. So it is! And of course, from the new understanding in the head of the traveler there must be born a new road for him and distinct from his initial journey. Let it be this way! But only it is somewhat more incredible for the foot to indicate inclination, friendship and selfish desire.

It seems this can be noticed just as much with others as with the words of Habakkuk, "The Lord my God is my strength and He orients my feet for climbing and leads me to a high place in order to grant me victory in his song."[667] I understand that many can ruminate and expel the fragrant spirit and then return to the number of those of whom it is written, "Many of his disciples walked away and no longer associated with him." And I know that the Lord needs only a few and without having to give reason, so that the animal dedicated to him would be beyond chewing the cud or having a cloven hoof, and because not always will this be pleasant to our taste, what it is we eat. But what is required is for us to be hunters with good teeth. But for what reason do we identify the appetite as the foot? What a marvelous style.

Pamba: Beloved friend! Train your taste to the food of the Bible. There is nothing more useful or sweeter, although its curves are not pretty corners. But first I ask of you to acquire a better opinion regarding this gloomy wisdom that has created for itself a house of 7 pillars. As much as it is externally unsightly and contemptible, to the same extent internally it is important and majestic. Wisdom selects words from you that are applicable to your encompassing manner of interpretation, for example: feet, hands, eyes, head, clothes, bread, vessels, house, soil, cattle, land, water, air, fire. But it does not ever itself wander in the surroundings, but strikes directly at the point that is the most perspicacious and principle of all that

---

[667] Hab 3:19

surrounds it, and which has the sole intent of bringing you to it. Wisdom speaks only with your words, but it is not yours. Using your flute and using your song it sings, "That I may gain the victory in his song." This is the very thing that will bring you out of your fated mud and from your encompassing superficiality to your very essence and the truth that is the immaterial and indivisible composition of that point in the high places of which wisdom itself wills to state, "My exits are exits to life."

To this exaltation and resurrection, meaning to restore you upon new feet while lying in the darkness of your extreme superficiality, you utilize bodily words that extend you like a hook for a fish, wound about whatever it is you may catch yourself on, knowing that you are unable to chew anything at all and that nothing is tasteful to you and not edible, except for the outer flesh. Have you heard of the tree called the date-palm? Imagine that it grows in your native land. Look through your window at a beautiful apple tree. Do you notice that with its branches, as if having many hands, and with its leaves it is decorated and towering? But tell me, what is it that you do not see? Its roots are not visible to you. Until you heard these words regarding its roots, you did not think about its secret area. But now, not seeing, you see something else. In silence its branches cry in your presence, witnessing to its roots that draw moisture and distribute it to its highest parts.

O, you, my friend, a definite apple tree! I see your branches, but I do not see the roots of your heart, your soul, your thoughts. It is all hidden in the ground of your superficiality. I see the outside of your eye, as if a mitten on your hand, but I do not see the eye itself. It is hidden there. Where? O, don't ask! How shall I say this? I don't know. How can I tell you? It is enough for you to know that it is not here, but there. Will you understand what *here* means? I do not think so. So what are you asking? Why do you want to know what *there* is? Will you be able to understand? If you comprehend the *here*, you will comprehend the *there*. Grasp what *lowly* means, and you will understand what *high* pertains to. View the night, and then the morning will dawn upon you. If you consider the morning to be night, and then call night the morning, then the result is darkness. How can you grasp the concept of dry material land if you have not understood liquid, which is a material opposite to soil? The same eyes can view black and white. One ray of mental vision can ascertain what is stable and what is unstable. Remove the cataract from your eyes, take the mittens off your hands, remove the boots from your feet and you will see the location of *there*.

But I will tell you only one item now: the place from which all of your externality evolves. This seams annoying to you that the Bible calls the human desire a foot. But it also calls a person – a tree, like the date-palm, and also a fig tree. And if you chew and keep chewing you will see that what you call a foot is nothing other than some outer naked dust, like a twig from a tree that grows from the ground, like a lump of clay, and as if boots for your feet that witness to your outside that resides in the hidden roots of your heart, and all the dust is like your boots that you wear on your feet. And this is the target I think to which Job aimed here, "You placed my feet in rebuke, protected all my actions, you entered the roots of my feet." And of which root Isaiah writes, "Their root will become like dirt." And that he called the heart a root, listen to this, "Look that their heart is just dust, and they go astray." Note this: there the root is called dirt, while here it is called dust. The heart is a root. Your foot resides in it, and its boot is its outer dust.

This is why the Bible calls heartfelt desire the foot! This is specifically the foot, although it is clean, although not clean as the poet teachers. "The desire of the wicked is crime, the root of the pious is firm." And David calls very properly a foot the heart that by pride is haughty due to ambition. "Let not the foot of the arrogant step on me." As soon as the foot that is your heart is inflated, immediately the shoe upon it follows the head and conforms to it, just like a copy of an original document. And if this is surprising to you, that your heart and foot is one and the same, then it will seem all the more surprising to you if you notice that not only the foot, but also the hands and eyes and ears and tongue and all of your external members, is nothing more than a complete superficial cover of the internal person. But the precise members are securely hidden in the heart.

So here you are, poet, all of the thoughts of your heart placed together with your treasure. "The eye of the vixen, tongue of the criminal, the hands that spill innocent blood, and the heart that generates evil intents, and the feet that drive forward to do wrong, will all perish." Raise your ability to hear a little and meditate on what this means, "Who has ears to hear... If you eye causes you to go astray. Mortify your members" But is it possible to prick the eye? Mortify your members? It is possible. Bah! It is easily possible. There is nothing easier, but only for that person who has somewhat comprehended himself. But if you have not comprehended yourself, how will you prick it? How will you cut it? How will you heal yourself and recover? Do you not hear where your hands, feet and eyes are located? That which you consider your foot has never ever been one. You are blind. You are a snake slithering on your belly and always eating the dirt and the dust. So can you severe your earthly members? Are you asking me this, my friend? It is not possible, not at all possible. How is this? Let me tell you this, how it is. Because it is stupid. Why is this? O, destitute person! What a poor opinion you have of God. Is not your answer that He cannot be sufficient for you? So why are you separating impossibility from harm, and benefit from capability? It is all the same: it is impossible and unbeneficial.

Do not think bad of God's mercy toward you. This blessed essence you can develop to your benefit. It would have been possible to do this a long time ago, if it were beneficial. It would be impossible for you to breathe if it were not for spirit; is there any place not to find it? And if air was not beneficial, of course you would have a hard time finding it. And here you need to be satisfied with the answer given you. It was said, there is no reason to severe it. Do not ask any further to know why this is not beneficial. And this should not be done because it is not beneficial. Do you still not understand? You have a poor opinion of God's mercy, and your understanding is completely torpid.

But once you resolve this issue with yourself you will grasp this passage of Jeremiah, "Profound is the heart of a person, worse than all, and you are just human and who can fathom him?" And you will not be surprised that David's heart possessed lips and says that his tongue rejoices and his feet are joyous. Who has ever seen a tongue rejoice? The one who has comprehended himself. And of course it is the poor who have not penetrated considerately within themselves, whom Christ and his friends call melancholic. As a result the senseless question arises: Did Christ ever laugh? This question is very parallel with the following wisdom: Is it possible to have something hotter than the sun? What are you saying? Christ is the very son of Abraham, Isaac, that is laughter, joy and happiness, sweetness, peace and festivity. A person's heart that is enlightened by the wisdom of divine law is like the root of a tree that is planted along streams of water, while the violator of the law is a cursed fig tree. What use is a leaf superficially green if its root is deprived of life-providing fluids? It will soon whither. What joy it is if ostensive laughter opens the jaws showing its teeth to visitors, while your heart is cramped due to torpidity? Just as it writes, "Do not rejoice in crime!" Enlarge your heart and open wide your inner lips with David, "My lips I have opened and attracted the spirit." At this time and without a superficial smile you will always laugh with Sarah, "Give me laughter, Lord." And with David, "You provided me joy in my heart."

If the heart was able to speak in secret, then it is also able to laugh in secret. At this time you become just like a tree in winter that has no leaves. But they are concealed in the root, protected by that life-providing water of which the poet writes, "Deep water is the counsel in a person's heart." And David likewise, "The thoughts of his heart continue generation after generation." But without this, it is not yourself, but just only the dead lips of your skin that smiles. And is there anything that can be more opposing or tasteless to such laughter than hypocrisy? Here is home-born laughter! Listen, "Jesus rejoiced in the spirit."[668] Here Samuel's mother laughs over virtue, "My lips are enlarged at my enemies. I rejoice in your salvation."[669] So exactly does Paul laugh, "Your lips are opened unto us, Corinthians. Our hearts are expanded. Expand yours also to us."[670] So is David's smile. "In my sorrow you have expanded me; you have expanded my heart." But this is surprising that even his own tracks have expanded. "You have expanded my footsteps." It is as if his tracks have expanded and his footsteps laugh with him.

So what type of miracle is this? You did hear from Jeremiah that the person is specifically his heart. All the members are in his heart! So why should not all of his members laugh when he says himself, "My heart rejoices and my tongue is made joyous." The culmination of a heart's joy fills all of his members to fullness with a flood of bliss. "You have nourished me at calm waters." And even Job speaks of laughter, "The Lord will not reject the non-violent. He will not accept any gift from a criminal. He will fill true lips with laughter."[671] But with great sympathy God calls to those who lose the indescribable treasure of such a heart – the salvation or prosperity of their soul – in the words of Isaiah, "Approach me you who destroy the heart, who reside distant from justice."

Luke: The Bible seems to be like a terrifying cave where once a hermit lived, whom my brother once visited. "Tell me dear brother, what is it that keeps you in this gloomy residence?" After these words the hermit opened a curtain hanging on the wall. "Oh my God," cried the guest, having seen the majesty that surpasses and transcends the capability of any human mind. The hermit responded, "Here brother is what occupies

---

[668] Luke 10:21
[669] 1 Sam 2:1
[670] 2 Cor 6:11-13
[671] Job 8:21

my time." Then the brother remained to live with the other brother to the end of their lives, there in a residence that outwardly appeared sparse and gloomy.

Just as wisdom that enters a person's heart is wrapped in an old rag, yet it is incomparable in value to anything else. With its sparseness its high divine ladder descended to a street where simple-people resided, to make it accessible for everyone to climb and lead them to the very highest pinnacle of heavenly comprehension. And is not this what the poet inspires us? "It is on the highest edges, standing in the middle of the road." This is that folly to which Paul refers to the Corinthians.[672] Open the veil and you will see that this is the wisest of all, but only covered by stupidity.[673] But oh, my beloved friend! Now I recognize that you will not open the curtain until you comprehend yourself. Not having comprehended yourself, how can you seek this? "He acquired what he desired." And without this person Paul cries, "The cover will not cease to cover. He alone opens our eyes and transfers us from the ground to the heavens."

Kvadrat: The entirety of the book Exodus leads us to this place, to comprehend ones self. If the exodus unto wisdom is the exodus unto life, it is apparent that the migration from Egypt signifies the exit from death and unto life, from knowledge and unto more knowledge, from strength and unto more strength, until the God of gods appears in Zion. But where is this life? Listen to Paul, "We are given to death for the sake of Jesus, so that the life of Jesus will appear in our dead body." God is everywhere. What is the reason to move from place to place, from one superficial arena to another? So where can He be closer sought than within you yourself?

Anton: But does not Isaiah interpret this sufficiently, the meaning of this exodus? "You will leave in joy." What does it say further? "And you will learn in joy." Transfer your thoughts, O, person, from one understanding to the other. Do you see what David crossed? "Our soul has crossed the stream. Our

---

[672] 1 Cor 1:21
[673] 2 Cor 3:16

	soul will cross the constantly flowing water." But what to be learned is how to cross it. To learn aimlessly is to migrate aimlessly: it is all the same, and you can only go astray if your heart goes astray. This is what Paul teaches about walking, "I witness for the Lord, that you would no longer walk as other pagans walk in the vanity of their mind, their darkened thinking, being alienated from the divine life due to ignorance and the hard hearts that reside in them."[674]
Friend:	Israel walks the royal path, not inclining to the right or the left, but circumventing all that is perishable. It crosses over the regions of paganism and destroys all obstacles; not rivers, not seas, restrain him. He divides all in half[675] and manages to everywhere find the divine path. To state this briefly, he does what Abraham did, severing the bodies in half.[676] But what does this mean, if not this? "Seek and you will find." Israel labored to comprehend itself. Now look as to how one strove to attain this, "Forgetting what is behind, I strive toward the future, to the intended vein, to the honor of the high divine calling in Christ Jesus."[677] Divide yourself in order to comprehend yourself. Here! God teaches Jeremiah how to divide. "If you separate the worthy from the unworthy, you will be as my lips."[678] Research what in you is vile and what is valuable.
Pamba:	Israel walks between the thick walls of the sea upon dry ground. But where is he going? There, where David indicated, "When will I arrive and appear before God's presence."[679] Go and find, do not error, pay attention.
Anton:	Abraham in one place did the same that Israel did during its exodus. There Israel walked between 2 halves of water, while here Abraham holding burning lamps passed between the bodies severed in half. This is what Abraham foresaw,

---

[674] Eph 4:17-18
[675] referring to the division of the Red Sea and the Jordan River for crossing.
[676] Gen 15:10
[677] Phil 3:13-14
[678] Jer 15:19
[679] Ps 95:5-6

something he did not see from birth. Comprehend yourself, please, you will see what has never yet been seen.

Kvadrat: If someone wants to understand these burning lamps let that person contend with Zechariah. "On that day I will install the governors of Judah as a burning log among the wood pile and as a burning lamp in the sheaves, and they will devour all the surrounding people from the right and from the left."[680] And second also Nahum, "Watch the road, gird your waist, become courageous and strong. For the Lord will restore the majesty of Jacob and the majesty of Israel." What does he says further, below? "Their appearance is as burning lamps and flashing as lightning. There has not been such as them from the beginning of time."[681] Then Joel the third repeats the same song, "Every face you see looks like a burning pot." This is what Abraham saw in the severed bodies: he saw a new generation of people born of God. Then the Lord bequeathed him a covenant and soon an heir was born to him, not limited by any expanse. What are you thinking? I am the fourth and what shall I sing to you? Similar is born from the same; what is born from the appearance of lightning appears as lightning. Pay attention! Here you will find this, of which is said, "Our God is a consuming fire."[682]

Seek here his entire family. Daniel saw him in himself and this is what he sang, "I raised my eyes and saw one person standing there. He was clothed in a linen garment, and his waist was girded with a band of bright gold; his body was like the stone beryl, his face was like the sight of lightning, his eyes were like burning lamps."[683] This is the family. But where will you find it, this blessed generation? Listen to the answer that the Lord provided to Rebecca, "And the Lord said to her, Two nations are in your womb, and the 2 peoples in your womb will be divided, and one people will surpass the other people, and the greater will be enslaved to the

---

[680] Zech 12:6
[681] Nahum 2:1-4
[682] Heb 12:29
[683] Dan 10:5-6

younger."[684] Look, my friend, right in your midst. The firstborn Esau resides in you. Here is also Jacob grasping the heel of Esau, or more correctly stated, he holds Esau's heel of which David says, "The crimes of my brother's heel will circumvent me. I will take caution of my heel."[685] Comprehend yourself, having ascertained between the man of blood and the man of God, and say, "The first person was from the decaying ground, the second person is from heaven."

Pamba: Of course, of these 2 people who have an indivisible unity generated between themselves God said to Job, "Who will disclose to it their rebuke? Who will enter into its chest? Who will open the doors of its face? Surrounding its teeth is terror; his back is made of rows of metal, sealed one to another so tight that air will not penetrate. They are joined one to another, connected and they will not tear. It's sneezing flashes light. Its eyes are the vision of the dawn. Out of its lips proceed burning torches, sparks of fire. From its nostrils pass the smoke of a furnace, burning with the fire of coals. Its soul is burning coals and fire and proceeds from its lips. On its neck resides strength."[686]

Friend: Now you have explained, Pamba, the following verses, "As the sun was in the west, there was a flame, and behold a smoking stove and burning torches! It passed between the severed pieces." Now it is obvious what it was that scared Abraham so much. "When the sun set, terror fell upon Abraham; and a great dark fear fell upon him." In the division he saw the following, "Surrounding his teeth was fear."[687] How can he not shudder? Did he see Him? The lightning sneezes; the dawn watches; the sparks breath and the coals burn.

Anton: Isaiah was also no less scared by an awesome man, "I have seen the Lord. O, what a cursed man am I! The house was filled with His glory." Then he tasted of the sweetest coal from the Lord's altar, which cleansed his lips and his crimes

---

[684] Gen 25:23
[685] Ps 41:9, 49:5 (as in the Russian)
[686] Job 41:14-22
[687] Gen 15:12, 17

	were erased and he became an apostle. "Whom shall I send? Here I am! Send me."[688] Abraham bequeaths a covenant, while this person comes an apostle. Blessed is the person who finds his tribe in Zion.
Kvadrat:	Isaiah as if points with his finger at those who have not comprehended themselves. "Woe unto those who consider darkness – light, and light – darkness. Woe unto those who think they are so wise and so intelligent in their own presence."[689] All they now need to say is that it is all in their own flesh.
Pamba:	It is apparent from the following that he definitively cries at such people. "And the reed will burn completely from hot coals and the dry grass will be consumed by fire. Their root is just as their flesh, and their flower will convert to dust, since they have not wanted the law of the Lord Sabaoth."[690]
Friend:	Yes, and further down it says that the Lord will raise a flag for the nations that have gone astray from their homes to the ends of the earth, and he will call to them with his whistle. The separated peoples who have gone astray and are found in the field or forest will be summoned with a whistle, and they will react lively at the sound and return. "They will not hunger, not weary, not slumber, not sleep, not loose their waistband from their waists and not tear the laces from their sandals. They are sharp arrows and their bows are ready. The shoes of their horses are strong like rock. The wheels of their chariots are like the storm; they are ferocious as lions and present themselves as young lions."[691] Do you notice that this generation is not the same, since, "They look to the land and behold a thick darkness surrounds their incomprehension." Abraham was a member of this generation. "Terror fell upon Abraham." So from where does this incomprehension and terror come? It is due to the division of light from darkness. The fear of the Lord produced Israel.

---

[688] Is 6:5-8
[689] Is 5:20-21
[690] Is 5:24
[691] Is 5:27-29

Anton:	Jacob came to my mind. He likewise, awakening from sleep, was afraid and said, "How terrifying is this place."[692] Paul also came to mind, upon whom the light of heaven shined while on the road, trembling and afraid he says, "Lord what should I do?" But the beloved bride says in important terms, "Love is strong as death; fierce as hell is its jealousy. It wings are the wings of fire; fiery coals create its flames." It is apparent all of this is related to Israel. It separated the waters, found fire with Abraham and fell in love with him. "Many waters cannot drown love." It will not terrify but will melt from love.
Kvadrat:	The bride has long grasped the matter, comprehending herself, and she is not the first to speak as David did, "The light of your face shined upon us." But first she cried, "Fear and trembling encompass me."
Pamba:	It is the very truth. It has earlier and long ago said, "My soul delves into Your word." It has proceeded and found that although heaven and earth will pass away, His word will not. It sought the night but did not find it. And the light shined in darkness, and in this manner it interpreted for us the significance of the Book of Exodus.
Friend:	The Book of Leviticus is completely in agreement with our song. And if a book was not in agreement with the Lord, His virtue and kingdom, then such a book was long not included in the number of religious books. "God is spirit. The Lord is spirit. Sing to the Lord." But take care that the song be a new one. Bring it to the Lord, but that all of it should be clean. All that is old, decaying, unclean, will pass away. Give what is new to the new, clean to the clean, the secret to the invisible. Present yourselves as a most beautiful, fragrant garden on the mountains, filled with comfort that is incessant. How desirable it is for guests to enter it; but there is no room for strife. Impassible thickets, imperious thorns and sharp crags surround this paradise. O, precious paradise! The sweetest truth of the Lord! When will we finally arrive there? The

---

[692] Gen 28:17

bramble bush of ceremony does not permit us. We have entangled ourselves in it.

But you on this side of this cruel wall barely shine, our joy. So who will guide us and lead us through his wilderness? Blessed who comprehends himself! He alone has a shepherd and a leader. David with him climbs over the wall not fearing in his immediate presence the shadow of death. The inner iron spear for David was his word. With this spear he ascended the mountain of God's kingdom and its virtue. The fear of God leads to the inner curtain of the Bible and to the Bible, and to you especially, taking you by the hand, it leads you into the inner chamber which you from birth have not seen, and leads you to another friend of whom Solomon said, "To be a virtuous person is an important matter and especially the man who provides charity. To be a man of integrity is something worth attaining." Likewise the poet wrote in the past, "Brother helping brother is like a strong city." The Bible is this brother. It was born for our protection, for its brethren. The Bible speaks to all of us corporately and not just to Jeremiah, "Human! I have made you a guard over the house of Israel." Do you not hear what the bride sings, "You have made me a guard in the vineyard." You wander not knowing where along desolate fences, while she is attempting to lead you into her mother's chamber. The same is likewise prudently written about Christ, "She thought that this was the gardener." Of course, he looked like a gardener. All the theological prophets were as if protectors of the garden.

We have heard Isaiah that the vineyard of the Lord Sabaoth is the house of Israel. We are also in the same situation, and we also as individuals are the house of God. They guard us so we would not leave the master and his house with the prodigal son to a far country or else to Jericho with the foreigner who fell to criminals. All of these guards reside solely in a person, I am the spirit in all of them. Here is the one! And the first guard returns to his house. Here is the other, "Come my people, enter into your chamber."[693] Here

---

[693] Is 26:20

are the Cherubim with fiery weapons protecting our inner self, the path to the tree of life, and their arrows are sharp; their appearance is as fiery lamps; faces as burning pots delivered from the Lord; Seraphim carrying the coals of divine wisdom. And just as they are the wheels and the throne of the Lord who lives within them, so it is with us who have wandered to the ends of the earth, they return us to our inner self, to that tree of life, to our head, as if to a safe ark of which the poet writes, "The tree of life is like the strength of the Lord for all those who retain it and venerate it." Obeying it this is what we hear, "You are my friends because you do what I command you." From this point on we hear nothing unless it leads us into the most inner tabernacle of revelation that resides within us. There is my paradise of sweetness and where the fruit of the tree of life and waters reside for me. This is sufficient! Nobody must say anything further to me.

Pamba: Bring to the Lord, to the son of God. The son of God brings Israel to his living God as an offering and gift. For what reason? Lest his soul fail. Ascertain this, Lest his soul fail. Allow me Lord, if even just a little, to taste of what this signifies. "Let him slaughter the calf in the presence of the Lord," it says there. But do not slice it! Listen to me, do not slice it! Comprehend yourself! Listen to Isaiah, "What use is the multitude of your sacrifices? Says the Lord. I do not want the fat of lambs and blood of calves and goats. Who requires this from your hands?"[694] Have you forgotten that our God is a fire? What stupidity is it to bring meat before his eyes, before the fire-emanating eyes of him who consumes and burns every flesh like straw. "Bring to the Lord glory and honor."[695] If you can taste the flavor here in something you have never yet chewed, then you can also love what you have not yet understood. Comprehend yourself! He is here.

Anton: The foolish pagan priests did not understand this. They thought that the matter consisted in slaughtering calves and creating an excellent feast. Isaiah writes of their stupidity,

---

[694] Is 1:11-12
[695] Ps 29:1

"They made joy and happiness, slaughtering calves and fat sheep, eating meat and drinking wine, saying, Let us eat and drink for tomorrow we die."[696] Amos calls such fattened cattle – cows of Bashan's pastures.[697] Listen, you priests! Listen to this word, you cows of Bashan.

Now listen to the type of calf that is slaughtered and cooked for love unto the Lord as Moses writes in Deuteronomy. "And your sin that you committed was the calf, and I took it and burned it in a fire, smashed it and crushed it until it turned as fine as powder."[698] Slaughter the sin in you, O, person. Mortify your arrogance and pride that discredits the voice of the supreme law. Remove it and burn it with the fire of your love toward God. Listen to Moses and uproot the bad from inside yourself. Here is the sacrifice! This is the fragrant odor unto the Lord! Understand all of this all of you who forget God. Listen to what is said, "Glorify Me with a sacrifice of praise, and I will show him the path and unveil to him my salvation."[699]

Kvadrat: We can state with the son of Sirach the following words regarding calves' obstinacy toward God, "Do not exalt yourself with the counsel of your soul, lest your soul be carried away like the young calf."[700] It is impossible to dedicate an obstinate young calf unto God.

Pamba: Jeremiah likewise calls them calves and bulls. "Rejoice and yell, stealing my legacy. Skip like calves on the grass and ram like bulls." Of course, God in the Book of Leviticus speaks threateningly of such calves, "If you will not obey me and not observe my commands, not submit yourself to them, and if you soul disdains my revelations, I will remove you from my inheritance."[701] While here is the divine legacy, "He inherited your revelations forever."

---

[696] 1 Cor 15:32
[697] Amos 4:1
[698] Deut 9:21
[699] Heb 13:15
[700] Sirach 30:21
[701] Lev 26:14-16

Friend:	Stephan in the Acts also cries against such obstinate bulls, "Stiff-necked and uncircumcised in heart."[702] But here is the humble and circumcised calf. "The distressed and humble heart."[703] God finds such a heart when he accepts your offering on His altar.
Anton:	O, acceptable young calves! To such calves the words are spoken, "Take my yoke upon you."[704] O, sweetest yoke! "Blessed is the person, weeps Jeremiah, who takes the yoke in his youth. It is good for me that You have humbled me."[705] How will a young person rectify his ways? This is how, When he observes My words.
	Discard, my friend, the calves and goats. Reconcile this with yourself. Kill for God within yourself this bull-type obstinacy. A different bull will remain within you. And here it is, "Moses said to Joseph, His land be blessed by the Lord, from the beauty of the heavens and the dew, like the firstborn bull is his beauty, with the horn of the ox he rams all the nations, all of them together to the ends of the earth."[706] Here is an undefiled male.
Kvadrat:	The Bible is a person and you are a person. It is a young calf and you are one also. If you can grasp this concept, the one person and the one calf will be within you. First comprehend yourself. With an idiot this is stupidity, but with a saint this is holiness; for the busy-body – a fall, for the good person – an ascension. Comprehend yourself. Separate good from bad, the valuable and good from the vile and bad. You should be able to ascertain this, otherwise you will just ingest poison. Without doubt here is the calf: Abraham who presented himself to the most-eminent triune guest. Wisdom defines this calf, "Your sacrificed animals summon you." This is what the father presented to the prodigal son at the time when he returned home.[707]

---

[702] Acts 7:51
[703] Is 66:2
[704] Matt 11:30
[705] Lamentations 3:27
[706] Deut 33:13, 17
[707] Luke 15:23

	This is the calf to be brought to God. This is the only way to gain his propitiation and be cleansed of all your errors, and not by actually offering meat. You will sanctify him and you will eat with him, because this is the beautiful calf that he possesses. First comprehend yourself. Do not meander about planets and starts. Return home. Here is your father and the calf that he will present for you: God is God, rectitude is rectitude, truth is truth. Truth will radiate from the earthly body of a calf, while the rectitude of your father will penetrate from heaven. At this time virtue and peace will meet and greet one another. Then you will say, "We have peace with God."[708]
Anton:	"Let him lay his hand on the head of the calf in the presence of the Lord."[709] This was only to be performed by an anointed priest. But first, what does it mean to be anointed? Listen to this, 'The Lord's spirit is upon me, He has anointed me."[710] An anointed person places his hand upon another person to be anointed; a spiritual person upon a spiritual calf, because the carnal person cannot grasp that this pertains to God's spirit, and to him it is foolishness, and it is apparent he cannot lay his hands upon it.

Please, comprehend yourself. Realize within yourself the father placing his hand upon the son. No one can approach this calf unless the father first draws him. Listen to Paul, "The spirit tests all things, even the depths of God." Paul, comprehending himself, was anointed by the spirit, "It is not the spirit of this world we have accepted, but the spirit that is from God."[711] Then he approaches the mysterious calf, saying, "We know what God has gifted us." The Holy Bible is the calf of salvation given to us by God. |
| Kvadrat: | Here is a calf for you. Ezekiel, "The Lord's hand was upon me and I saw…" Who has not comprehended himself is blind to Ezekiel. Comprehend yourself, be anointed with the spirit, |

---

[708] Rom 5:1
[709] Lev 1:4
[710] Is 61:1
[711] 1 Cor 2:12

have his hand placed upon you, and you will suddenly say, "And I saw..."

And what did he see? Among other things he saw the figure of a calf.[712] O, my friend! If you approach a prophet without God's spirit then he is blind and deaf to you. Is it possible for you to see in him the power of God, the hand of God, if you have not seen this already within yourself. As David writes, "Your hands have created me."[713] Comprehend yourself and perhaps He – the God who is residing in you – will lay his hands upon you. The spirit will recognize the spirit; brother helps brother; a hand knows another hand. How can a body deprived of spirit approach the spirit? If you comprehended yourself, you could say the following along with the prophet, "The Lord's hand was upon me, and he led me in the Lord's spirit, and placed me in the middle of a field, and behold, it was filled with people's bones."[714] Ezekiel vivified the dead bones, attaching to them tendons, flesh, skin: all new and with the spirit of life. The massive group stands on their feet. The bones signify the biblical house, and you are this house. How can you prophesize to dry and lifeless bones if you do not yourself possess the spirit? One thing I say about this: All depends on you. Comprehend yourself. You are the calf. Place your hands upon your inner self, then upon your brother, and you will be like a confirmed strong kingdom.

Pamba: What about the evangelist Luke? Was he not also a calf? The calf was Moses; the calf was Isaiah; the calf was Paul. All of them were from the Lord's herd, chewing the cud and with cloven hooves. Together with Ezekiel they saw the vision of the Lord's glory, "I saw his glory." The Lord's hand was with all of them, and they entered and played as calves loosened from their bridle.[715] All of this resides in the Lord and the Lord is in them. Select one of these calves, the best you have and sacrifice it, but sacrifice it to the Lord, since the calves are the Lord's. Eat them with the Lord and in the presence of

---

[712] Eze 1:10
[713] Ps 139:13
[714] Eze 37:1
[715] Mal 4:2

the Lord. Do not mix something of your own in with them. Here is what Moses teaches, "And you will eat there in the presence of the Lord your God and you will rejoice over all that you possess and have brought in the your hands, you and your household, just as the Lord your God has blessed you. And you will not do here as you were doing there in the past, every person what is right in his own eyes."[716] Please eat with discernment.

Pay attention so you do not eat blood, but only what is written, what is new and clean and what is the Lord's. Do not think that the eyes, ears, feet and hands are yours. They are not yours but all is God's, to the last very thread on your shoelaces. How can they speak of the flesh of those who were not born of flesh or its lust, but of God? The entire Bible is full of examples of virtuous men, the divine species of calves for your cleansing. Your obligation is solely to take one beloved animal as a sacrifice and place your hands on it. But first look within yourself. Your hand is not your hand. Discern this on your own and seek within yourself the strong hand and high arm. Then following it you will be consoled with the supreme mind of this immortal dinner. If you cannot do this on your own, bring to the person anointed of the divine spirit an interpretation and this divine servant will serve you. "Since the lips of the priest, says Malachi, preserve intellect and people seek the law from their lips, for he is the angel of the Lord Almighty."[717] All of this will be accomplished when you begin to comprehend yourself, and without this occurring in no manner will you be able to provide legitimate sacrifices.

Friend: "The entrails and feet of the offering will be washed with water."[718] The following passage is parallel with washing the calf's entrails. "God, create a clean heart within me and spirit."[719]

Anton: And here is another example! He washes others and is being cleansed himself. "Wash and you will be clean."

---

[716] Deut 26:10-11, 12:7-8
[717] Mal 2:7
[718] Lev 1:9
[719] Ps 51:10

Kvadrat:	Yes, and here is a third, "Jacob said to his household and all that were with him, Discard your foreign deities that you possess and are among you, and be cleansed and change your clothes and arise. We are to enter Bethel and there we will perform a sacrifice to God who heeded me on the day of my sorrow."[720]
Pamba:	Here is another beautiful calf for you! The bride's brother, "I have washed my feet; how can I dirty them?"[721]
Friend:	So why are you silent about the unclean? Ah, when did these increase so much? "I will place my laws in their minds, and upon their hearts will I write them, and I will be to them God and they will be my people, and each will no longer say to his associate, saying, Know the Lord. Because they will all gain knowledge of me, from the smallest of them to the greatest."[722] "I will pour of My spirit upon all flesh, and your sons will prophesize and so will your daughters."[723] O, sweetest prophets! When will the time arrive for us to also be the same type of calves? Woe unto us if we have not comprehended ourselves. And what resides within us, the inner higher presence, is here spoken by Joel, "And you will see that I am in the midst of Israel, and I am your Lord God and there is no other than Me." And then the following words supplement, "My people will never again be shamed."[724] And then the subsequent words, "I will pour of My spirit on all flesh."
Anton:	Here is the passage that Habakkuk provides regarding the unclean calf. "In malice you tell a tree, Be encouraged, arise! And to a rock, Be exalted!"[725] This is just a fantasy, the forging of gold and silver that is deprived of all spirit.
Kvadrat:	This calf is perfectly appropriate for idols. It knows nothing of itself or of its house, just as our clean calf Habakkuk

---

[720] Gen 35:2-3
[721] Song 5:3
[722] Jer 31:33-34
[723] Joel 2:28
[724] Joel 2:27
[725] Habakkuk 2:19

	consistently says, "The Lord is in His holy temple. Let all the earth fear His face."[726]
Pamba:	This calf possesses an inherent defect. It does not chew the cud and its hooves are not cloven, and so Israel cannot eat this calf.
Friend:	The pagan calves are much different than Israel's. They chew only once and the structure of their hooves are merged as one; their nature requires this of them. The pagans are identified with the name Babylon, and this signifies mixture or merging. They only see the outside flesh and are amazed by it; they write about it, measure it. But not knowing spiritual truth those who reside in the flesh mix it together with the flesh and call it a fantasy. But our perspicacious watcher, the calf Habakkuk, noticing that he calls every tree, rock and silver and all outer flesh a fantasy, foresees in it the imperishable divine truth that is opposite to all this, and having made his house aware of all of those lovers of superficiality, he soars about the clouds transcending fulfillment. And this is what is means to be a prophet, to be wide and open-eyed and perspicacious.
Anton:	Here is the words of Baruch regarding these counterfeit calves that are dedicated to idols, "Lord, open Your eyes and look at those who are in hell, as though dead, whose spirit has departed from their inner person, who provide You not glory and justification, Lord. And attend to the soul that sorrows regarding the immensity of evil, who walks stooped and hurting and whose eyes fail and whose soul hungers to provide You glory and righteousness, Lord."[727]
Kvadrat:	Baruch speaks of both types of calves: the clean and the unclean. These are the unclean, "Whose spirit has departed from their inner self." Now tell me, how will they be washed? They could not find a way since they lost the spirit within them. God's Kingdom and His virtue has been taken from them. It was taken because they could not find it, and they did not find it because they did not comprehend themselves. But

---

[726] Habakkuk 2:20
[727] Baruch 2:17-18

	is not the following person the hungry soul? "Blessed are those who hunger and thirst." They weep and hurt with David; they disdain malice and walked stooped, and their eyes fail as they seek God's salvation. When will you comfort me? "May your kingdom come!" Such at their own time spoke together with Isaiah, "For this reason my soul is against Moab. I will announce this like a lyre. My inner person is like a wall that you have repaired."[728]
Pamba:	This blessed renewal of the entrails is provided by Ezekiel, "They will sprinkle clean water on you and you will be cleansed of all your defilements and all of your idols, and I will give you a new heart, and a new spirit I will give you."[729] And where is this fortunate person of whom the following can be said, "You have been washed, you have been justified."? Where are these dove's eyes resting, awaiting the recession of the waters, as the poet writes, "If whoever is thirsty let him come to me and drink. Rivers of living water will flow from his entrails. This he spoke of the spirit."[730]
Friend:	Such clean calves can bring as an offering the most holy calf to the Lord just as Abraham brought Isaac. But those who are not washed by this water and – to define this better – have ruthless hearts cannot place their hand on the head of the calf. They have lost the head of their lord residing within them and so who will bring them to the calf? Having lost this in themselves they seek it in something else. Here is the manner of laying the hand, "Sing to him to magnify the Lord. And Moab will strike their hand on the vomit and become a joke."[731]

Can the heart mixed with paganism separate the flesh and blood of this calf from the spirit, and separate death from the life, and the useless from the fat? Can you place wood and fire on the altar while not knowing and not seeing in your own home the non-fabricated tabernacle of the Lord's revelation?

---

[728] Is 16:11-12
[729] Eze 36:25-26
[730] John 7:37-38
[731] Jer 48:26

This is the wood, "And the Lord showed me a tree."⁷³² Its wings are wings of fire." Now view the altar. Listen, "We have an altar."⁷³³ Here is the separated fat, "May God give unto you the dew of heaven and the fat of the earth."⁷³⁴ So what is this fat? Listen to Moses, "I led him to the strength of the land, fed them with the village produce. They sucked honey from rocks and oil from hard stones, along with butter and sheep's milk and the fat of lambs and rams, calves and goats, with plenty of wheat and the blood of grapes, meaning wine."⁷³⁵

The Bible is the promised land. Upon it grazes the clean and divine flock, which is Israel. And the calf's son was the beautiful Joseph who sustained his brethren during the famine with the fat of wheat. Here is another son of a ram, a lamb, "My flesh is indeed flour." Here is the fat, "The flesh means nothing." Did the Baptizer not know that he was washing the lamb? But do you want to enter the goodness and the fat of God's land? This is how, "Behold I send My Angel before your face, before your eyes, in front of your forehead, and he will protect you along the way and lead you into the land that I have prepared for you. Attend to him and obey him."⁷³⁶

Do you want to bring a calf or lamb as a sacrifice to your God? "Pay strong attention to this, that you eat no blood, and it will be well for you and your sons after you forever." Do not become drunk with the blood, meaning the material wine. Drink the virtuous blood, the Lord's blood, the spiritual blood. In this manner will you ascertain the true spiritual person created after God in righteousness and likeness of truth. The number of godless people will increase, as the poet writes, "Son, do not allow criminal minds to deceive you. They say, Come with us and participate in murder; we will criminally hide the righteous person in the ground; we will devour him alive like hell and remove his memory from the

---

⁷³² Dan 4:10
⁷³³ Heb 13:10
⁷³⁴ Gen 27:28
⁷³⁵ Deut 32:13-14
⁷³⁶ Ex 23:20-21

	land."⁷³⁷ Such a sacrifice is an idolatrous abomination, and not a fragrant odor to the Lord, since God is love.
Anton:	Regarding those who have attacked Israel, this is what Isaiah sings, "Those who have attacked you have eaten your flesh and drank your blood as though it was new wine and become drunk on it."⁷³⁸ And these are the wolves who leave nothing behind in the morning. "Let us eat and drink for in the morning we die."
Kvadrat:	The daughter of Jerusalem was the same at one time in the past, and this is what God said to Ezekiel about it, "Your root and your sprout come from the land of Canaan. Your father was an Amorite and your mother was a Hittite and so you were born. On the day you were born, your umbilical cord was not cut and you were not washed with water to cleanse you. You were not rubbed with salt and not wrapped in diapers." And then further he says to her, "And I stretched my wings over you and covered your shame and swore to you and entered into covenant with you, says the Lord Adonai. And you were mine and I washed you with water and rinsed your blood from you and smeared oil upon you."⁷³⁹ The daughters of Jerusalem are the following: Ruth, Judith, Esther, Susanna, Miriam.

So you are able to bring to the Lord a selection from these beautiful calves and high-skipping goats as a sacrifice. Comprehend first he who is speaking in you, "And he covered your shame." Otherwise without this you will become like the old men who lusted after Susanna,[740] or as what occurred to Judah's firstborn son Er, "He was evil before the Lord and God killed him." The same occurred to his younger brother Onan.[741] The beautiful Tamar lived with him as a wife, but this prodigal brother did not want to raise offspring for his brother, and so God killed him.

---

[737] Pr 1:10-13
[738] Is 49:26
[739] Eze 16:4, 8-9
[740] Susanna 8
[741] Gen 38:7, 10

	Listen to Ezekiel, "The spirit of life was in the wheels." Listen to David, "The voice of thunder is in the wheels. The Lord's judgments are true, they are more desirable than gold."
Pamba:	The Bible does not say anything at all unless it pertains to a person. Jeremiah speaks to confused doves, "Leave the city and reside in the rocks, residents of Moab, and be like doves nesting in the rocks, at the entrance to caves."[742] These are the rocks that caused the old men to stumble, those who lusted after Susanna, and among whom is the brainless bird Shebna, who built for himself a house and whom Isaiah was to banish, "Why are you here and what do you have here? You have carved out for yourself a sepulcher and there you will die."[743]
	Such adulterers attempted to force the chaste Susanna – the Bible – into immorality. Captivated by their flesh and converted into dissolution, they descend into hell. In Jeremiah, "Their adultery was nothing to them and they defiled the land and fornicated with every rock and tree."[744] So does the poet write, "Men's souls and those of women's hunger, always learning, but never becoming educated."[745] But they are themselves to blame, not being able to recognize the evil tongue and separate it from the good. For this reason the poet also writes further, "The lips of a fool bring him to evil; his bold lips summon death."
Anton:	So who is the clean dove? Here is one for example, "Who will give me wings like a dove." Proceed, my beloved friends before my light and airy eyes that are quick and sharp as a dove's. These words of Isaiah annoy me, "They will feel the wall as a blind person does and will arise like the dead who have no eyes, like the bear and like the dove they will proceed together."[746]

---

[742] Jer 48:28
[743] Is 22:16
[744] Jer 2:20
[745] 2 Tim 3:6-7
[746] Is 59:10

Kvadrat: So here we have for you one messenger that flies from the ark. "And the dove returned to him toward evening and it had in its beak a branch with leaves from an olive tree."[747]

Pamba: O, blessed are your eyes! They have seen the dry ground, they have seen the earth that gives birth to an abundance of greenery providing seed after its likeness and image. Who separated for you the dry ground from the waters? Tell me, my beloved! My father, my Noah, my peace. I know him. I am with him in his house. I sat in the ark and did not fly without him across this world flooded with criminals – those who whitewash sins. He sent me himself to this sea, to the flood of divine intellect and his wisdom, to the waters of the Sacred Scripture. Truth sent me to mercy and peace to virtue. And this is the reason the depths of the sea did not devour me as it did the others. Here it is! I carry a branch of the olive tree from there, from where many are: ruin, gall and death.

Mercy and truth met and after 7 days the waters subsided from the face of all the earth. "The earth is the Lord's and all that fills it."[748] At that I will no longer take shelter in the ark, resting in the premise that all is in all. And I will fly and rest.

Friend: It is difficult to see this land. Twelve elders were sent by Moses to ascertain, to investigate, to view it. But of all of these selected spies only 2 commended the place – Caleb and Joshua – while the others corrupted the people's minds. The precious Caleb was one perspicacious dove and note what he said, "The land which we spied is very good. If the Lord loves us he will lead us into this land."[749]

Anton: In order to inspect this blessed land God led Moses upon a high mountain. This mountain was Abarim, which signifies Passover. On this mountain he rested with the dove and his eyes did not lose their vision.

Kvadrat: The dry ground is separated from the waters, the promised land is separated from the pagan. There the dove rests, while Israel rests in the high hills, as it says, "The land ceased from

---

[747] Gen 8:11
[748] Ps 24:1
[749] Num 14:7-8

	war. The land rested from strife."⁷⁵⁰ O, precious land! But meanwhile you are naked! Who will proclaim you among us? Where is the dove? Where are the spies?
Pamba:	Where are the silver wings of the dove? Where are the beautiful feet evangelizing peace upon the mountains, evangelizing goodness?⁷⁵¹ Who will at least tell us about this high and distant land of which it says, "God, your animals live upon it, when they approach you in the presence of your people." Then it will be for the sake of Your guidance that the land will shake and separate in half and we will see the dry land. The skies will provide dew, which will cause the earth to bring its produce.
Friend:	Who has comprehended himself will be given the word to evangelize the King of power, of whom the poet writes, "The righteous king will exalt the land, while the criminal will be digging in the dirt." This land is very difficult to view; listen to Peter, "It is hidden from those seeking to know." And what does this mean? This is what, "The heavens were created first." And then what? "And by the divine word the land was derived from the waters and in the midst of the waters."⁷⁵² Only Israel thirsted for it and saw it, "Like the soul thirsting for pleasantly tasting cool water, so is good news from a distant land."
Pamba:	Who shall quench our thirst? Where is that of which is it spoken? "The eyes that see goodness will gladden the heart; a good reputation will fatten the bones."
Friend:	Behold the evangelists fly to you! Listen to Isaiah, "The Lord Sabaoth commanded the pagan warrior to come from a distant land, from the far ends of the sky. The Lord and his warrior have destroyed all the world." Bringing this to mind He calls them a bird, "All that I have bequeathed I will accomplish, calling a bird of prey from the east and from the distant

---

[750] Josh 11:23
[751] Is 52:7
[752] 2 Peter 3:5

	land."⁷⁵³ Now remember also these birds that in the presence of Abraham landed on the carcasses divided in half.
Anton:	Watch, Kvadrat! Here is another dove, Hezekiah in Isaiah, "Like a swallow I sing and like a dove I learn. My eyes lose their vision to view the Lord in the heavenly heights, He who has delivered me."⁷⁵⁴ This is completely in accord with what David says, "Remember the years of time passed and learn from them.⁷⁵⁵ Remember what occurred first from the beginning of time, that I am God and there is no other than Me who proclaims what is to occur beforehand, and states what is to happen and then it does."⁷⁵⁶ Do you notice what the dove's eye sees? The hope of eternity. The entire heart of David relocated here since he never thought about what is temporal.

Here is the olive branch, "According to your mercy, according to your destiny for me, liven me." |
| Kvadrat: | I thank you for this pair, for Hezekiah and David. And their brother is also a very beloved dove. And this brother spent 3 days and not in a whale's belly, but in a stone sepulcher. This was our new Jonah, meaning a dove, who was so merciful and spoke the following, "You, my dove, in the shelter of rocks present your appearance unto me and allow me to hear your voice, because your voice is sweet and your image is beautiful."⁷⁵⁷ This rock shelter where he spent his time was not a cave, but another cave that transcended this one, and even higher than the one that Shebna carved for himself. Even then the angel appearing as bright as lightening said, "He is not here! He is risen!"

Seek what is above! What is at the highest bounds. Meditate on the celestial. Why do you slither in the vile dirt with the snake? You are subtle like a snake, yet you do not have that sharp and undefiled eye of a dove, of which Habakkuk spoke, "You are of such pure eyes that you cannot |

---

[753] Is 46:11
[754] Is 38:14
[755] Ps 77:5
[756] Is 44:7-8
[757] Jer 48:28

	gaze on evil and do not view the pain people cause to themselves. Obstinacy and pain resides in their heart. But I retain your counsel in my soul."[758]
Anton:	Ah! You have burdened my soul with your bird! I will repay you entirely with Isaiah's words, "Who is this that flies like a cloud, like a dove with its young toward me?"[759]
Kvadrat:	It is as if he speaks to them with outstretched and hugging arms as to a bride, "You are my dove.[760] You are my friends. The slave does not know what his master is doing.[761] Blessed are your eyes. The light of lights, dove of doves, father of sons; and spirit greets spirit. Raise your eyes and see your offspring gathered from distant lands."
Pamba:	Jonah was a dove. Isaiah was a dove, and so were all the seers and prophets. Bring one of these doves as an offering unto your God. Another dove you can eat, but only comprehend yourself. Comprehend yourself.
Friend:	Wash the lamb that is dedicated as a sin offering. The Baptizer saw God's spirit descending like a dove and settling on him. Spirit to spirit, like approaching like. But this would never have occurred if he had not earlier comprehended the voice speaking within him, "This is my beloved son. The beginning and the end." Comprehend yourself.
Anton:	"He sees God's spirit descending like a dove."[762]
Kvadrat:	The dove is every person, but we must listen to Zephaniah, "O, radiant and delivered city, my dove." And the calamity that is further spoken of, "You did not hear the voice, you did not accept punishment, and you did not draw near to God."[763] This is the reason they did not draw near to God: They did not listen to the thunderous voice saying, Comprehend yourself.
Pamba:	So he will bring as his gift a dove or pigeon. What is this dove? What will a dove do for God? Let them go free for hunters to catch! But you comprehend yourself and all that

---

[758] Habakkuk 1:13
[759] Is 60:8
[760] Song 5:2, 6:9
[761] John 15:15
[762] Matt 3:16
[763] Zephaniah 3:1-2

pertains to you. You are a dove yourself! Within you is a dove! Comprehend yourself and you will discover this dove. "How beloved are your settlements, Lord of hosts!" This dove does not sleep or sigh as it sits on distant branches. "I will not allow my eyes to sleep." All flesh is sleep. But its sharp vision disdains all of what is not worth viewing, and it turns its eyes away from vanity. "Whatever I have in the skies. My heart and my flesh rejoice over the living God." I see your courts and vanish in them: they are my nest. "There the birds nest." At the ends of the skies! Here are your doves! Dedicate them to your lord. Comprehend yourself! Your Lord is there and all resides in him.

Friend: Watch, Pamba! My dove has caught up to yours.

Anton: And was Jacob not a dove? He placed his tent on a mountain just as a dove locates its nest.[764]

---

[764] Gen 31:25

GRIGORI SAVVICH SKOVORODA

DISCUSSION OF THE FIVE TRAVELLERS REGARDING TRUE HAPPINESS IN LIFE

(Short Selection)

Grigori: It is impossible for us to be happy.
Afanasi: For what reason?
Grigori: We are not able to find happiness.
Jacob: Why is this?
Grigori: Because we do not desire this and cannot desire it.
Afanasi: Why?
Grigori: Because we do not understand of what it consists. The principal of the matter is to comprehend where the desire is born, which is from desire of truth, and then we can receive it. This is prosperity, meaning the acquisition of what is to your benevolence. Now understand what wisdom means.
Jabob: I often hear this word – wisdom.
Grigori: The matter of wisdom consists in comprehending what happiness consists of. This is the right wing, but virtue takes effort to find. For this reason it was considered among the Greeks and Romans courage and strength, and this is the left wing. Without these wings in no manner will you be able to take off and fly toward prosperity. Wisdom is like the telescopic and perspicacious eye of an eagle, while virtue is like a person having courageous hands with the agile feet of a deer. This divine marriage is vivaciously portrayed with the following fable.

Jacob:	You have taken this right out of my mouth. Of course the fable is about 2 travelers: one lame and the other blind.
Grigori:	Of course I had you in mind when I thought of this.
Afanasi:	Tell me this in more detail.
Grigori:	A traveler name Observator, having traversed many lands and countries, was deprived of the use of his feet. Then it came to his mind to return to his father's house. So he, utilizing his hands, with great difficulty continued his journey and now homeward. Finally, reaching the top of a mountain, from which he was able to see his father's house, he was deprived of the use of his hands.

    From that summit his keen eye jumped with eager joy at the sight beyond the rivers and forests, the wind blowing across the pyramid-shaped mountains and their summits where majestic fortresses set, and then his father's palace in the distance on the summit, the home of his peace-loving family, the end and crown of his entire journey's effort. But the calamity was that our Observator had neither the use of his hands or feet, and he sat there tormented, just as the rich person as he looked upon Lazarus.[765]

    Meanwhile, he looked behind him and unexpectedly saw an amazing and destitute spectacle: a vagrant blind was stumbling along, touching the right and the left with his staff, and was walking as if he was drunk, continually straying from the road. As he came nearer he sighed, "My days have vanished in futility. Woe is me, how my arrival seems to be taking forever." And he recited other such words to himself, sighing, while continuously stumbling and falling.

"I am afraid that I might have scared you, my friend. And who are you?" asked the seeing seer.

"This is the 34th year of my journey, and you are the first person that I have so far met," replied the blind. My migration into various ends of the world only led me into exile. The unusually hot rays of the sun in Arabia deprived me of the use of my eyes, and so I am returning blind to my father."

---

[765] Luke 16:23

"And who is your father?

"He lives in the palace on the top of that mountain, which is called Peace-City. His name is Uranus, while mine is Practik."

"My god! What are you saying to me? I am your blood brother," cried the enlightened crippled. "I am Observator."

Such extraordinary happiness is always sealed with tears, and after both shed many tears the blind with his tearful eyes said to his brother, "Sweetest brother! I have only heard rumors of you, but now my heart's eyes see you personally. Have a kind heart and end my destitution, be a guide to me. I will tell you the truth, that it is difficult for me to be happy, because stumbling every minute decreases my strength."

"I am so sorry that I cannot help you, my beloved soul," replied the seeing crippled. I am a traveler having circumnavigated the entire world upon only my feet. They have successfully carried me everywhere, but rocky areas and mountains have caused me to lose their use. So I then depended on my hands to continue my journey, and right at this point I have lost their use. I am no longer able to walk or to even to crawl along the ground.

"So is there a way to make the best of a bad situation, if it be possible?" said the blind. "Since you are just a light torso and beloved to me, I will take you upon myself. Your good eyes will be a guide for my body and the head for all my members. You will in this manner curb the torture of my darkness and I will be a horse for you to ride upon. Sit on my shoulders and direct me, most precious sir and brother."

"I will sit, my brother, and willingly to display to you the truth of the written divine word that the poet relates, A brother has help from a brother, as a strong and high city.[766] It is strengthened as an established kingdom. Now look at the marvelous works of God: from 2 people one is created. One traveler is created from 2 relatives without any merger, and each mutually serves the other. This traveler – which none has yet seen on earth – will not stray to the left or to the right but stay directly on the road, and will successfully cross rivers, forests, potholes and streams, cross mountains with their crooked paths, and with joy will ascend the heights of the peaceful city, which a bright and fragrant air encompasses, there to meet serene people in peace and the residents inhaling love, clapping their

---

[766] Pr 18:19

hands. Waiting for us on the doorsteps and accepting us into the blessed bosom at our arrival will be Uranus, the Ancient of Days."

GARDEN OF DIVINE SONGS

SONG 12

I will not enter the city of the wealthy.
I will live in the fields.
I will spend the length of my life,
Where time quietly passes.
>O, oak grove. O, greenery. O, my birth mother.
>My life in you is joyful.
>In you is calm and quiet.

The majestic cities,
High upon the sea of sorrows,
And beautiful gates,
Wide and leading to unwanted bitterness.
>O, oak grove. O, greenery. O, my birth mother.
>My life in you is joyful.
>In you is calm and quiet.

I do not want to travel beyond the sea,
I do not want beautiful clothing.
Because under it is hidden sorrow,
Misery, fear and strife.
>O, oak grove. O, greenery. O, my birth mother.
>My life in you is joyful.
>In you is calm and quiet.

I do not want to follow the beating of drums,
Or to take cities captive.

I do not want a government post
To impress lower level officials.
> O, oak grove. O, greenery. O, my birth mother.
> My life in you is joyful.
> In you is calm and quiet.

I do not want new sciences,
Other than a healthy mind,
Other than the mind of Christ,
In whom resides the sweetness of thought.
> O, oak grove. O, greenery. O, my birth mother.
> My life in you is joyful.
> In you is calm and quiet.

I am in want of nothing
Except bread and water.
Poverty is a friend to me,
And long have I been united to it.
> O, oak grove. O, greenery. O, my birth mother.
> My life in you is joyful.
> In you is calm and quiet.

Of all my bodily possessions,
The calm of my will is holy.
Other than the eternity of the heavens,
Only this one life is holy for me.
> O, oak grove. O, greenery. O, my birth mother.
> My life in you is joyful.
> In you is calm and quiet.

And if I should reach that end
And I need to gain the victory over sin,
Then I do not know if
I will gain the advantage here.
> O, oak grove. O, greenery. O, my birth mother.
> My life in you is joyful.
> In you is calm and quiet.

Welcome, my dear rest!
Forever you will be mine.
It is good for me to be with you,
You are my lifespan and I am yours.
    O, oak grove. O, freedom!
    In you I have found wisdom.
    My nature has reached unto you,
    And in you I wish to die.

SONG 21

Happiness, where do you reside?
Tell me, little dove!
Are you tending your sheep in the field?
Let me know, little dove!
    O, happiness, our clear light.
    O, happiness, our bright light.
    You are the mother and home,
    Appear, disclose yourself.

Happiness, where do you reside?
Tell me, wise men!
Do you drink beer in heaven?
Scholars, tell me.
    O, happiness, our clear light.
    O, happiness, our bright light.
    You are the mother and home,
    Appear, disclose yourself.

All the scholars are silent,
The birds likewise say nothing.
They tell us not where mother is,
All of us are without such knowledge.

> O, happiness, our clear light.
> O, happiness, our bright light.
> You are the mother and home,
> Appear, disclose yourself.

Happiness is not on earth,
Happiness is not in heaven.
It is not in warm coals,
It is nowhere to be sought.
> O, happiness, our clear light.
> O, happiness, our bright light.
> You are the mother and home,
> Appear, disclose yourself.

Heaven, earth and the moon,
All the stars, I bid farewell!
All of you were a foolish haven to me,
Await me no more.
> O, happiness, our clear light.
> O, happiness, our bright light.
> You are the mother and home,
> Appear, disclose yourself.

I have migrated through the heavens,
Let me acquire what is distant.
And including the nether-world,
Give me the chance to visit it.
> O, happiness, our clear light.
> O, happiness, our bright light.
> You are the mother and home,
> Appear, disclose yourself.

Behold my beloved is swift,
He skips as a young deer.
Higher than the sky, higher than the mountains,
My lilies are clean and new.

> O, happiness, our clear light.
> O, happiness, our bright light.
> You are the mother and home,
> Now do I see; now do I hear.

His sweetness is in his lips,
The eyes of the dove.
He is filled with love in Haran,
Having hands of crystal.
> O, happiness, our clear light.
> O, happiness, our bright light.
> You are the mother and home,
> Now do I see; now do I hear.

Do not approach me,
Immediately you will acquire me.
Do not acquire me from elsewhere,
Immediately you will find me.
> O, happiness, our clear light.
> O, happiness, our bright light.
> You are the mother and home,
> Now do I see; now do I hear.

O, turn to me your sight;
It will provide me wings.
Higher than the elements, higher than
The mountains, he leans upon me.
> O, happiness, our clear light.
> O, happiness, our bright light.
> You are the mother and home,
> Now do I see; now do I hear.

Let us sit together, my brother.
Let us sit to converse.
Your sweet words are life,
I am cleansed of all sorrows.

> O, happiness, our clear light.
> O, happiness, our bright light.
> You are the mother and home,
> Today do I see you; now do I hear you.

At noon you sleep on the mountains,
You tend your sheep in the meadows.
Not in the fields of Gergesenes,[767]
And not in their valleys.
> O, happiness, our clear light.
> O, happiness, our bright light.
> You are the mother and home,
> Now do I see you; now do I hear you.

SONG 22

Remember the conclusion of your life and you will not sin.[768]
There is a path that seems right to a person but the end thereof is hell.[769]

Expand your vision into the distance and grasp the rays.
And remember what is to occur at your end.
All of your actions are like an arrow aiming at a target.
Watch all of your extreme desires.

Upon what items have you founded your house?
If it is a rock, then your house will survive.
If it is on sand it may begin as a mansion,
But a hurricane will sweep it from the face of the earth.

All flesh is sand and all glory is secular.
And all of its passion will freeze.

---

[767] Matt 8:28
[768] Eccl 11:9, 12:1
[769] Pr 14:12

Love the narrow path; flee the general morality.

Lord, let me have a portion along with David.
And you are my portion, Lord.
The God of my heart and my portion, God, forever.

If I must return to Zion,
Live in this city, as it is the mother of us all.
Then why should I condescend to the world?
The road to Jericho is dangerous.

If you should descend onto this road,
God will quickly barricade the road.
You know that many have descended into the abyss,
The mind has not joy in the evils of the abyss.

O, you, who consist of spirit,
The number of your years will not be meager.
May the spirit rid us of disorder,
May your storm destroy the net to snare us.

SONG 24

O, our heavenly peace!
Where have you hidden yourself from our eyes?
You are beloved to all of us in common,
And have directed us to another different road.

For your sake the sails expand in ships,
So these wings can seek you in foreign countries.
They march after you, destroying cities.
Dropping bombs all the age,
But will they ever attain their goal?

It seems they live in sorrow in their majestic homes,
But a small house has greater comfort,

If all the necessary amenities are available.

Ah, but we seem to be never satisfied:
This is the source of all sorrows.
The various minds have one invention:
This becoming the source of all strife.

Unrestrained is the insatiable spirit.
It torments completely the short age we possess!
What will the famous bounds provide us?
You are still just a person.

Know that sorrow everywhere flies
Along the ground and along the water.
The demon like lightning all the faster
Can apprehend us anywhere.

We will be what God has destined us,
For his sake will be shatter the sorrow with laughter.
Enough for us to be devoured by worms,
Which is the cup for all people.

Glorious for example are the heroes,
Although defeated on the fields.
Who live long in tranquility,
Will suffer in the old age to come.

God has gifted you with a foundation,
But you still can possible fall from it.
But my destiny is with the poor,
And God has provided me wisdom as my portion.

POEMS

An Astronomical Fable[770]

As soon as the sun set in the evening
And the entire sky became noticeable dark,
The stars of the firmament shined beautifully,
Like precious bits of diamond.
Thales shouted, "O, precious old woman!"
"Why do you shout? Foolish wisdom."
"I have had enough of sitting in this one spot;
Lead me to look at the stars."
The precious old woman proceeded ahead of him
And after her follows foolish wisdom.
They went where the hill was at its highest summit,
From where the sphere of the stars could best be seen.
"Ah, old woman," the wise man muttered, "I have gone astray,
Falling into a hole and bruising my ear."
"You would not have fallen into a hole, you absurd old man,
If you would have been following close after me.
How did you manage not to see the pit in front of your nose?
But yet you manage to stare at the stars, you absurd head."
Having such speculations the old woman led him,
The wise man, back to his house without an ear.

---

[770] Regarding Thales of Miletus, a Greek philosopher and scientist, for whom Skovoroda had considerable respect.

A Philosophical Fable

A certain old man Filaret in the wilderness,
Live his entire life in a thick oak grove.
A certain young man who called himself Filidon,
Approached the long-bearded elder,
Having heard much good about him,
That the hermit was holy and full of wisdom.
He greeted the honorable elder,
"Welcome," said the elder, "And be healthy, my son."
"Do not be angered at me, merciful father.
Do tell me the road to a holy and solid life.
My mother and father have left me,
And I have long fulfilled a requiem on their behalf.
Can you be to me a father in their place?
And can you be, and if you will, a mentor to me?"
"Son, I myself am meager in wisdom.
I only know that the path to life is difficult."
"O, silver-headed, be considerate.
I will remember all you say. I am not a bag with holes."
"It is dangerous, my son, in dealing with the world.
Avoid harmful circumstances with people,
And do not learn good and evil from your own experiences.
For example, if you see a thief who is beaten,
Learn from him, that theft will cause you quick sorrow.
Do not struggle with a person who is not inclined toward goodness.
Associate with the holy, and you will become holy.
Whatever you do, do not chase after the wind,
But after what the intent of the law commands.
The person whose ethics radiate,
Will never be destitute in this world."
Filidon, sensing that the elder was clapping,
But not with his hands, felt lonesome.
"Thank you, silver-headed elder."
"May God be with you, my son." And he left for home.
"This wisdom is holy, but hardly practical,"
He though to himself.

After, now finding the truth
From this true friend, he delved into instruction
To acquire a complete mind.
But he was conscripted into the navy,
When war against France began.
But when a dozen years passed
Fate finally led him home again.
He began his march to the forest again to Filaret,
Remembering his wise directives.
"Greetings, father."
"And what person are you?"
"Do you remember, holy father, Filidon?"
"Ah, how you have become a mature figure."
"The world's storms have completely anguished me."
"What do you have bandaged over your right eye?"
"This is because a bullet passed into it."
"And what is that strange hole in your forehead?"
"Another shot from a weapon."
"And what are the two scars on your cheek?"
"These are wounds I incurred in a fight."
"At the front?"
"No, while in a bar during relief."
"So why is something attached to the end of your nose?"
"It was severed by a Frenchman."
"I think it was more probably a Frenchwoman.
So what covers all of your face?"
"It is a scab."
"And I notice that your walk with a limp."
"I fell from a horse and twisted my knee.
And in addition to all the above doctors cared for me,
While an illness weakened all of my muscles."
"So why are you weeping? Crying will not help you any."
"O, my God, my God. Please help me, holy father!"
"Now I cannot, beloved son. You have not heeded my counsel.
Ask society and the world for help."

Where is Virtue?

It is difficult to subdue anger and other's passions.
It is difficult not to abandon yourself to the body's demands.
It is difficult to tolerate criticism done in vain to you.
It is difficult to leave your home to follow Christ.
It is difficult to move your mind from the earth and to the heavenly mountains.
It is difficult not to drown in the abyss of this world.
Who can defeat all the ancient malice?
The king, the strong ruler, through the strength of your soul.

Of Imaginary Satisfaction

If a light shade should cover you, and should it soon vanish,
The heat will affect you.

If a house should shelter you, you will find rest there,
Day and night. So is bodily sweetness.
You taste the sweetness of honey, but when it departs
Like a shade, your stomach becomes filled with acidity.

O! Flee, flee, person beloved of God, from bait.
Because in it a hook is concealed.
Bait is quickly hidden, but a greedy hook remains.

But virtue is not the same.
It makes the soul courageous.
Initially it may be bitter as gall,
But then will your stomach settle.

So it is when you unwillingly accept medicine tasting bitter.
However after every swallow, food becomes more pleasant.

And do this if you want to avoid a fever leading to delirium,

And causing hallucinations.
Then the joy of health will return to you.

Whoever endures winter from beginning to end,
Will enjoy a pleasant spring.
Whoever has rain early in life, then fog will set in for him.

God is everywhere just, measuring all items.
What is bitter is covered from above by what is sweet.
But what begins as sweetness will have a bitter end.

But the person capable of swallowing misfortune,
Will taste sweetness in the end.

The weak in heart are still strong enough to begin life sweetly.
But only among excellent people is labor crowned by sweetness.

GRIGORI SAVVICH SKOVORODA

KHARKOV FABLES

Beloved friend!

During the seventh decade of the present decade, having retired from my teaching obligation and isolating myself in forests, fields, gardens, villages, settlements and aviaries, all lying near Kharkov. Here I studied virtue and learned the Bible. Then I occupied myself with edifying projects, writing about 50 fables, none of which you are familiar with. And now in the village Babayakh,[771] I increased the number by an additional half. But meanwhile as I was composing the additional it seemed as if your presence was always here and was encouraging my thoughts and as if participating in their composition. So I gift to you 30 fables, to you and those like you.[772]

Sweetness is confined in the sorrow of a father's punishment, while strength is hidden in a wise toy.

People incur futile importance in appearance and this opens the door to laughter, while an intelligent response will seal an important conclusion. There is nothing more funny than some person's intelligent appearance with empty intestines, and nothing more humorous than a person with a laughing face having some clandestine intent. Remember the proverb, "Bricks do not make a house beautiful, but well-baked cakes."

I myself do not live the perverted mask of such people and their activities, and the Russian proverb can be applied to this, "Knock, shout, make noise. And who is there? The dead head of a bore is running." Those who are wealthy and eloquent may speak, but there is nothing to which to listen. I do not like such empty haughtiness and inflated vanity, but love what ascends and descends, and what may appear on the outside falsity, but inside it is truth.

---

[771] This village was also the home of Priest Jacob Pravitzki.
[772] The translator has selected the initial 12 fables for this volume as representative.

My friend, do not disdain fables, since a fable and a parable is the same. Do not judge a treasure by what is in the purse, but judge the matter justly. Fables only become fantasy and eccentric when applied in a vile and vain manner, and without good intent, just as a nut that has no kernel. These are the old wife's tales that Paul warned Timothy of.[773] So please chew on these words of Paul, "Do not heed Hebrew fables or commands of people who stray from truth."[774] Just as a rite possesses no divine strength and is emptiness, so is a fable without truth. But if it possesses truth, then who is bold enough to deny it? "To the clean all things are clean. To the defiled and unbelieving nothing is clean, and their mind and conscience is dirty."[775] These people are sick, deprived of any fear of God. It is vile spiritual food that has defiled their mind and conscience.

This type of entertaining and figurative writing was the best means of household philosophy for the ancient people. So the sages were intelligent in entertainment and truthful in exposing falsity. The truth to their sharp vision was not something distant and leaving them with empty minds, but it presented itself clear as a mirror, and they saw the living image and utilized it with various bodily figures.

Not only colors explain a rose or lily or narcissus, as much as their purpose and beauty that portrays divine invisible truth, a shadow of the heavenly and reflections of earthly matters. As a result there evolved hieroglyphics, emblems, symbols, rites, parables, fables, similitude, proverbs. And it is not surprising that Socrates, when his inner angelic guide ordered him to writes verses, while Aesop selected fables.

The sun of all the planets is the Bible, it is the queen of all divinely-inspired allegorical figures, parables and similitude. Although it is molded out of clay, but in this clay resides the spirit of life and wisdom. To configure, allegorize and contrast is all the same.

So accept with your friendly heart, my beloved associate, this tasteful water: the thoughts of your friend. These are not specifically my thoughts and I did not think of all of these alone: truth is beginningless. But I love what is mine and if you love then they will be yours also. I know that your bodily figure is far different than my scarecrow, but the same liquor can fill 2 bottles of different constituency, that one soul and one heart can

---

[773] 1 Tim 4:7
[774] Titus 1:14
[775] Titus 1:15

abide. This is true friendship, having identical thoughts. Eventually all will perish and our material figures included, but only our thoughts are always with us, and only truth is eternal and we reside in it. We are concealed just as an apple is inside its seed.

We feed on our friendship. Accept it and eat it with Peter with the clean food he has eaten all his life.[776] May God bless you! With him not even pagan poison will harm you. Taste of it and continue until God should provide you better.

Your beloved associate! Your trusting servant, a lover of the Holy Bible, Grigori Skovoroda.

1744 in the village Babaev, on the eve of Pentecost.

Fable 1
Dogs

At the master's house in a village lived 2 dogs. On one occasion some unfamiliar person was passing near the gate. One of them jumped and barked until the person disappeared from sight, and then he return back into the yard.

"So what did you accomplish doing this," asked the other dog.

"At least it rid me of some boredom," he answered.

"But what else?" answered the more intelligent dog. "You need to first consider that a passer-by is an enemy of our master, otherwise you will also fail in your obligation. Nonetheless, last night I did the same and a wolf bit my leg. To be a dog is not bad, but to bark at anything and without reason is stupid."

Moral: An intelligent person knows what to censure, but the foolish babbles without differentiation.

---

[776] Acts 10:14

Fable 2
The Raven and the Finch

Not far from a lake where toads could be seen, a finch was sitting on a branch singing. A raven nearby was also chirping, and seeing that the finch would not stop singing it said, "Why did you ascend up here, you toad?"

"And why are you calling me a toad?" the finch asked the raven.

"Because you are green exactly like that toad over there."

And the finch said, "If I was a toad, then you are a frog, since your chirping sounds exactly like a frog's."

Moral: A person needs to bear witness to his heart and ethics, the type of person he is, and not based on outer qualities. A tree is known by its fruit.

Fable 3
Larks

During ancient eras, at the very time that turtles would learn to fly among the eagles, a young lark sat not far from this place where the successful flight of one of the above-mentioned turtles (as the wise Aesop related) was interrupted when he landed on a rock with a loud noise and crash.[777]

A child becoming afraid of what occurred ran trembling to his father and said, "Father! Of course near the mountain sat an eagle, of which you told me about earlier, that it is a bird that is more awesome and stronger than all other birds."

"And how did you guess this, son?" asked the old man.

"Father! When he landed! I have never seen such speed and noise and crash."

"My beloved son," said the old man, "It is your infantile mind. Know this, my friend and always sing to yourself this short song."

> It is not an eagle that flies high.
> But the one who lightly lands.

---

[777] It was not unusual in Russia for an eagle to grab a small turtle and drop him from the sky to break the shell for food.

Moral: Many begin actions without forethought of nature, and they end badly. The verdict depends on a good intention and the conclusion of the matter.

Fable 4
The Head and the Torso

A torso was clothed in majestic clothing that was embroidered with many expensive decorations, and boasted of itself to the head and criticized the head saying that it was not worth even 1/10 in comparison to the value of the torso.

"Listen, you stupid! If the mind was able to fit inside your pants, then this would occur because of your dignity, and not because you can exist without me," said the head.

Moral: The fable pertains to those who depend on superficial adornment as their honor.

Fable 5
The Siskin and the Goldfinch

A siskin was able to fly to its freedom, and flew to meet his old friend the goldfinch, who asked him, "My friend, how were you able to gain your freedom? Tell me."

"It was an interesting situation," answered the freed captive. "A rich Turk arrived with messengers into our city and, walking though the marketplace out of curiosity, entered the bird store. There were about 400 of us birds all cooped up in hanging cages. The Turk looked at all of us, as we were singing one to another, and sympathetically said to the store owner, "So how much money are you asking for all of them?"

"25 rubles," he answered.

The Turk, not saying a word, put the money on the counter and ordered that he be given every cage, one by one, and he emptied every cage setting us all free. He was comforted by the sight of all of us flying to our freedom in different directions.

"So what enticed you originally into captivity?" asked the friend.

"Sweet food is a pretty cage," answered the fortunate bird. "And until the day I die I will thank God with the following song:

Better for me is dry bread with water,

Than sugar with misery."

Moral: Who does not enjoy trouble must learn to be satisfied with living plainly and poor.

Fable 6
The Wheels of the Clock

One wheel on a clock's mechanism said to the other, "Tell me, why are you not rotating in the same direction as I am, but in the opposite rotation?"

"This is how the master built me," answered the other. "And not only do I not bother you on this matter, but I even assist you, so that our clock turns in agreement with the rotation of the sun."

Moral: The path of life varies according to natural inclinations. However all have the same conclusion: honor, peace and love.

Fable 7
The Eagle and the Magpie

The magpie said to the eagle, "Tell me, do you not get dizzy always flying in circles in the highest parts of the sky and then into the mountains and then straight down, as though descending a circular staircase?"

"I would never descend to the ground, "said the eagle, "unless it was for some bodily need."

"While I would never fly away from the city, "said the magpie, "If I was an eagle."

"And I would do the same," said the eagle, "If I was a magpie."

Moral: If a person was born to eternally entertain himself, it is better for him to live in the fields, forests and gardens, than to live in the cities.

Fable 8

The Head and the Torso

"How would you stay alive," the torso asked the head, "If I were not to provide you with life-giving juices and did not have you connected to me?"

"This is very true," said the head, "But to defend you I provide you with an eye as a light and I assist you with counsel."

Moral: The people must serve and feed their rulers.

Fable 9

The Worm and the Pig

A pig and a worm were arguing as to which of them was the wealthier. A nearby ox was to be witness to their justifications and was assigned as arbiter.

"And do you have much grain to eat?" asked the pig with a proud grim. "Tell me, most honorable person."

"I have half a handful of the best clean grain." As soon as the worm said this both the pig and the ox laughed out loud.

"So then let the ox be the judge of this matter," said the pig. "He has spent 20 years plus performing judicial matters with great merit, and can state something with his excellent knowledge of arithmetic and algebra. His nobleman will soon resolve this matter. And he even knows Latin."

After these words spoken by the wise animal, he immediately began to count and mentally calculating he came to the following conclusion.

"Since the poor worm only has one handful of grain, of which he very courteously informed us, and since he consumes nothing else except seed, while Mr. Pig here has an entire barn that consists of 300 handfuls of grain and more, it seems to me in all rights of a proper evaluation that..."

"You did not count it correctly, Mr. Ox," interrupted the worm. "Put on your glasses and count the expenses as opposed to the income."

They began to argue and the matter was regulated to a higher authority: violence.

Moral: A little food used satisfactorily is fine, and when you are satisfied it is the same as being wealthy.

Fable 10
Two Chickens

A wild chicken had the opportunity to fly to a domestic chicken.

"How are you doing, sister, living in the forests?" asked the domestic chicken.

"Nothing much to say, the same as all the other forest birds," answered the wild chicken. "The same God feeds me as the one that feeds the wild pigeons."

"I notice the they are able to fly well," muttered the domestic.

"This is true," said the wild, "And I for the same reason fly and I am satisfied with the wings God has given me?"

"This is something I cannot believe, sister," said the domestic, "Because I hardly have enough strength to fly to that shed."

"I do not debate this," said the wild, "And allow me the courtesy to say this, my little dove, that you from a young age, from the time you were born, walk about the barnyard scratching the dirt, while I was forced to fly daily to gain experience to hunt."

Moral: Many, if they are unable to do something because they lack the strength, do not believe another can do it.

Fable 11
The Wind and the Philosopher

"I hope you go to hell, cursed."

"Why are you reviling me, Mr. Philosopher?" asked the wind.

"Because," said the sage, "Because as soon as I open the window, to rid my house of garlic smell, you blew with your cursed wind and knocked over everything in my room and even the last bottle of wine that I had standing, and the dust you blew in ruined all the food on my table."

"But did you not know," said the wind, "That this is what I am like?"

"How could I not know?" cried the Philosopher. "But I would place you at the bottom of the natural acts of the heavenly planets. You are just an empty shadow."

"And if I am just a shadow," says the wind, "Then this means I have a body. And true I am just a shadow, but the invisible power of God in me is definitely a body unto me. And so how am I not to motion if our common creator invisible is always moving all existence?"

"I know," said the Philosopher, "That in you is a substance relative to your position as wind."

Moral: Whoever is angered at the weather opposes God who created all of this.

Fable 12
The Sharpening Stone and the Knife

A knife was talking with a sharpening stone.

"Of course, sister, you do not want to be one of us, a knife."

"If I was not capable of sharpening," said the whetstone, "I would not deny myself your advice and follow it. But I love you just the same even if I was not one of you. And of course, if I was to become a knife, I would not be able to cut nearly as much as the other knives and swords that I myself sharpened. I would regret not being a whetstone anymore."

Moral: Some are born who do not want to serve in the military or get married, while others will encourage them to do so.

SELECTED LETTERS[778]

Letter 2
To Mikhail Kovalinski
July 9, 1762

My most desirable friend, Mikhail!

You are already discarding us. So depart to wherever virtue and usefulness summon you. Go under the shelter of Christ and return likewise under his guidance. May Jesus grant you success for you to find both of your precious parents at home healthy and prosperous. May you have no anxieties and may all reside in peace! May the supreme guard of Israel preserve your footsteps and your dear brother, that no misfortune overtake you on the journey. Rest at home, but flee excessive idleness, have moderation in all things.

From super-satisfaction is born from excessiveness, and from super-satisfaction – boredom; and from boredom – inherent bitterness, and who suffers from this cannot ever be called healthy. There is never a time that would not be useful for a person to involve himself in practical sciences, and the person who moderately but consistently learns subjects that are useful in this life as well in the one here after has an education that is not a burden, but a pleasure. Who thinks about science loves it; and who loves it will never cease to learn, although outwardly you may seem to be idle. Who genuinely loves something, as long as the beloved subject is with him, enjoys at least a moderate amount of pleasure. And the torture he feels if he has to depart from some beloved subject is the same as dealing with the torture of having to depart from a loved one. Why is it this way? Because if you do not love useful sciences with all your soul, then every effort will be futile; on the contrary, love searches and meditates even if in

---

[778] Letter number coincides with the list of letters in Complete Works, volume 2.

a dormant stage; and the more it departs from occupation, the stronger it strives to it.

I am sufficiently aware of the amount that you love scientific experiments, and I do not see the need to state that you need any compulsion, since on your own personal desire you more than sufficiently show zeal in courses of science. Especially since such compulsion is out of place in the present chronological period of your life. I write of this only for you to know how I feel. And I am the type of person who can never be satisfied listening to friends' chatter. Think about this, that people who love virtue are especially pleasant, young men with a clear conscience, adolescents gifted by nature with fortunate inclinations. And Socrates usually calls them children of gods. For this reason I also send gratitude to your excellent grandfather and Proto-pope, the most honorable father Peter, because he acquired for me the opportunity to become woven with your friendship, and for which I count myself very fortunate.

Your new friend, Grigori Skovoroda

Letter 18
To Mikhail Kovalinski
November 15, 1762

Mikhail! The most desirable brother in Christ!

If you are well, I rejoice; if you are likewise happy, I rejoice even more, because joy is the health of a well organized soul. But the soul cannot be joyous if it is affected by some type of vice. I know how slippery the path of adolescence is, how immoderately the typical Christian person has celebrated yesterday. I fear much if you have joined yesterday to some type of company and have fallen into poor associates. If there is no reason for me to worry myself then I rejoice at your great prosperity. If it is not this way, then do not be distressed in vain. It is sufficient for you to hate vices. Christ forgave, but as long as the decision to no longer sin materializes in you. I know that for you it is difficult to hear such words. I know well the morals of young people: but not all is poison that is pleasant to the taste. One item I will only tell you: if you cannot interpret these worries of mine as expressions of my great love to you, you will be profoundly disappointing to me. May Christ in the best possible manner preserve your growth in safety and protect you from all vices and may he direct you to all that is best.

Grigori Savvich, who loves you greatly.

It is the dawn of November 15.

Of what you have asked me in your previous letter, all will be, as long as it is likewise pleasing to Christ and you are yourself firm in the activity you have started. Write to me shorter letters, because I know that you do not always have sufficient time. Take care of your health, especially your eyes.

Letter 19
To Mikhail Kovalinski
November 23, 1762

Greetings, friend.

You asked me my opinion about the plans you intend for your life, your future position, especially the type of friends with whom you should have association. You prudently act by being concerned with your future while the present is opportune. But of your position in life we will discuss at a later date, when Christ should inspire me. Now we need to speak about associations. With whom should you have associations, you ask. With good people, I answer concisely. And of the good people, just those to whom you are naturally inclined based on the secret influences of your heart. This is the best norm for deciding friendship. Food is good, but what will you do if your stomach disagrees with it? It is not amazing that it harms you. And if there only was, my Mikhail, as many good people as there are good foods! But this is something we can only desire; to have is another matter. Truly a good person, that is, a Christian, is more rare than a white raven. To find such a person, you will need many Diogenes' lamps. What should be done? The next step is to extend association with those having less stupidity than others, who in general can be considered just plain people. I would select the tranquil, consistent and plain. I heard said regarding the tranquil soul that it is completely void of envy or malevolence, which is malice. Plain people are not stupid, but frank, not fake, not imposters or vain. Such people I would not hate to release to hell.

O, if we only had less of them! What would we do if the entire world, that is, the majority of people, consisted of such as these?

"The world is a cage of fools and marketplace of vices," as our Palingen sang.[779] For this reason my most proper advice would be for you to acquire friends dead to the world, that is, those alive in the Sacred Scriptures. Among the number of the living you will only have those who are cunning, sly and dishonorable rascals, whose youth has deceived them. They have poured their poison upon the innocent plain and especially attacking the simple, because the snake is so near to them wanting the spoils of his victory. But even a dog will not eat a dog lover. Be fearing of such! What damage I have suffered with my good morals having been deceived by these messengers of the devil. How stealthily they crawl into your trust, that it will take the course of some 5 years that you will feel the results.

Take advantage of my experience. I am the sailor, having been thrown on the shore after a shipwreck. I warn in a timid voice also my other brethren who are preparing to take this same journey; for them to beware of sirens and monsters, and watch the direction to hold the path. For others have drown and passed into eternity. "But," you will say, "I am able to stay prudent myself under the blows of fate." O, my most valuable friend! Do you not know that many suffer shipwreck, while very few survive – maybe 3 of a hundred. Can you really assure yourself that you will be the one to survive? If you have medicine, then should you by your own free will drink poison instead? There exists sufficient disasters if you want to try them due to carelessness.

The bell has rung calling me to my Greek class. So if you want and are free to converse with me on this subject, then write to me soon. So we will continue to carry on our conversation on sacred subjects and during this time improve our style. Take care.

Grigori Savvich who loves you immeasurably.

November 23, at the museum.

---

[779] Marcel Palingen, philosopher of the 9th century who wrote the book Zodiac of Life.

Letter 24
To Mikhail Kovalinski
Beginning of January, 1763

Greetings most pleasant youth and the most dear to me Mikhail!

A new year has started. For this reason I write to you in Greek and consider this a good premonition. Christ said the following in the Gospels, "The Lord's Spirit is upon me," and so forth. May the crown of this year bless you and protect you in good health and prosperity together with those who are precious to you.

You devoted friend prays over this.

Grigori Skovoroda, 1763.

Letter 25
To Mikhail Kovalinski
January 23-26, 1763

Most precious Mikhail!

Some, says Socrates, live to eat and drink, but I am on the contrary. Further, the majority completely do not know what it means to live, and although they make use of food in order to sustain life, however they cannot live this way because the greatest and likewise the most difficult art of all is to learn to live as the art teaches and only Christ can provide this. As long as I know that you greedily read my letters, I will not cease to write to you and speak in terms similar.

Quiet, quiet is the narrow trail. Ascend to the raised tower and disclose in your soul what the rabble rebels. You will see that one suffers due to scabies; another due to convulsions; a third due to gout; a fourth due to epilepsy; a fifth due to tuberculosis. One person has a tooth infection; another has pain inside; some are so miserable that it seems they as if possess not a body but a living corpse. Yet I will not speak about the easier items, such as a cough, exhaustion, bad breath and the similar. These are what the world consists of, that is, of leprous members. So if you should see among them people with a healthy body, then these latter belong to that group which – being recently entrapped in a trap – have not yet reached the point of which we spoke about above, however they are driving in that direction, even running furiously, prepared to accept a glorious reward. But we must flee these sick and are correct to do so, lest they infect us by touching us. However we willingly continue association with those who are up to this point healthy, even though their minds are damaged and drunk full of poisonous teachings. But this will not cause us to become sick in the body, as long as first we do not become sick in the soul.

What advantage is there to distance ourselves from the filth and stench of the fornicator if we associate with those who are infected with the spirit of fornication? The former causes a destitute body that infects the soul. You flee him who acts disorderly due to drunkenness, and you watch for gluttons who invite you to their inopportune and immoderate consumption of vast amount of meat and wine. Why do you run from rivers but draw near to fountains? You fear fires, but you seek a candle. You curse hot coals while you walk following sparks and hot ashes. You fear touching a wound, but walk among knives and scorpions. You flee tuberculosis, gout, syphilis, yet you do not depart from unrestraint, the mother of all disasters.

But Socrates in the midst of a plague remained unharmed, having accustomed himself to the holiest manner of life, to a plain and moderate diet.

Fire seeks only the place where it senses the presence of naphtha. So illness, every infection and fever cannot attach itself if the body is cool, deprived of mucilage and in general has healthy lungs. The majority of people eat meat to the point of madness and with every kind of drink. And does it amaze you if all this does have a bad effect on them? Namely because of this unnecessary substance all of the earlier misfortunes have occurred. Quiet, quiet is the narrow trail. Flee the secular murdering spirit, flee these scorpions; do not harm, do not destroy your body lest you sin in the process; do not emaciate yourself by curbing your regular diet, and flee from the fire which is called wine. All the soul's vices evolve from the above and later they become illnesses of the body. It is not plain fodder that kills a steed, but who feeds him many oats and does not ride him moderately. We load ourselves with food and wine and then for a long while remain on some type of alarming thoughts. Following this is premature ageing, if not something else also bad.

Now I need to stop at this point, since it is already sufficiently detailed because, as I see it, very many, even those clothed in authority, are not satisfied with ruining young men with the deceit of their examples and their bait and eloquence, and excite them to gluttony, and then find excerpts from the Holy Scripture to use as justification. If you desire to listen to me for a while then be assured that as long as you observe moderation, you will preserve your health and shame and reputation, which is a most valuable treasure. Do they manipulate you to unrestrained conduct? I hope you did discard shameful activities that defile you, so do not attempt to reply with a direct refusal. Instead train yourself to this holy stubbornness and say, "This is not beneficial for me, although you say that for the clean all things are clean. And if Paul says that it is not permitted for him to eat meat out of love for others, then likewise can't I out of love for myself observe a partial fast or select my own food." So estrange yourself from the bile and poison of their words sweetened with honey.

Does boredom lead you to extravagance? Take the holy book, sing sacred hymns, pray. If this seems insufficient, invite decent friends and spend the time in joyous and good conversation. Or come to visit me or even invite me to visit you. What have you to fear? If you are ashamed to do something, then beware of doing it. If it is not this way, overcome disgraceful conduct and fear that leads you away from orderly activities. O, if we were only so disgraced and embarrassed in our shameful conduct, just as we often are cowardly and falsely embarrassed in materializing orderly conduct! May Christ preserve your immense gift unblemished from secular infections and may he prepare you for his residence! Be well, my dearest!

The person immeasurably inclined to you, Grigori Skovoroda.

Letter 33
To Mikhail Kovalinski
End of February to beginning of March, 1763

Peace to you my brother.

I wrote this yesterday in a disoriented and scattered condition and even then very quickly. It is not amazing that what is written to you is not satisfactory, especially if you were to pay serious attention to the significant difficulty of your question. I recognize your gift and your zeal in science, and I like your virtue and I rejoice over this. But let us try anyway if we can resolve your question, if Christ will condescend to us inspiration.

However it is sufficient to want to resolve a large matter.

Nonetheless you say that virtue preserves moderation. If it is not this way then in striving for a rule nothing appears that is mandatory. If it is this way then why does one surpass another in virtue? Such are your thoughts. But first of all it is needful to know that there exists 2 classes of people zealous of virtue: one class are the perfect, the other are novices, or as Paul says, they are children.

Based on this we can made the conclusion that there exists 2 type of virtue: one type is the one that clenches what is called virtue in its genuine sense, to which, as if to a goal, the other virtues pertain. These latter consist of the second type. But the perfect are adults (from this point virtue receives its appellation of perfection) and they inherit a castle or fortress of virtue. There is no moderation of it just as there is no saturation of it. We then conclude that one has a supremacy over another, because in a castle there exists levels of ascension, and the more that someone surpasses another, the greater benefit he brings to the human race and becomes more pleasing unto God, whose goodness has no end, no measure, no amount.

From this point on Paul, if I am not in error, counts 5 classes of the elect, and namely in respect to merits. It seems the more estranged a person is to all the earthly, the closer he is to the heavenly and to the very source of light. David's verses, which I often sing, pertain to this, "Just as He has affirmed the heavens high above the earth."[780] Virtues in their genuine sense are those by which the Lord will reveal himself as the existent one or as God. Such are faith, hope and – the greatest of all and not having and end – love. For God himself is called love. All of them are infinitely creative. The quality of faith can be noticed or understood; and the more that someone notices it the more he hopes; and the more that someone hopes, the more fiery the love. In joy he does what is good as much as widely possible, without any restrictions or moderation.

O, if you, my soul, would at some time attain this fortress. O, how little is the number that are allowed to near this Corinth. Do you want to attain it? For this a foundation is needed, which you call the means. What are the means? They are the following: knowledge of Greek and Latin

---

[780] Ps 102:25

literature, which is acquired by study at night; to flee from the masses and secular activities; a contempt of wealth; also to fast and have restraint; or in short, subjection of the flesh in order to acquire the spirit. And I already refer to you as having taken these means.

Finally, such activities as well as the customary virtues are inherent even in disorderly people. Otherwise, if you in just one night of unrestrained riot will ruin your eyes and lungs, how will you later be in a condition to read or converse with saints? What path will you gain from them in regard to God? Faith sees God and is itself divine. In order to attain it, observe moderation at nights and at work, and acquiring the spiritual take care so you do not kill your body, and especially when your body can lead you to something better.

Does not the person who begins a long journey, and does not take measures along the road, act foolishly? Undoubtedly, he will not reach Jerusalem: illness or even death will interrupt his journey. For this reason watch, so that your howling – not having a limit – will not throw you into calamity. O, it is difficult for me to forewarn you of the bad that may occur. You, my Mikhail, are earning the most acceptable destiny. Do you flee the crowds? Preserve moderation in this also. But he is also a fool who avoids people to the point that he completely has no one to talk with. Such a person is stupid and not holy. Watch with whom you speak or to whom you make promises.

Do you fast? Does not the person who provides for his body something poisonous seems to you mentally deranged? Curb excess food, so your inner wild donkey will not surface, that is, the flesh. From another aspect, do not starve yourself either, so he can carry you the passenger. Such are beautiful things, which without moderation become very bad. At such an age as yours, some excessively drink wine, and there are such who excessively are occupied with horses and dogs and a lavish manner of life. There are also those on the contrary who lead an excessively ascetic life. The result of this is a beautiful and divine rule: Do not do anything beyond moderation.

Write in a letter and reply what your thoughts are on this matter so I would know whether any of this is agreeable to you. O, if Christ, who promised to be in your presence always, where 2 or 3 are gathered in his name, would consider us worthy enough to join us in our conversation. From another aspect, without him, all is futile.

Take care of yourself, my Mikhail.
Yours entirely in the Lord, Grigori Savvich.

Letter 36
To Mikhail Kovalinski
First half of March 1763

Greetings, my valiant new soldier of Christ's army, my beloved Mikhail!

Having read your short letter with great satisfaction and not without some laughter, I meditated much about myself, or more truthfully said, I silently conversed with you, and having prepared myself for sleep I thought much about it. And suddenly its seems to me that I was hearing this inner voice, "Your life is a military service." Because the devil, since he was unable to deceive you either with meagerness or with pleasures and so harm your soul, perhaps he can harm your health? This is indubitably so and is actually wisely stated, "From 2 evils it is best to choose the lesser." This old sly entity knows that some of the best minds are very inclined toward vanity, especially at such an age as your, and by doing this he has often hurried the time of someone's inopportune death or has harmed his health beyond recovery, such as the eyes or the lungs. And so not having succeeded in the first manner he attempts to act in another manner.

In order not to lose sight of the interests of your valuable health, at this time fulfill these – as they appear to be – foolish and vain, although very difficult, demands. It is better to sacrifice your ambitions. This will occur if you will labor and exercise a certain moderation that will be sufficient for a middle-school pupil and for your discipline, and without any fervent complaints.

But I turn toward our honorable perfector, master and friend. You, my dearest, reside under the wings of your leader Christ. Be healthy in him!

Your Grigori Savvich.

Letter 49
To Mikhail Kovalinski
From Belgorod.
July 18, 1763

Most beloved friend, Mikhail! Rejoice in the Lord!

It has been 3 days now since the ode that I promised you has been ready. What pertains to me is that I have not spent even one day without conversing with you. This lion – the devil – never sleeps, and for this reason we must always be vigilant. An enemy will strike at the body at some unexpected moment, so will this spiritual enemy never cease to throw into our souls his fiery arrows of lust and to strike us dead. You will extinguish them if you think about all that you possess, the strength by which you can become great, that is, a holy man.

For what reasons would you want to be tormented, to suffer? Is it because you do not participate in all-night booze parties with gluttons? That in royal palaces you do not gamble playing dice? That you do not dance? That you do not enter military service? If these pitiful items compose an object for your ecstasy, then you have not yet attained wisdom and are just one more person among the many. You are not yet virtuous if you are seeking some goodness outside of yourself. Gather within yourself your thoughts and seek true goodness within your very self. Dig within yourself a well for that water that will shower your house and the neighbor's house. Within yourself is located that base, as Plutarch says, the fountain of tranquility. Strive to cleanse this fountain, scooping from it not as if from a pig's mire, but from the holy books of holy people.

Do not allow the crowds to lead you astray as they chase the seas and lands for what is inconsistent, but instead reside in your own home watching what occurs, the bad and good. What good is a scepter or palace or gold if you will lose and destroy you valuable soul, that is, yourself. Is it not due to mental anguish that bodily illnesses are borne? As soon as sinful passions inflame your soul, know this, that it has been attacked and even died. So why do you not worry about discarding passion from yourself – the death of your most valuable members? Why do you go astray mentally? Why do you lust when within yourself you possess all goodness and if you intend to be prudent? Why do you attend feasts and join the crowds of unworthy groups? What do you see there that is good? Suppress and restrain the passions of the soul and now accustom yourself to being a king.

O, if I only had a spiritual sword I would hew from you lonesomeness and would destroy luxury and the spirit of drunkenness; I would strike at ambition and destroy vanity. O, holy vigilance! O, benevolent poverty! O, tranquility of the soul! How little do people know about you! If you do not already know that all appearances of evil are contained in sin, you are no longer wise, not possessing the evangelic belief. However belief is not by seeing. If you do not already see that the entire paradise is confined in sturdy protection and the observance of God's commandments, you still do not have God's grace. Believe however and proclaim with David, "Open my eyes and I will understand."[781] As long as you have understood even what I have not said and the benefit inherent in it, there is no reason for you not to say, "I have inherited your revelations as my compensation." Seek this as Virgil summons. If you will seek this with all your heart you will find it. Should you strive for this? How can this be wrong? Do not allow yourself to be lead astray.

May Christ the Lord preserve your soul and your body from the poison of your compatriots, from all filth, from the fiery arrows! Care for your health, my dear, and reply in a letter! I thirst to know how matters are with you.

Your Christian friend, Grigori Savvich.

July 18, from Belgorod.

Letter 73
To Mikhail Kovalinski
July – August, 1767

Greetings, my treasure, my most precious Mikhail!

Perhaps, and you may feel the same, my dear, that during these past few days I was upset and burdened and caused myself to be agitated. Because when I am melancholy, when I am sorrowful and irritated, I cannot look at you and I cannot approach you with our usual friendly

---

[781] Ps 119:18

manner, to the point it is amazing if you were to feel the same something in us that was inappropriate. Then I begin to feel sorrowful, my friend, as though one of my most important joys and one of my comforts was suddenly stolen from me. No one provides me more pleasure in friendliness: this is my sole joy and treasure. What is amazing in this matter is that I have not taken measures when I gave myself over to sorrow. We excuse the person who is weeping, having lost an expensive horse, or the sorrow of a person who lost his possessions in a fire. You need also to excuse me, because I do not see this and fear that something else is drawing near to me. The more the human soul and friend is outside of any doubt, the more valuable are possessions. If he was in a more safe place, I would be less upset. Now it is a palace – a den of deceit and crime.

A person at your young age is inexperienced and easily succumbs to deceit and the influence of bad morals. I have myself experienced this and so am the more alarmed. I am alarmed and I have the right to be alarmed. What am I to do with my life than to route my spirit to decide about what to worry? Not to worry about anything, not to be annoyed over anything, means not to live but to be dead. All worry is movement of the soul, while life consists of movement. One worries about one matter, another about another matter. My allotment is to worry about what has been assigned me, and the souls of those young men and adolescents who consider me their friend. Where the corpse, there is demise. Where the worry, there is happiness.

The miser worries about money, he suffers for the sake of acquisition, but he will never be satisfied with the amount of money he has. But to find satisfaction he devotes himself to money and rejoices, now consumed by these worries. In a similar vein is that I love my soul to be agitated over my friends' prosperity, so that I may at some time also experience such satisfaction and joy, although I already experience all of this at present. So what can be sweeter than to be beloved, than to be the subject of the attraction of a good soul? What can be more pleasant than a friend's love? A desolate matter is unpleasant to me, unless it is tied with love and philanthropy. For me there is nothing more valuable or sweeter than a soul that loves me, even if all else should depart from me. While my worry and joy and credit and – I would even say – life, and referring to eternal life, what is all this? The friendly soul is the soul that loves me, the soul that remembers me. I prefer it to pyramids, mausoleums, and other royal memorials.

But what is nobler than a noble soul and what can persist longer than eternity? Because of this I am troubled over my dear Yasha[782] and worry over him, that perhaps at some time he did love me, even though at the present he does love me. So love summons more love, and wanting to be loved I earlier myself did love. And who would not love the soul of this child? Imagine for yourself the large amount I would be distressed if something bad should occur to you, even though you are not a child but an adult. I say this frankly, it is for your sake, only for your sake I left my very pleasant tranquility, and entrusted myself to storms; over the course of 2 years I experience so much animosity, subjected myself to such slander, such hate. Otherwise some religious hierarch, some archimandrite, would have lured me away from such sweetest tranquility to the detriment of my reputation and health, if I had not seen you significantly prior to their influence and demands, if you did not become so beloved to my soul at first sight.

I think you remember how indignant I became when they removed you from the class in Greek language, and how they invited you to their palace when you almost became a teacher of the German language, when – as I say – I became indignant. So this occurs also when lion cubs are removed from the lioness, or they remove a child from its loving mother. I have also experienced such feelings because I saw how close you were to ruin, having become a pedagogue in a palace or official teacher of some foreign language. All were surprised and suspicious, while my enemies laughed at me. So what is the matter if I worry about someone more than I would over a relative? So if my concern over the fate of my Jacob bothers me so much, will the person whom you present to me out of incident or maneuver love me also? And if others made use of my productive efforts, then all of them are likewise obligated to you, the only person who drug me from refuge, or more concisely said, it was my love to you that drug me.

Even though I loved you so much that you became my enemy, but I could not hate you or deny you anything that was beneficial to you. As I see it, I am of this particular nature, that, finding myself in a condition of a present anger, applying equally to the most vile of enemies, I immediately

---

[782] diminutive for Yacov or Jacob, but no indication who this is specifically.

softened, this occurring as soon as I noticed even the most insignificant indication of a good attitude toward me. As soon as I notice that someone loves me, I am ready to devote to him half of the days of my life, if this would be possible and permissible. Nonetheless, who voluntarily for the sake of a friend subjects himself to danger will in a certain manner expend his life for him. On occasion he can show that I am angered at certain people who are precious to me. Ah, but this is not anger, but exceptional fervor that summons love and perspicacity, because I see more than you do those things that must be fled and those things we must strive for.

And so while I comprehend myself, as long as my soul directs the body, I will worry only about what will with all possible means summon love in me toward noble souls. This is my treasure and joy and life and credit. Love summons more love, which engenders good inclinations and goodwill toward a union with philanthropy. But you are most precious to me of all, and I will not regret my solitude – although my health has become weaker – as long as you should remain my friend. Be healthy my precious friend.

Your Grigori Skovoroda

Letter 97
To Vasili Maksimovich

Beloved friend Vasili Maksimovich!

A person's merit is an invaluable treasure. We do right when we preserve wealth that is honorably acquired or if we happen to discover what was stolen from us. Such virtue requires of us to earn a living using honorable means and preserving for ourselves a merit, and also to strive to return to ourselves what was stolen by criminal fingernails. You my friend I think will believe the number of malicious slanderers I have. If they were to just attribute to me regular crimes I could tolerate it. But such ruthless people breathe at me with unlimited damage exiting their tongue. Other than just extremely ruining my ethics with their rumors, they also make me a murderer or heretic, and for this reason they forbid their subordinates to listen to my conversations. This I cannot tolerate and so have made a short clarification that I am sending to you, my friend. Although it will not be able to block their yelping jaws, however I think it will at least twist their tongues a little, so that those who are kind and right-hearted will have to endure less of such deceit.

Your friend, Grigori Skovoroda.

First they are saying that as if I have influenced certain young people telling them that this or another such human manner of life is harmful and deleterious, and then contrary to this, that I have attributed existential virtue to certain compositions. But is it really possible for me to have such foolish and harmful opinions? Those who know my inner person are sufficiently assured that I have the same opinions as did St Maxim the Confessor. He says that no malice exists anywhere, within anything, ever. How can this be if we see that malice exists almost everywhere? He teaches that malice is nothing else but good items created by God that have been put to a purpose other than its intended. So for example someone places a boot on their head, and a hat on their foot. The disorder is genuinely wrong, but who can say that a hat or boot is not useful to the human life? And as much as I have noticed that such disorder for the most part depends on the period of time that such occurs, and place, extent and persons. For example, during a hot summer mid-day to drag a pipe without a worthy reason; or has someone fallen asleep when he should not have; or overslept, or slept where he should not have. Profanity can be labeled disorderly conduct, but not sleep or anger. All of this is yet good.

And yet do I not understand how wise people can compare a human's life to a comedic game? I can say that you as a person by nature cannot present himself as such in the theater. But can I assume that him, or another person just as comedic, is harmful, if an intelligent composer will assign it such? And great persons were assigned to wear original masks in this important life of our comedy by the wise creator. Ascertaining the character of your nature, if I may use as an example, you would be unsuccessful as either a healer or cook. But when did I ever say to someone that the healing science and culinary mastery are harmful? Many times I have spoken that it is not your nature to be a priest or a monk, but I have never yet have said that the priesthood or monasticism is harmful. Who by his own nature is a busybody or meddlesome, to such a person I can say for him to be a city official, where they are incessantly inclined to anger and nonsense. But can I ascertain that due to some arbitrary reason it is not proper to be a city commander? Have mercy on me. I was not born for such base understanding, to descend into such immense wild behavior.

Many call me an intelligent person, but such deliberations cannot arise except in some demonic head.

If I am able to assure virtuous and non-pretentious hearts that it never occurred to me or entered my mind to call essentially harmful a certain mode of life, and that I always taught people to inspect their nature, or to say this in short, to comprehend yourself and your purpose in birth, then God has offended nobody. Now I bequeath this very truth to minds possessing love to ascertain: to which blasphemies or praises am I worthy? I must take a very contrite attitude in discernment, where from among the nations did such disorder, upheaval and restlessness arise? Is it not in accord with the proverb that many were not born for the priesthood but have crawled into robes, and not being mushrooms they crawled into the basket? It is due to this reason that for some the priesthood was gracious for them, but for many it has made them cursed.

The following now occurs, that even the most base of conduct becomes a reason for prosperity for any person, if it conforms to his nature. If every person presents his own person to the public as being right and good, then why are there so many premeditated struggles on the theater stage? From this evolves failure without doubt, while failure irrefutably evolves from a nature that is inherently dissident. Many refined people would have become merchants or farmers if they had not accepted as a vocation what was contradictory to their nature. Others would have become professional lawyers if they did not take vows as a monk, where they now struggle worse with nature that has become for them temptation, and more temptations than 5 virtuous persons can remove, as regularly occurs in comedies.

This is my opinion and intention, for which reason I always provide counsel to young people with their nature, so that they on the theater of our life could observe orderly conduct as a professional actor, a proper one. And if the occasions should arise to wear a mask, one that is not entirely conforming to his proper nature, this could always be to his success, as long as he is conducting himself outside of temptation, and even though having a certain number of complaints among their countrymen, his grievances toward God regarding his condition would decrease.

I would myself and today discard my condition and enter into another if I felt that I was not adaptable to my unsettled and melancholic nature toward the most vile and corrupt and isolated mask. If I am unable to serve my beloved fatherland in any manner, then at least with all my strength I will strive to not be harming to anybody in any manner.

There is another slander directed against me that is more important than other statements, and namely they say that as if I condemn the consumption of meat and wine. And this is definitely a heresy of the Manicheans, who were long ago declared anathema by the holy ecumenical councils. Others ascribe to me the attitude that as if gold, silver, expensive clothing and other such similar items are in themselves detrimental and that I call them useless. But those that know my heart, after hearing such stuff, just laugh. It is true that there was a time and it is still this way on occasion, that for my inner economy I restrain from eating meat and drinking wine and even during permitted days.[783] But then why does the local healer advise against for example garlic, when a person is suffering from an eye infection? This is well known that of all the good things created by our all-generous creator not all of them are useful and not for everyone in every situation. It is true that I have advised some people that they should conduct themselves cautiously in regard to meat and wine, and on occasion I have steered them away from them entirely after realizing the extreme zeal of their youth. It is the same as a father who removes from his young son's hand a knife or does not allow him to utilize a pistol, even though he as an adult will utilize these instruments. Does not this clearly indicate that they have not yet reached a maturity in regard to the proper use of these items that will be beneficial and for the reason they were manufactured? This is the basis for these people to consider me a disciple of the Manichees.

Definitely every type of food and drink is useful and good, but it is necessary to ascertain the proper time, place, amount to consume and the person you are. And would it not be sad and interwoven with laughter if someone was to pour vinegar into a bottle and give it to a baby lying in a cradle to drink; or to give a 8 year-old child a bottle of some distilled liquor to drink; or to give a glass of sweet milk to an elderly soldier returning from war? So have these people incorrectly labeled me a Manichee, and it is not because of any of my merits, but by claiming I was odious to wealth or odious to people, a person fleeing association with society.

---

[783] The reference is that in the Russian Orthodox Church, both Wednesday and Friday are meatless days.

When God assigned me a basic mask to wear in my theater then I must wear the entire costume, and in the company of worthy people I must observe decency and always remember my humility in the presence of others. This is what I strive to observe myself and have advised others to do the same, and as a result I have fallen into reproach. I hope that with the help of prudent and kind hearts I will be released from such calumnies, and even if just part of them. Then my innocence would grant me safety from these ruthless rodents with their gnawing, and would make it more conducive for me to fulfill the Lord's command, "Love your enemies," and others.

Letter 100
To Yakov Ivanovich Dolganski
Sent from Kharkov to Ostrogozhk, 1772

Tell me what this phase of your means, "You have compelled me with coercion." And likewise the following, "Why is this news not comfortable for me?" Are you opposing my effort to compel you? I am not a despot and you are not my enemy. Or rather should Paul have stated instead that we prefer our elders' opinions, instead of the rectitude that is pleasing to God?[784] It seems to me that you have recited these words not as loving friends, but as servants who are disobedient to the Bible's rectitude. Have you been defeated by something to state this? If this is so, discard the servitude residing within yourself, and then love as though a son. I can guess something: has the inner secret whisperer almost attached himself to the one of whom is written, "Angels stood." It is possible to recognize this with the singing of the bird; correlate this with the secrets of the heart. Has not the snake crawled into those thoughts that, seeking the Lord's truth, reside on a high pillar? But I say with Augustine that he has everywhere placed nets, even at the very heavenly table, inside the very chamber where those who seek rectitude feast. Friend, he is the very one that is the reason for this weeping incident that you have entered. Can a person stand in the presence of this table while not wearing wedding clothes? Can he willingly eat while someone is saying something to me that is very inappropriate? Or

---

[784] Phil 4:9

do you need to force him to eat? I have no desire for this. Comprehend this yourselves, what these items are: spirit, friend, day, today and home.[785]

Circumspect this intently. A person's enemies are his own household. Because I love you, I formidably love not what resides in you. He wants to have prejudice against such food as a result of you, to crawl toward you, and it seems, to whisper. Why should such affluence affect you? And you really do not have the strength to understand this, and perhaps this is not yet even born, which is all the more harmful to you. Be satisfied with what you have, and all of this is confirmed by the sacred words that can be supplied by the sacred books, and draw you away from what resembles the snake. This is gathered from these very flowers from which bees gather nectar, the divine juice, even though they have the ability to convert this into a poison to sting, such is the nature of bees. He puts us through trials. The snake never seems to have been ashamed of the people he has stung, but we have a Savior who resides in us and we in him. Tell me, he says, to turn these breads into stone, so what is the use of agonizing regarding this issue? It is enough for the flesh. Here is another. Our Christ tells us that bread alone is insufficient to satisfy our hunger: there exists 2 births and 2 lives. As strong as the evil snake becomes in order to overthrow the destiny of our salvation, this good person resides in celestial places attaining to the Lord, to the spirit, to God, and so he [the snake] leaves him behind, since he [the believer] cannot descend from the heavens to the ground. The divine spirit ascends to the divine spirit, while evil descends to the ground.

I now say this and have said this long ago that the sacred scripture needs to be read with the fear of God, leaving behind all of your base and secular and bodily superstitions in the same manner as Abraham left his donkey with his servants when he ascended God's mountain with Isaac. At this time you will not be saying, This is not acceptable to me; or, It is repulsive to my opinions; or, It causes me to follow a different direction; or, It seems it is not so necessary anyway; or, So why even debate the issue. Did not God test Abraham, that is, did he not afflict him with the word of his holy truth? How was it possible for the benevolent spirit of God to demand the death of his only-born son?

But my God! So what was occurring in the devoted heart of this mild-mannered soul at the immediate time? "This is what should be done! Or

---

[785] These 5 items all begin with the same letter **D** in Russian,

should I debate it, as if I do not know that you are actually the more wise, even though I would consider this not advantageous." I do not understand this; my mind is weak in this area. But is it possible that I have thought bad of you and of your word? Permit me to speak: I have only one heir, and for your sake I will butcher him. It is more tolerable for me to be deprived of all that is in the world than your friendship; this consists in the agreement of opinion and you are my leader.

Tell me please if God should not disclose the issue to such a heart? O, how destitute we are with our servants and our donkeys! There! To the mountain we will rise, that is, those who have the strength, but those with possessions are not allowed. Discard your opinions, wash the mud and change your clothes. Remove all of your vileness and then ascend. But as long as you carry your possessions and brag of them, this bragging of yours is blasphemy unto God. Let your clothing be white.[786] And what is this clothing? Listen to Isaiah, "Array yourselves in garments of joy."[787] What is this joy? Listen to Sirach, "Fear of the Lord will provide joy to the heart."[788] This is the rod that divides the sea, let us not reduce it with slag. This is the key that opens and it remains opened, and if someone should close it, it remains closed.[789] "Fear of the Lord is a gift of the Lord. To be loved of the Lord is a glorious wisdom. Wisdom and punishment are the fear of the Lord."[790] Even though wisdom is unveiled to many, not all are aware of this, and it is shared in visions.

Letter 101
To Yacob Ivanovich Dolganski
February 25, 1773, from Babaev.

My good friend, Yacob Ivanovich!

I have received your letter. In it you ask me to more intelligibly discuss items with you. Even in your absence, my friend, the friendship is still active and enlivening. This is most true. If the friend does not write to you, then he is just like a friend that is close to you, however dumb.

---

[786] Eccl 9:8
[787] Is 61:3
[788] Sirach 1:11
[789] Rev 3:7
[790] Sirach 2:15

Conversation is the communication of thoughts and as if the mutual kiss of hearts. With the company of salt and light, it is a consummation of unity. But just as it is impossible for a garden to communicate to a friend without greenery or branches, so it is impossible for a friend's thoughts to be carried into the soul and migrate through it and increase, except through a seed or the person speaking, or words inscribed on paper. But just as a seed in its essential nature is small and insignificant, but it has the capability of creating 1,000 trees with the hidden source of the reproductive divine spirit within it. So it is with a word when it is expelled into the air or inscribed on something, it seems to be irrelevant, but due to the strength of the hidden spirit within it sown on the heart, it has the capability of producing a new creation and new activities that are of most importance. The seed of this world's evil crimes produces weeds that torment the soul. Good conversations decay due to bad habits. Who sows death reaps the soul's decay. But on the opposite hand, the seed of a good word flourishes in the heart: love, joy, peace, endurance.

There is no more a bitter calamity than pain in the soul. It hurts when thoughts hurt. And thoughts hurt when the following is born in the heart. "Lest there be among you a root growing on the hills producing bitterness and sorrow."[791]

These are not the conversations that Isaiah heard, who said, "Lord. He accepted it into his entrails and had pains and gave birth to the spirit of your salvation." We will not fall, but those living on the earth will fall.

Living on the earth is not thinking about anything at all, except how to become wealthy, eat and drink lots, be clothed. Flee the conversations of those who strive to gain wealth. In their heart a bad seed resides that produces gall and a snake's poison that can be fatal to the soul.

And if the seed should fall (and this cannot but happen since every interlocutor is a sower), watch that a cursed idol-worshiping root not rise from the ground. Counsel is the beginning of an action; it is the seed and head. Pray for him of whom it is said, "And he will crush your head." The good seed is the Holy Scripture. "The farmer went to sow." The evil seed is the contemporary fashion. And I will put enmity between the seed of the snake and the seed of the woman. And so what is the woman? It is the evangelic wisdom and the entire Bible. Listen to Sirach, "He will greet her like a mother and accept her as a wife married when a virgin, and will feed

---

[791] Deut 29:18

him with the bread of intelligence and give him the water of wisdom to drink."[792] And also read the 14th chapter. Of course, this is the woman, "Come, eat my bread and drink."[793] Yes, goodness will flow and we will be the sons of that mother of us all.

And I, as I was in the past and so am today, a traveler, collaborator, and most humble servant.

Grigori Skovoroda

Letter 104
To Ivan Grigoryevich Diskom
November 20, 1778,
From Burluk, Izyumski Province.

Most merciful sir, Ivan Grigoryevich!

Remembering your love of humanity and your old love toward me, all of a sudden I thought to bring greetings and a deep bow to you and to your entire house. If you are still alive, then I thank you greatly. Death is torture, but to others rest. Up to this time I still wander, bearing this dead body. My protective shield is my high ethic and innocence, and my comfort is love toward God and to his wisdom. I live as though I possess nothing, but yet possess everything. I have learned to be content with little. And it is as if I was seaworthy to travel, always watching if I will see some sweetest harbor to secure me from calamity, and the worst is death. My hope is my Lord who resides within me. With His wings I will escape the autumn. To Him I entrust you and your entire household.

Merciful sir, from your faithful servant.

Grigori Skovoroda

---

[792] Sirach 15:2-3
[793] Proverbs 9:5

Letter 105
To Artem Dorofeevich Karpov
From Gusinski Wilderness, Poltava Province, Prilutzski County
February 19, 1779

My beloved sir, Artem Dorofeevich! Greetings and rejoice!

My guardian angel now with me rejoices in this wilderness. I have been born for it. Old age, destitution, humility, worry-free and contriteness are my companions at my residence. I love them and they love me. And what do I do in this wilderness? Do not ask. Not too long ago someone asked another about me, "Tell me, so what does he do there?" If I was in the wilderness to recover from some bodily illness, or caring for bees, or sewing clothes, or hunting animals, then it would seem that Skovoroda was occupied with activities. But I do none of these, they think I am idle and so they are without reason surprised at me.

It is true that idleness is heavier than the Caucasus Mountains. So are the only matters that pertain to a person to sell, buy, marry,[794] be given in marriage,[795] war, struggle, sew, build, catch animals? So is our heart here always incompatible with this? The destitution of our reasoning seems to be now so apparent, that we, having driven our entire heart into the acquisition of the world and into the sea of bodily comforts, we do not have time to look into ourselves, to cleanse and heal the master of our body, our soul. We have forgotten about ourselves, with the exception of our slave – the undependable fat on our body – our soul concerns us day and night. This is similar to a gigolo who is concerned about his shoes and not about his feet; about the color of the hot coals and not the cake baking on it; about a gold purse and not whether any money is in it. Can we fathom the futility and vanity of such a person? Have we all become opulent? It seems that good only pertains to the body. As we have a saying: He is just a wagon without wheels. As a result we have no soul remaining in us. Although it is true that we do possess a soul, but it is the same type as the one found in a leech or a person with gout. It is weak in us, coarse, unethical, cowardly, envious, greedy, satisfied with nothing,

---

[794] referring to the groom
[795] referring to the bride

angry at itself, gaunt, poor. Exactly this, like a patient at a hospital. Even if such a soul was clothed in velvet, it would just be a velvet coffin.

If the most secret place, meaning the very center of the soul, is full of puss and pain, who or what will provide joy? O, my sir and beloved friend! Float upon the sea and raise your eyes to the haven. Do not forget yourself in the midst of your abundance. You have one bread that is sufficient for you; would not another be too much for you? Your slave is satiated, but is Rebecca satisfied? This applies, "A person will not live by bread alone." It is in regard to the angelic bread that Skovoroda worries. He loves this type of bread more than all other types. I would give a piece of my bread to all of Israel, even if it should leave me with hardly a piece for myself.

This is what he does residing in the wilderness.

Beloved sovereign! I am always your most humble servant, and also the same for our beloved Stepan Nikitich Kurdumov. Give regards to father Boris and his son if you can, and to Ivan Akimovich.

Letter 106
To Vasili Mikhailovich Zemborski
From Gusinski Wilderness
February 21, 1779

Merciful sir!

A Polish proverb says, "Krakow was not suddenly built." Little by little recover from your illness. Let the body hurt. Ice was created to melt. Take care to save yourself, meaning your soul. To say this more clearly your thoughts and heart that your body possesses is just like a body wearing clothes.

There is nothing worse and even in hell than to bear pain inside yourself, and the darkest parts of our inner body is the abyss of our thoughts, waters that are more expansive than the heavens. Even what is furthest inside the most inner part of us is a tempest of the mind, while the center is a haven and our peace is the sweetest name Christ, our God.

Pay attention to yourself. Not because it rests in the very most inner point inside us, but as it has ceased from work and so fulfills an internal Sabbath. Leave this thought for children and fanatics, and not because they are as if very small mentally, like a poppy-seed, and even smaller so they cannot expand into our hands, feet, hair, to run along the chamber walls, along the palace fences, in forests, fields, the skies, and through the entire Copernican planetary system. Leave this for the insane and those suffering high fevers. This is why their inner person is so small: it is invisible and inaccessible. It invites because it realizes no destruction and ruin can reach it and nothing will agitate it; but it is always vigilant and lively and it will not be deprived of years. It has no height, no depth, no width, but everywhere and always existing. While a seed is formed because as a seed can produce 1,000 trees, so does it form creation out of itself and into the public.

Pay attention to yourself. Now we have found a haven of salvation in the destitute mode of life we have – this turbulent sea. Rejoice with me, my friend! Do you see and do you believe and we have found a most dark treasure in the dust of our body's little house? Yes, and acquired it. Why do you weep? And you weep in the secret recess of your heart. Is not this a fire and worry and anguish? Let the branches of your hand and feet whither and vanish! Do not fear; it will hide inside its seed, from which it evolved. Do you notice that we have found Abraham's seed? O, our hope and consolation! And sweetest are all who believe in you and are of you.

Do you notice the truth said to Abraham, that his seed is eternal? Do you want to be part of the generation of Abraham? Believe in his seed; not his specifically, but God's. Abraham and we are just dust. This very Abraham saw and rejoiced, and we believe, rejoice and boast.

Weep for the time being and ask for medicine. Within you is the divine person, not somewhere across the sea. The person is close to the Lord. Do not ask of the slave that evolves from you flesh, meaning your body. The flesh is nothing; it is dust and death and darkness and clothing and clay. You will be laid to rest in some superficial corner, in the darkness outside. The further it is from the chambers of our king, the more the evil is occupied. For you this is the Samaritan and the tavern and paradise and the haven. Here is where the ark of the blessed Noah rests.

Do not fear! It is not very far away! Just clothe your thoughts in the wings of belief and divine love. And I have been bringing him long already with Mary and this portion is sufficient goodness for me, existing exceptionally, my beloved friend.

Your most humble servant.

Grigori Skovoroda to Vasili Mikhailovich Zemborski, in Kharkov.

Letter 108
To Osip Yuryevich Soshalski
From Gusinski Wilderness
1781

Beloved sir, Osip Yuryevich!

Today's travel of Ms. Alekseeva brought to my heart Paul's following words, The root of all evil is love of money, as a result of which occur strife, war, poisoning, murder, counterfeiting, conniving, animosity, failure, sorrow, despair, alcoholism, duels, and etc, and the most vile of all is the use of tobacco. This root of defilement was born from apostasy, meaning from unbelief in God, which destroys providence pertaining to us. Our father sits high but due to trampling upon the most precious pearls they violate the third of the 10 commandments, "Do not use the name of the Lord your God in vain." So did God interpret this commandment as part of our divine education or catechism, and which now lies before your very eyes.

My heart flew from these thoughts to the furthest of meditations, that such people, having forgotten the good fortune of the rock, "Let your will be done," depend on themselves, on their own will and on their own subtlety, and will finally entangle themselves in an inescapable destructive labyrinth. At this time they lose the entirety of light and the most valuable of wealth, "My peace I give unto you. A heart's joy is a person's life. Son, protect your heart." At least it seems they calmly sought their ruin. And this is how calmly, "They walked in the inaccessible paths." This is how calmly, "Like a deer shot by an arrow."

Ascertain the matter, are they not all insane that they wander in cemeteries, marshes, and along village fences. The following words seem to be only a joke and nonsense to such demonized people, "Who will lose his soul will gain it." Christ speaks to such demonized and lost people with almost the same words, "Return to your home," meaning, Son, protect your heart. Or simply said, Aleksei, do not strive to acquire korban, but the heart's tranquility. Lose the soul, sever from yourself the lust of your barns. This is a noble loss and true circumcision, and the praise is not from people but from God.

Do you not understand that what enters a person cannot defile him. But this will: immorality, murder, theft, and greed, which is love of money. Paul calls the seed of the serpent powers and authorities and spirits of malice, and that our war is not against flesh and blood. If someone is genuinely a soldier of Christ and fought these spirits, then his heart will rejoice and his face will shine. This is what it means to lose your soul. This is the significance of baptism.

This is also the chrism, the anointment, joy for the weeping. If a person does not return home, does not look into his heart and does not lose his cursed soul, or to say it more correctly, the demonic regiment, then the heart becomes for such a person a turbulent wind like a hurricane. O, woe unto them for they walk in the path of Cain. And it is not surprising that they, not having mortified what is evil, mortify the innocent soul.

Letter 109
To S. I. Kurdumov in Kharkov
From Taganrog, 1781

Love is the source of all life and the work of every creature and so not in vain are the words recorded, "God is love." God is our fire and the paraclete signifies this for every person filled with spirit. This is also comfort, but dreariness is laziness. This is the paraclete and he has set me on fire.

Please, out of mercy send to me a pair of winter shoes, with red laces, and appropriate for snow. Grigori Ivanov at the beginning of winter will be traveling to Petersburg through Kharkov from Ekaterinoslav.

Give Artem Dorofeevich my deepest regards.

I regret for not having written to you earlier. Just laziness.

O, paraclete.

Letter 114
To Grigori Ivanovich Kovalinski[796]
From Veliki Burluk to Taganrog
September 23, 1781

Alyosha writes that you are sick. If it is bodily pain, this is nothing. If it is psychological at the same time, and for the same reason as you would have, I am empathetic toward you. Because to have psychological pain is a worse illness. May Christ recover you from your illness, especially your spirit.

Learn to slowly depart from the world. In this manner you will reduce your worries, and likewise the pain of spirit and body. Do you not know that a person possesses 2 natures: master and servant, spirit and flesh, heart and body? Why do I say this? So that you would understand that you need to yield a certain extent to the body, as much as reasonably possible, but not to the extent to what the servant of the body wants – lust! So if you were to yield to the body more than just the required necessities, then you will please its lusts, and you will never live happily. Why is this? Because when you yield something extra to the flesh, you reduce yourself as its master. Who is the master of the flesh? It is the spirit, a brother to you. Further, whoever has severed a brotherly attachment has never and ever lived pleasantly. To be able to take advantage of brotherly peace or agreement is to be satisfied with yourself, and this meaning to have a prosperous self-sufficiency, which is what Apostle Paul insistently recommends to Timothy.[797] Apparently this is same as the passage, "If our hearts do not condemn us we have boldness toward God."[798] We learn to comprehend ourselves through him as our means.

I desire for you my valuable friend the one and blessed peace. I entrust you and all of your family to Christ, who is our peace. Amen. From one of those who desires good for you, the elder Grigori Skovoroda.

Incline your ear and give attention to my request. View the writer of this letter with the eye of your most inner self and promise me even some

---
[796] uncle of Mikhail Kovalinksi
[797] 1 Tim 6:6
[798] 1 John 3:21

small amount for my sustenance. I know You who rains on the good and the bad.[799]

To the merciful sovereign, Grigori Ivanovich Kovalinski in Taganrog.

Letter 118
To Grigori Giorgievich Yurupin
From Veliki Burluk to Kharkov
July 2, 1790

Beloved friend, Grigori Giorgievich! May peace be upon you and upon your household.

Do not forget my friend that today the first quarter of the heavenly moon of August is passing. Comprehend what I am saying: Give way to the wise person and you will become even more wise. Listen to the Latin proverb, A mother does not weep over a cowardly son. Do not slumber! Our life is a sea. Take care that you walk not dangerously. May the Lord protect you in the right course that you take. As you sail may you reach the haven of the anointed old age. The crown of praise is old age! So what is this oil that will anoint you with a prosperous old age? What is the crown? Listen! God has anointed us with his spirit. With the oil of joy he has anointed him.[800] The eternal joy upon the head of the saints! What better way is there to sweeten old age than with God's anointing oil? Here is oil for you! A good reputation is better than the softest bread.

Do not think my friend that a good reputation is the same as a secular newspaper that no one is reading, or that someone is heralding your wisdom, strength and wealth as he walks through the streets. Let not the wise person boast of his wisdom.[801] From this oil David flees: Let not the oil of the sinner be poured upon my head. The criminals are smeared with this oil. They paint the walls and bodies, and not their hearts. And there they are. O, hypocrite! Wash first your inner cup. Now here for you is the true oil that paints the heart and nourishes it. The light of your face has been sealed and indicated so on our heart. You have provided joy in my

---

[799] Matt 5:45
[800] Heb 1:9
[801] Jer 9:23

heart, from the produce, wheat, wine and oil and other items, meaning that we have become wealthy with the decoration and nourishment of our heart.

Have the ability to separate false merit from the true, like counterfeit money, and you will become blessed. A merchant praised by Christ. He preferred the precious pearl more than all of his possessions. Although he sold all he had, it was solely to acquire this item. And so exactly what is this unique and marvelous pearl?

This is it! The radiant commandment of the Lord. Fear of the Lord is pure. Here it is! I have taken pleasure in the paths of your revelations, just as with every type of wealth. Here it is! Open my eyes and I will fathom its value. Here it is! I am a migrant in the land. Here it is! A good reputation puts fat on the bones. Here it is! Your heart will cling to you. Never will I forget your laws. It is better to be a naked righteous person than to be a wealthy criminal. I do not fear the person who will strip naked the body, but is unable to strip naked the soul.

A beloved friend and true person who desires the best for you. Your most humble servant, elder Grigori Savvich Skovoroda.

Please send to me a knife and some gloves.

Give my deepest regards to Prokopi Semeonovich.

Letter 119
To Ivan Ivanovich Ermolov
From Gusinski Monastery to Kharkov
Second half of September 1791

Most merciful sir, Ivan Ivanovich!

For God's sake please help me with acquiring a winter coat in the Yaroslav style. Winter is approaching and I have long attained old age. What I need is to be warm and comfortable and need to buy such even with my meager capital. Do not worry about the money, this letter will bear witness of my intended payment. If I should die, then even my friends will not permit any to criticize me, although just a corpse, and will repay my debts, of which I only have just one.

My God! How stupid I am to worry about a great coat, as if residing with it will provide me bliss. Enough of mentioning this! My beloved friend, we are timid, and as far as our bodies are concerned we are careful and adaptable. But would I not be in a better position to reconcile my soul with the Lord if I was wearing a thin coat during winter, than if I was a criminal heart and my body was covered with sables? Nothing is more torturous than psychological pain, to be tormented in the heart, for the soul to be ice cold and teeth chattering, and in a state of depressed despair. But it has been a long time since I have feared frost in its entirety.

Inner comfort, born from a peaceful conscience, is so strong that in the midst of difficult bodily disappointments that do not seem to disappear, prove true the following words, "Do not fear who will kill the body." Whatever is harmful and vexing will kill. I think that if someone is happy, then he is well even if sick. Not every person who is well in the body lives happily. It is apparent there is a difference between physical health and the soul's happiness. If a healthy person sometimes lives without happiness, then why should a weak person not also have access to the same happiness.

Are we not to be identified with salt? We have one body, while the soul is another issue. Let the decaying body – as it was born to do such – continue its pain, but let the soul rejoice. It is only the flesh that decays, but we are renewed in our soul. In our body we are nothing, but in our soul we are somebody, and even great on occasion. It is forever with us and we are with it and in it.

Do you see with what the hermit occupies his time? And he is full of love.

To my most merciful sir, Ivan Ivanovich Ermolov.

Letter 122
To an unknown recipient

It is good for us to gather together and place the fear of God and belief in Christ next to each others as though pictures in order to determine whether there is a great difference between them. The fear of God is to fear God, belief in Christ means to believe in him. Fear, fearing God, is loving Him, and belief, believing, hopes to love.

Fear fears Him who is omnipresent; belief believes in a creator who creates all. Fear fears Him who is invisible; belief, not seeing, sees the same. Fear of God relies on God; belief relies on Christ. The fear of God is a gift of the Load.[802] Belief is a gift of God.[803] Fear of God is the same as belief in Christ as the rock, since he was the rock.[804] Fear of God is the head and flower of prosperity; belief retains prosperity and salvation. Fear of God is a crown of wisdom; belief is the creed, statement, and seal of the Christian. Fear of God leads to the promised land; by belief did they cross the Red Sea.[805] Fear of the Lord adds days.[806] Belief shall endure forever.[807] Fear of the Lord is a fountain of life.[808] The righteous shall life by his belief.[809] Fear of the Lord drives away sin.[810] Belief leads to fulfillment of the commandments.[811] Fear of the Lord, fearing your master, is to believe in Him; belief, believing your master, is to fear Him. Fear of God proclaims peace. Having been justified by belief, we have peace with God.[812]

How can you believe God not fearing Him? How can you fear not believing? God and Christ are the same; the will of God and command of Christ are the same.

It is apparent that belief and fear of God are one and the same. Fear of God is that spirit of God in a person. The fear of the Lord will fill him.[813] The belief of Christ is also the inner spirit of Lord. Having this spirit of belief.[814] Through God we fear God and through the spirit we see the spirit. The Father inclines us toward the Son, and the Son toward the Son. But the Father is in the Son, and the Son is in the Father. Fear of the Lord resides in belief, and belief resides in fear. Fear of God is the inner witness to His son. Belief in Christ is an ostensive proof in the presence of people. His Father sets as a rock, a monument of revelation. Whoever believes in the rock of revelation has the fear of God within him; but whoever destroys the inner witness honors a false son of God. Whoever believes in

---

[802] Sirach 2:8
[803] Eph 2:8
[804] 1 Cor 10:4
[805] Heb 11:29
[806] Proverbs 16:27
[807] Sir 40:12
[808] Proverbs 14:26
[809] Habakkuk 2:4
[810] Sirach 1:21
[811] 1 John 3:23
[812] Rom 5:1
[813] Is 11:3
[814] 1 Cor 9:13

the son of God has the witness in himself; but whoever does not believe in God accuses Him of being a liar.[815]

If someone was to ask me the manner that he could inherit fear of God, I would respond to him with the words of the son of Sirach, "Having desired wisdom, observe the commandments and the Lord will gift you." Wisdom and fear of God is the same. And if you would again ask me the path to attain belief, to be able to see the invisible majesty of God, I would answer with the words of John, "Everyone who sins has not seen Him and has not recognized Him."[816] Now ask me again and now about the manner to receive the legacy of the most important of commandments. I would answer with the words of David, "Blessed is the person who fears the Lord and is zealous in His commandments." Do you see that the 2 passages noted above agree, while the third solely deals with fear of God and the belief in Christ and the life-giving commandments. Fear of God and belief motivates an observance of commandments, while the spirit of the commandments crowns both of them. Fear of God is the head and principle; belief in Christ is the field and seed. The sweetest commandments are the life-giving fruit of the tree of paradise, which provides fruit at its proper season.

With the witness of the rock – the Bible – we have concluded fear of God and belief in Christ as the same, while David places fear of God alongside the commandments. Fear of the Lord is pure, the judgments of the Lord are true. Who has the boldness to separate the treasure of the immortal deity – the commandments of God – from the indivisible divine pair? They are the fruit, the pinnacle and consummation of everything, having no end; but the end and beginning is all the same. God is the beginning of everything and God is the means. God is the end of everything. No one can derive something better out of God than He is Himself, for which reason He is God, the best of everything. How can I become filled with the best commandments? Where? In heaven or on earth? When? In this age or in the future one? True, I would have left both of them behind if I were to find something better than them. But I cannot because I do not want to and do not want to because I cannot. This is my God, paradise and eternal life. "I take pleasure in the paths of Your revelations just as I would of every treasure." "Sorrows and needs have

---

[815] 1 John 5:10
[816] 1 John 4:20

enveloped me, however Your commandments are my instruction." They who fear You will see me and rejoice, just as in the words, "Much peace is upon those who love Your law." "I will not ever forget your revelations, as they have enlightened me and educated me."

There also exists another type of fear of God. It does not provide joy, but torments; does not provide bliss but ruins; is not life for the soul but a fierce death. It is called godless and slavish and resides in 2 categories of people. David speaks regarding the first selection, "The fools says in his heart." His son the Christ speaks regarding the second selection, "Every person who is sinning is a slave to sin." The first sort does not recognize the Lord and leads a war against God's camp. The second recognizes Him, but fears Him as a torturer rather than as a father. Opposing His will and living according to their blindness, their fear is defined, "The wicked flee when no one is chasing." The wicked are agitated and unable to rest, and there they have become afraid of fear, where the entire life of the wicked person is only caring for himself. "His fear is in his ears." (Note that this is his own personal fears, and not any fear of God.) The sting of death is sin. One fears so that what is decaying will not further decay; another worries over sin, and both are tormented. This fear can be called infernal and not godly. And just as fear is ruinous, so is belief vain, hypocritical, demonic, slavish. Belief obviously believes that God exists, but as Paul writes, it can be noticed through activities and by those fruits that will witness to belief in Christ hidden in you, just as a seed in the heart. He says with his lips, "Lord, Lord," and does not observe His will. "Show me your belief through your activities," cries the Apostle James. It is one matter to believe that God exists and another matter to believe in God with love, having reliance on Him and a godly life. Demons definitely believe that God exists and they tremble. But do you see belief residing in demons, do you see fear residing in demons? Such belief does not reside in them and they do not walk according to such belief as the path of prosperity. Criminals believe that a civil court exists and fear it, but they do not live according to its laws, and indicate their distrust of it, and rather take their personal path to some imaginary personal prosperity.

The rich person is not the one who believes that gold is to be found in the nether-regions of the earth, but the one who has chased after Him, loving Him, and gathering His fruit becoming rich in it, strengthening his home and entrusting himself to Him. So the believing Christian is not the one believing in the fact that God exists in the world, but who follows Him, loving Him, and bases the prosperity of his home on the love of God, affirming it by the observance of His gracious will, assured that his home will not shift forever, as if founded upon a rock as rigid as a diamond. This is the treasure by which he is rich. The law of Your lips is a benefit to me. This is what the betrothal of belief with the Lord consists of according to the words of Hosea, "I will betroth you in virtue and in justice and in mercy and in generosity, and will wed you in faith, and you will then know the Lord."[817] Do you now see that belief is not separated from virtue, justice, mercy and generosity. What is virtue? Listen to David, "Your rectitude is forever rectitude, and Your law is truth." What is justice? "You have executed justice and rectitude. I stand in fear of your judgments." What is mercy? "Enliven me according to Your mercy and Your judgment." What is generosity? "Your generosities are many, Lord." "Enliven me according to Your judgment; whoever believes in Me possesses eternal life." What is life? Listen to the Father, "I will not forever forget that in them You have enlivened me." Here is life for you; this is what will enliven the dead stung by death. How long should you wait until deciding to believe in this life? How long should you suffer before allowing the light and peace of His commandments? O, blind of heart and unfortunate of mind! His commandment is the seal of friendship. "You are my friends if you do what I command you."

123
To an unknown recipient

This is something you cannot grasp, Separating yourself from the unity of belief. You are so misunderstanding; has the following statement already been expressed, Wickedness evolves from your lusts, and such statements are about the one and same type of people? Such unfortunate people who base their blessedness on superficial ceremonies, lead their life according to their lusts. So what is this lust? Listen to Paul, The following are the lusts of the flush, which are fornication, promiscuity, defilements, shamefulness, idolatry, sorcery, animosity, compulsion, envy, anger, irritation, argument, deceit, heresy, jealousy, murder, alcoholism, mayhem,

---

[817] Hosea 2:19

profanity and matters similar.[818] Every ceremony is a carnal matter, although not leading to anything mysterious, as though a primer for reading, and reading to understanding strength. But these gray doves abandoning all strength and the results of ceremony and their souls, have erected their homes on sand, as though on ice, depending on a sandy foundation, and not on a firm and rigid rock, as David writes, "The first that I learned from your revelations was that they were established to last forever."

Paul likewise cries regarding them, "Having an appearance of piety but denying its strength." So does Jude speak, "Separating from the unity of belief." So what Paul and the prophets call a rock or solidity, the theologian calls love or unity. Love and unity are the same. This is what our Jude calls unity, this signifies the rock of the Lord's commands, "For You have placed me upon the rock of belief." And for this reason such gods are called bodily, fleshly and unfortunate, that is, not having solidity, as Isaiah writes, "Know that their heart is dust and deceptive." Remember the person who built his temple on sand. Sand is not an individual item, but of various particles mixed together. But a rock is a whole item and so is firm. Such people who depend on ceremony can state they have belief because they depend on this, but this is not stable but is fleshly. This is why our Jude states in its entirety, "You, beloved with your faith," that is, one that is not sandy, but one that observes God's love. True belief leads to its consummation. What is this end? What love is – when from a pure heart and good conscience and unfeigned faith – is stated to Timothy, "Do not be in debt to one another, only to love one another, because he who loves has fulfilled the law."

---

[818] Gal 5:19-21

BIBLIOGRAPHY

(All in Russian or Ukrainian)

Багалій, Дмитро (Dmitro Bagali), *Український мандрований філософ Григорій Сковорода* (The Ukrainian Wandering Philosopher Grigori Skovoroda)

Данилевский, Г.П. (Danilevski, G.P.), *Украинская старина* (Ukrainian Heritage), Kiev, 1926.

Зеньковский, Василий (Vasili Zenkovski), *История Русской Философии* (History of Russian Philosophy), Eksmo Press, 2001.

Ковалинский, Михаил И. (Mikhail Kovalinski), *Жизнь Григория Сковороды* (Life of Grigori Skovoroda), 1796.

Лощиц, Юрий, (Yuri Loschitz), *Сковорода биография* (Skovoroda Biography), Moscow, 1972.

Милюков, Павел (Pavel Miluikov), *Очерки по Истории Русской Культуры* (History of Russian Culture), Volume 2. Moscow, 1994.

Сковорода, Григорий (Grigori Skovoroda), *Сочинения в Двух Томах*, (Collected Works in Two Volumes), Moscow, 1973.

Эрн, Владимир (Vladimir Ern), *Сковорода Жизнь и учение* (Skovoroda, Life and Teaching), 2000, Moscow.

Яковенко, Борис В. (Boris Yakovenko), *История Русской Философии* (History of Russian Philosophy), Republic Press, 2003.

GRIGORI SAVVICH SKOVORODA